Alcohol

Alcohol

A Social and Cultural History

Edited by
Mack P. Holt

Oxford • New York

English edition
First published in 2006 by
Berg
Editorial offices:
First Floor, Angel Court, 81 St Clements Street, Oxford OX4 1AW, UK
175 Fifth Avenue, New York, NY 10010, USA

© Mack P. Holt 2006

Berg is the imprint of Oxford International Publishers Ltd.

Library of Congress Cataloging-in-Publication Data
A catalogue record for this book is available from the Library of Congress.

British Library Cataloguing-in-Publication Data
Alcohol : a social and cultural history / edited by Mack P.
Holt.—English ed.
  p. cm.
Includes bibliographical references and index.
ISBN-13: 978-1-84520-166-1 (pbk.)
ISBN-10: 1-84520-166-3 (pbk.)
ISBN-13: 978-1-84520-165-4 (hardback)
ISBN-10: 1-84520-165-5 (hardback)
 1. Drinking of alcoholic beverages—History. 2. Alcoholism—
History. 3. Bars (Drinking establishments)—History. I. Holt,
Mack P.
  HV5023.A53 2006
  394.1'309—dc22   2005034777

ISBN-13 978 1 84520 165 4 (Cloth)
       978 1 84520 166 1 (Paper)

ISBN-10 1 84520 165 5 (Cloth)
       1 84520 166 3 (Paper)

Typeset by Avocet Typeset, Chilton, Aylesbury, Bucks
Printed in the United Kingdom by Biddles Ltd, King's Lynn.

www.bergpublishers.com

Contents

Notes on Contributors

Ken Albala is Associate Professor and Chair of the History Department at the University of the Pacific in Stockton, California. He is the author of *Eating Right in the Renaissance* (University of California Press, 2002), *Food In Early Modern Europe* (Greenwood, 2003), *The Banquet* (University of Illinois Press, 2006) and is currently working on a book about beans for Berg. He is also editor of Greenwood's *Food Culture Around the World* series.

Jack S. Blocker Jr. is Professor of History at Huron University College and Adjunct Research Professor at the University of Western Ontario. He has authored or edited six books on alcohol and temperance history, the most recent of which is *Alcohol and Temperance in Modern History: An International Encyclopedia* (ABC-Clio, 2003), which he co-edited with David M. Fahey and Ian R. Tyrrell.

Thomas Brennan is Professor of History at the United States Naval Academy in Annapolis, Maryland. He is the author of *Public Drinking and Popular Culture in Eighteenth-Century Paris* (Princeton University Press, 1988) and *Burgundy to Champagne: The Wine Trade in Early Modern France* (Johns Hopkins University Press, 1997).

David W. Conroy has taught at Northeastern University, the University of Massachusetts at Boston, and the University of Connecticut at Storrs. His publications include *In Public Houses: Drink And The Revolution Of Authority In Colonial Massachusetts* (University of North Carolina Press, 1995), and an article on law and popular culture in seventeenth-century Massachusetts in *Drinking: Behavior And Belief In Modern History* (University of California Press, 1991) edited by Barrows and Room. Taverns figure prominently in his current manuscript on race relations in Connecticut between 1740 and 1820.

Paul A. Garfinkel is Assistant Professor of History at Simon Fraser University in Burnaby, British Columbia. He is presently completing his first book manuscript, *Juridical Culture and Criminal Law in Liberal and Fascist Italy*.

W. Scott Haine is Adjunct Professor of History at the University of Maryland University College in Adelphi, Maryland. His books include *The World of the Paris Cafe: Sociability Among the French Working Class, 1789–1914* (Johns Hopkins University Press, 1996, paper ed. 1998); *The History of France* (Greenwood Press, 2000), and *The Culture and Customs of France* (Greenwood

Press, forthcoming). His articles on cafés, sociability, and youth leisure have appeared in *Journal of Contemporary History* and *Journal of Family History.*

Patricia Herlihy is Professor Emerita of History at Brown University and Research Professor at the Watson Institute of International Studies at Brown University. Her publications include *Odessa: A History, 1794–1914* (Harvard University Press, 1986); *The Alcoholic Empire: Vodka and Politics in Late Imperial Russia* (Oxford University Press, 2002); "'Joy of the Rus': Rites and Rituals of Russian Drinking," *Russian Review* 50 (1991): 131–147; and "Odessa Memories," in Nicolas Iljine (ed.) *Odessa Memories* (University of Washington Press, 2004).

Mack P. Holt is Professor of History at George Mason University in Fairfax, Virginia. His publications include *The Duke of Anjou and the Politique Struggle during the Wars of Religion* (Cambridge University Press, 1986); *The French Wars of Religion, 1562–1629* (Cambridge University Press, 1995; 2nd ed. 2005); and as editor, *Renaissance and Reformation France, 1500–1648* (Oxford University Press, 2002). He has also published articles on wine in the sixteenth century in *Past & Present* and in *Food and Foodways* and is currently completing a book on wine and the Reformation in Burgundy.

Diane Kirkby is Reader in History at La Trobe University in Melbourne, Australia. She has published extensively on women and work, including *Alice Henry: The Power of Pen and Voice* (Cambridge University Press, 1991) and *Barmaids: A History of Women's Work in Pubs* (Cambridge University Press, 1997). She has also edited *Sex, Power, and Justice: Historical Perspectives on Law in Australia* (Oxford University Press, 1995). Her most recent publications include articles on beer drinking and licensing laws in Australia, and she is currently writing a history of the Australian pub.

Charles C. Ludington is Visiting Assistant Professor of History at North Carolina State University and Duke University. His dissertation (Columbia University, 2003) was entitled "Politics and the Taste for Wine in England and Scotland, 1660–1860." His publications include "'Be sometimes to your country true': The Politics of Wine in England, 1660–1714," in Adam Smyth (ed.), *Drink and Conviviality in Early Modern England* (Boydell and Brewer, 2004); and "'A good and most particular taste': The Consumption and Meaning of Luxury Claret in Early Eighteenth-Century England," in A. Lynn Martin and Barbara Santich, eds., *Culinary History* (East Street, 2004).

A. Lynn Martin founded the Research Centre for the History of Food and Drink at the University of Adelaide in 1997 and served as its first Director from 1997 to 2004, where he established the Graduate Program in Gastronomy. His publications include *Alcohol, Sex, and Gender in Late Medieval and Early Modern Europe* (Palgrave, 2001), as well as a prizewinning article on fetal alcohol syndrome in *Food and Foodways*, and as editor with Barbara Santich, *Culinary History* (East Street Publications, 2004) and *Gastronomic Encounters* (forthcoming). He is currently a research fellow at the University of Adelaide.

Kim Munholland is Professor Emeritus of History at the University of Minnesota. He has published *Origins of Contemporary Europe, 1890–1914* (Harcourt, Brace & World, 1970) and *Rock of Contention: Americans and Free French at War in New Caledonia, 1940–1945* (Berghahn Press, 2005). He served as historical consultant to Don and Petie Kladstrup, *Wine & War: The French, the Nazis and the Battle for France's Greatest Treasure* (Broadway Books, 2001), which led to his current interest in wine and health as part of French identity.

Madelon Powers is Associate Professor of History at the University of New Orleans, Louisiana. Her publications include *Faces Along the Bar: Lore and Order in the Workingman's Saloon, 1870–1920* (University of Chicago Press, 1998) and "Decay from Within," in Susan Barrows and Robin Room (eds), *Drinking: Behavior and Belief Systems in Modern History* (University of California Press, 1991). She has also written on bar culture for *Encyclopedia of Recreation and Leisure in America* (Charles Scribner's Sons, 2005), *International Labor and Working-Class History* and *History Today*.

Introduction

Mack P. Holt

This volume brings together a collection of chapters on the history of alcoholic beverages in the West from the Renaissance to the present. As such, it makes no pretence to being comprehensive even within this Western perspective; nor can it do more than point to the general outlines of recent research on the subject, of which there has been a great deal in many languages. The goal, however, has been to produce a volume that outlines the broadest and most basic changes over time in the drinking patterns of Western Europeans and their colonial counterparts over the last five centuries. But what is "a social and cultural history" of alcohol? For the most part, the social and cultural history that follows will focus much more on the consumption side of alcohol rather than the production side, though that aspect cannot be completely ignored. All of the contributors are also professional historians, meaning that our interests and methodologies will be geared toward seeking to explain changes over time in drinking patterns and how alcohol functioned in Western culture. Obviously, all the authors are also keen to make sure that the history of alcohol over the last five centuries is not isolated from the overall history of the West during that period, for in many ways alcohol is a very useful lens through which to explore larger and more obvious historical changes such as industrialization or the rise of the state. Thus, the essays that follow will try to contextualize and situate alcohol into the larger historical picture at every opportunity.

To paint the most general of pictures in the broadest of strokes, this volume will analyze several different changes or transformations in the period from 1500 to the present: (1) changes in the nature and kinds of alcoholic beverages Westerns consumed; (2) changes in the venues, environments, and circumstances in which Westerners consumed alcoholic beverages; and (3) changes in the ways in which alcoholic beverages functioned to delineate and define various social and cultural phenomena in the West such as religion, class, politics, or health and disease. What alcoholic beverages did Europeans drink at the beginning of the sixteenth century? The answer, surprisingly, is quite a lot. In addition to wine and beer—which, with the addition of hops, was already beginning to replace ale by 1500—there were numerous other drinks such as mead, hard cider, not to mention a host of distilled spirits, though spirits were used largely for medicinal purposes in the sixteenth century. The most ubiquitous beverages, however, were wine, especially in southern Europe where grapes were bountiful, and beer (or hopped ale), more predominant in northern Europe where grapes were not as easily cultivated as cereal grains and hops. We need to keep in mind that the terms wine and beer encompassed a wide variety of different beverages in the sixteenth century. For example, the nobility consumed a very different quality of wine from the poorer classes, who had to make do with a second pressing or *piquette*, if they could afford wine at all.[1] Most wine was distributed and consumed locally, though already by 1500 certain wines from Gascony in southwest France, which the English called claret, were being exported to the British Isles as a result of the English occupation of the region during the Hundred Years War, while some of the best wines from Burgundy were being exported to the Low Countries where the fifteenth-century Dukes of Burgundy had established their courts. And beer was also usually consumed locally. It tended to keep longer and proved more stable than the unhopped ale it replaced, though both could be produced domestically in a well-stocked kitchen. The variety of distilled spirits available—primarily gin, vodka, various whiskeys and brandies (*eau de vie*), and eventually rum—only began to appear in any significant quantity in the seventeenth century. Le Roy Ladurie notes that it was only in 1663 that a drink of brandy was included in the wine harvester's daily meal ration in Béziers, while the following year was the first time ever that the *mercuriale* of that town (the annual list of official market prices) included "spoiled wine for the making of brandy."[2] According to Fernand Braudel, however, spirits did not become a truly popular beverage, that is, widely consumed by all social classes except the very poor, until the eighteenth century.[3] The introduction of spirits not only revolutionized drinking habits, but it also led to a dramatic increase in alcoholism in the West, forever the dark side in any history of alcohol. Fortified wines from Portugal and Spain also began to be consumed in significant quantity by the affluent in this period. And while all of Europe's grape vines were nearly destroyed by phylloxera insects in the late nineteenth century,[4] replanting with grafted vine stock from North America enabled the wine industry not only to recover fairly quickly, but also to increase production significantly. And in the twentieth century new specialty drinks and American-style "cocktails" only added to the variety of ways alcohol was consumed.

In terms of where people consumed alcohol, it is clear that ale and beer was originally a domestic product, usually brewed at home by the woman of the house, and also consumed at home. When hops were added to ale to make beer as early as the thirteenth century, the process became slightly more complicated but it was still largely a domestic industry until the introduction of alehouses provided new outlets for the lower classes to consume alcohol in the sixteenth century.[5] Wine was much more labor intensive than beer and was usually purchased at a wine shop or tavern. There is evidence of a wine merchants' guild in Paris going back to the thirteenth century, though it was not formally recognized until 1587. By the mid-eighteenth century, however, there were 1,500 wine merchants in the French capital licensed to sell wine, and maybe 3,000 total purveyors of alcoholic beverages of one type or another, or roughly one for every 200 inhabitants of the city.[6] In sixteenth-century Augsburg, a city of about 30,000 people, there were roughly

100 taverns, or roughly one for every 300 inhabitants.[7] Yet taverns and alehouses were for the most part only frequented by the popular classes. More respectable folk tended to drink at home or in private clubs. The creation of the restaurant and the advent of the coffeehouse, or café, in the late eighteenth and early nineteenth centuries, however, would eventually offer the leisure classes more public places in which to imbibe. By the beginning of the twentieth century, in fact, the café had replaced the tavern altogether, and had become a place where the middle and the working classes could even begin to mix to drink wine.[8] The elimination of social barriers was hardly uniform across Western culture, as many English pubs, for example, maintained their strictly divided public bars for working-class men and lounge bars for women and everyone else until the 1970s. Moreover, as changes in the nature of work and leisure have transformed post-industrial society, the consumption of alcoholic beverages has declined overall in the West. It has been estimated that before World War One France had more than half a million cafés licensed to sell wine, or roughly one for every eighty inhabitants. By the 1990s, however, this number had declined to only 160,000 cafés, or roughly one for every 360 inhabitants of France.[9]

Finally, alcohol has resonated and functioned in a variety of ways in the West since the Renaissance, helping to define and shape our culture. As the following chapters will show, looking at how we have consumed and understood alcohol provides an interesting window into our past. This volume is divided into three sections, which represent three of the most fruitful areas of recent research by social and cultural historians in the last decade or so. Part I focuses on morality and health, two areas that clearly overlap in the area of drunkenness and drinking to excess, but they are also linked in the way that both concepts were historically constructed over time by Western culture. Both church and state were active in the continual effort to regulate alcohol consumption for reasons of both morality and health. Part II centers on the general concept of sociability and how alcohol has functioned as both lubricant and astringent in cementing and regulating social relations since the Renaissance. Several historians have demonstrated, for example, how sites of alcohol consumption like the tavern and later the café helped create a public space where not only the various social classes could make contact, but also where they could influence and even shape public opinion. Indeed, all the chapters in this section underscore in one way or another that in order to maintain proper sociability, Westerners were constantly creating new public spaces to drink alcohol with one another. Part III focuses on the state and the rise of nationalism, and here some historians demonstrate how different governing elites in various Western states have used alcohol as a means of attempting to create national identities, while others show how some elites used alcohol to get or remain in power. There are no clear boundaries between these three sections, however, as it will be readily obvious that many of the chapters link up very nicely with many other chapters in the volume. But given that these three areas are the focus of much of the most important research by historians of alcohol in the last decade or so, it made more sense to highlight these themes for the general reader rather than attempting to weave them together superficially into a more general narrative. The outlines of such a narrative do emerge from this volume, however, and the thoughtful reader should be able to see that from the Renaissance to the present efforts by the intelligentsia, the church, and the state to dictate how alcohol should be consumed and perceived by the masses in Western society have met with only limited success. In fact, if there is a common theme running throughout the entire volume, it is that the culture of the consumption of alcohol cannot be unilaterally dictated to the masses from above—with the failure of the policy of prohibition in the United States in the 1920s being the most obvious example—and that the culture of drink in the West has always been the product of negotiation between the ruling elites and the drinking population at large. I do not mean to suggest that a crude and mechanical model of market forces is the driving force of history—which is simply another from of historical determinism that most historians would rightly eschew—but simply that alcohol consumption has been so ubiquitous in our past that no single group or institution, no matter how powerful, has been able to control the meaning and culture of drinking.

In Part I on "Health and Morality" Ken Albala offers a fresh survey of medical opinion about wine in the sixteenth century and shows that the controversy over whether wine is healthy or harmful was just as robust in the Renaissance as it is today. He demonstrates how Renaissance medical opinion was shaped by social and cultural suppositions as it came to define wine as a healthy beverage. At the same time, the same humanist scholarship that trumpeted wine's value as medicament or palliative could also harshly condemn excessive drinking as unhealthy and even dangerous. My own chapters on the impact of the Reformation on European drinking habits clearly highlights this side of this debate, as various Protestant Reformers ardently campaigned against excessive drinking and drunkenness. A few of the more radical Reformers, largely Anabaptists, even advocated total abstinence from alcohol, marking out what would remain a strident moralist view, though very much in the minority, but one that would survive into the twentieth century. During the Reformation of the sixteenth and seventeenth centuries it was clear that morality and health were explicitly linked, as the radical Reformers who advocated total abstinence from alcohol maintained that purity of the body was just as important as purity of the spirit. David Conroy introduces the tavern in eighteenth-century colonial America as a public space where politics intervened. Conroy shows how Whig opposition to the Crown's attempts to curb the consumption of rum in the colonies made use of taverns as sites of opposition leading up to the American Revolution. Moreover, his chapter also demonstrates that by the eighteenth century it was the state that had taken over from the church the principal role of attempting to regulate alcohol consumption for reasons of health and morality. And Conroy's chapter also links very nicely into themes stressed in Parts II and III of the volume. Finally the two chapters by Paul Garfinkel and Kim Munholland show how two different modern states could take completely different views of alcohol consumption in an effort to promote their own political agendas. Garfinkel demonstrates how the liberal magistrates of the government of early twentieth-century Italy tried to introduce strict temperance laws by exaggerating the problem of alcoholism in an effort to paint themselves as the architects of a new and more modern Italian state. Not only did these liberal efforts fail, but Garfinkel points out the irony that is was the fascist Mussolini who was more successful with a similar campaign after World War One. Munholland, on the other hand, shows how French medical opinion at the turn of the twentieth century took the opposite view in its efforts to shape government policy, by maintaining that drinking wine was good for health. But he shows that French physicians relied less on medical evidence to support their claims, of which there was very little at the time, and more on efforts linking wine-drinking with French identity. As such they tried to exempt wine from the charges of being the cause of rising alcoholism in France. Thus, neither for the first nor the last time did doctors allow social and cultural pressures to shape their diagnoses and health policies.

In Part II on "Sociability" Lynn Martin focuses on the diary of an English mercer in Lancashire to draw conclusions about drinking patterns in seventeenth-century England. Whereas in the sixteenth century so much of the social life of the community centered around the parish church—the feasts and celebrations following baptisms and weddings being the most obvious examples—by the seventeenth century most of these rituals of sociability had shifted to the ale house, as the English Reformation had not only ended the practice of church ales but had also significantly diminished the social elements traditionally connected to the sacraments. The chapters by Thomas Brennan and Scott Haine take us directly into the debate surrounding the concept of the public sphere. Originally developed by the German sociologist and philosopher Jürgen Habermas, what he termed the public sphere was first created in the eighteenth century with the aid of print culture that circulated among the bourgeoisie in English coffeehouses. The result, he argues, was a dynamic bourgeois public opinion that came to shape public policy and force its way into political debate that heretofore had been dominated by the gentry and aristocracy at court and in Parliament.[10] Some cultural historians of eighteenth-century France have taken Habermas's concept of the public sphere and adapted it to the salons of Paris in an effort to come up with a new explanation for the French Revolution. Replacing the older Marxist explanation based on class conflict, this new cultural explanation focuses on the public discourse of print culture emanating from the salons. As such it tends to reify the intelligentsia and the elites in general and virtually ignores social and material life. This notion of the public sphere has also been attractive to German and other European historians as well.[11] The model has not gone unchallenged, especially by some historians of eighteenth-century France, who argue that political culture in general, and the French Revolution in particular, cannot be completely explained by a study of language.[12] The benefit of the chapters by Brennan and Haine is that, like Conroy's chapter on eighteenth-century America, they demonstrate that the public sphere extended to the tavern in the eighteenth century and to the café in the nineteenth century. Not only do these essays extend the concept to the popular classes who populated these drinking sites, but they also reintroduce material and social life back into the discussion of how public opinion was formed and how it operated as a viable political force. Brennan's chapter is the more theoretical, though he does demonstrate that the public sphere was not the exclusive property of the salons and private homes of the bourgeoisie as Habermas's followers have tended to suggest. Haine's chapter focuses on the social life of drinking in the café, and he shows how drinking wine in Parisian cafés became a marker of social class in the nineteenth century. Finally Madelon Powers looks at bar-room and saloon culture in the United States in the late nineteenth and early twentieth centuries and shows how mass migration of both foreign-born and native-born citizens to American cities in this period, combined with industrialization and urbanization, reshaped American drinking customs and norms of sociability. Her chapter is especially good at demonstrating that not only were saloons and bars a valuable lens through which to view larger historical forces shaping Western culture, but that they were actually significant sites of the negotiation of social relations between new immigrants and locals.

In Part III, "State and Nation," we see how alcohol was used in places as diverse as Scotland, Russia, Australia, and the United States both to help create a national identity as well as shape public policy. Charles Ludington asks an intriguing question about drinking patterns in eighteenth-century Scotland, wondering why England and Scotland, united politically in 1707 and with equal duties on imported wine, nevertheless experienced very different drinking patterns by the mid-eighteenth century. While the English taste had turned from French wine to cheaper port, the poorer Scots were still drinking more expensive French claret. His conclusion is that Scottish drinkers used French wine as a means of distinguishing Scottish national identity from being submerged in the political union with England after 1707. Patricia Herlihy demonstrates that drinking vodka in a nineteenth-century Russian tavern served as a political marker linking the state and the drinker. While theoretically regulated by the state, Herlihy shows how Russian taverns still managed to distribute vodka to their customers even when they were not officially allowed to do so, with the result that both the state and the drinking public each had a means for expressing its political will to the other. And while Herlihy does not invoke Habermas explicitly, her chapter does resonate with some of the same themes as the essays by Conroy, Brennan, and Haine. Diane Kirkby provides an overview of Australian drinking patterns in the twentieth century that clearly parallels many of the same changes and transformations described elsewhere. Above all, she shows how the impact of the exploding wine industry in Australia after World War Two served to replace beer with wine as the nation's alcoholic beverage of choice. In the process wine not only transformed the Australian economy but helped create a new national identity as well. Finally the chapter by Jack Blocker is a brisk synthetic overview of four centuries of drinking in the USA. Among the many and various changes and transformations he out-lines, he shows that over the last 400 years the beverages of choice shifted from distilled spirits early on to fermented beverages—beer and wine—more recently, while the principal site for most drinking was originally in the home, which later shifted to public drinking spaces in the nineteenth and early twentieth centuries, and then came full circle back to the home in the late twentieth century. Much like Kirkby does for Australia, Blocker's chapter resonates with the wider social and cultural changes ongoing in the United States that provide the context for the drinking of alcoholic beverages.

Throughout, this book attempts to situate alcohol in its social and cultural set-tings so as to better understand its functions in our culture over the last 500 years. As our culture as well as out standard of living have been transformed during that span by industrialization, urbanization, and since the end of World War Two, glob-alization, so has the way we have consumed alcohol in all its many forms. If efforts to curb and occasionally even ban the drinking of alcohol remain with us as a con-stant throughout our history, there seems little doubt that alcohol is here to stay for the future. It seems equally clear that how we consume it is likely to change as much in the next 500 years, however, as in the last 500. And even if today's drinkers seem to be caught in the middle of the ongoing battle between the forces of globalization and anti-globalization—the wonderful documentary film "Mondvino" immediately comes to mind here—I think we need not be overly pes-simistic. If the history of alcohol in the West has anything to teach us, it is surely that not even the commercial interests that control the production of alcohol can totally regulate, much less control, either the meanings or myriad functions of alcohol in Western life.

Notes

1. Emmanuel Le Roy Ladurie, *Les paysans de Languedoc*, 2 vols. (Paris: Ecole Pratique des Hautes Etudes, 1966), Vol. 1, p. 177.

2. Ibid., Vol. 1, p. 521.

3. Fernand Braudel, *The Structures of Everyday Life: The Limits of the Possible*, vol. 1 of *Civilization and Capitalism, 15th-18th Century* (New York and London: Harper and Row, 1981), p. 241.

4. Rod Phillips, *A Short History of Wine* (London: Allen Lane/Penguain Press, 2000), pp. 281–7.

5. See Peter Clark, *The English Alehouse: A Social History, 1200–1830* (London: Longman, 1983), pp. 24–34.

6. Thomas Brennan, *Public Drinking and Popular Culture in Eighteenth-Century Paris* (Princeton: Princeton University Press, 1988), pp. 76–9.

7. T. Ann Tlusty, *Bacchus and Civic Order: The Culture of Drink in Early Modern Germany* (Charlottesville: University of Virginia Press, 2001), p. 35.

8. Rebecca Spang, *The Invention of the Restaurant: Paris and Modern Gastronomic Culture* (Cambridge, MA: Harvard University Press, 2000); and Scott Haine, *World of the Paris Café: Sociability Among the French Working Class, 1789–1914* (Baltimore: Johns Hopkins University Press, 1998).

9. Phillips, *Short History of Wine*, p. 310.

10. Jürgen Habermas, *The Structural Transformation of the Public Sphere: An Inquiry into a Category of Bourgeois Society*, trans. Thomas Burger and Frederick Lawrence (Cambridge, MA: MIT Press, 1989).

11. For a general discussion of this literature, see Craig Calhoun (ed.), *Habermas and the Public Sphere* (Cambridge, MA: MIT Press, 1992), and the review essay by Anthony La Vopa, "Conceiving a Public: Ideas and Society in Eighteenth-Century Europe," *The Journal of Modern History* 64 (1992): 79–116.

12. For example, see the article by M. Jay Smith, "No More Language Games: Words, Beliefs, and the Political Culture of Early Modern France," *The American Historical Review* 102 (1997): 1413–40.

Part I
Morality and Health

–1–

To Your Health

Wine as Food and Medicine in Mid-sixteenth-century Italy

Ken Albala

In the late twentieth century wine drinkers suffered a barrage of conflicting messages regarding the role of wine in promoting health. On one hand medical research, not uninfluenced by the wine industry, proclaimed the antioxidant virtues of wine. At the same time every bottle bore a strident warning on the dangers of alcohol consumption.

In the mid-sixteenth century a comparable controversy arose with equally mixed motives during a period in history when growing population and the expansion of trade encouraged the vigorous promotion of wine as a nutritious and medicinal beverage.[1] This was also in the midst of the Reformation when not only was the traditional role of wine in the Christian sacrament reexamined on the basis of biblical authority, but its place in a balanced diet was reevaluated. Some writers were critical of medical authorities and offered fresh new insights, others attempted to restrain an apparently drunk and unruly populace by threatening them with innumerable diseases that result from drinking. This controversy over wine reveals the anxieties that faced sixteenth-century drinkers as they tried to negotiate the rival claims of health, morality, and pleasure.

Then as now, the medical arguments were informed by deep cultural suppositions and authors had their own particular axes to grind, some praised wine by force of habit and cultural prejudice; others carefully crafted their arguments with the aim of curbing consumption as a means of social control. The Reformations, both Protestant and Catholic, and their insistence on public decorum and morality also had an effect on early modern attitudes toward wine. The argument for regular wine consumption was never bereft of supporters. First, according to medical authorities, from ancient times to the early modern period, wine was considered a necessary nutrient. As the closest physical substance to human blood, it was thought to convert easily into blood and is thus easily assimilated into the human body. In his *Alimentorum facultatibus* Galen settled the question in a sentence. "Everyone agrees that wine is among that which nourishes; and if everything nourishing is a food, it must be said that wine too should be classed as a food." And "Of all the wines the red and thick are most suited for the production of blood because they require little change before turning into it."[2] This was accepted without question as a fact.

Yet physicians could not agree on how wine affects the body. According to the tenets of humoral physiology anything which is nourishing must be hot and moist since life itself is defined as the confluence of vital heat and radical moisture. Logically wine heats and moistens the body, something that can be empirically verified both on a cold day after a drink and after a cool draught to quench a summer's thirst. With equally empirical evidence wine also dries the body due to its diuretic properties and in excess can accidentally chill the body. On top of this, due to its volatile nature, wine sends cloudy vapors into the brain which obfuscate the intellect, cause stupor and in extreme cases inebriation and loss of consciousness. In the end can wine be said to promote health or hinder it? Is it simply that wine in moderation is good for you, but in excess is harmful, or do the color, texture, flavor, and age of wine make a difference? Does the time of day we drink, the place of wine among other foods, or our physical constitution and age determine how we should use it?

There was a certain reassuring similarity between the words *vitis*, the genus of wine grape, and *vita*, meaning life. Among its unmistakable virtues it incites joy and perhaps less obviously aids digestion, provokes urine which cleans the body out and resolves clogs by means of its incisive and scouring qualities. Wine not only serves to "provoke Venus" as they politely put it, but to increase sperm production (which is after all manufactured from a plethora of blood) and thus it fosters conception. As a hot and moist aliment it is particularly suited for those prone to melancholy, those of a cold and dry complexion, and those Saturnine personalities such as scholars and artists, as well as the aged who are also cold and dry. *Vinum lac senum est* (wine is the milk of the aged).

Yet the question of the temperature of wine remained somewhat knotty. Temperature refers not to the tactile and measurable heat on a thermometer, but rather the effect that a food or medicine has on the human body. In other words how do wines humoral qualities (hot or cold, dry or moist) ultimately affect ours? Classical sources appear to have settled the question without much difficulty. Why the question was reopened in the sixteenth century appears to have been the result of gaining direct access to a number of conflicting sources at once and trying to reconcile their opinions or arrive at a definitive solution. It was in fact the rigorous tools of textual analysis used by medical humanists that were used to examine this question. In the end many authors struck out with their own reasoning, and their own cultural prejudices.

The first significant discussion on the temperature of wine was composed in the 1530s in Verona. A physician named Giovanni Battista Confalonieri attempted to clarify the question and his efforts were published both in Venice and Basel in 1535. First, he recounted the various positions: some have argued that wine is hot and moist, some say it is dry, others cool. Some insist that it depends on the type of wine and its flavor. Sour wines are colder and styptic or tannic wines are drier. He used this term precisely as we use the word dry today and its meaning comes directly from humoral theory. Unlike Hippocrates and Galen, Confalonieri points out that Aristotle was keenly aware that different wines have different faculties, and we should follow his lead in investigating these rather than merely relying on the authorities.[3]

With a rare appreciation for the role of *terroir* on the ultimate quality of wine, Confalonieri adds that the location of the vineyard, the exposure to the sun and properties of the soil are the crucial factors that will determine not only the flavor of wine but its use in promoting health. Even the water nourishing the vines affects its quality since some water tastes of "alumina, some is bitter, some sulfurous, some salty, some unctuous, some tastes like asphalt ..."[4] All of this determines the medicinal virtues of various wines. He says "There are some wines that aggravate the head or cause pains, others that either remove pain or cause sobriety."[5] It is not then merely a matter of the quantity consumed, but the quality of the wine which will either leave you refreshed and invigorated or give you a nasty hangover. He admits that it would be ideal to have physicians investigate what properties are common to all wines, but that seems futile in light of the incredible diversity of types. Unlike the ancient authorities he refuses to make a bold and general statement about all wines.

Nor is there a simple way wine affects people of varying constitutions. It can heat those that are frigid, dry those that have superfluous humidity, and also cool and refresh the bilious. Depending on the complexion of the drinker the particular elements of which wine is composed may also influence its role in a healthful diet. A watery wine will affect the phlegmatic person differently than the bilious; a hot and volatile wine will make hotter constitutions drunk quicker because vapors (the aireal elements) rise more easily to the brain than in colder (and usually heavier) bodies.[6] In other words, effects that we would today ascribe to alcohol content, metabolism and body weight were still perfectly intelligible in humoral terms. By this logic passing out is merely the result of the wine overcoming and suffocating the innate heat, just as water puts out a fire.[7]

The inherent differences among individuals also explain why some people like sweet wines and some like bitter.[8] Our own humoral makeup determines which kinds of wine will be most effective at balancing our constitution and which our taste buds will respond most favorably toward. Taste preferences are thus predetermined and never absolute. In practice cold and dry people should enjoy hotter and moister (i.e. sweeter) wines while cold and moist people will prefer austere and tannic ones which will dry out their superfluities.

Confalonieri also settles the question of nourishment. Keep in mind as a native of Verona he had a vested cultural interest in wine. It is still one of the major wine producing regions in Italy. He contends that because it has such an affinity to our own substance, it nourishes first, particularly in those with tempered constitutions, and only secondarily serves as medicine for the infirm.[9] Robust individuals should have no trouble concocting (that is digesting) wine and thus it should be part of our daily fare. Wine is first and foremost a food and should be a regular part of a balanced diet.

Apparently unsatisfied with this simplistic promotion, within a year fellow gentleman of Verona, Antonio Fumanelli, had his own *Commentarium de vino, et
facultatibus vini* published in Venice. Ranging across the full gamut of authorita-
tive opinions both ancient, Arab, and medieval, Fumanelli examines Galen's very
circular logic that proves wine is hot and moist. "Food that nourishes is assimilated
into the body, what we eat is thus familiar. Wine therefore nourishes greatly and is
extremely familiar to humans. Since it is similar to the human body and the human
body is hot and moist, then so is wine."[10] By reading the text closely he was able
to point out that Galen's position does not seem entirely consistent, because he prescribed wine for cold and moist diseases, which would mean that wine must be hot
and dry.

In fact many authorities did suggest that wine is hot and dry. This is why
Hippocrates recommended it for women, who being moister should drink uncut
wine and drier foods to balance their constitutions.[11] Aristotle and Galen used
wine for ulcers to dry and clean their viscous humors. How wine can be both moist
and dry is only solved with some simple logic chopping: wine's substance is
indeed liquid and thus it is moist and quenches thirst. But the effect it has on the
body is to dry it out, thus qualitatively it is drying.[12] Actual properties should be
distinguished from potential or accidental effects, or as Galen called them, primary
versus secondary qualities. The contradiction here is only apparent, not real.
Another way to put it is that wine's active properties are hot and moist (and thus it
is nourishing) while its passive properties, the way it alters us, is hot and dry. Thus
wine is not only an aliment, but a medicine too.[13] Wine increases our substance
quantitatively, but changes us qualitatively. Or yet another way to put it, its extensive properties (expanding our corporeal substance) should be thought of sepa-
rately from its intensive properties (the ability to alter our humoral balance).[14]

To those who contend that wine is cold Fumanelli answers that this is only the
case when water is added. The wine acts as a vehicle carrying the water faster
through the body and this is why it refreshes, even more than ordinary water
would. Some believe that "wine with water added more easily inebriates, since
water promotes the distribution of wine." But in fact it is the wine that helps the
water penetrate by means of its subtle penetrating force as well as an occult property.[15] By that he merely means an unseen force in wine that causes it to course
faster through the body than other substances. Even more surprisingly, Fumanelli
insists that wine does also moisten the body, even more so without water, because
it nourishes the moist parts of our body and satisfies them in a way that water
cannot.[16]

Another problem surrounding wine concerns the role it plays in inducing sleep.
According to standard theory drowsiness and sleep are caused by the brain
growing colder and moister, the result of all the nourishing hot and dry spirits
having been dissipated in the course of daily activity. Spirits are in a sense a rar-
efied distillation of blood, exactly as spirits of alcohol are a distillate of wine.
(Incidentally physicians in the next century would explain how coffee keeps you

awake with a similar logic—it is the hot and dry volatile spirits that have an affinity to our own and agitate the molecules.) But if wine heats the body, then why does it make us drowsy?[17]

The standard explanation runs as follows: it is not wine's qualities that cause sleep, but its mechanical effect on the brain. Mental acuity depends on light and flowing spirits in the brain. Wine in the process of digestion creates cloudy vapors and these can seep up from the stomach and cloud the brain, causing sleep not from a quantitative deficiency of spirits, but by crowding and obscuring them. In extreme cases it causes total drunkenness.[18]

Fumanelli next explains that despite its medicinal virtues, wine is also nourishing, and is even more nourishing than solid foods. "It is quicker and more easily concocted in the stomach, converted into blood in the liver, and sent through the veins, and easily in every particle of the body digested and quickly assimilated into the members ..."[19] It penetrates quickly because of its heat and subtlety. Later he continues that it is finally in the body converted to light and abundant spirits, thus in a way lifting our spirits—in the other sense of that word, making us joyful. While the reader might have expected Fumanelli to recommend wine primarily as a medicine, and in only in moderation, in the end he promotes it even further than Confalonieri, as the ideal aliment and an invaluable medicine.

These works seem to have caught the attention of a greater medical luminary. The renowned Girolamo Fracastoro, also from Verona, soon jumped into the fray with his own *De vini temperature sententia*. It was dated September 9, 1534, so he must have read Fumanelli before it was published.[20] Fracastoro, among other things, is credited with the first theory of contagion and for having written a long poem about the latest new venereal disease which he gave the name: syphilis. Fracastoro begins by directly addressing his predecessors and wondering why there has been this enormous debate over the temperature of wine. First to allay some of the confusion, he says he will not discuss watered wine, which is quite different, nor very young, very old wine, or any with extreme medicinal properties, just ordinary drinking wine.

He makes the same distinction between actual and potential qualities made by Fumanelli. This explains why water even if served hot, cools the body, and why lettuce, though cold can if converted into blood offer us heat. This served to clarify why it is that no one really argues over the primary qualities of wine, which are hot and moist, but rather they disagree about its effect on the body.[21] Fracastoro insists that a further distinction must also be made, between potential (future effects) that are active and those that are passive. That is, some result from the natural processes of our body, like converting wine into blood, but some merely happen to us down the road, sometimes altering us with no participation on our part. Hence the medicinal effect of wine—whose qualities can be other than hot and moist.

Being among the first generation of medical writers with complete access to the works of Galen and a willingness to criticize him, Fracastoro points out that Galen did often contradict himself. Sometimes he said it is an aliment and not a medicine,

yet he included it among medicines. Clearly it is both.[22] Here Fracastoro criticizes
the opinion of Bartolomeo Gaiano who apparently took part in this controversy but
whose work on the topic does not appear to have been published.

With this formal distinction between actual and potential, active and passive
properties, Fracastoro can state confidently that wine is liquid and moist. But it
still dries us accidentally, and that is its proper medicinal role, and that is why it is
properly used in cold and moist diseases, which would include coughs, colds,
catarrh—but not hot ones like fevers or gout.

One by one he counters the arguments of ancient authorities arguing that wine
is hot and moist, and concludes in the end that they are all plainly wrong. When
we speak of the qualities of a food or drink, we refer not to the fact that it is nourishing, but how it changes us. Whether as a food or medicine wine does dry the
body and is in all cases therefore hot and dry.[23] Although Fracastoro offers no
experiment or concrete empirical evidence, it is nonetheless his actual medical
experience with wine which dehydrates the body that led him to this bold pro-
nouncement contrary to the classical authorities and his own colleagues.

Finally Fracastoro concedes that Fumanelli deserves credit and understands the
topic better than his opponents, but he nonetheless calls it a dubious victory.[24]
Presumably Fracastoro was called in to settle this question in the first place, but in
the end his own conclusion is quite different from Fumanelli's, and only serves to
leave the topic wide open. Rather than promote wine as the ideal aliment, his discussion actually restricts its use from a medical point of view.

The next major work to address the question is much larger and far more extensive than the three preceding books. It was also written by someone of a very different cast. A native of the Bergamo region and thus born maybe fifty miles from
Verona, and a few decades younger, Gulielmo Grataroli was also a Protestant.
Hunted by the Inquisition, he eventually took up practice in Basel. In 1565, after
writing numerous dietary works, his massive *De vini natura* was published in
Strasbourg. He immediately announces in it that he is well acquainted with the
works of all three authors discussed thus far.[25] In fact in another work he calls
Fumanelli "that famous and excellent Grayehead … of Verona" which suggests
that he may have known him.[26]

But unlike his predecessors one of Grataroli's major concerns is to lash out
against drunkenness. It seems that he found the customs of his adopted Germanic
city particularly odious. Wine does of course make you glad, as the Psalm says:
"*Vinum exhilarat cor hominis.*" But that should not invite drinking to excess "like
vulgar Germans and many others, who are accustomed to this particular vice,
which makes men forgetful, overwhelms their internal and external senses, and
suffocates their energy."[27]

Grataroli in many of his works comes off as positively puritanical, and it is
perhaps not surprising that some of them were translated into English. His trans-
lator rendered this passage on wine as follows "But being immoderatelie drunken
and ingluuiously swilled (as now adaies many use to do) it is most hurtfull and the

special cause of many grievous diseases" and it "doth too much humect and moisture the whole bodie."[28]

Grataroli also complained about the custom of drinking the best wines at the
end of meals with fruit, which causes the undigested food to be pushed into the
veins prematurely where it mixes with the blood and corrupts.[29] By the later sixteenth century condemning the common practice of drinking wine with fruit, or
even worse with ice or snow, would become a major preoccupation among medical
authors.

This is not to say that Grataroli ignored the various virtues of wine. It does
convert into good blood, aids digestion, revives the spirits, provokes urine, helps
expel gas, increases the natural heat, stimulates the appetite, opens obstructions,
and the list goes on.[30] But all this is only in moderation. In excess wine does
exactly the opposite: it cools the body by suffocating the natural heat and leads to
apoplexy, paralysis, tremors, stupor, convulsions, vertigo, lethargy, phrenitis, etc.
It perturbs the senses, ruins the memory, makes men libidinous and "fetid drunkenness makes men into irrational beasts."

Clearly Grataroli's motive here is not only to discuss the dietary virtues of wine
but to frighten people into drinking less. His book becomes a tool of his puritanical desire to control people and make them more rational. He continues that it is
obviously a drink inappropriate for children and especially women, who are naturally less endowed with reason. Wine only makes them more prone to lascivious-
ness and "they more easily commit debauchery or adultery."[31] Despite any avowed
nutritional and medicinal uses, the dangers of excessive wine consumption seem
to outweigh the advantages.

Perhaps addressing his new neighbors, he adds that getting drunk on beer is
even worse, because it emits crass vapors that take a long time to dispel from the
brain, so you actually stay drunk longer.[32] That is not perhaps as bad as what
Muscovites get drunk on, or the swill that others quaff mixed with cloves, darnel,
poppy seeds, or belladonna in wine to get drunk (or rather drugged) quicker.

For those who care to prevent drunkenness he suggests either roasted lungs of
sheep, seven bitter almonds on an empty stomach, raw cabbage (that was
Aristotle's favorite), celery seeds, or saffron. But with the latter you run the risk
of succumbing to such intense hilarity that you might resolve the vital spirits and
perish. Fatty meat, salted herring or better yet olive oil work much better because
they prevent fumes from rising to the head.[33] Drunkenness is conceived of
entirely as vapors clouding the brain, so anything that suppresses the vapors
should work.

Drunks appear to have been among Grataroli's regular customers as well,
because he offered tried and true hangover remedies. For severe headaches and
especially after vomiting he suggests wrapping the head in linen soaked in vinegar
and rosewater (both humorally cold) and sleeping in a quiet room. For women he
suggests wrapping the breasts, for some reason.[34] Sounder advice is to drink a lot
of water. Whether he could clearly conceive of the dehydrating effects of wine here

or was merely intuitively countering the heating effect with cooling water is not clear, but this would certainly have had some positive effect.

Most revealingly he condemns the "hair of the dog" approach. "Most pernicious however and truly most alien to reason is that precept to overcome yesterday's hangover with guzzling in the morning."[35] In any case, what promised to be a medical discourse on the properties of wine had descended into a tirade against alcohol abuse. He even suggested ways to make the profligate drunk hate wine: by giving him wine in which an animal has been killed, perhaps an eel, or in which peacock feces has been steeped.[36]

To be fair, Grataroli does devote considerable energy to discussing different types of wine and the various effects they have on health. New wine is colder, older is hotter. Wine separated from the lees (*defoecatum*) is stronger but doesn't keep as well. Vines that get a lot of sunlight on hillsides are drier in nature and conversely those grown in the plains are moister.[37] All these factors influence the ultimate temperature of the wine and its effect on us. Even the color is important. *Ruffum* or what we might take to be a claret makes the best blood, but darker wines such as *nigrum* are crass, bitter, hard to digest, and generate thick blood. *Palmeum*, which is clear and aromatic, generates the clearest blood and is good for all ages and complexions.

Wine must of course be chosen according to one's constitution, but contrary to custom, some wines are not actually good for you. Old wines in particular, he claims: "Wine quite old, that exceeds seven years, offers little nutrition, and is heating in the third degree and drying, and has the force of medicine," meaning that it does not make a good food.[38]

The rest of Grataroli's book contains practical advice for making, storing, testing, and correcting wine, including medicinal recipes. This is not directly relevant, but suffice to say that he addresses the question of the temperature of wine but that concern is subsumed in his obsession with inebriation, and his comments seem more a form of social control than medical discourse. Moreover the entire question of the temperature of wine and its role in a healthy diet remains wide open. If anything, the failure of physicians to decide the question definitively leaves room for wide speculation that veers far from medical orthodoxy.

For example Alessandro Petronio, who was physician to Pope Gregory XIII and Ignatius Loyola, seems to have picked up the idea that wine is drying, but further concluded that it therefore slows concoction in the stomach. "Every sort of wine slows concoction because it toughens food in the stomach and renders the chyle thicker, which water does not do."[39] He even suggests a little experiment of placing one fig in wine and another in water. The former will become tough and only the latter soft. Better then to drink water with dinner. Furthermore, drinking wine without water during meals is a very bad idea, and doesn't speed digestion as many people think. This advice runs contrary to all medical opinion and marks the beginning of a slow and steady erosion of humoral physiology as it gives way to empirical observation and experimentation. Most significantly he suggests that wine is not harmful because it sends vapors to the head as some think but because it is dehydrating and as he puts it, dissipates the body.[40]

An indication that these Latin medical treatises were not merely sterile academic exercises but had an effect on popular perceptions of wine and its effect on health can be gauged by contemporaneous vernacular works on wine. For example Giovanni Battista Scarlino's verse *Nuovo Trattato* which discusses the various wines that were imported to Rome mid century also includes medical opinions. Scarlino notes that while most people prefer Greco, he believes malvagia is superior because it comforts the brain, the chest, and the heart, and invigorates the pulse during every sickness.[41]

In a section on the utility of wine, he reveals his familiarity with the medical literature: wine gives the face a good color, provokes urine "*e 'l coito incita.*" It sharpens the wit, chases wrath, generates blood, resolves clogs, provokes the appetite, and has a host of other virtues. But Scarlino, like Grataroli also offers dire warnings on the dangers of excess: it leads to headaches, premature old age, lethargy, spasms, stupor, vertigo, tremors, and nervous disorders.[42] For an author writing in Rome in the midst of the Catholic Reformation, one can only suspect that he feared too enthusiastic praise of wine without some qualifying pronouncements would never pass censorship. His fears do seem genuine though, particularly in a passage where he complains that some vulgar people think that drinking good strong wine will preserve you from death, a perverse opinion bereft of all reason, and obviously a simplified corruption of medical opinion.[43]

Also appearing mid century was a fascinating vernacular dialogue that encapsulates the raging controversy as it was perceived at the popular level. It is deceptively titled *L'Humore*. Its author, Bartolomeo Taegio, a popular agronomic author, here sets up an argument with a friend whose ranting denunciations of wine are systematically confuted. The friend's logic is clearly a parody of sour medical advice with which readers were familiar: "wine burns the blood, destroys the seed of generation, diminishes energy, suffocates the natural heat" and leads to "an infinity of diseases such as dropsy, falling sickness, paralysis, gout, stupor, spasms, tremors, vertigo" and so the list goes on.[44] Beyond that, wine ruins morals and makes people contentious, lazy, dishonest, furious and homicidal. Water is a much more healthy drink.

Taegio meanwhile, who had been spewing out poems in praise of Bacchus, finally refutes the warnings with another medical argument. Just as you would not blame the sword for murder, so you should not blame wine if someone drinks to excess. In moderation wine is digestive, nourishing, provokes urine, stimulates the appetite, increases the natural heat, opens clogs, etc. His list sounds as if it was taken directly from a medical tract.[45] By this point his interlocutor has been reduced to curt questions while Taegio rattles off the other miraculous uses for wine. It is good for young frail girls, as an antidote for poison, and then he describes the effects that aging has on wine, how to judge it by the aroma, liberally seasoning his encomium with classical references.

Like the Veronese physicians Taegio, a landowner and winemaker as well, had a vested interest in promoting wine consumption. His dialogue shows that although advice could obviously be skewed, Italian readers were indeed still being ʼpresented with conflicting arguments in favor and against wine. The dialogue was essentially a long amusing advertisement.

The same could be said for a comparable Latin dialogue written by a physician from Sicily, Jacobus Praefectus. The dialogue takes place among four men over the course of a banquet and symposium that follows, and eventually is dominated by the physician among them. He offers standard warnings, how wine can lead to greater vices. In his opinion rulers at every level of government should abstain from wine, as should all public functionaries.[46]

He next criticizes the idiotic idea that guzzling wine before a meal is good for health and prevents aging. Apparently some so-called doctors were making just this claim and people seem to have willingly adopted the custom.[47] But wine does have its medicinal virtues, one must merely pay attention to the temperature of the wine, some types are hotter, some drier, some cooler, etc. Some are useful for health, others harmful. For example, wines whose taste he describes as austere (sour) are cooler and should be given to those of a bilious complexion or to those who perform manual labor or live in hot regions.[48] Sweet wines, on the contrary should be given to cold and humid people whom it will warm. Wine does have a medical role, but most people do not understand how it should be used.

The physician answers many other questions about wine, exploding other popular misconceptions, such as why Germans are all drunks, which he claims has to do with their more robust bodies and the colder climate. He also makes a remarkable claim that drinking uncut wine is useful for pregnant women, especially those with cravings.[49] He denounces the custom of drinking wine chilled with snow or with saltpeter, which harms the brain, but approves of drinking wine with peaches, which prevents the fruit from corrupting.[50] He also explains why you get a headache from wine flavored with sandalwood, rose, amber, musk, and other aromatics.

In the end, Praefectus offers nothing new, and in fact he is a fairly orthodox Galenist, but his dialogue is good evidence that wine was being used and abused for health purposes, and that conflicting opinions invited consumers to use alcohol for practically any ailment. His opinion in the end is that wine can be useful, but people should learn how to use it properly.

It is ironic also that the largest and best-known of all sixteenth-century books devoted to wine, Andrea Bacci's *De naturali vinorum historia* printed in Rome in 1596, devotes many chapters to the question of wine as nourishment and medicine, and the temperature of wine, but in a sense quells any productive discussion on the topic. He had apparently read about the controversy in Verona, raging while he was a young boy, via Fracastoro, and in a brief paragraph dismisses it all.[51] Relying on the authority of Galen, here and elsewhere, Bacci merely claims that wine can be hot and moist, hot and dry, cold and dry, etc. and it all depends on the color, odor, age, flavor, latitude of cultivation, and a number of other factors. There are in fact no universal properties common to all wines. Moreover the ancient authorities, above all Galen, were never inconsistent about wine, they were merely referring to different varieties when prescribing wildly different applications. In the end we should trust their opinions rather than range abroad with our own wild speculations. Bacci was, therefore, not much more than a hack. He merely wrote authoritatively and studded his prose with classical references. On the topic of viticulture and wine varieties, his work is unparalleled, but regarding the nutritional and medicinal use of wine he brought the controversy and fruitful dialogue to a grinding halt.

It was not until the late seventeenth century that new chemical theories and mechanical theories reopened the entire question of the role of wine in a healthy diet. Just as in the sixteenth century, wine would have its ardent supporters and rabid detractors, and medical questions here as always were formed by social and cultural suppositions. The same would be the case in nineteenth century with new nutritional discoveries, and is, of course still the case today.

Notes

This chapter was originally presented as a paper at the Convivial Journeys conference in Adelaide, Australia in July 2004. The author wishes to express his thanks to the organizer (A. Lynn Martin) and fellow speakers at that conference, the staff of the Biblioteca Apostolica Vaticana and to the International Association for Culinary Professionals Foundation and Martini and Rossi for funding this research. Thanks also to Sean Thackrey, winemaker, who let me use his astonishing private collection of wine books.

1. Tim Unwin, *Wine and the Vine* (London: Routledge, 1991); Rod Phillips, *Wine a Short History* (New York: Harper Collins, 2000). As in the work of B. Ann Tlusty, *Bacchus and Civic Order* (Charlottesville and London: University Press of Virginia, 2001), which explores the physical setting of drinking establishments in Augsburg and shifting official attitudes toward drunkenness, I hope to describe the medical literature on wine as a series of conflicting voices which could either promote alcohol for health or condemn it as a means of social control. This was not a simple matter of elites with a reforming or "civilizing" attitude cracking down on the unruly masses. Physicians, themselves a cultural subset of elite society, could adopt a remarkable range of attitudes, showing, especially in the case of Italy, that alcohol consumption was not only an integral part of daily life, but something considered indispensable to health and well-being. In contrast to the German example, Italian elites seem to have been consciously searching for new ways to promote wine.

2. *Galen on Food*, tr. Mark Grant (New York: Routledge, 2000), p. 188.

3. Giovanii Battista Confalonieri, *De vini natura disputatio* (Venice, n.p., 1535), p. 8.

4. Ibid., pp. 13–14.

5. Ibid., pp. 5–6 "sunt et queadam vina quem illico caput, aut aggravarent, aut dolore afficiant, alia quem dolorem aut tollant, aut sobrietatem adducant."

6. Ibid., p. 21.

7. Ibid., p. 23.

8. Ibid., p. 57.

9. Ibid., pp. 32–5, "Vinum homini proprium esse alimentum summaque cum sanguine nostro affinitatem habere", p. 48.

10. Antonio Fumanelli, *Commentarium de vino, et facultatibus vini* (Venice: Patavini et Venturini Rossinelli, 1536), pp. 3–3v.

11. Ibid., pp. 6v–7.

12. Ibid., p. 14.

13. Ibid., pp. 18v–19, 23.

14. Ibid., p. 27.

15. Ibid., p. 43.

16. Ibid., p. 44. "Vinum non dilutum magis humectat, quoniam ut materia substantiam auget humiditam, quae venae et venter quae inanitia sunt indigent."

17. Ibid., pp. 48–9.

18. Ibid., p. 75v.

19. Ibid., pp. 53–4.

20. Girolamo Fracastoro, *Opera Omnia* (Venice, Iuntas, 1555), p. 244.

21. Ibid., p. 228.

22. Ibid., pp. 231v–2.

23. Ibid., p. 234. "vinum simpliciter calidum et siccum est pronunciandum: sive ut medicina, sive ut cibus, et alimentum sumatur."

24. Ibid., 234v.

25. Guglielmo Grataroli, *De vini natura* (Strasbourg: Theodosius Ribelius, 1565), p. 3.

26. Grataroli, *Directions for the Health of Magistrates*, tr. Thomas Newton (London: William How for Abraham Veale, 1574), C2.

27. Grataroli, *De vini*, p. 9

28. Grataroli, *Directions*, G2v.

29. Ibid., H.

30. Grataroli, *De vini*, pp. 10–11, 17

31. Ibid., p. 22.

32. Ibid., p. 31.

33. Ibid., pp. 34–6.

34. Ibid., pp. 39–42.

35. Ibid., p. 52 "Perniciosum autem et à ratione vera alienissimum est quorumdam praeceptum, hesternam crapulam matutina ingurgitatione profliganda esse."

36. Ibid., pp. 55–6.

37. Ibid., pp. 58–64.

38. Ibid., pp. 13–14.

39. Alessandro Petronio, *Del viver delli Romani* (Rome: Domenico Basa, 1592), p. 58.

40. Ibid., pp. 60–1.

41. Giovani Battista Scarlino, *Nuovo trattato della varietà, e qualità de vini, che vengono in Roma* (Rome: Valerio Dorico, 1554), Bii.

42. Ibid., Civ vo, Diii vo.

43. Ibid., Div.

44. Bartolomeo Taegio, *L'Humore* (Milan: Giovanni Antonio degli Antonii, 1564), p. 10.

45. Taegio, p. 18

46. Jacobus Praefectus *De diversorum vini generum* (Venice: Jordani Ziletti, 1559), p. 19v.

47. Ibid., p. 22.

48. Ibid., p. 32.

49. Ibid., p. 36v.

50. Ibid., pp. 32, 49.

51. Bacci, Andrea. *De naturali vinorum historia* (Rome: Nicholai Mutii, 1596), pp. 55–6.

–2–

Europe Divided

Wine, Beer, and the Reformation in Sixteenth-century Europe

Mack P. Holt

When historians of food and drink look at a map of Western Europe in the sixteenth century, they see a Europe divided between a largely beer (or ale) drinking culture in northern Europe, stretching from the British isles, across the North Sea to the Low Countries, Scandinavia, and the German Empire, and a largely wine-drinking culture in southern Europe, stretching from the Iberian peninsula across the Mediterranean coast from France, the Italian peninsula, and the Balkan region to Greece. There were large areas, of course, where the two drinking cultures overlapped in a wide belt right across the center of the European continent. Much of France and the German Empire falls into this category, for example, where both cereal grain and grape production were both significant components of the local economies. It was not the same geographic distribution of viticulture as we see today, however, as grapes were grown and wine was produced in quantity much farther north in Europe in the sixteenth century than is the case today. In sixteenth-century France, for just one example, grape vines were planted not only throughout the Paris region, but were also a significant part of the local economy as far north as the region around Beauvais.[1] Nevertheless, the pattern was still fairly striking: a largely wine-drinking south and a largely ale (or increasingly beer) drinking north divided Europeans into two different drinking cultures in the sixteenth century, with a band in the middle of the continent where the two cultures met and even intermingled.

Religious historians of the sixteenth century also see a divided Europe, though the geography is slightly different. Whereas most of northern Europe had turned to various forms of Protestantism by the end of the sixteenth century, most of southern Europe had remained loyal to the Roman Catholic Church. England and Wales had turned to its own *sui generis* version of Protestantism (the Church of England), and Scotland had converted to a Presbyterian form of Calvinism unlike England's church altogether, despite the fact that England and Scotland shared the same king after 1603. The Dutch Republic had evolved into its own reformed version of Calvinism, while nearly all of the northern German Empire—Saxony and Brandenburg being the most conspicuous—and all of Scandinavia had converted to Lutheranism by the end of the century. Small communities of more radical Protestants, pejoratively called Anabaptists, also dotted the European land-scape. At the same time, the entire Iberian peninsula, nearly all of France, the whole of the Italian peninsula, and most of the southern German Empire remained Catholic. To be sure, there were areas where Catholicism, Lutheransim, and the Reformed churches coexisted tentatively and often nervously: Hungary and Poland, as well as certain free Imperial cities being the obvious examples. But all in all, Europe in the sixteenth century was divided into northern and southern cultures by religion as well as by drink.

The obvious question, then, virtually poses itself: Is there any relationship between these two seemingly independent cultural geographies? I propose to address this question in two ways. First, given that the geographic divisions of wine and beer predated the Protestant reformations of the sixteenth century, I want to begin by exploring several possible hypotheses that might link wine to Catholicism and beer to Protestantism. I certainly do not intend to suggest in any kind of mechanical or determinist way that what Europeans drank largely deter-mined their religion. But there are a number of areas in which wine was linked to the Catholic Church that may help explain the sharp religious division in Western Europe. I am much more interested, however, in examining the relationship between drinking and religion from the opposite perspective: not so much how the different cultures of wine and beer impacted the geography of the religious refor-mations of the sixteenth century, but how the religious reformations of the six-teenth century impacted the geography of the wine and beer drinking cultures of Europe. Thus, most of this essay will examine the ways in which the various ref-ormations of the sixteenth century affected and influenced the drinking patterns of Europeans in sixteenth-century Europe. But first it is important to examine some of the links between the wine industry and the Catholic Church at the time of the Reformation.

Wine and the Catholic Church on the Eve of the Reformation

The most obvious link between wine and the Catholic Church was the doctrine of the Eucharist. While the doctrine evolved somewhat from the first century AD, there is no question that the Eucharist and its doctrine of transubstantiation had become one of the principal tenets of Christian faith by the High Middle Ages and that on the eve of the Reformation the Catholic Mass was the central rite of Christianity in the West. All Western Christians believed that the wine of the Mass literally turned into the blood of Christ when it was consecrated by an ordained priest. It was considered so holy, in fact, that ordinary lay men and women were not even allowed to drink it at the time of the Reformation, though they had cer-tainly done so in earlier centuries.[2] The consecrated wine was reserved for the clergy during the celebration of Mass, while the laity had to make do with the con-secrated Host, or unleavened bread. This made it all the more special for most laity, who almost everywhere in Europe usually did get some wine to wash down the unleavened bread, just not wine from the consecrated chalice blessed by the priest. Above all, the Mass was the central rite of the Catholic Church and it expressed in a very symbolic way the community of Christ as well as the social community of the parish. They all ate bread from a common loaf, while the priest consumed the consecrated wine on their behalf, the whole designed to underscore the collective Christian community of which they were all members. Thus, the Mass represented their spiritual communion with Christ as well as their social communion with each other. It symbolized to all Catholics and represented for them the very nature of their community.[3] When Luther and Calvin came along and told Catholics that the Mass was a sham and that the doctrine of transubstantiation was just a magic trick conjured up by the priest, it was more than an attack on the central belief of their faith; it was an attack on the very notion of community that the Eucharist purported to represent. Thus, for many Catholics conversion to Protestantism meant above all a willingness to abandon the notion of Catholic community fostered by the Eucharist in order to accept Protestant notions of community based on the idea of the elect and predestination. Many Catholics in Europe, especially in beer-drinking northern Europe, did convert, however, so this was not an impossible hurdle to overcome. The real question is whether it was really a significant barrier in southern Europe where wine was actually produced.

Economic motives certainly complicate this picture, to be sure, but I want to emphasize the cultural links of religion more than base motives of material gain. One way that religious culture and material culture were interconnected, for example, is the way that wine served as a medium of exchange and remuneration for Masses for the dead in pre-modern Europe. Although I am drawing on my own research in Burgundy (central eastern France), this practice seems to have been widely prevalent in other parts of Europe where wine formed one of the principal components of the local economy. The system worked as follows: when anyone wanted to fund perpetual Masses for the dead to be performed by a local priest— either for a recently deceased relative or for one's self—the Masses were paid for in wine futures. Thus, the local priest was promised that he could have the profits every year from the sale of wine from a particular parcel of vines owned by the endower of the Mass in return for the priest saying a special Mass for the designated person or persons on a specific date every year in perpetuity. Thus, the clergy became middlemen, or brokers, in a system of wine exchange in which they purchased wine futures in significant amounts, not for consumption themselves or for speculation, but in order to fund the needs of their parish. The owners and workers in the vineyards—called *vignerons* in French—even funded other special Masses, not for the release of souls from Purgatory into Heaven, but for the protection of their vineyards from the natural predators in this world: from the hail, storms, drought, insects, etc. so common to viticulturists in all periods and places. Thus, there is clearly an economic motive here linking wine to the Catholic Church, though I would argue that it is too centrally tied to the culture of the Catholic religion to be treated as purely a secular factor.[4] Nevertheless, it would be possible to make a case that these economic and cultural ties that the wine industry had to the Catholic Church in the sixteenth century made it more likely that Europeans in the wine-producing areas of Europe might be less willing to abandon their traditional practices and beliefs for Protestantism. What speaks against this theory, however, is that some of the most significant exceptions to this link occurred in some of the heaviest wine-producing areas of Europe. In southern France, for example, the region of Languedoc was home to some of the most intensive viticulture in all of France. Nevertheless, Calvinism took root there in a number of villages and towns where wine was the backbone of the local economy. Although a clear majority of vineyard workers remained Catholic even in Languedoc, it is equally true that the links between wine and the Catholic Church did not prevent others from converting to the new religion.[5] Also in parts of the Rhineland where grapes were produced in quantity in the sixteenth century—areas of Alsace near Strasbourg and the region of the Palatinate near Heidelberg, not to mention the Swiss cantons in the Lower Rhine, being obvious examples—Lutheranism and later Calvinism also took root.[6] So drawing any simple conclusions between wine drinkers and Catholicism, or conversely between beer drinkers and Protestantism, is fraught with difficulties.

Another possible geographical difference dividing northern and southern Europe in the sixteenth century was the practice of penance and its link with Carnival. Carnival was the week-long period ending on Shrove Tuesday (called *Mardi Gras* in French-speaking Europe and *Fastnacht* in German-speaking Europe) that marked the end of feasting and indulgence and the beginning of a period of fasting and penance during the period of Lent, leading up to Easter Sunday. In contrast to Carnival, Lent was a period of fasting and abstinence: *carne*, or flesh, and *vale*, meaning farewell, from which the English word carnival is derived, was forbidden. It was not just the consumption of animal flesh that was forbidden during Lent, but the indulgence in human flesh in the form of sexual relations was also prohibited during Lent, even between legally married husbands and wives. Thus, Carnival was a period for the indulgence of the flesh, while Lent was a period of the denial of the flesh. The sins of the flesh—gluttony as well as fornication—were slightly more acceptable during the one week of Carnival, so that they might be better identified and more easily eradicated and confessed during Lent. The Carnival regime of fasting and sexuality was thus one half of its structural opposite, Lent, which joined together the carnal and the penitential activities of the pre-Easter period. Sixteenth-century Christians had to confess their sins and do penance before receiving the holy feast of the Eucharist on Easter Sunday, and the whole properly began by singling out the sins of carnality in the Carnival period preceding Lent itself. What is curious, however, is the geographic division of how Europeans practiced Carnival. In southern and eastern Europe in the sixteenth century, Carnival was practiced more or less like it still continues to be practiced today in the New World variants in New Orleans and Rio de Janeiro. That is, carnality was represented by a carnival figure, a king or prince, who dominated a procession and a feast. Sometimes it was represented by fat sausages or other symbols of lechery such as bears or cocks, and in Nantes in western France *Mardi Gras* was dedicated to St. Gobillard (St. Vomit), who seems an appropriate patron for the entire feast of Carnival. The king of Carnival was invariably a fat man who encouraged lots of eating and drinking. In northern and western Europe, however, none of this excess of the flesh seemed to make much of an impression. In the British Isles, northwestern France, most of the Low Countries, virtually all of Scandinavia, and most of the northern German-speaking lands, there was generally only a one day celebration marking the beginning of Lent with nothing more lecherous or gluttonous than a ritualistic eating of pancakes on the night of Shrove Tuesday itself. We cannot explain this as a result of the Reformation, since this social and cultural division in the practice of Carnival predated the Reformation. As John Bossy has suggested, it appears that the reason for this division lies in the history of penitential practice in pre-modern Europe. Where the practice of individual penance and the penitential tariff had been invented in the High Middle Ages in northwest Europe, Carnival was a low-key affair. Where penance was still a public sacrament, however, that is in southern and eastern Europe where both confession and the act of penance signifying forgiveness were public and communal rituals, Carnival was also a more public and communal ritual focused on the sins of the flesh.[7]

Bossy's evidence for this geographic division is supported at least in part by Anne Thayer's study of penitential sermon books circulating in Western Europe on the eve of the Reformation. Thayer examined dozens of different sermon collections in hundreds of editions that were written to be used during Lenten sermons on the theme of confession and penance. Although she never explicitly tries to link her findings with the geographical division in the practice of Carnival as Bossy has done, Thayer has found that in southern and western Europe where Carnival was strongest the preachers stressed the power of the sacrament to work forgiveness and emphasized the role of the priest above all. In other words, the preachers placed a less demanding role on the penitent. In northern and eastern Europe where Carnival was less widely celebrated, however, the preachers stressed a more rigorist line and emphasized the importance of contrition and satisfaction, holding the penitents much more responsible for the forgiveness and satisfaction of sin. Thayer's point is that such a rigorist penitential system that stressed the role of the sinner and reduced the role of the priest in the process of forgiveness might have made Lutheranism and Calvinism more attractive in the Holy Roman Empire and in southern France where Protestantism flourished.[8]

But there appears to be no link whatsoever between the geographical division of Europe regarding Carnival and a wine-drinking culture of the flesh in southern Europe and a more ascetic beer drinking culture of penance in northern Europe. And as most scholars of the Reformation now fully accept, the confessional divisions of Europe into Protestant and Catholic areas was just as much he result of politics and the political choices of kings and princes as it was a result of the religious choices (not to mention drinking choices) of sixteenth-century Christians. Indeed, the idea of a magisterial Reformation, where a prince or magistrate had to support the Protestant religion in some overt and explicit way in order for it to survive anywhere in Europe is one of the common clichés of current scholarship. To be sure, in many cases popular pressures from below were pivotal in determining which religious choices princes and magistrates made. The case of England is a typical example, where by the reign of Elizabeth (1558–1603) the crown had opted for a public and permanent break with Rome and for a church that was doctrinally Protestant, even if the liturgy and calendar still looked remarkably Catholic in appearance. The English people went along with this transformation largely without violence or serious opposition, and in many ways they helped lead Elizabeth to this compromise.[9] In France the opposite was true, as the monarchy clung tenaciously to the Catholic faith, ultimately forcing French Protestants—or Huguenots as they were called—underground or abroad. French public opinion forced Henry of Navarre, the Protestant heir to the throne, to convert to Catholicism in 1593 in order to be accepted as king by French Catholics. By 1598 when the crown finally recognized the right of the Huguenots to exist legally in the kingdom, they made up less than 5 percent of the total population.[10] Thus, it seems pretty clear that any direct or facile link between the north-south division of beer drinkers and wine drinkers in the sixteenth century and the confessional divide between Protestants and Catholics is simply illusory.

The Impact of the Reformation on Drinking Patterns

What, then, is the relationship between wine, beer, and the Reformation? Rather than looking for ways in which Europeans' drinking patterns affected the Reformation, it is probably much more fruitful to analyze the ways in which the various reformations of the sixteenth century impacted European drinking patterns. One way to do this is to try to look at the Reformation less as a confrontation between Protestants and Catholics and see it more as a transformation from a generally unified though fractious traditional church into a series of reformed churches (including reformed Catholicism). What all these new reformed churches shared in common was not just the desire to eradicate the abuses within the traditional church, but they also wanted to remake society into a more godly kingdom of Christ on earth. Thus, social and moral discipline became a central concern of all the reformed movements both Protestant and Catholic. And central to this new disciplinary focus was a renewed effort to regulate the consumption of alcohol.[11] All the new churches waged war on drunkenness and unruly behavior, though it tended to be the most radical Protestant Reformers who were the most outspoken. Because wine in southern Europe and beer in northern Europe were so much a part of the diet as well as the culture, no mainstream Protestant church or government ever sought to eradicate alcohol consumption altogether. Several individual radicals did advocate total abstinence, however, and eventually a small number of

Anabaptist communities also tried to enforce prohibition. While most Reformers tended to argue over where the proper boundaries should be between the sacred and the profane, the most radical Reformers sought to eliminate these boundaries altogether, making everything sacred in a true kingdom of Christ on earth. Claiming to take a literal interpretation of the Bible as their guide and a spiritualist approach to divine revelation as their principal methodology, these Protestant militants declared war on alcohol.

This is very strange in one sense, because the Bible never even hinted that drinking alcohol was a sin. To be sure, drinking to excess was a sin, and drunkenness was excoriated in the scriptures of both Jews and Christians alike. Drinking wine, however, was part of the cultural and historical heritage of the Mediterranean basin where both Judaism and Christianity were born. Wine was just as central an element of the Passover Seder as it was of the Christian Mass. Moreover, the first thing that Noah did after spending forty days on the ark was to plant a grapevine.[12] And the very first miracle mentioned in the New Testament was Jesus's turning water into wine at the wedding feast at Cana.[12] Furthermore, Paul even explicitly advised Timothy that drinking wine was good for his health.[14] So, any literal interpretation of the Bible that claimed a total abstinence from alcohol only serves to show that a literal interpretation is still just an interpretation. It is nevertheless true that several of the Protestant reformations of the sixteenth century spawned a variety of different sects and communities that attempted to severely restrict alcohol in their community as both sinful and dangerous.

It has to be said that public declarations for the outright prohibition of alcohol and its complete removal from society were extremely rare during the Reformation. Most Reformers called for the policing and regulation of drinking more than outright prohibition. Nevertheless, there were such minority voices and they appeared almost immediately after Martin Luther and Ulrich Zwingli began their ministries after 1520. Two such Reformers were Ludwig Haetzer and Sebastian Franck. Both began in the mainstream of the Protestant Reformation, yet they eventually found themselves pushed to the radical fringes of Protestantism when they discovered that the kind of reformations being advocated by Luther and Zwingli were not as thoroughgoing as they had hoped. Both also ended their careers as outspoken radicals shunned by their former colleagues. That each came out so militantly against alcohol reminds us that there were always Reformers who wanted much more than just a cleansing of the church of doctrinal abuses and immoral practices. Many wanted a more immediate social revolution that would transform society into a kingdom of Christ on earth in its fullest sense.

The first Reformer to denounce alcohol publicly was almost certainly Ludwig Haetzer (ca. 1500–29). Haetzer was a young priest from Thurgau who had already attracted attention in 1523 as the author of a treatise condemning images. This got him noticed in Zurich, where Ulrich Zwingli commissioned him to work on a number of translations because of his language skills. While in Zurich Haetzer is probably best known as the scribe who copied down the proceedings of the famous

Second Zurich Disputation on October 23, 1523, when the Great and Small Councils of the city called upon the clergy and laity to debate the use of images.[15] Two years later in Augsburg Haetzer published his treatise against the consumption of alcohol, titled *On Evangelical Drinking*.[16] Haetzer believed that the entire world had succumbed to excessive drinking, because Satan had praised drinking and carousing as part of the freedom of a Christian. Therefore, he was not surprised to see that it was the evangelicals in Saxony and Zurich who were drinking the most. These evangelical drinkers were, in his mind, more interested in drinking than in worshipping God. The first Christians came together, he continued, not to drink, but to worship the Lord. They were brought together not by Bacchus, but by the Holy Spirit. Alcohol was thus to be shunned, and he went on to suggest that any evangelical drinkers who refused to conform should be expelled from the community. Haetzer's views on drinking were not his only ideas that were out of the mainstream of evangelical Protestantism. He was forced out of Zurich and he later fled to Augsburg, Basel, Strasbourg, and eventually Constance. By this time he had become linked to various Anabaptist communities and had become acquainted with the spiritualist Hans Denck, who had already denounced Luther's view of salvation and insisted on free will. In 1528 Haetzer was finally arrested by Protestant authorities in Constance, technically on charges of adultery, but in truth for his anti-Trinitarian views. There in the town square of Constance, the same city in which he was originally ordained as a priest, he was executed on February 4, 1529. His outspoken views on the prohibition of alcohol were not what got him into trouble, though they do reflect the explicit strain of prohibitionism that would later mark many—though clearly not all—radical Reform groups.[17]

While Haetzer's views on alcohol were not so widely known, another radical Protestant soon joined him in denouncing the consumption of alcohol. Sebastian Franck (1499–1542) published a more widely read treatise in 1528 called *Concerning the Horrible Vice of Drunkenness*.[18] Franck was from a family of weavers in Donauwörth, who was attracted to theology and eventually became an ordained priest. It was not long before he was attracted to Lutheranism, however, and he quickly became a Lutheran pastor and chaplain near Nuremberg. Like Haetzer, Franck despised the sin of drunkenness, and he made the abolition of alcohol a central part of what he saw as a much-needed reform of morals in the German-speaking lands. For Franck, drinking alcohol to excess brought on "a wild confused mind, dizzy head, bleary eyes, a stinking breath, bad stomach, shaking hands, gout, dropsy, weeping leg sores, [and] water on the brain." Alcohol only added further to a person's already impaired reason; and because it led to sin, it also damaged men's souls. Thus he reasoned that those who drank alcohol were "heathens and not Christian, who do not show forth the fruits of faith."[19] Franck was so despondent because he saw that so many kings and princes were drunks, he attributed a variety of social ills to alcohol, including blasphemy, idolatry, theft, murder, and even the German Peasants' War of 1525. The situation was so acute, he believed, that God's final judgment would soon punish all humankind for their sins of drunkenness, as a chapter entitled "How boozing, gorging, and drinking are a certain sign before the end times" makes clear. The only remedy for Franck was a prohibition of alcohol altogether. And those who refused to abide by it, he argued, should be expelled from the community:

> Oh misery! We are not alone drunk from wine, but drunk, drunk with the lying spirit, error and ignorance. One should punish the public vice, preachers with the word and ban, the princes with the sword and law. For so long as no ban exists, and is in place, I recognize no Gospel or Christian community to speak of. One must remove the impure from the community of God.[20]

What Franck most desired was a church of visible saints who were constantly on their guard against sin. Unless sin and vice could be eliminated altogether, then he believed that there could be no Christian community. And because there seemed to be neither preacher nor prince willing to heed his advice, he believed that the day of judgment was at hand. "Our destruction is nearer than we believe," he warned, "and the ax is already laid to the roots of the tree."[21]

Both Haetzer and Franck found that their views on alcohol were more widely shared by some Anabaptist groups than by either Luther or Zwingli. The very earliest Anabaptist confession was the "Seven Articles of Schleitheim" in 1527, written by Michael Sattler of the Swiss Brethren group of Anabaptists. Article 4 explicitly prohibited the patronage of taverns and other drinking houses on pain of ban from the community, as drinking alcohol was included in a litany of sinful activities, "which are highly regarded by the world yet are carried on in flat contradiction to the command of God."[22] And some individual radicals, such as Peter Riedemann of the Hutterite Bretheren, echoed this sentiment. In his "Confession of Faith" written in 1540 Riedemann condemned all drinking establishments and tavern-keepers for luring men into sin by serving them drinks. "It is the cause of evil and transgression of the commandments of God," he argued, "for thereby is the man moved and lured on to drink when he otherwise would not do so. Therefore it is against nature and is sin and evil ... It is an invention of the devil to catch men, drawing them into his net, making them cleave to him and forsake God and leading them into all sins."[23] Not all Hutterite communities demanded total abstinence, and it is clear that some even grew their own grapes and hops to make wine and beer. The same was true of Mennonites, followers of the Dutch Anabaptist leader Menno Simons (1496–1561), who were strong opponents of drunkenness without totally abstaining from alcohol altogether. Nevertheless, it was the few outspoken radicals such as Haetzer, Franck, and Riedemann who gave all Anabaptists the collective reputation of being drinkers of water rather than of wine and beer.

Another common misperception, in fact, is that it was John Calvin's efforts to instill moral discipline in Geneva in the 1540s, 1550s, and 1560s that established the foundation of Protestant attempts to regulate alcohol. The execution of the

Spaniard Miguel Servetus in 1553 for heresy as well as the notorious oversight of the city by the Calvinist consistory has consistently given Calvin the reputation of a proto-Puritan killjoy. This is patently unfair, however, as Calvin was a moderate man who never thought about trying to eliminate alcohol from Geneva. While he did undertake a brief experiment of placing Bibles in the taverns in Geneva, he ultimately chose to regulate drinking and drunkenness by attempting to transform the tavern from a place of sociability. In 1547 at Calvin's urging, the city council passed a new drinking ordinance: "There is to be no treating of one another to drinks, under penalty of 3 *sous* ... There are to be no carousals, under penalty of 10 *sous*."[24] Though Calvin was clearly trying to undermine the sociability of drinking together with friends, he was by no means attempting to eliminate alcohol from Geneva altogether. The real opponent of alcohol in the Reformed (Calvinist) tradition was not Calvin at all, but one of his predecessors. Martin Bucer had befriended Calvin in Strasbourg for three years prior to Calvin's invitation to Geneva in 1541. The much older Bucer had a strong influence on Calvin and helped him see the necessity of policing and enforcing moral discipline in any godly community. He showed the younger Reformer how a consistory could work to maintain discipline in a congregation in a much larger city, ideas that Calvin certainly took with him to Geneva.[25] But Bucer went much farther than Calvin did in terms of alcohol and drinking. As he wrote in his principal work, *On the Kingdom of Christ*, Bucer felt that a true kingdom of Christ on earth had to regulate eating and drinking very carefully. Bucer was especially fond of fasting, since it was so highly recommended by both Jesus and the apostles of the New Testament. But for Bucer, fasting was not enough: "There should be abstinence not only from illicit pleasures of the flesh but even from permissible pleasures."[26] This was all part of a larger goal of creating a kingdom of Christ on earth by eliminating sin from a godly community. Every member of that community who professed piety was required to abstain from "all luxury, pomp, and excess in housing, clothing, ornamentation of the body, food and drink, and all things contributing more to the delight of the flesh than to the virtue of spirit." Moreover, he maintained that for all true Christians, "whether they eat, or drink, or whatever else they do in word or in work, everything is to be done in the name of the Lord Jesus for the Glory of God."[27] Although Bucer opposed all pubic drinking places in principle, he recognized the need for public inns in order to house out of town visitors. Even there, however, he demanded that innkeepers must be men of decency and good character, and that they should "take an interest not only in the physical well-being of the guests but also in the holiness and integrity of life and morals."[28] Bucer spent the last decade of his life in England, where he dedicated *On the Kingdom of Christ* to the young Protestant King Edward VI when it was published in 1549. And the legacy of his views on the regulation of drinking are clearly evident in the Puritans of late sixteenth-century and early seventeenth-century England.

The term Puritan, much like the term Anabaptist, is fraught with ambiguity and confusion because it encompassed so many different views, individuals, and groups. Nevertheless, it is certainly true that after the Anabaptists, the Puritans were more militantly hostile to alcohol than any other sect or denomination in early modern Europe. All were members of the Church of England, though most considered the Elizabethan Settlement much too Catholic to suit their tastes, with bishops, the liturgical calendar of saints' days, clerical vestments, etc. being at the top of their long list of complaints. They also expected Elizabeth to enact a much more thoroughgoing "reformation of manners" than what the Thirty-Nine Articles had brought about. Thus, drinking and alehouses were obvious targets of Puritan condemnation. Puritan hostility only increased in the early seventeenth century, as economic dislocation, forced migration, and urbanization caused many of the poor to turn to drink in order to meet more and more of their dietary needs. The Puritan preacher William Vaughn made a typical attack in 1611, claiming that alehouses "breed conspiracies, combinations, common conjurations, detractions, [and] defamations." The Puritan magistrates of the local corporation of Northampton complained constantly that "the horrible and loathsome sin of drunkenness does daily increase to the dishonour of God [and] the impoverishing of this town and commonwealth." At Preston in Lancashire Christopher Hudson claimed in 1631 that alehouses were "nests of Satan where the owls of impiety lurk and where all evil is hatched." And finally, in the county of Kent justice William Lambarde exclaimed that alehouses and the excessive drinking they produced were dangers not just to proper religion but to orderly society as well: "your children and ser-vants be corrupted in manners, bastards be multiplied in parishes, thieves and rogues do swarm in the highways, the lawful pastimes of the land be abandoned, and dicing, cards, and bowling be set up in place."[29] As historian Peter Clark has indicated, there was a broad consensus of opinion among many Puritans—largely made up of the middling and the respectable classes—that excessive drinking in alehouses bred not just drunkenness and ungodly behavior, but that alehouses were sites that generated crime and social disorder. "In other words," Clark writes, "the alehouse was perceived as the command post of men who sought to turn the tra-ditional world upside down and create their own alternative society."[30]

It turns out, however, that despite the Puritan excoriations against alehouses and excessive drinking in seventeenth-century England, drinking houses were hardly guilty of the charges of unruliness, crime, and disorder that were leveled against them. To be sure, drunken and disorderly conduct was common in English ale-houses, but there is no statistical evidence to correlate crime and disorder with ale-houses.[31] Moreover, ironically the Puritans themselves were partly responsible for the rise in popularity of English alehouses as a result of their intense pressure to reform manners and behavior. Before the Reformation it was the parish church and the churchyard that served as the central focus of most village and community life. The parish church was usually at the literal and figurative center of the community. It was there that much of the ritual life of medieval Christianity took place. Over and above the sacraments that took place inside the church, outside in the church-yard was where religious processions assembled, where guild and fraternity members met, and where parish feasts and church-ales took place. It was also the site of plays and performances, as well as May games and other rituals that had nothing to do with religion *per se*. English Reformers in general and Puritan activists in particular sought to eliminate all these activities, especially church-ales—the selling of ale or beer in the churchyard after services in order to raise money for the parish—as being ungodly and not worthy of a kingdom of Christ on earth. The alehouse then became an efficacious alternative for all these communal activities once they had been eradicated from the parish church. From the early seventeenth century, then, alehouses became for the poorer half of society the only alternative they had to the rituals of sociability that had formerly taken place on parish church property. We are speaking here of much more than a space for the buying and selling of beer (hopped ale), as various games, mummers, and other social activities that once took place in church now took place in the local ale-house.[32] The principal point to be stressed here, however, is that the Puritan opponents of drinking and everything that they (largely falsely) believed was associated with it came to transform drinking patterns in England in significant ways. While Puritan authorities, even during the height of Puritan influence in the 1650s, were never able to implement the kind of reformation of manners that they had hoped for, their voices and their scrutiny of daily life was both significant and intense.

Conclusions

Above all, the hostility to drink of many Anabaptists in the German Empire and Puritans in England contrasted sharply with attitudes towards drink in most of southern, Catholic Europe. Catholic reformers were equally committed to fighting against drunkenness and the unruly behavior that usually accompanied it, but they never tried to eliminate alcohol altogether as a few radical Protestants did, nor did they ever initiate the kind of reformation of manners associated with Puritanism in early modern England. Thus, the north–south divide in European drinking patterns with which I began this essay is not really so much a division between a wine-drinking culture and a beer-drinking culture, as it is about a split between a northern culture of ascetic Protestantism that excoriated the drinking of alcohol in the sixteenth and seventeenth centuries and a more tolerant southern culture, almost entirely Catholic, in which drinking was considered more a natural part of social life and community rather than some demon to be excised. It is clear that there was a large middle ground in which both cultures coexisted nervously and tentatively, but there is no doubt that the harshest and most vocal critics of alcohol during the Reformation came from the Protestant side. There are obviously exceptions to this general trend, as Charles Ludington's essay on Scotland in this very volume shows; though located in northern Europe, Scotland's drinking attitudes of the seventeenth century resembled the Catholics of southern Europe much more than the English Puritans.[33] It should also be added that Puritan influence in England disappeared along with the Protectorate at the Restoration in 1660.

This leads me to ask one final question about the Reformation's legacy on European drinking patterns. Social and cultural anthropologists have long since recognized a geographic division in contemporary Europe between a "wet" drinking culture in the south and a "dry" drinking culture in the north. What they mean by this is that in southern "wet" Europe drinking alcohol is more a part of daily life and alcohol is consumed with meals on a regular basis as a form of sociability as well as a vital element of commensality. Children are reared with expectations of drinking alcohol with meals and of learning how to participate in this "wet" culture from an early age. Moreover, alcoholism and diseases associated with excessive drinking are proportionately rarer and less problematic than elsewhere in the West. In "dry" northern Europe, however, drinking alcohol is perceived as something less connected with mealtimes and more associated with drinking in the tavern, pub, beer hall, or even at drinking parties at home. There also appears to be much more alcoholism and drinking related diseases than in southern Europe. Of course, the very definitions of alcoholism and problem drinking are cultural constructions, as these same anthropologists are quick to point out. Nevertheless, their research suggests that alcoholism and drinking problems are most acute in societies in whose norms and values about drinking are the most severe.[34] This obviously raises the question of whether the northern European enemies of alcohol in the sixteenth and seventeenth centuries, such as the Anabaptists and Puritans described above, may have contributed in some indirect way to this contemporary division in European drinking patterns. There is no obvious answer, nor can I offer any corroborating evidence even to suggest such a historical link. But as drinkers in the United States were forced to discover in the 1920s, most historical attempts to prohibit the drinking of alcohol altogether have proved to be counter-productive. The Protestant Reformation obviously did alter the drinking habits of some Europeans in the sixteenth and seventeenth centuries, but it is not clear at all that these changes were necessarily what the Reformers had hoped for.

Notes

1. For Paris see Jean Jacquart, *La crise rurale en l'Ile de France, 1550–1670* (Paris: Armand Colin, 1974), and for Beauvais see Pierre Goubert, *Beauvais et les Beauvaisis de 1600 à 1730* (Paris: Ecole ds Hautes Etudes en Sciences Sociales, 1960). Also see Roger Dion, *Histoire de la vigne et du vin en France des origines au XIXe siècle* (Paris: Flammarion, 1959).

2. Wine was withdrawn from the laity in the twelfth century as a means of elevating the status of the clergy *vis à vis* the laity. See Joseph A. Jungmann, *The Mass of the Roman Rite*, trans. Francis A. Brunner, 2 vols. (New York: Benziger Brothers, 1951–5), Vol. 2, pp. 382–6. Also see John Bossy, "The Mass as a Social Institution, 1200–1700," *Past & Present* 100 (August 1983): 29–61.

3. See my own article, "Wine, Community and Reformation in Sixteenth-Century Burgundy," *Past & Present* 138 (February 1993): 58–93.

4. See my article "Wine, Life, and Death in Early Modern Burgundy," *Food and Foodways* vol. 8, no. 2 (1999): 73–98.

5. See Emmanuel Le Roy Ladurie, *Les paysans de Languedoc*, 2 vols. (Paris: Ecole Pratique des Hautes Etudes, 1966); and Raymond A. Mentzer, *Heresy Proceedings in Languedoc, 1500–1560* (Philadelphia: American Philosophical Society, 1984).

6. See the article by Tom Scott on "German History" in Jancis Robinson, ed., *The Oxford Companion to Wine* (Oxford: Oxford University Press, 1994), pp. 429–41.

7. See John Bossy, *Christianity in the West, 1400–1700* (Oxford: Oxford University Press, 1985), pp. 43–5, as well as the same author's article, "The Social History of Confession in the Age of Reformation," *Transactions of the Royal Historical Society*, 5th series 25 (1975): 21–38. Also see Thomas F. Tentler, *Sin and Confession on the Eve of the Reformation* (Princeton: Princeton University Press, 1977).

8. Anne T. Thayer, *Penitence, Preaching, and the Coming of the Reformation* (Aldershot: Ashgate, 2002), especially pp. 184–95. This theme is nicely summarized in her article, "Judge and Doctor: Images of the Confessor in Printed Model Sermon Collections, 1450–1520," in Katharine J. Lualdi and Anne T. Thayer, eds, *Penitence in the Age of Reformations* (Aldershot: Ashgate, 2000), pp. 10–29.

9. See Ethan H. Shagan, *Popular Politics and the English Reformation* (Cambridge: Cambridge University Press, 2003), as well as Eamon Duffy, *The Stripping of the Altars: Traditional Religion in England, 1400–1580* (New Haven and London: Yale University Press, 1992).

10. Mack P. Holt, *The French Wars of Religion, 1562–1629* (Cambridge: Cambridge University Press, 1995; 2nd ed. 2005).

11. The literature here is vast, but for an entry into it, see Ronnie Po-Chia Hsia, *Social Discipline in the Reformation: Central Europe, 1550–1750* (London: Routledge, 1989). And on the regulation of alcohol, see Peter Clark, *The English Alehouse: A Social History, 1200–1830* (London: Longman, 1983), especially chap. 8; B. Ann Tlusty, *Bacchus and Civic Order: The Culture of Drink in Early Modern Germany* (Charlottesville: University of Virginia Press, 2001; and A. Lynn Martin, *Alcohol, Sex, and Gender in Early Modern Europe* (London: Palgrave, 2001).

12. Genesis 9:20.

13. John 2:1–11.

14. 1 Timothy 5:23.

15. See Donald J. Ziegler, ed., *Great Debates of the Reformation* (New York: Random House, 1969), pp. 35–69, for an English translation of the highlights of this debate, as well as Haetzer's role in recording it.

16. Ludwig Haetzer, *Von dem Evangelischen Zechen und von der Christenred*

aus heliger geschrifft 1525 dem Konstanzer Bürger Achatius Froembd gewidmet (Augsburg, 1525). This is a very rare work, and I was unable to locate a copy in the United States.

17. For more on Haetzer, see Fritz Blanke, "Reformation und Alcoholisimus," *Zwingliana* (1949): 75–89; the article by Christian Neff on Haetzer in *Mennonitisches Lexikon,* 4 vols. (Frankfurt and Karlsruhe, 1913), Vol. 1, pp. 226–7; and the biography by J. F. G. Goesters, *Ludwig Haetzer* (Güttersloh, 1957). There is little in English on Haetzer, but see George Hunston Williams, *The Radical Reformation*, 3rd rev. ed. (Kirksville: Sixteenth Centure Studies, 1992), pp. 181–6, 255–60, and 301–3; and Charles Garside, "Ludwig Haetzer's Pamphlet Against Images," *Mennonite Quarterly Review* 34 (1960): 3–19.

18. Sebastian Franck, *Von dem greulichen Laster der Trunkenheit* (Nuremburg, 1528). There is a very good discussion of this treatise in English in Patrick Hayden-Roy, *The Inner Word and the Outer World: A Biography of Sebastian Franck* (New York: Peter Lang, 1994), pp. 19–25. All quotations that follow come from Hayden-Roy's translations.

19. Quoted in Hayden-Roy, *The Inner Word*, pp. 20–1.

20. Quoted in ibid., p. 21.

21. Quoted in ibid., p. 23.

22. See Williams, *The Radical Reformation*, pp. 288–94 (quote on p. 292).

23. Peter Riedemann, *Account of Our Religion, Doctrine, and Faith Given by Peter Riedemann of the Brothers Whom Men Call Hutterites*, trans. Kathleen Hasenberg (London: Hodder and Stoughton, 1950), pp. 127–9.

24. "Ordinances for the Supervision of the Churches dependant on the Seigneury of Geneva, 3 February 1547," in *Calvin: Theological Treatises*, ed. and trans. J. K. S. Reid (Philadelphia and London: Westminster Press, 1954), p. 81.

25. For Bucer's impact on Calvin, see William J. Bouwsma, *John Calvin: A Sixteenth-Century Portrait* (New York and Oxford: Oxford University Press, 1988), especially pp. 21–4; Amy Nelson Burnett, *The Yoke of Christ: Martin Bucer and Christian Discipline* (Kirksville: Sixteenth Century Studies, 1994); and Diarmaid MacCulloch, *The Reformation: A History* (New York and London: Viking, 2004), pp. 231–6.

26. Martin Bucer, *De Regno Christi*, in William Pauck, ed. and trans., *Melancthon and Bucer* (Philadelphia: Westminster Press, 1969), p. 254.

27. Ibid., p. 354.

28. Ibid., p. 34.

29. All quoted in Peter Clark, "The Alehouse and Alternative Society," in Donald Pennington and Keith Thomas, eds, *Puritans and Revolutionaries: Essays in Seventeenth-Century History Presented to Christopher Hill* (Oxford: Oxford University Press, 1978), p. 47.

30. Ibid., p. 48. Also see his *The English Alehouse*, pp. 145–78.

31. Clark, "The Alehouse and Alternative Society," pp. 57–9.

32. On the rise of the alehouse see Clark, *The English Alehouse*, 24–34; and

Clark, "The Alehouse and Alternative Society," 61–2. For the various activities that would become a part of alehouse sociability attacked by Puritans, see Ronald Hutton, *The Rise and Fall of Merry England: The Ritual Year, 1400–1700* (Oxford: Oxford University Press, 1994), especially pp. 99–100 and 111–53; Keith Wrightson, *English Society, 1580–1680* (London: Hutchinson & Co., 1982), pp. 167–70; and David Underdown, *Revel, Riot, and Rebellion: Popular Politics and Culture in England, 1603–1660* (Oxford: Oxford University Press, 1985), pp. 241–44. Finally, see the essay by A. Lynn Martin in this volume, "Drinking and Alehouses in the Diary of an English Mercer's Apprentice, 1663–1674, pp. 93–106.

33. Charles C. Ludington, "To the King O'er the Water: Scotland and Claret, c. 1660–1763," pp. 163–84.

34. For a review of the literature, see Dwight B. Heath, "A Decade of Development in the Anthropological Study of Alcohol Use, 1970–1980," in Mary Douglas, ed., *Constructive Drinking: Perspectives on Drink from Anthropology* (Cambridge: Cambridge University Press, 1987), pp. 16–68, but especially p. 46; Mac Marshall, ed., *Beliefs, Behaviors, and Alcoholic Beverages: A Cross-Cultural Survey* (Ann Arbor: University of Michigan Press, 1979); Michael W. Everett, Jack O. Waddell, and Dwight B. Heath, eds, *Cross-Cultural Approaches to the Study of Alcohol: An Interdisciplinary Perspective* (The Hague: Walter De Gruyter, 1976); and Thomas M. Wilson, ed., *Drinking Cultures* (Oxford: Berg, 2005), especially chap. 5 on Norwegian drinking patterns.

–3–

In the Public Sphere

Efforts to Curb the Consumption of Rum in Connecticut, 1760–1820

David W. Conroy

Printer and Federalist Timothy Green (1737–96) of New London, Connecticut usually found space in his newspaper for a finely wrought criticism of the use of rum. In 1788, he reprinted a piece originally published in a Pennsylvania paper in his *Connecticut Gazette*. Here a "Friend to Family Happiness" calculated the amount expended by a drinker of a pint of rum a day over a period of ten years. He found that this amount would not only buy the drinker a small farm and stock, but "enable him to purchase" a "small collection of books" and subscribe to "a newspaper" with which "he might improve himself and entertain his family."[1] Yet many of the readers of the *Gazette*, as Green well knew, continued to visit local taverns in order to read the news or hear it read aloud. Back in 1744, gentleman traveler and physician Alexander Hamilton had come across such a group in a tavern in Milford, Connecticut. He contemptuously noted that while "I was there the post arrived so that there came great crowds of politicians of the town to read the news, and we had plenty of orthographical blunders."[2] Patronizing taverns in order to read newspapers continued to be customary into the 1790s. Militia Captain Thomas Allen kept a coffeehouse and tavern in New London from at least 1773 to 1793 in two locations. He not only provided current issues of newspapers but also kept back issues in seven "bound Newspaper Books" in his tavern at his death about 1793.[3] Using Green's newspaper (published by his son Samuel after 1796) and that of neighboring printer John Trumbull (1750–1802) in Norwich, this chapter explores the effort by printers to reduce the consumption of spirits in society and at labor in southeastern Connecticut between 1760 and 1820. The forms and efficacy of this criticism deserve more attention not just as harbingers of the later temperance movement, but as sources for understanding the political and social contexts of consumption.

Such an inquiry can help us to understand the shifting boundaries of the nascent "public sphere" during these years. Jürgen Habermas first conceived of how a "bourgeois" public sphere began to coalesce through debates and discussions in London coffeehouses in the early decades of the eighteenth century. London had 551 coffeehouses in 1739 by one count, which still sold mainly alcoholic beverages as well as the novel new drink of coffee, and most possessed a regular clientele.

Discussion of new ideas of the Enlightenment popularized by periodicals like the *Spectator* brought traditional assumptions and beliefs under question. Members of these companies, before whom some writers presented new ideas, began to think of themselves as members of a broader "public" which might legitimately criticize acts of state. For Habermas, coffeehouses "presumed a kind of social intercourse that, far from supposing the equality of status, disregarded status altogether." There, of course, existed limits to this temporary suspension of status. This self-conscious "public" coming together outside of institutions of state " was still extremely small" in relation to the mass of the rural population and the poor illiterate people in the towns. Most of the population of London consumed drink in the approximately 6,000 alehouses in the 1730s. At the start of the eighteenth century, more than half of the population lived on the margins of existence, and could not purchase literature of any kind. Nevertheless, Britain's freedom of the press allowed for the creation of the most well-developed and self-conscious "public" in western Europe, and Britain serves as a point of reference for Habermas in tracing the development of public spheres on the Continent.[4]

Elsewhere, I have shown how public houses in colonial and Revolutionary Massachusetts became the settings for the still more rapid and diffuse development of a critical public in a wider cross section of public houses.[5] Indeed the issue of the creation of a wide public, and the growing conviction that all adult white males should be kept informed about issues hitherto the province of a narrow elite, became a central theme of the American Revolution. All of the new urgency to become informed via reading newspapers in taverns became focused on the perception of an alleged conspiracy by Governor Thomas Hutchinosn and other royal officials to misrepresent colonists to the Crown and reduce their liberties. The "aggrandized upstarts" of "low extraction" that Hamilton loathed in New England tavern companies in 1744 gradually constructed a public where consciousness of rank and degree were not just temporarily suspended but rhetorically repudiated during the Revolution.[6] Still, representations of this raw, new public assembled in taverns also came under more vehement criticism by public observers because high levels of consumption of spirits accompanied the rapid decentralization of political authority. The birth of a "public" in a new republic seemed drowned in rum. A writer to Green's newspaper in 1768 criticized militia elections as one of the worst symptoms of the corruption of republican virtue. For Connecticut as a whole, he observed, the "entertainments" by "the captains and inferior officers ... cost this colony not less than 7 or 8,000 pounds annually." Training Days had become "frolics" that ended in drunkenness.[7] Instrumental as taverns had become in the diffusion of authority to criticize affairs of state, social observers lamented the impact of consumption of spirits on the capacity of new citizens to read and judge reasonably. Timothy Green and fellow printer John Trumbull in Norwich perpetuated and refined appeals for temperance after the Revolution in secular terms. They defined intemperance as less of a "sin" and more of an impediment to the self-fulfillment and social well being of enlightened men. Measuring the impact of their entreaties can tell us more about the volatile mix of print and rum in the public sphere in the early decades of the Republic.

Timothy Green inherited his printing shop from his Uncle, also Timothy, in 1763. His uncle had started a newspaper entitled *The New London Summary* in 1758 to answer the demand for news of Connecticut soldiers serving in the Seven Years War, and for the convenience of merchants involved in the expanding Atlantic trade of New London and Norwich. By 1772, Green had a more exalted sense of the mission of his newspaper, now called *The Connecticut Gazette*. In what would become a regular commentary on the importance of newspapers for all households, Green esteemed the papers as the printed matter consumed by the public with the "greatest avidity." The newspaper "flies around the land into the very mouths of the gaping multitude" and therefore "cements a friendly intercourse betwixt neighbours throughout all their vicinities—everyone can read, or hear them read" without the benefit of "classical learning."[8]

Green also helped to develop the public sphere in eastern Connecticut by the books he sold. He was the major bookseller between New Haven and Providence, and it is likely that some of the extensive libraries collected by New London County tavernkeepers were constructed through purchases from Green. His grandfather, named Samuel Green, who had been printer for the Colony from 1714 to 1757 in New London, had printed and sold mainly sermons. Indeed Samuel had avidly attended meetinghouses in the tradition of Samuel Sewall to hear sermons that might be worthy of publication. But the religious revivals of the 1740s had ultimately divested the colony's government of its traditional role as upholder of orthodoxy by exciting different preaching styles leading to the formation of new denominations. The revivals left a fractured religious establishment in its wake and more receptivity to secular and skeptical points of view. A need for more secular offerings coalesced that would eventually aid in the reconceptualization of relations between church and state, and transcend extreme exhibitions of religious feeling and behavior. When Samuel Green died in 1757, it was said (as related by printer Isaiah Thomas) that he left behind such a large quantity of sermons as "dead stock" that "they were put into baskets, appraised by the bushel, and sold under the value of common waste paper." Just five years later, Green's father advertised "Books and Pamphlets" for sale of which less than half had a religious focus. They included a six-volume "Select Collection of Novels," an eight-volume collection of the *Spectator*, and a three-volume "Select Collection of Plays from the best Authors" at a time when no playhouse existed in Connecticut or New England. Green and his nephew gave the public sphere in eastern Connecticut a cutting edge. John and Samuel Trumbull contributed to this shift to secular works by establishing the Norwich Circulating Library in 1796. The Library opened at John Trumbull's printing office and offered books for loan on "Divinity, History, Biography, Voyages, Travels, Novels, Poetry, Miscellany," and others. In 1797, the *Packet* announced the addition of 300 more volumes to the library, "consisting principally of the latest wrote and highly estimable Novels and Romances, most of which were a few weeks since imported from Europe" together with works on travel, history, biography, and voyages.[9] Novels became the genre most in demand.

While establishing the Enlightenment as a new foundation for knowledge and behavior, Timothy Green may never have read any of the principal works associated with this shift in perspective. His personal library at his death in 1796 was small and not strikingly modern.[10] Of course, he may have read some of the books he advertised for sale, but it is probable that he read mainly newspapers when not preoccupied with the business of operating the print and the press. His newspaper regularly offered reprints of news gleaned from London newspapers as well as colonial newspapers as far south as South Carolina. So his close readings of subscribed newspapers made his periodic commentary on the importance of household subscription to newspapers, as opposed to tavern readings, to be more than just a self-interested effort to win more subscribers, but a reflection of his own path to personal enlightenment.

Green and Trumbull became more fervent advocates of the temperate use of spirits as the resistance to British imperial initiatives swelled into Revolution. Green published over thirty letters, essays, poems, and dialogues on Anglo-American drinking habits between 1763 and 1793 despite the increasing need for space to cover the expanding array of issues taken up by politically transformed "citizens." Green's son and heir Samuel published temperance pieces less frequently but regularly from 1793 into the 1810s. They printed items as they came to their knowledge either through writers to the press or from other newspapers. Only occasionally does the senior Green appear to have composed a piece on drinking habits himself. Green and other printers may have preferred an anonymous, disinterested, and republican tack on this issue so as not to offend the sensibilities of the majority of readers who read his paper at taverns while consuming rum. Nevertheless Green, his son, and Trumbull presented the consumption of rum as an issue of wide-ranging concern across the Atlantic world which must now come to the attention of readers in southeastern Connecticut.

During the course of the Revolution, criticism of the consumption of tea eclipsed the already controversial consumption of rum in Massachusetts. Attacks on rum and tavern-haunting became muffled as Whig leaders engaged the support of tavern assemblies to maintain order in resistance. Like printers in Boston, Green provided space for the new opprobrium for tea as a species of "female" excess that must be suppressed in the name of social unity and health as well as for "constitutional" reasons. In 1769, as the merchant boycott crumbled, Green published a long, misogynous diatribe against tea proclaiming that "Eve's daughters encourage merchants to import this fatal plant." Indeed, "Eve's daughters" had become "most violently addicted to it, and use all their persuasions to entice their Adams to perpetuate" this "vice." Tea drinking, after all, is a "custom" usually "practiced in a company of women, exclusive of men, as Eve was inspired by the serpent, and sinned in absence of her consort."[11] Proscribing tea, also considered a beverage for those who aspired to "gentility," helped to sanction gatherings to drink rum and hear news by men.

Yet Green was not comfortable with this simple dichotomy in consumption defined by Whig leaders. In 1771, he decided to borrow a piece from a Portsmouth, New Hampshire paper about a drunken man dying in the road. A woman had refused the man's pleas for help "not thinking him near death" because "people in his condition" had become "not so great a curiosity as formerly." Amidst political mobilization in which taverns played an important role, Green decided to give space to a notice emphasizing the perception that drunkenness was a condition becoming more prevalent. This was "a warning" to "caution people against drinking too freely." The same year Green published a notice about an Annapolis, Maryland man dying in the woods of drink.[12]

In 1772, alarm over proposed salaries for Crown officers in neighboring Massachusetts prompted the formation of the Boston Committee of Correspondence. The Committee wrote to Connecticut officials, and Connecticut towns eventually emulated those of Massachusetts. But Green, busily engaged in a close reading of the expanding press of the colonies, became alarmed by new levels of consumption and crowding at taverns within his own observation. He published a letter declaring the use of rum and other spirits to be "one of the prevailing Vices of the Country" that is "destructive of the Estates, Health, Morals and Lives" of not just colonists but "mankind." It "highly concerns everyone," the writer continued, "who has at Heart, the interest of his Country" to use "his utmost Endeavours to put a Stop to this most threatening and growing Evil." But it was difficult for such sentiments to sway anyone involved with the heady atmosphere of posturing and bold, unlettered speech at nascent representations of the public in taverns. Still, Green had become so dismayed at levels of drinking that he in effect repudiated his earlier tirade against tea in order to recommend it as an alternative to rum. In 1772, he published a piece from "Medicus" defending tea from its detractors and praising it as "a most happy ... substitute in the place of toddy to which many people of both sexes have long been habituated." This writer recommended that tea, a beverage previously associated strongly with gatherings of women, should be taken up by men. "You will seldom see a thirst for RUM and a thirst for TEA in the same person." Upon the whole, Medicus concluded, "it is my opinion that for a single Person whose life has been lost by tea, thousands have been slain by Rum."[13] In publishing this social critique by an anonymous republican writer, Green transcended the popular boundaries of public discourse that demonized tea (consumed mainly by women) at gatherings tempered by rum (consumed mainly by men).

Again in contrast to Boston printers, he leveled more pointed criticism of rum in 1773, the year of the Boston Tea Party. In May, a letter appeared on the front page of the *Gazette* noting the great and increasing expense for spirits "respectively remarked upon in your Paper," but "to little good Purpose, as to Effect." This writer identified himself as a malster intent on recommending the replacement of spirits with beer. Since it is highly unlikely that a malster lived locally in New

London County, the writer may have been Green himself taking the persona of a very literate tradesman. Another front-page letter in December of 1773 deplored the resort to rum for so many reasons—including the effort by drinkers to "drive off their uneasy feelings." Indeed the "greater part of mankind" has formed "so strong an attachment" to rum "that it becomes the principal ingredient of their happiness." Here the writer insists that a clinical addiction among the populace at large had become so apparent that it now must be addressed critically. Certainly drinkers had found a multitude of occasions and reasons to imbibe. According to folk wisdom, it "is good for almost every thing." But this writer thought it "good for almost nothing." Rum even had become necessary at elections. When "the soldiers are about to vote," it is "debated among them, whom to choose." One is named, but "he won't do," for "he does not treat well," so they choose another who "brings out his two case bottles of rum and distributes it" and "they call him one of the cleverest men that ever existed." It is "almost incredible" what sway "a little generosity of this sort has, among drinking people." To emphasize Green's esteem for this letter, or to deflect suspicions that he composed it himself, Green added that "the Printer would be glad of an Interview with the Writer of the Piece" on "distilled Spiritous Liquors."[14] Green threw the full weight of what social authority he could muster as a "printer" behind these sentiments questioning the legitimacy of the interweaving of drink and civil society.

Indeed, Green was ready to place at risk his authority as an outlet through which the new public might speak in his pursuit of a reversal of the new prominence of drinking assemblies. In February of 1774, just little more than a month after the Boston Tea Party, he published a letter by "Home Manufacture" actually critical of the event. The writer prefaced his letter with the observation that he considered it his "duty, to say every Thing, in favour of firm, rational and Consistent Opposition to ministerial Oppression." But he went on to say that "every controversy, whether public or private," should be "conducted with a seriousness and dignity adequate to the importance of it," and "in such a manner that the managers on either side, may review their conduct, when past, without uneasy and disagreeable Sensations." He asked rhetorically "whether when the duty was fix'd on Glass as well as Tea, it would not have been a very extraordinary resolution, to have determined on breaking all the glass in America, and to send round committees to put it in execution." The "jingling of windows, and devastation of furniture," accompanied by "huzzas and bonfires," might be orchestrated "to keep up the attention and spirit of the populace." But, he asked, "is this a spirit to be relied on?" Our patriotism, he continued, should not "degenerate" into "wild or childish licentiousness." And to this purpose, "Home Manufacture" declared, tea should be encouraged as "an antidote to the love of spiritous liquors." Indeed, the colonies should cultivate tea themselves so as to avoid duties like that levied by the Tea Act. Further, the writer compared the drinking habits of the colonies unfavorably with those of China. There "tea is the constant liquor" in a nation "which is supposed to contain more inhabitants than all of Europe put together." And the "people are remarkably alert, ingenious and artfull" for "rum is unknown among them, and neither wines, malt or spiritous liquors of any kind" consumed. The writer wished the colonies to repudiate rum-inspired activism like the Tea Party in favor of a "universal standing drink" of the Chinese.[15] Green went so far as to publish not just a criticism of the violation of property at the Tea Party, but an Enlightenment inspired, quasi-sociological, comparison of custom in both the Pacific and the Atlantic worlds that found the latter wanting. The colonies should look to Asia for the reformulation of custom.

But the strength of the ongoing elaboration of drinking customs continued to inform and define the creation of an active public. This is reflected in Green's publication of an excerpt from a sermon condemning the distribution of drink by officeholders. He deemed it necessary to publish it in the newspaper because such a sermon "will not come into so many hands as were to be wished." Now printed "over again", it might be read in taverns. The anonymous author admitted that laws had become useless against a "mischief" not "easy to come at." But he still declared that "no man" who drinks habitually "will ever be good for much." He "will discharge no office, as he ought to do." Indeed, the question voters should ask "when a man stands a candidate for any preferment," is whether or not it "be known" if "he be a friend of the bottle or no?" Further, a "sober man" will never "choose any but a sober man to represent them." But this minister measured the influence of tavern assemblies to be so great that sober men must actually organize as an alternative. They must "form societies for reformation, and associate to stop the flood which threatens" because "Drunkards are solden together as Thorns" and "have their clubs."[16]

The influence of such clubs is reflected in a poem published in the *Packet* in January of 1775 about a farmer's dream of visiting Boston to see all the troops "intrenching," and then to meet "Tom" Gage at a tavern. The poem stigmatizes troops and loyalists by associating them with the habits actually politicized by Whigs:

> His friends all around him, and if you think fitting,
> I'll tell you the posture the club was now sitting:
> There was Tom, Dick, and Will, with several more,
> I thought in the whole, they would make nigh a score;
> Sat round a large table, but all in a pause,
> To think of a plan to inforce the new laws,
> I wonder'd at this and asking old Brattle,
> (not knowing the Villain was apt for to tattle),
> Who honestly told me what was the true reason,
> The devil, said he, is gone for a season,
>
> To help his friend North, project a new plan,
> And when this is done we expect him again.[17]

Trumbull and the anonymous poet cast the new premium on wide knowledge of decisions made by men of high rank in a negative light insofar as this information was dispensed through the medium of drink round a common table.

But printers like Trumbull and Green received reminders as they set type for their papers of how Revolution sanctioned consumption. In 1776, Green published the information that every Connecticut enlistee had a right to receive a "half pint of rum … every day, and discretionary allowance on extra duty and in time of engagement." Such was the expectation of citizen soldiers of their commanders. The selectmen of nearby Norwich recognized the power of custom when they took pains to limit the prices charged by tavernkeepers for "mugs of flip or toddy" made with West India rum, bowls of "sour punch," and gills of "French brandy and foreign Geneva."[18] The decade-long agitation by Green against imported liquors did not prompt officials to consider permitting prices of them to rise out of the reach of the common man.

The founding of a republic, and the radical break with so many habits sanctioned time out of mind, placed drinking habits under new scrutiny. Green had already compared Anglo-American drinking habits unfavorably with that of the Chinese through featured letters. He had dared to exalt tea amidst an effort to demonize anyone who used it, even as Whig leaders presided over elaborate drinking rituals using rum to engage and temper popular support. Now Green deemed it more important than ever that heavy consumption of rum be repudiated for habits that he himself had cultivated as reader of and subscriber to a number of newspapers. Drinking customs "have crept into Society" that "exist only from habitual, hereditary principles." And since "our infant country is now happily extracted from the British Yoke," and we are left at liberty "to adjust unprejudiced a system of manners consistent with reason," we may "abolish many disgustful, embarrassing destructive English customs."[19] To this end, Green presented a rough, cross-cultural, and comparative sociology of drink over the next decade as the information became available to him. Such essays and letters simplified the drinking mores of various groups and nations. Yet insofar as these pieces compared American drinking habits unfavorably with those of others, they perpetuated the spirit of international Enlightenment that prompted Green to exalt tea over rum, Chinese over English habits, before and after the Boston Tea Party.

One group in or near the new United States whose habits came readily to mind in comparative inspection was the Indians. The toll which rum had taken in relations among Indians and between them and Whites, behind and on the frontier, had long been a subject of commentary in the colonies. Connecticut had outlawed the sale of spirits to the Mohegans in 1733 in response to the entreaties of Sachem Ben Uncas. Mohegan leader and ordained minister Samson Occom singled out drinking as the most pressing problem that Indians faced in the execution sermon he delivered in 1772 upon the event of the hanging of Indian Moses Paul for the murder of a White outside of a tavern.[20] In 1777, printer John Trumbull borrowed from *The Connecticut Journal* a long piece condemning the love of rum in the new republic for the front page of his *Norwich Packet*. Here this essayist declared that there existed nothing "more superfluous and unnecessary" than rum. Further, "the aborigines of America were entirely destitute" of rum before the English introduced it and "where shall we find a more robust and healthy race of men than they were?" But rum has "swept them away in great numbers." Moreover "our forefathers "had little to do with rum" for "many years after the settlement of the country," and "they were more healthy and virtuous than their degenerate sons."[21] Thus the histories of a people, and the comparison of one people's history with another, and what one people could do to another by the introduction of an item for trade such as rum, became the stuff of first page news in the early republic. Trumbull added detail to this commentary by publishing the statistics of one White trader in Pittsburgh with the Indians. A subtext implicit to the statistics is that the Indians on the frontier now hunted diminishing game to buy more whiskey. The trader had acquired 2,173 summer deerskins, 419 muskrat skins, 278 raccoon skins, 94 bear skins, and dozens of other animal skins, all "mostly paid for in whiskey and flour." In 1794, Green presented an elaborate statistical calculation as a lesson on the cost to the country of the army on the frontier engaged with the Indians. The article attributed incidents that incited the war to drunken settlers killing drunken Indians.[22] This of course simplified the complexity of the cultural conflict occurring behind and on the frontier. Still, observers took the step to transcend ethnicity and race in their investigation of the issue of alcohol, a first step to inquiry into the latent causes of violence on the frontier.

Critical self-inspection of American drinking habits also underlay Trumbull's decision to publish a piece on Russian habits halfway around the world. In Russia, the writer contended, the "vice of drunkenness is common to both sexes, and as it is the only felicity" that "they conceive in this world," they generally drink spirits "of which they are fond of even to madness." The Russian peasants are not lazy, "but they do not work for themselves," and consequently do every task "imperfectly." The lesson for Americans by this cursory overview lay in the attribution of such habits to a "slavish" society. They have "for each other that kind of politeness which is taught by slavery." This "constant habit of bowing and scraping" leads them in proportion "to prostrate themselves, and cast their body at full length on the earth before their lords, or those from whom they request any favour." And "pleased when used with mildness, they are totally insensible to opprobrious language" for "wretches inured to the cudgel cannot be moved by mere words." The Russian boyar has "a right to inflict on" their serfs an "arbitrary punishment."[23] Before the Revolution, New Englanders commonly displayed postures of deference to men of superior social rank, but now such bows and "scraping" could be fixed as characteristics of a hierarchical society. At the same time, description of this regimen imposed by Russian aristocrats on their serfs implicitly condemned the slave society of the southern states for similar callous disregard for life or feeling. Intemperance thus became by such comparisons symptomatic of an "unrepublican" society.

But the still powerful social hierarchies of France and Italy remained the thorns in these novel but simplistic comparisons. In 1781, when France reached new heights in popularity among Americans, Green reprinted a letter stating that the "ridiculous custom of drinking people's healths" no longer prevailed as formerly in France, and "we seldom see anyone disguised with liquor, except porters."[24] But this letter focused on the manners of "polite" society. Another set of "reflections" on drinking published by Trumbull in 1788 before the outbreak of the French Revolution also drew unfavorable comparisons between American and European habits in the higher echelons of society. In Italy and France, where "man are allowed to have the quickest and most subtile wits, the bottle is never called in to make them shine." Sherberts, lemonades, and low wines are drunk at their meeting rather than rum. A "man heated with liquor in those countries, would be thought fitter for a bed than conversation." A display of wit "is only commendable when well applied" with a "sprightly saying" on a "proper occasion" while "a string of jests is only fit for a buffoon." [25] Trumbull even went so far as to publish extracts from a letter critical of the temper of tavern conversation written by a "British traveller of distinction in this country to his friend in Europe." Sitting in a public house, "in company with a number of plain gentlemen belonging to the vicinity," he soon heard them complain of 'hard times" as "it is common in New-England, for it is their darling theme."[26] Although sometimes simplistic and naïve, the novel new comparisons of Anglo-American drinking habits with those of other nations and ethnic groups served to identify the consumption of rum at home in a wide variety of contexts as a recently adopted habit. By these juxtapositions, Green and Trumbull declared that such habits might and should be abandoned in a society in the process of reinventing itself.

Still, unfavorable comparisons of America with other nations might be lost on those immersed in habits that fixed and reinforced their political identities. And the drinking of healths at taverns had become a popular means of mental and physical devotion to the abstract entity of a new republic. Therefore Green and Trumbull also published criticisms set in terms that might be more readily seized by the semi-literate as convincing. In 1783, he presented a series by "Philo-Pat" or "Philosopher-Patriot," also known as "fill-pot" which satirized the mixture of punch and politics to make the point that rum is a principle source of impoverishment of artisans and sailors. In 1784, the leader of the drinking "company" of neighbors complains of "old Phil-Pat" and announces that "I have had serious tho'ts of sending to the printer, to let him know, that I will not read his paper any longer, if he don't silence old Phil." The latter "has affronted us all" even as we "began to feel the effects of his exports and imports" and got into "good humor." Further, good neighbors, "what with old Phil's talk, and more of my own inclination, I have dip'd pretty deep in debt," and have had a "miss-crop, and sickness in my family, too." Indeed, he confessed that he could not "steer our own family matters, so as to shun rocks and breakers" while "neighbor Never-think" and

"Run-in-debt" have "executions out against them, for more than they are worth." Such satires might have a biting sting, but they also placed entreaties on the consumption of rum into the vernacular of tavern camaraderie to make the lesson that the advice of a vocal drinking fellow might proved disastrous over the long term. Poems against drinking, and dramatic representations of "Intemperance" as the "prime-minister" of "Death, the king of terrors," introduced fresh, secular forms of temperance propaganda.[27]

With the crisis of the Confederation and the debate over the proposed Constitution, temperance entreaties took a more urgent tone. The new availability and eagerness to employ statistics crystallized in Trumbull's *Packet* with the announcement in 1786 that 3,332,270 gallons of rum had been imported on an average annual basis by the new United States from the West Indies since the treaty of peace with Britain.[28] This amounted to over five gallons per every adult White male in the republic. The Revolution had therefore wrought no reformation in drinking habits, as the continuing return to the issue by printers already suggested. The next year, Trumbull published a piece in his *Norwich Packet* taken from the *Connecticut Magazine* that broke this sum down to unnecessary state and family expenses for Connecticut households. He concluded that the £23,530 sterling wasted in government expense paled in comparison to the £90,000 expended on rum. So "say not a word" about taxes, judges, lawyers, and "women's extravagance." Your government, courts, lawyers, clergymen, schools, and the poor "do not cost you so much as this one paltry article, which does you little or no good." Such a conjecture based on the statistic on importation may have seemed suspect to some. Still, the essay did not call for abstinence from spirits, but merely a reduction in consumption. The farmer essayist allowed his family "but two gallons of rum a year" which is "enough for any family and too much for most of them." This of course could be supplemented by cider and beer of the farmer's "own manufacture." One may "have two or three frolicks of innocent mirth" a year, and keep some spirits for medicine, but "let your common drink be the produce or manufacture of this country."[29] A poem defaming the retail "Dram Shop" stated that every "morning" such shops draw "a lounging circle," placing consumption during the day in shops on attack. Newspapers in New England also began to stigmatize West India rum as the product of slavery in the 1780s. It "is indeed a ten fold child of the devil" for "it is manufactured by slaves, and it either creates slaves, or reduces its votaries" to "beggary." Most African-Americans in Connecticut remained enslaved at this date, but a gradual emancipation act enacted in 1784 at least promised to purge the state of an institution that had come to be defined as inhumane.[30]

Green may have thought that a definitive change in habits had occurred as a consequence of the ratification of the Constitution in Connecticut and the country. In August 1788, he did take care to record "for the information of strangers and posterity" news of a political celebration that took place without the consumption of rum. An estimated 17,000 people "assembled on this green"(presumably in

New London) on the of July 4, "without intoxication or a single quarrel" because "they drank nothing but Beer and Cyder." Readers should learn to prize the latter beverages as "Federal" liquors as opposed to "antifederal" spirits. This is the same year that Green reprinted a calculation of the savings to a tradesman of ten years abstinence from rum, including his ability to subscribe to a newspaper.[31]

Sentiments in favor of a reduction in the occasions for the distribution and consumption of rum did begin to penetrate the ranks of tavern companies. The unrelenting return to this theme by printers like Green had some impact. And Green's turn to poems and dialogues to diffuse temperance entreaties also coincided with new pressures and initiatives to claim "gentility" through dress. Almost one half of a poem entitled "The Dram Drinker" dwelt on the toll that habitual drinking could have on the appearance one could cut in public, and particularly the clothes one could maintain or purchase:

> An old black rusty waistcoat, and his shirt
> Was, what remain'd a perfect patch of dirt:
> His coat ... which his great grand sire wore when young,
> In rags and tatters on his shoulders hung.
> Upon his head a rusty felt he wore,
> Which his short matted locks, scarce cover'd o'er,
> These form'd the wardrobe of our once gay friend ...
> These are the fruits that LOVE OF GROG attend.[32]

This man had once "shone" in his "circle," presumably as many men had first asserted themselves politically, in debates and readings at taverns. But now it had become conventional wisdom that the "love" of rum could destroy a man's capacity to cut a bold figure in the public sphere and thus transcend all the traditional restrictions of inherited social rank.

The startling new course of politics set in motion by the ratification of the Constitution may have helped to inspire the formation of the "Association for discouraging the Use of Spiritous Liquors" in the Connecticut town of Litchfield in 1789. Green prefaced the publication of the Society's vows to abstain from the consumption and distribution of rum with a short historical lesson on civilization focusing on the decline of Spain. Once Spain had no equal for her "industry, her agriculture, her manufactures, and her commerce." But "luxuries" introduced into her society had sapped the energy of the state and people and they had quickly sunk into indigence and poverty. Green believed that rum had come to pose such a threat over the past century of its introduction into the Anglo-American world. The Litchfield farmers declared at a meeting at Mr David Bull's house, possibly a tavern, that a "mistaken idea" concerning the fortifying agency of rum had come into common currency. Distilled spirits are not "necessary" for "labouring men" to "counteract the the influences of heat" and "give relief from severe fatigue." An entire "class of citizens" has been lead to adopt "a habit of such dangerous tendency." In 1790, Green reinforced the lesson of the Litchfield Association imploring farmers to forbear distributing rum to their laborers at harvest. Instead, he enumerated a list of substitutes including strong beer and cider.[33]

It was not just men performing manual labor who must be denied rum. Those who went to taverns to accomplish business must not linger. Mr "Frugal never goes to a tavern without business, nor tarries longer than to finish the business that called him there." If "he meets a friend whom he is glad to see," he "invites him to his house." Some "men invite their friends to the tavern, because they love the place themselves," but "then by tavern expenses they are become so poor, that they cannot entertain a friend at their own houses."[34] The entire compass of male tavern fellowship for a variety of purposes came under attack habit by habit.

Taverns had given birth to the physical representation of the "public sphere," of gathered members of a wider public that could never be fully assembled. Here hierarchy could be softened or suspended, as in England, and actually repudiated in favor of a concept of citizenship, as in the new United States. Buoyed by the burst of print born of the Constitutional debate, printers like Green and Trumbull now called for a separation of the public from the tavern in favor of more individual, family-based, and private readings and subscriptions. Satire of the Revolutionary importance of taverns occupied the front page of *The Connecticut Gazette* in 1789, borrowed from the *Federal Gazette*. "Rum, like death, is an universal leveler," for it "leads the merchant, the lawyer, the doctor and the beggar to meet upon equal terms in taverns and tippling houses." One cannot forget or ignore the "influence" of rum on "government." It is this which "unites the tongue, the hands, and the feet of the country politician." Rum "inspires him with eloquence and furnisheth him with all his ideas of the horrors of aristocratical, and kingly power." It is this noble liquor that "pulls down old governments," and "which opposes the establishment of new ones, when they run counter to the inclinations of the people." So men may continue to drink their "two quarts" per day.[35] Such was the intensity of feeling on this issue that Green came close to praising "aristocracy" in the face of the continuing decentralization of political authority in the new republic. On the front page, he satirically and contemptuously communicated his conviction that as long as rum remained the staple drink of Americans, Congress will be thwarted from acting in its new authority to protect republican liberties. If Americans gave up rum, they might recognize the wisdom of the new Constitution, accede to the wisdom of and need for centralization, and welcome the legitimate exercise of power by the new federal government.

In the same spirit, Trumbull printed a few years later a letter originally published in *The Hampshire Chronicle* asking if "the publick will give me a short audience." A repentant "toper" told of a typical evening on Saturday when he "took a walk up the streets" about sunset to overtake "Lem Lovegrog." They walked on while "discoursing of the affairs of the town," and ended up at landlord Punch's. There we "drank and discoursed of our riches, and felt as big, important and independent, as though we were a couple of absolute monarchs." The letter writer could not

"recollect as the thought of going once entered my mind until our good landlord"
bid them goodnight.[36] The custom of "discourse" over public affairs in taverns
must be abandoned as much as rum at celebrations. The tavern reader who recognized himself and reformed his habits, the notice implied, might also ultimately be
capable of writing a letter to the newspaper.

Now that the Constitution had been ratified, and political chaos averted, editors
like Green and Trumbull believed that politics grounded in taverns and drink might
be left behind. Certainly when political celebrations such as the one on New
London green could take place without rum, and farmers could resolve to purge
the harvest of its use, the issue had come to occupy a new place in the political
spectrum. The moment had arrived, or so Green implied by his printings, for the
public to reformulate itself free of rum-soaked assemblies. The Constitution
should not only mark the beginning of a new political configuration, but the abandonment of habits that had hampered its construction.

Or so printers like Green hoped. But he died in about 1796 just as the controversy
over the character of the French Revolution attracted fresh waves of drinkers into
taverns to hear and read the news. His son Samuel Jr. published pieces reiterating
pleas for reform that his father had hoped would take place during his lifetime. In
1794, official advertisements to provide rations for the army stipulated that con-
tractors must supply half a gill of rum, brandy, or whiskey per day. The range of
distilled liquors on the market had widened. The same liquors were officially
rationed in 1798.[37] And the distribution and consumption of these liquors continued to punctuate labor, evident from the publication of pieces critical of these
habits. A short essay in 1801 recommended more frequent meals to discourage
"the use of spirited or fermented liquors, so general among labourers of all kinds."
In 1802 another essay again asked farmers not to distribute distilled liquors to
laborers during the harvest. The "pernicious effects of this growing practice are
very numerous," including the diminishment "of the strength of the laborer." In
1806, an essayist estimated that one-third of the earning of day laborers is
expended on spirits. The $75.00 per annum spent on spirits might be replaced, the
writer suggested, with 100 gallons of beer costing only $25.00 a year. The town of
Saybrook advertised for a Blacksmith in 1808 who does not "drink a quart of Rum
a day." In July of 1812, a retailer advertised to "inform the Farmers that he will
draw Rum per keg, or bbl., remarkably low through the season" for distribution to
laborers. Another retailer advertised in 1816 that he would sell his New England
rum by the hogshead, barrel, or less. Hence "Farmers in particular for their haying,
would do well to call." In 1813, the Connecticut legislature was still trying to
outlaw the distribution of rum at militia elections. And in 1820, agricultural societies in Connecticut were still trying to promote "American" beverages.[38]

Consumption at taverns also continued to set the course of sociability. The
"Rambler" wrote for the *Packet* in 1797 of his observations of "mechanics"
drinking in public houses. The "Landlord makes the flip & delivers it to the person

who called for it who politely hands it to one of his comrades present," after which a long "discourse" begins on "hard times" while the mugs are handed from one to the "last gentleman's mouth." The rambler concluded that it was a "shame to human nature" that "any man can be so devoid of all reason and feeling, as to visit a tavern, two or three times a week." They spend "for such useless articles, all what they earn" to the "distress of their needy families." But consumption at taverns continued to help define mass political activism, and so to some extent also defined manhood. In 1793, Trumbull complained of men who "cannot afford to take the newspapers." One complains "they are too expensive, but goes to the tavern, once a week, to hear the news." Such a man "spends ninepence, when he might have a newspaper delivered at his door for two pence."[39] Such groups continued to provide the physical sensation of membership in a transcendent public composed of free males.

Drinkers continued to look to tavernkeepers as trusted purveyors of oral and printed news. In 1787, a Norwich tavernkeeper named Azariah Lathrop advertised for the return of six specific books, two of them multi-volume novels. He also issued a general call to "the Persons who have Books in their possession, that belongs to the Subscriber," to return them. Apparently after some discussion of the books with local customers, Lathrop had loaned books to individuals for private home readings. But the contents of his personal library at his death suggest that he saved pamphlets to be read, like the newspapers, at his tables. Along with James Addison's *The Freeholder* and twenty-nine other books, he owned "50 Small Books & Pamphlets" suitable for reading at the tables in his public rooms. And in 1801 Democratic-Republican Lathrop hosted "a respectable number of the Republican citizens of Norwich and from the adjacent towns" for the "purpose of celebrating the election of Mr. Jefferson." They drank fifteen of those maligned "healths," now called "toasts," to various political maxims and statements. Eleazer Lord, the keeper of a modest tavern in Norwich at his death in 1809, had "40 old Pamphlets."[40]

Continuity of high consumption in New London County is reflected in the advertisements of retailers in the same decades. Ezra Chappell had seventeen pipes, or 2,142 gallons, of French brandy for sale in 1797. Lathrop and Eels had three varieties of West Indies rum (St. Croix, Demarara, St. Vincent's) for sale by the pipe (126 gallons) or barrel (32 gallons) in 1798. In the same issue of the *Gazette*, another retailer advertised the sale of forty puncheons, or 3,200 gallons, of a fourth variety of rum, Grenada. Samuel Haynes had ten hogsheads, or 630 gallons, of a fifth and sixth variety: Tobago and Jamaica. Advertisements into the 1810s reveal a steady importation of West Indies rum. The Brig Victoria landed 247 puncheons, or 19,760 gallons, of Barbados rum in 1816, sold by Martin Lee. At the same time Lee advertised 11,760 gallons of Demerara rum. In the same issue, William Belcher had available "Old Cognac Brandy, Old Jamaica Spirits, Pure Holland Gin," and West Indies and New England rum. New London County had a population of just 34,707 in 1810, little more than in 1774 because of emigration to the west. Nationally, estimates of consumption rose from an annual average of 5.8 gallons of absolute alcohol per capita (for people aged fifteen or older) in 1790 to 7.1 gallons in 1810, where it remained about level until 1830.[41]

Yet advertisements also suggest that the consumption of a non-alcoholic stimulant, coffee, also rose in New London County after 1790. Of course, coffee had become available in some New England public houses, a few called coffeehouses, in the early eighteenth century. And these coffeehouses had become leading settings for the definition of a new public sphere. But most public houses through the Revolution did not sell coffee at all, and those that did so continued to sell rum in greater quantity.[42] In 1797, Samuel Green suggested that coffee should have its own poetry like that of other beverages and opiates including wine and opium. In "Miltonian" or "heroick" verse, a poet should "relate the natural history of the shrub," and describe its effects "to invigorate the body, and clarify the mind." Such a poem, suggested Green, "would be a charming breakfast companion," and presumably serve to help alter the habit of morning alcoholic draughts. By, 1805, this appears to have happened when an increase in popularity in coffee received notice. While only a "few years back" the article of coffee had been "looked upon as a luxury," it is "now considered from the great use made of it, as one of the necessaries of life." It had become so popular that the price had doubled since 1793 according to this article.[43] The same year Perkins & Starr advertised 1,000 lb of coffee for sale along with 2,480 gallons of rum. In 1812, Charles and George Starr advertised 4,000 lb of coffee. In 1813, Daniel Deshon had 50,000 lb of coffee for sale in hogsheads, barrels, and bags. In 1814, another store had 10,000 lb of coffee for sale. In 1816, Robert Coit advertised "W.I. Rum, Coffee." In 1812, "Probatum" wrote to the *Gazette* with directions as to how to make one's "morning" coffee grounds last longer. Thus, he concluded, "you will not only live cheaper, but you will also live better."[44] The writer implied that coffee had become a staple morning drink even among households that must make calculated choices as to beverages.

The inventories of taverns confirm the rise in popularity of coffee. Captain Thomas Allen kept a coffeehouse for "gentlemen" from the time of the Revolution until 1794. At his death he owned coffee pots, a coffee mill, and plenty of cups and saucers. But the diffusion of this genteel drink is apparent in the inventories of tavernkeepers Eleazer Lord in 1809 and Azariah Lathrop in 1810. Lord kept a modest tavern in Norwich, but could provide nine "blue and white coffee cups and saucers." Some patrons had begun to read his forty "old pamphlets" with coffee instead of rum. Lathrop, the Democratic-Republican proprietor of a prominent tavern in Norwich, had twenty-eight cups and saucers explicitly labeled as for "coffee," and another nineteen "cups and saucers." He owned fifty "small books and Pamphlets."[45]

Back in 1773, Timothy Green had daringly printed letters lecturing New Englanders that they should consume more tea like the Chinese and less rum at a time when tea had become demonized as the taxed luxury drunk mainly by women.

Meanwhile men of low rank increasingly used rum and taverns to confirm their new status as vocal, critical and active citizens. Green compared them unfavorably with the Chinese tea drinkers, and later to the habits of the French and Italians. All of his entreaties did not stop the rise in consumption of distilled liquors that accompanied the further decentralization of political authority after the Revolution. But these new efforts by printers to crystallize the issue of temperance, and so promote a separation of the act of reading newspapers from the consumption of spirits, helped to prepare tavern companies for the wider introduction of the stimulant of coffee. To have coffee with one's newspaper, either at home or at taverns, had reached new popularity on the American scene by 1810. In the more hurried and distracting commercial climate of the decades after 1790, American men turned to coffee to "clarify" the mind. It was no longer a genteel luxury, but fast becoming a consumer staple. This occurred before the introduction of heavy machinery requiring unremitting human attention. Male participants in the public sphere had not yet shed bowls of punch and quarts of rum periodically during the day. Nor did laborers give up their "fortification" at regular intervals. But an alternative habit of far-reaching consequences on society and the economy had begun to grow in popularity, and would become an important variable in the new social relationships constructed during the temperance revolution of the 1830s.

The Greens and Trumbull acted to define temperance in the secular terms of the Enlightenment during the Revolution and the early decades of the republic. They placed drinking habits in historical perspective in the Anglo-American world, compared them with those of other nations, enumerated statistics for consumption, and sought to bridge chasms in understanding by creative uses of vernacular speech. Foremost, they stigmatized "excessive" drinking as an impediment to the expansion of the act of reading that they celebrated and promoted as printers of newspapers for a wide and politically active public. Directly and indirectly, they sought to wean readers of newspapers from the tavern-based collective readings so instrumental in forging a new public during the Revolution. While largely unsuccessful in popular terms, the elements of their approach would be incorporated with the more evangelical spirit of the more explicitly organized mass temperance crusade in the 1830s. Withdrawal from taverns into temperance societies became less of a reasoned choice one should make, and more of an urgent, necessary conversion experience. Still, the emphasis on the diffusion of new information based on print and statistics pioneered by printers like the Greens and Trumbull continued to influence the cultivation of new habits deemed appropriate for a modern society.

Notes

1. *The Connecticut Gazette*, August 29, 1788, no. 1294.
2. "The Itinerarium of Dr. Alexander Hamilton" in Wendy Martin, ed.,

Colonial American Travel Narratives (New York: Penguin, 1994), p. 300.

3. Inventory of Captain Thomas Allen, 13 January 1794, Probate Records, Connecticut State Archives.

4. Jürgen Habermas, *The Structural Transformation Of The Public Sphere: An Inquiry into a Category of Bourgeois Society* (Cambridge, MA: MIT Press, 1991), pp. 32–43, 36–7, 38; Roy Porter, *The Creation Of The Modern World: The Untold Story Of The British Enlightenment* (New York: Norton Press, 2000), pp. 35–7; Thomas Munck, *The Enlightenment: A Comparative Social History, 1721–1794* (New York: Oxford University Press, 2000); Dorinda Outram, *The Enlightenment* (Cambridge: Cambridge University Press, 1995), ch. 2; James Van Horn Melton, *The Rise of the Public in Enlightenment Europe* (Cambridge: Cambridge University Press, 2001), ch 1, 7; John Brewer, *The Pleasures of the Imagination: English Culture in the Eighteenth Century* (New York: Farrar, Strauss, & Giroux, 1997), pp. 34–50, 161–4; Peter Clark, *The English Alehouse: A Social History, 1200–1830* (London: Longman, 1983), ch. 1, 12, 13.

5. David W. Conroy, *In Public Houses: Drink And The Revolution Of Authority In Colonial Massachusetts* (Chapel Hill: University of North Carolina, 1995).

6. *Colonial American Travel Narratives*, p. 316; Bernard Bailyn , *The Origins Of American Politics* (New York: Vintage, 1968); Bailyn , *The Ideological Origins of the American Revolution* (Cambridge, MA: Harvard University Press, 1967), pp. 44–159; Bailyn, *The Ordeal Of Thomas Hutchinson* (Cambridge, MA: Harvard University Press, 1974), ch. 4.

7. *New London Gazette*, January 20, 1769, no. 271.

8. Isaiah Thomas, *The History Of Printing In America with a Biography of Printers and an Account of Newspapers* ed. Marcus A. McCorison (New York: Weathervane, 1970), pp. 295–303, 307–9; *Gazette*, October 2, 1772.

9. Isaiah Thomas, *History of Printing*, p. 296: *New London Summary*, June 18, 1762, no. 202; The *Summary* becomes *The New London Gazette* in 1763 which in turn becomes *The Connecticut Gazette* in 1773; Richard Bushman, *From Puritan to Yankee: Character and the Social Order in Connecticut, 1690–1765* (New York: Norton, 1967), ch. 14; *Norwich Packet*, July 14, 1796, no. 1165; July 18, 1797, no. 1218.

10. Inventory of the Estate of Timothy Green, August 20, 1796, Connecticut State Archives.

11. Conroy, *In Public Houses*, pp. 260–3; *Gazette*, June 9, 1769, no. 291.

12. *Gazette*, April 26, 1771, no. 389.

13. Richard D. Brown, *Revolutionary Politics in Massachusetts: The Boston Committee of Correspondence and the Towns, 1772–1774* (Cambridge, MA: Harvard University Press, 1970), p. 181, n. 247; *Gazette*, January 31, 1772, no. 429; March 13, 1772, no. 435. See also Brown, *The Strength Of A People: The Idea Of An Informed Citizenry In America, 1650–1870* (Chapel Hill, University of North Carolina, 1996).

14. *Gazette*, May 7, 1773, no. 495; December 3, 1773, no. 525.

15. Ibid., February 25, 1774, no. 537.

16. Ibid., August 19, 1774, no. 562.

17. *The Norwich Packet*, January 26 – February 2, 1775, no. 70

18. *Gazette*, June 7, 1776, no. 656; *Packet* April 13, 1778, no. 237.

19. *Gazette*, April 30, 1781, no. 929.

20. Petition of Ben Uncas, October, 1733, Indian Series I, Vol I: 161, Connecticut State Archives; Harold Blodgett *Samson Occom* (Hanover: Dartmouth College Publications, 1935), pp. 138–43.

21. *Packet*, March 24 – March 31, 1777, no. 183.

22. Ibid., September 28, 1786, no. 622; *Gazette*, January 23, 1794, no. 1036.

23. *Packet*, February 9, 1786, no. 589.

24. *Gazette*, August 31, 1781, no. 929.

25. *Packet*, 28 February 1788, no. 696.

26. Ibid., June 7, 1787, no. 658.

27. *Gazette*, November 28, 1783, no. 1046; December 19, 1783, no. 1049; January 16, 1784, no. 1053; *Packet*, October 21, 1784, no. 520; *Gazette*, December 2, 1785, no. 1151.

28. *Packet*, June 15, 1786, no. 607; Patricia Cline Cohen, *A Calculating People: The Spread Of Numeracy in Early America* (Chicago: University of Chicago Press, 1982).

29. *Packet*, January 11, 1787, no. 637.

30. Ibid., September 4, 1788, no. 723.

31. *Gazette*, August 8, 1788, no.1291; August 29, 1788, no. 1294.

32. *Packet*, September 11, 1788, no. 724.

33. Ibid., June 5, 1789, no. 793; *Gazette*, June 19, 1789, no. 1336; *Packet*, July 23, 1790, no. 851.

34. Ibid., July 6, 1791, no. 903.

35. *Gazette*, December 18, 1789, no. 1362.

36. *Packet*, March 15, 1792, no. 938.

37. *Gazette*, July 10, 1794, no. 1600; December 12, 1798, no. 1831.

38. Ibid., June 17, 1801, no. 1962; September 22, 1802, no. 2028; February 19, 1806, no. 2206; August 10, 1808, no. 2333; June 10, 1812, no. 2537; July 3, 1816, no. 2747; July 7, 1813, no. 2591; October 25, 1820, no. 2972.

39. *Packet*, March 23, 1797, no. 1201; July 4, 1793, no. 1007.

40. Ibid., January 15, 1787, no. 639; Inventory of Azariah Lathrop, May 26, 1810, Connecticut State Archives; *Packet*, March 10, 1801, no. 1409; Eleazer Lord, August 11, 1809, CSA.

41. *Gazette*, June 28, 1797, no. 1755; October 10, 1798, no. 1822; August 28, 1816, no. 2755; Stella M. Sutherland *Population Distribution In Colonial America* (New York: Columbia, 1936), p. 22; *Gazette*, February 6, 1811, no. 2465; Mark Lender and James Martin *Drinking in America* (New York: Free Press, 1987), p. 46.

42. Conroy, *In Public Houses*, pp. 73–4, 89–95, 121, 125, 132, 161–2, 177–9.

43. *Gazette* March 10, 1797, no. 1740; June 26, 1805, no. 2172.

44. Ibid., June 26, 1805, no. 2172; October 23, 1811, no. 2502; January 1, 1812, no. 2512; October 26, 1813; January 5, 1814, no. 2617; June 19, 1816, no. 2745.

45. Ibid., May 28, 1773, no. 498; March 29, 1776, no. 646; Inventory of Captain Thomas Allen, January 12, 1794, Connecticut State Archives; Eleazer Lord, August 16, 1809, CSA; Azariah Lathrop, May 26, 1810, CSA.

–4–

In Vino Veritas

The Construction of Alcoholic Disease in Liberal Italy, 1876–1914

Paul A. Garfinkel

In the first decade of the twentieth century, incidents of alcohol-related crime filled the pages of newspaper police blotters and district-attorney reports across Italy. Among them, episodes of drunken violence appeared most frequently. Two inebriated brothers in Bologna, for example, got into a fistfight with a pair of policemen and then tried to kiss them when being arrested. According to the district prosecutor of Palermo, *tocco*, a popular drinking game played with cards, had sparked so many killings, beatings, and brawls in the city's taverns that the police finally had to outlaw it. In Lucca, a man stumbled home drunk from the tavern one evening to find another man passed out naked on the floor. Convinced the intruder had violated his wife, the owner of the house fatally stabbed the unconscious trespasser and threw his corpse into the street. And in a town near Naples, a man under the influence clubbed his girlfriend to death simply because she had insisted that they stay longer at a party.[1]

While accounts such as these were common throughout Europe at the time, they produced an unusually strong reaction in Italy, and especially among its jurists, who were already convinced that theirs was the most lawless country in Europe. As in other nations, the legal establishment in Italy associated criminal intemperance with acute social problems, including poverty, malnutrition, illiteracy, and unsanitary conditions in both town and country. But the lawyers, doctors, and other professional elites who made up the Italian juridical order consistently emphasized—and greatly exaggerated—still other connections. For one, they identified alcohol not only as a product of these social ills, but also as a leading cause. Drunkenness, they contended, led to frequent outbreaks of popular unrest; many of them blamed alcohol even for the army's embarrassing defeat in Ethiopia in 1896. Still more importantly, they saw alcohol-induced lawbreaking as a manifestation of the political, moral, and cultural backwardness of Italians. Like recidivism, violence, insanity, and juvenile delinquency, alcohol-related criminality gave jurists yet another explanation for why Italy failed to emerge as a first-rate industrial power after Unification in 1861. It was this all-consuming juridical preoccupation with criminal inebriety and national ascendancy that set Italy apart from other European nations concerned about intemperance.

In the quarter-century before the Great War, Italian legal experts shaped public debates about drunkenness by defining it not as an individual vice, but as a collective disease. As they drew upon homegrown criminological knowledge and foreign temperance initiatives, jurists claimed confidently to know the causes of and solutions to the problem, and they seemed to have the hard data to prove their case. At the same time, they argued that the broader trend across Europe during this period also applied to Italy, at least in the developing North: higher consumption followed increasing industrial prosperity, and as wages rose and prices fell, more people could afford to drink. On these grounds, the juridical establishment urged the state to regulate the flow of alcohol and to criminalize insobriety. But the heightened anxiety about criminal intemperance did not necessarily correlate with an actual social pathology, nor did juridical perception mirror social reality. Although jurists maintained that they had the quantitative evidence linking alcoholic excess with unlawful behavior, statistics were either unreliable or nonexistent; in fact, official figures on alcohol-related offenses did not even appear until 1909. Indeed, the ambiguity between juridical certainty and statistical uncertainty suggests that something else was driving the obsession with drunken lawlessness. Why did jurists suddenly begin to worry about immoderation in the late nineteenth century? Why did they attempt to institutionalize remedies to the problem? Why did parliament eventually pass a temperance bill in 1913, but why only in a diluted form?

The temperance movement in unified Italy faced many obstacles and dilemmas. In the first half of the nineteenth century and before, drinking assumed a central place in the lives, beliefs, and customs of people throughout the Italian territories. Viticulture figured as an important sector in local and regional economies and stood to suffer from governmental regulation. Inhabitants drank wine almost exclusively in regions lacking potable water, while doctors prescribed alcohol to treat illnesses such as pellagra, malaria, and tuberculosis. Peasants and workers thought of wine as "liquid food" that provided energy and nourishment in lieu of more expensive foodstuffs like meat and cheese. At harvest time, rural laborers often received the fruits of the vine as legitimate—and preferred—recompense for a day's work.

By 1870, when the annexation of Rome completed the political union of the kingdom, Italians seldom considered drinking to be a problem.[2] Both popular and medical opinion tended to equate overindulgence with factory labor and urban poverty, conditions still rare in the predominantly agrarian country. Many people, moreover, believed that their Latin roots and agricultural way of life, as well as the Mediterranean climate, predisposed them to sobriety. Still more reasons explained this nonchalance: physicians made the case that the quality, rather than the quantity, of liquors caused drunkenness; and since Italian peasants consumed natural, fermented alcohol, they poisoned themselves far less than northern European industrial workers and city dwellers who routinely ingested manufactured spirits.[3] This general lack of concern about immoderation found reflection in the various penal codes on the peninsula. From Turin to Palermo, traditional jurists defined *ubriachezza* as a mitigating circumstance in some cases, and grounds for exoneration in others. Given the attitude of both the new state and its citizens, it should come as no surprise that when a Turinese doctor in 1864 tried to establish a temperance society in his city, his efforts came to naught.

While Italians cared little about excessive drinking throughout most of the nineteenth century, physicians throughout Europe were worriedly investigating the effects of alcoholic pathology. Physiologists took the lead, linking alcohol intake to organic diseases and nervous disorders. Alienists, too, theorized extensively. They connected dipsomania to behavioral anomalies, and particularly to insanity and suicide. By mid-century, Swedish doctor Magnus Huss had coined the expression "chronic alcoholism" to differentiate more serious alcohol addiction from the ordinary vice, "acute alcoholism."[4] And in his 1857 treatise on degeneration, French doctor B. A. Morel went a step further by classifying habitual drinking as both an individual and a social disease.[5] In labeling overindulgence as such, Morel both conveyed anxieties in France about the moral, physical, and hereditary consequences of intemperance and promoted public hygiene as the means to thwart the major social ramifications of industrialization. The emergence of Darwinian evolutionary theory in the 1860s gave physicians in Europe only greater reason to fear inebriety: because of alcohol's potential to debilitate both the individual and the social body, it stood to reason that people could eventually drink their way to extinction.

Only in the late 1870s did the Italian medical establishment begin to fret about the newly established disease of alcoholism. This sudden preoccupation reflected mounting disaffection with the political struggles of the Liberal state: uneven industrialization in the north, chronic underdevelopment in the south, and sluggish movement toward a national social program. It also signified political elites' ongoing ideological conflict with the Vatican and their attempts to erect a lay ethos in an overwhelmingly Catholic country. Anticlerical jurists and physicians sought to wrestle moral authority away from the Church by replacing spiritual truths with scientific ones. Alcoholism, according to secular legal experts, was to be understood organically as a sickness, not metaphysically as a sin. Cesare Lombroso, a Jewish surgeon from Verona and the founder of criminal anthropology, put forward this claim most loudly. Lombroso and his following sought to prove empirically that some people were born with a predisposition to delinquency. On this basis, criminal anthropologists demanded new standards defining legal accountability as well as specialized prisons, hospitals, and labor colonies to confine lawbreakers predestined to a life of crime.[6]

Following his publication of *Criminal Man* in 1876, Lombroso led the way in framing criminal inebriety in medical and criminological terms. The "criminal alcoholic" stood out prominently in his elaborate taxonomy of delinquent types. Alcohol, he explained, triggered a wrongdoer's latent proclivities to madness, suicide, neurasthenia, and especially cruelty. And since even the healthy and

wealthy could succumb to drink and turn spontaneously violent, liquor posed a
still greater social danger. According to Lombroso, alcoholism caused poverty,
crime, disease, and a loss of moral sense; it endangered both individual and public
health; and it compromised hereditary fitness, for alcoholic parents would beget
only defective children.[7] Within a few years, Lombroso's medical and criminal
anthropological colleagues, such as Antonio Marro and Virgilio Rossi, tried to cor-
roborate his hypotheses.[8] Some sought to extend them by joining alcoholism to the
potential for political upheaval. They held intoxicated workers responsible for the
revolutionary violence of the Paris Commune in 1871, an event that demonstrated
to them how drunkenness—whether spontaneous or pathological—could threaten
the public order. Other doctors went so far as to claim that the main reason why
the Germans won the Franco-Prussian War was because they were more sober than
the French.

   At a public conference entitled "Il vino," held in Turin in 1880, medical opinion
began to coalesce on the perils of immoderation. Some of Italy's leading physicians, scientists, and intellectuals delivered a series of eleven lectures, four of
which centered on alcohol's cause-and-effect relationship to organic disease, poor
hygiene, and criminal behavior. These connections reflected the speed with which
many Italian physicians had begun to welcome the early criminological ideas of
Lombroso and his coterie. Giulio Bizzozero, a Lombard hygienist who later
became a senator, joined Lombroso in branding alcoholism as a "terrible social
scourge" that especially "has an evil influence on the lower classes."[9] His paper,
"Wine and Health," combined physiological and sociological interpretations of
alcohol's influence on class, sex, and the body. He beseeched parliament to enact
legislative remedies that could prevent the Paris Commune from happening at
home. Physiologist Angelo Mosso detailed the ways in which alcohol irritated the
nervous system, a process that caused accelerated blood flow, anomalous cerebral
stimulation, and the eventual loss of moral consciousness.[10] In the penultimate
address, Lombroso applied Mosso's theories to describe how alcohol drove people
to suicide, madness, crime, and spontaneous acts of violence. He predicted that
industrialization stood to make the already "lurid calamity of alcoholism" even
worse, and he warned that along with "our other plagues ... like those of malaria
and pellagra," alcohol addiction threatened to turn Italians into "the helots of
Europe."[11]

   Although doctors were the first to embrace criminological theories linking
alcohol and crime, secular jurists soon joined their cause. By the 1890s, lawyers,
magistrates, and public officials routinely cited alcoholism as a chief reason for
Italy's violent-crime problem and as both a cause and an effect of various social
woes wrought by industrial capitalism. Like their French counterparts, Italian
jurists did not impugn only industrialization: they also condemned rural alcoholism, especially in the center and south, where farmers and mountain villagers
were widely thought to be impulsive and belligerent by nature. On the basis of
their self-proclaimed sociological expertise, these jurists began to insist upon new

laws rooted in social defense, a concept also influenced by criminological doctrine. Social-defense jurisprudence, which emerged in the *fin de siècle* as the predominant philosophical orientation among Italian legal experts, came to signify three cardinal principles: crime prevention, public health, and state interventionism. Some extreme-left jurists and traditional legal scholars opposed social-defense theories on intemperance, but their voices would remain in the minority well into the next century.[12]

Jurists fueled the anti-alcohol craze in the 1890s for a variety of reasons. First and foremost, they disliked the Zanardelli penal code of 1889, united Italy's first standardized criminal law. Even though the new statutes proscribed public drunkenness for the first time on the peninsula, lawyers and magistrates loathed its categorization as a misdemeanor rather than a felony.[13] And because the *Codice Zanardelli* retained the traditional notion of inebriety as an attenuating or exculpatory condition, they argued that the law actually gave criminals an incentive to drink. General social conditions, too, caused jurists to view alcohol with still greater alarm. They feared that persistent social and economic crises threatened to bring down the Liberal order. Industrialization in the north sparked worries about trade unionism and urban mobs, and frequent episodes of popular protest had already caused the state to resort to political repression and martial law. Moreover, a new and ever-increasing body of social statistics seemed to bear out juridical elites' apprehensions about national decline. Parliamentary inquests into rural and urban living conditions confirmed that peasants and workers everywhere were still living in extreme poverty, while medical geographers painted Italy as a country plagued by endemic diseases and high mortality. Bodily measurements of military conscripts corroborated this evidence still more: recruits, especially those from the south, were so unhealthy and malformed that army doctors had to reject them in astonishing numbers. Even more worrisome, penal statistics indicated that crime was on the rise throughout the kingdom, thereby suggesting that Italy, rather than catching up to its European betters, was falling further behind. To jurists, alcoholism did not represent the only cause of such backwardness, but it did seem to be one of considerable significance.[14]

With his 1892 monograph, *Alcoholism: A Sociological and Juridical Study*, a text that remained the standard well into the next century, Socialist lawyer Adolfo Zerboglio synthesized these juridical beliefs.[15] The quintessential social-defense jurist, he turned to criminology, contemporary medicine, and social statistics to examine the causes and effects of alcohol abuse and to suggest the means to prevent it. He found that since the 1870s, rates of criminality and alcohol consumption had risen in direct proportion to one another. He discovered, too, that south of Rome, peasants drank mostly wine, while their countrymen to the north ingested hard liquor and beer as well, and in far greater amounts.[16] Northern drinking habits, Zerboglio maintained, helped to account for the prevalence of alcohol-related madness, disease, suicide, and mortality in those regions. He cited official and psychiatric data from Lombardy and the Veneto—where distilled liquors proliferated the most—to explain trends such as a fourfold jump in alcoholic psychoses and a threefold rise in insanity among women since 1874. These patterns seemed to substantiate jurists' fears that as Italians were becoming more intoxicated, they were also becoming more lawless and more sickly than ever before.

Although Zerboglio and other anxious jurists tended to overstate the case, they were not entirely incorrect: Italians were in reality drinking more alcohol than ever. In 1879, when parasites devastated the French wine harvest, many Italian landowners responded by turning over their fields from cereals to grapes. Their speculation proved profitable. Production levels soared, exports increased, and the domestic market improved in the short-term as prices began to fall.[17] Overproduction, phylloxera, and a tariff war with France slowed the wine trade by the early 1890s, but domestic prices had dropped even further, allowing more workers access to cheap wines and low-grade liquors. By the early twentieth century, viticultural yields hit record highs as vineyards in the north began to outperform those in the Mezzogiorno for the first time since the agricultural depression in the 1870s. Domestic breweries tripled their output during the same period, and after a brief decline in the 1890s, distilleries saw a 50 percent rise in production over the next decade.[18] Improved railways and storage methods also boosted consumption, for bottled alcohol could be transported to more of the peninsula and islands and could therefore reach a broader base of customers.

While uneasy about public health and overindulgence, social-defense jurists' greatest concern in the 1890s remained criminal intemperance. The data collected about consumption habits helps to explain its continuing priority. Since statistics on alcohol-related crime did not yet exist at this time, legal experts looked to the number of *osterie* (drinking establishments) per capita to quantify the interconnections between delinquency and crapulence. The government's investigation into factory strikes in one Piedmontese town in 1878 was the first to measure crime and disorder according to the density of taverns. The parliamentary commission studying the event determined that *osterie* in the town had doubled since 1864 and that this rise led directly to the local workers' unruliness.[19] In 1886, a more extensive inquiry into public-health conditions nationwide corroborated this alarming trend: taverns had increased 13 percent since 1874, and even more so in the urban north.[20] In Milan, for example, the number of taverns leapt by 31 percent between 1872 and 1877. Yet, even in a remote town such as Aosta in the northwest, there was one liquor establishment to every 174 people, a ratio made still more remarkable by the fact that it included women, children, and convalescents. This exponential growth of *osterie* provided jurists with the most compelling evidence of the catalyst for alcohol-related crime.

The solutions put forth by social-defense jurists in the 1890s anticipated those proposed in the new century. Zerboglio, for example, lobbied for preventative means, namely state-run inebriate asylums to confine habitual drunkards. Pathological drinkers, he argued, must be treated as a distinct class of offender unsuited for ordinary prisons and madhouses. In addition, Zerboglio recommended stricter regulation of the production, sale, and consumption of alcohol. He called for higher duties on wine and spirits, state monopolization of the liquor trade, and tougher licensing and inspections of drinking establishments and production plants. Above all, he promoted temperance leagues even while admitting that "they often have the defect of falling into hyperbole [and] making themselves look ridiculous."[21] He admired foreign associations that preached abstinence, founded journals, organized conferences, and awarded prizes to sober industrial workers. Zerboglio doubted, however, that a popular propaganda movement could ever really take root in Italy even though a small temperance organization had existed in Milan since 1882. Italians, he explained, "do not care about alcoholism, partly because of their deeply apathetic character ... and their belief that such a serious evil could never happen here."[22]

But Zerboglio soon ate his words. In the 1890s, anti-alcohol societies sprang up first in Florence and Lucca. *The Social Good*, Italy's first temperance journal, went to press. In Venice, considered to be the Kingdom's least sober region, local notables in the mid-1890s instituted public lectures for workers on the virtues of abstemiousness; in 1903, they established the city's first temperance association and hosted Italy's inaugural anti-alcohol congress. Another national conference followed in Verona in 1905, and a third took place in Milan two years later. By 1907, at least nine northern cities had established their own leagues, and in most cases psychiatrists, public-health officials, and politicians headed them. Regional and national interest groups endorsed these associations, and political conservatives and socialists jumped aboard. In 1907, these provincial bodies joined forces as the Milan-based Italian Anti-Alcohol Federation (FAI). The umbrella organization for the various regional chapters, it organized meetings, underwrote research studies, and published pamphlets, periodicals, and other propaganda. More importantly, the FAI turned the temperance movement into a national pressure group capable of influencing social policy in Rome. Its leadership was up to the task. FAI president, Malachia De Cristoforis, a Milanese senator and doctor, afforded the group immediate access to parliament. Indeed, the FAI was to be the main influence behind the 1913 anti-alcohol legislation.

Several factors explain the sudden enthusiasm and efficiency of the northern professional elites who participated in these groups. In temperance societies, Italians found a ready-made structure, based on the blueprint of foreign precedent. These associations opened the door for social-defense activism—and a secular solution to alcoholism—at the municipal level. They provided Liberal elites with an outlet for their knowledge and a means to organize quickly. In the absence of social policy emanating from Rome, the leagues gave provincial leaders justification to regulate civic affairs, improve social hygiene, and maintain public order in their own districts. At the national level, they allowed jurists to promote themselves as indispensable partners to the state, and especially in moralizing the masses without the Church's participation. It should come as no surprise that this moral mandate was most pronounced in those northern cities most affected by Italy's prewar industrial boom, which occurred between 1896 and 1907. League officials had little difficulty sensationalizing the physical signs of working-class misery during a period of rapid social change.

Despite lacking both grassroots support and the cooperation of labor unions, temperance organizations nevertheless continued to thrive before 1914. Their short-term success depended largely on their leaders' unfaltering faith that science and law could solve alcohol-related social problems. In 1903, Venetian league president Ferruccio Fiorioli proclaimed triumphantly that social medicine would conquer alcoholism, the "principal cause of somatic, psycho-moral and social degeneration."[23] Socialist doctor Alessandro Schiavi, a FAI commissioner, also invoked the language of contamination in a rather colorful analogy:

> Just as illiteracy is a social danger and a sign of personal inferiority, so is alcoholism a collective harm and an individual shame. And just as one does not have the right to spit in a closed place in order not to pass on infectious diseases to others, so does one not have the right to get drunk ... Society will not bear the weight of generations of sick people, epileptics and invalids produced by those who seek a moment of oblivion at the bottom of a bottle.[24]

Abstemious psychiatrists chimed in as well, using mental-hospital data to validate the temperance program. Alcohol-induced insanity, they claimed, had grown progressively worse in recent years. More than a quarter of all men who entered asylums suffered from alcoholic madness, and some hospitals reported that up to 50 percent of drinkers under their care presented hereditary predispositions to drink.[25] Linking these statistics directly to those on alcohol consumption, tavern density, and crime, temperance crusaders declared that the "alcohol epidemic" had thrown Italy into "viticultural anarchy," a condition that required immediate action.[26]

Foreign regulationist legislation and the resolutions of international professional conferences helped Italian temperance leagues to justify their growing presence. In the half-century before World War I, several countries in Europe and North America, many with the assistance of temperance societies, had passed laws to control liquor traffic.[27] Although some parts of the United States, Canada, and Scandinavia instituted total prohibition, most nations sought only to oversee the sale and distribution of alcohol or to implement specific bans, like those on absinthe in Switzerland and the Low Countries in 1908 and 1909. England and some Continental countries adopted indirect measures for reducing consumption, such as police surveillance, hygienic inspections of taverns, licensing restrictions, and age-of-majority statutes. By 1900, several nations began to experiment with state-run asylums to cure habitual drunkards. The 1898 Inebriate Act in Britain set the new standard for building these institutions, and other countries, Italy included, were soon trying to emulate this model. The quinquennial International Prison

Congress regularly encouraged moral persuasion, restrictive legislation, and detoxification wards as the optimal means to defend society from pathological and criminal inebriates. Delegates at the 1910 meeting, held in Washington, DC, went a step further by endorsing the indeterminate sentence as a valid scientific principle.[28] Italian temperance officials hoped to use this sanction both as a rationalization for their campaign and as a deterrent against problem drinkers.

The FAI's 1909 publication, with its leading title, *Is Alcoholism a Danger for Italy?*, revealed how and why temperance-league officials sought to apply these social-defense initiatives at home. Through various inquiries, questionnaires, and statistical analyses, the thick volume concluded that intemperance in Italy—at least in the north—had indeed begun to resemble that of northern Europe. On these grounds, FAI officials used the data in the study to call for regulation and prevention. They claimed that alcohol consumption nationwide not only had outpaced population growth since 1867, but it also had reached an all-time high in 1907. Temperance proponents noted that while people in Milan had drunk 81 liters of alcoholic beverages on average in 1867, they ingested 211 liters in 1907, or roughly 25 liters of pure alcohol.[29] Meanwhile, the number of taverns in the city had tripled during this period. In real terms, this growth meant that one could find approximately eight *osterie* on each of Milan's 634 streets and piazzas, or one drinking establishment per 110 people. The indices for Turin bore a striking similarity. One city councilor there reported that the 3,500 taverns throughout the regional capital were four times the combined number of bakeries, butcher shops, and delicatessens.[30]

To complement these statistics, the FAI publication attacked popular beliefs about the benefits of wine. In so doing, it revealed the medical profession's stunning about-face on the issue within just a few short years. It also showed one reason why temperance societies were gaining momentum among the professional classes: traditional medical attitudes had now given way to hard scientific proof. In the volume, doctors categorically denied that wine restored vital energy for workers, aided in digestion, or provided bodily warmth. Even more damning, they cited evidence that wine had neither nutritional nor medicinal value, and was therefore unnecessary for human sustenance. Some of Italy's leading public figures and intellectuals who replied to a FAI questionnaire gave the organization still more ammunition to assault traditional attitudes. As Benedetto Croce, Pasquale Villari, Francesco Nitti, Filippo Turati, and others boasted about their own moderation or abstinence, the FAI used their testimony to equate self-control with professional success.[31] The Federation also conducted an inquiry into Milan's elementary schools, one designed specifically to expose the perils of juvenile drinking.[32] Its findings, most likely fabricated, demonstrated that 83 percent of the students interviewed claimed at least to have wine with meals. Although some pupils said they drank only a bit at the table, many boys responded that they downed eight or nine glasses a day. One in four boys and one in ten girls claimed to get drunk often—even in school—and almost half the male respondents surveyed professed to ingesting hard liquors frequently. These firsthand reports only galvanized the FAI's demands for state interventionism.

While doctors put forth devastating evidence against the dangers of drink, jurists—in this case, prosecuting magistrates—went even further in their report on alcohol and crime. The sheer size and scope of their inquest laid bare the distinctive character of the temperance movement in Italy: not only did their survey constitute about 40 percent of the entire publication, but it was also its centerpiece. In addition, the decision to put Adolfo Zerboglio in charge of the study highlighted the Federation's explicit social-defense allegiances. Virtually all prosecutors, already Italy's most zealous social-defense jurists, emphasized the link between alcoholism and violence, estimating that drink played a role in up to 80 percent of all vicious crimes. Zerboglio, too, added theatrically that the "fumes of drunkenness" accounted for 90 percent of all tavern brawls.[33] And in a similar vein, a Milanese prosecutor, apparently with a keen sense of smell, charged that alcohol-related lawbreaking was so commonplace in his city that "the majority of criminal trials reek of wine and brandy."[34] Expressing the already popular belief that their fellow countrymen—and especially southerners—were aggressive by nature, investigating judges urged the FAI to do everything possible to avoid the combustible mixture of alcohol and fiery Italian blood.

More compelling than their presumed nexus of immoderation and aggression were prosecutors' causal explanations and regional breakdowns of alcohol-related crime. Such theories were necessary because when prosecutors divided the peninsula into a modernizing north, a developing center, and a barbarous south, they were faced with a curious quandary: if drinking caused delinquency, and especially violent crime, then why were southerners the most violent and yet the most temperate? And if modernity was supposed to reduce violence, then why were the numbers of brutal misdeeds still elevated in the industrializing north? The answer, magistrates claimed disingenuously, could not be extrapolated from statistics alone; rather, it was to be found in the combination of climatic conditions, the level of civilization, the quality of alcohol consumed, and the ethnic character of local populations. In short, magistrates fell back on personal biases and traditional attitudes when the numbers did not compute.

District attorneys argued that in the more developed north and center, alcoholic criminality was a moral problem caused by urban poverty and processed alcohols, the two inevitable evils of industrialization. They maintained that although factory laborers had become somewhat less violent through their contact with modernity, their level of civility still remained too low to eliminate their mental and moral depravity altogether. As a result, magistrates alleged, workers' rising wages went not to their families, but to tavern owners, and thus often led to violent crime. Prosecutors cited workers' particular thirst for low-grade liquors, induced perhaps by the cold climate, as another reason for violent crime in the North. The Procurator-General of Lucca explicitly blamed crime on such drinking habits. He condemned lawbreaking laborers for drinking up to sixteen glasses of moonshine in a single sitting, especially "an evil mixture of rum, chicory coffee, sugar and the essence of lemon."[35] A prosecutor in Leghorn insisted that the determining push to violence there was the maritime workers' heavy consumption of *torpedine*, a refreshing punch made of pure alcohol, diethyl ether, tannic acid, and cayenne pepper.[36]

According to magistrates, if urban squalor and the hard stuff were causing high rates of alcohol-related offenses north of Rome, there were other explanations for the patterns south of the capital. Peasants may have been drinking *vino buono* rather than "the poisonous mixtures found in [northern] cities," but as prosecutors pointed out, both wine consumption and the number of taverns were on the rise in the Mezzogiorno.[37] As a result, one Neapolitan judge asserted, the "fresh air [and] healthy smell of vegetation," the demands of farm labor, hot weather, and cultural remoteness no longer could keep southerners temperate. One prosecutor in the Abruzzi claimed in 1908 that pathological drinking had worsened in his district over the past five years and estimated that the "excitement of wine" figured in at least three-quarters of all violent transgressions.[38] A fellow *abruzzese* attorney argued that overindulgence there was chiefly responsible for over-stimulating southerners' "very inferior physical and intellectual characteristics."[39] Without so much wine, one Sicilian prosecutor ascertained, "it would not be so easy [for them] to stab with a knife or fire a revolver for such frivolous reasons."[40]

In the eyes of virtually all magistrates, emigration undermined most severely the long-standing checks on excessive drinking in the south. They believed that while the overseas departure of unruly, unemployed young men helped to reduce disorder in the short-term, returning emigrants offset this benefit in the long run. Seasonal work abroad, prosecutors argued, exposed formerly isolated peasants to the intemperate habits of North American and northern European workers. According to one Neapolitan procurator, having become "more evolved and aware" through these contacts, southern farmers underwent a "fatal transformation" that destroyed their "virtues of parsimony and sobriety, and that heroic and sacred affection for family and their little hometowns."[41] Magistrates maintained that these returning emigrants posed a particular danger to the public order because they coupled their inborn inclination to violence with ample savings, no work, and an acquired love for taverns.

The Federation's demands for reform seemed to culminate in December 1910 when then-premier Luigi Luzzatti introduced in the Senate Italy's first-ever temperance bill. An economist from Venice, Luzzatti authored the bill despite his position that a half-liter of wine per day benefited both individual health and the national till.[42] Bearing the unmistakable influence of both the FAI and international trends, the proposal aimed at three things: first, to impose drastic regulatory measures, the main one limiting the density of taverns to one per every 500 residents in any municipality; second, to sequester newly classified "dangerous habitual alcoholics" indefinitely in public inebriate hospitals; and third, to ban absinthe, weekend opening hours for taverns, and even the long-standing rural custom of paying wages in wine. It went still further by punishing producers and tavern owners who sold illegal or adulterated liquors, instituting temperance lectures in primary schools, and even striking recidivist drunkards from electoral and jury lists for up to five years.

These unprecedented constraints on drinking in Italy, however, were gutted almost entirely in the final version of the "Provisions to Fight Alcoholism," passed halfheartedly in 1913 under Prime Minister Giovanni Giolitti.[43] Expressing the dismay of temperance advocates, Socialist leader Filippo Turati carped to the Chamber of Deputies that the law turned out to be "not a defense against alcoholism, but a defense of wine producers."[44] Indeed, landowners and industrialists in parliament stripped the bill down to little more than a series of indirect bureaucratic controls. Few could stomach the economic consequences of penalizing viticulture, one of Italy's most profitable industries. The revised law subjected to weekend closings only those taverns that served drinks with an alcohol content above 21 percent. By establishing this artificial standard, wine shops were exempted from mandatory shutdowns, and stronger vine-based drinks like port and marsala fell just within the cutoff. Vermouth makers, meanwhile, could continue to use absinthe as a herbal aromatic. In addition, the "Provisions" permitted the payment of wages in wine and protected the right of vintners to sell their own produce tax-free. Most importantly, Giolitti tabled the plan for inebriate hospitals. Seldom a supporter of state-welfare prescriptions that hinged upon costly institutional reforms, he delivered the mortal blow to the initial bill's social-defense aspirations.

From its title, the "Provisions to Fight Alcoholism" seemed to be a notable achievement, especially in a country in which wine had such great cultural meaning and economic importance, and where popular opinion still questioned whether Italians truly had a widespread drinking problem. The new law promised to bring Italy into line with other Continental countries, the United States, and the British Commonwealth, all of which had passed similar but farther-reaching legislation. These apparent gains, however, pleased few temperance advocates, who viewed the 1913 Act as little more than parliament's evisceration of the juridical and medical ideas that had inspired the original Luzzatti proposal. To their dismay, the new decree—unlike many of the foreign statutes—did not recognize alcoholism as a disease, but simply as a public nuisance that required intensified supervision. Their perspective, as well as their predictions of the law's eventual failure, was not entirely unfounded. In 1916, the left-wing journal *Social Reform* reported that the number of drinking establishments nationwide had declined by only 2,000 since 1913. Given that this figure represented 0.01 percent of the more than 220,000 licensed taverns still open for business, the editor-in-chief predicted that it was going to take more than 100 years to reach the desired levels.[45] Meanwhile, the statutes fell into even greater disuse following Italy's entry into the Great War, and not until 1923 did parliament under Mussolini implement a new, if similar, temperance law.[46]

Although it resulted only in watered-down legislation, the Italian temperance campaign represents more than just a study in futility. To evaluate the movement only in terms of legislative success or failure is to overlook both the central role of juridical elites in formulating social policy and the broader problems of state-building in Liberal Italy. Legal experts urged temperance reforms for the same reason that they did their proposals to prevent crime: to assert themselves as the true architects of a nation that could finally make the grade as a preeminent world power. As their crusade against alcohol-related criminality demonstrates, jurists emerged as a key interest group in Liberal political culture even when they demanded solutions to problems largely of their own invention. Their anxieties may not have always translated into political action, but their conceptions of social defense came to dominate the juridical establishment as well as national debates on the crime question after 1890. The juridical order's appeals for crime-prevention legislation exposed many of the Liberal state's inadequacies, including its weak political center, insufficient institutional infrastructure, and meager financial resources. The politics of *trasformismo*, based on shifting personal alliances rather than established political parties, made ambitious social programs difficult to enact. Indeed, with twenty-three governments in power between 1870 and 1914, and eleven just since 1900, such initiatives consistently foundered. It is ironic that while Liberal officialdom did adopt jurists' crime-prevention prescriptions in part, it was only during Mussolini's dictatorship that they found full expression in the letter of the law.

Notes

1. Federazione antialcoolista italiana e Lega populare milanese contro l'alcoolismo, *L'alcoolismo è un pericolo per L'Italia?* (Milan: Ufficio del Lavoro della Società Umanitaria, 1909), pp. 48–9, 58–60, 87–8, 104–5. The Federation will be referred to below as the FAI.

2. Political and professional elites in the pre-unitary states often associated drunkenness and taverns with public-health crises and social unrest, but these concerns did not translate into the social or legislative action that began to take shape in the late nineteenth century. See, for example, Gian Mario Bravo, *Torino operaia. Mondo del lavoro e idee sociali nell'età di Carlo Alberto* (Turin: Einaudi, 1968), pp. 113–28. On diet and consumption habits in the nineteenth century, see Carol Helstosky, *Garlic and Oil: Politics and Food in Italy* (Oxford and New York: Berg, 2004), pp. 11–15.

3. Most Italian farmers drank *vinello*, a light, watered-down wine.

4. See the German edition of Magnus Huss, *Alcoholismus chronicus* (Stockholm and Leipzig: C. E. Fritze, 1852).

5. See Daniel Pick, *Faces of Degeneration: A European Disorder, c. 1848 – c. 1918* (Cambridge: Cambridge University Press, 1989), pp. 50–4.

6. For a more extensive analysis of Lombroso's ideas, see Mary Gibson, *Born to Crime: Cesare Lombroso and the Origins of Biological Criminology* (Westport, CT, and London: Praeger, 2002). In Italian, see Delia Castelnuovo Frigessi, *Cesare Lombroso* (Turin: Einaudi, 2003).

7. See, for instance, Cesare Lombroso, "Il vino e il delitto," *Archivio di psichiatria, scienze penali ed antropologia criminale* 1 (1880): 176–84; and idem, "Alcoolismo acuto e cronico," *Archivio di psichiatria, scienze penali ed antropologia criminale* 2 (1881): 285–309.

8. See Antonio Marro, *I caratteri dei delinquenti. Studio antropologico-sociologico*, 2nd ed. (Turin: Fratelli Bocca, 1887). Also see Virgilio Rossi, *Studi sopra una centuria di criminali*, 2nd ed. (Turin: Fratelli Bocca, 1888).

9. Giulio Bizzozero, "Il vino e la salute," in Arturo Graf (ed.), *Il vino. Undici conferenze fatte nell'inverno dell'anno 1880* (Turin: Ermanno Loescher, 1890), p. 354.

10. Angelo Mosso, *Gli effetti fisiologici del vino. Conferenza tenuta il 1 marzo 1880 nella Società di letture in Torino* (Rome and Turin: Ermanno Loescher, 1880), p. 33.

11. Cesare Lombroso, "Il vino nel delitto, nel suicidio e nella pazzia," in *Il vino*, p. 440.

12. See, for instance, Luigi Lucchini, *I semplicisti (antropologi, psicologi, e sociologi) del diritto penale* (Turin: Unione Tipografico-Editrice, 1886); Napoleone Colajanni, *L'alcoolismo: sue conseguenze morali e sue cause* (Catania: Filippo Tropea, 1887); and Amedeo Pistolese, *Alcoolismo e delinquenza. Studio sociologico-giuridico* (Turin: Unione Tipografico-Editrice Torinese, 1907).

13. Articles 488 and 489. The Zanardelli provisions resembled those of an 1872 public-drunkenness law in France.

14. Some of these inquests include Luigi Bodio, "Sui contratti agrari e sulle condizioni materiali di vita dei contadini," *Annali di statistica*, 2nd ser., vol. 8 (1879): 125–206; *Atti della Giunta per la inchiesta agraria e sulle condizioni della classe agricola*, 23 vols. (Rome: Forzani, 1881–6); Giuseppe Sormani, "Geografia nosologica dell'Italia," *Annali di statistica*, 2nd ser., vol. 6 (1881): 1–335; Direzione Generale di Statistica, *Risultati dell'inchiesta sulle condizioni igieniche e sanitarie nei comuni del Regno* (Rome: Tipografia nell'Ospizio di S. Michele, 1886); and D. Maestrelli, "Sulle condizioni sanitarie dell'esercito Italiano nel decennio 1871–1880," *Annali di statistica*, 3rd ser., vol. 13 (1885): 185–285.

15. Adolfo Zerboglio, *L'alcoolismo. Studio sociologico-giuridico* (Turin: Fratelli Bocca, 1892).

16. Many of Zerboglio's conclusions came directly from Enrico Raseri, a medical geographer-statistician and a former student of Lombroso. See Enrico Raseri, "Materiali per l'etnologia italiana, raccolti per cura della società italiana di antropologia ed etnologia," *Annali di statistica*, 2nd ser., vol. 8 (1879): 4–124.

17. See Christopher Seton-Watson, *Italy from Liberalism to Fascism, 1870–1925* (London: Methuen, 1967), p. 80.

18. See Istituto Centrale di Statistica, *Sommario di statistiche storiche dell'Italia, 1861–1965* (Rome: Istituto Poligrafico I.E.M., 1968), pp. 66, 77.

19. Zerboglio, *L'alcoolismo*, pp. 52–3. For a reprint of the inquest, see Commissione ministeriale d'inchiesta sugli scioperi, *Scioperi e conflitti sociali nell'Italia liberale: la relazione finale della Commissione ministeriale d'inchiesta sugli scioperi (1878)*, ed. Carlo Vallauri (Rome: Lavoro, 2000).

20. See Enrico Raseri's presentation in Direzione Generale di Statistica, *Risultati dell'inchiesta sulle condizioni igieniche e sanitarie nei comuni del Regno: relazione generale* (Rome: San Michele di Reggani, 1886).

21. Zerboglio, *L'alcoolismo*, p. 270.

22. Ibid., p. 164.

23. Ferruccio Fiorioli, *La lotta contro l'alcoolismo* (Udine: Tipografia Cooperativa, 1903), p. 3.

24. Quoted in FAI, *L'alcoolismo*, p. vii.

25. See, for example, Paolo Amaldi, "Sui rapporti tra alcoolismo e nevropsico-patie in Italia," *Rivista sperimentale di freniatria e medicina legale delle alienazione mentali* 35 (1909): 72–91. Also see Giulio Pelanda and Alessandro Cainer, *I pazzi criminali al Manicomio provinciale di Verona del decennio 1890–99* (Turin: Fratelli Bocca, 1902), pp. 27–36. FAI committee member and asylum director Andrea Verga reported that, between 1879 and 1905, admissions for alcoholic insanity in his hospital had more than doubled for men and quadrupled for women. See FAI, *L'alcoolismo*, p. 151.

26. FAI, *L'alcoolismo*, p. xv. Also see Pelanda and Cainer, *I pazzi criminali*, pp. 35–6.

27. For a comparative overview, see Jean-Charles Sournia, *A History of Alcoholism*, trans. Nick Hindley and Gareth Stanton (Oxford: Basil Blackwell, 1990).

28. See *Proceedings of the Annual Congress of the American Prison Association, Washington, D.C., September 29 to October 8 including Abstracts of Papers and Resolutions of the Eighth International Prison Congress* (Indianapolis: Wm. B. Buford, 1910), pp. 262–3.

29. FAI, *L'alcoolismo*, pp. 129–30. The data also suggested that by 1907, liquor intake had doubled and beer consumption had increased fivefold.

30. Ibid., pp. 127–34, 138.

31. Ibid., pp. 106–18.

32. Ibid., pp. 11–23.

33. Ibid., p. 27.

34. Enea Noseda, "Il codice penale e la lotta contro l'alcoolismo," *Rivista di diritto e procedura penale* 2 (1911): 202.

35. FAI, *L'alcoolismo*, p. 55.

36. Ibid., p. 61.

37. Ibid., p. 88.

38. Ibid., p. 69.

39. Ibid., p. 71.

40. Ibid., p. 103.

41. Ibid., p. 91.

42. See Filippo Virgilii, "Il problema enologico nazionale," *La riforma sociale* 26 (1915): 712.

43. R.D. June 19, 1913, n. 632.

44. Quoted in Renato Monteleone, "Socialisti o 'ciucialiter'? Il PSI e il destino delle osterie tra socialità e alcoolismo," *Movimento operaio e socialista* 8 (1985): 17.

45. Giuseppe Prato, "I primi rilievi dei provvedimenti repressivi dell'alcoolismo," *La riforma sociale* 27 (1916): 101.

46. R.D. October 7, 1923, n. 2208.

–5–

"Mon docteur le vin"

Wine and Health in France, 1900–1950

Kim Munholland

The title for this chapter comes from an elegant booklet, *Mon docteur le vin* that was published in 1936 by the Nicolas wine firm.[1] Raoul Dufy provided illustrations, which has made *Mon docteur* something of an art collectible. Nineteen eminent doctors provided testimonies to the health benefits that could be expected from drinking moderate amounts of wine. Among these nineteen medical experts was Doctor Georges Portmann, Dean of Medicine at the University of Bordeaux and Senator from the Gironde, who was at once a distinguished eye, ear, nose, and throat surgeon and a staunch advocate of wine's role in medical practice. Portmann assured the clients of Nicolas that "More than all other medications … wine revives one's strength and acts like a heroic remedy" presumably for a wide range of ailments. In this illustrated booklet art and medical science combined to promote wine consumption, and it reflected an ongoing discussion of wine's importance as part of a French national identity that had emerged at the turn of the century.

As for the military benefits of wine consumption, Marshal Philippe Pétain composed an "Hommage à vin" as preface to the booklet in which he assured readers that "of all the supplies sent to the army during the war, wine was surely the most highly anticipated and appreciated by the soldier."[2] Wine was thus presented not only as a pleasure (Dufy's illustrations) and healthy drink (the doctors' testimonies) but also as a martial tonic that had contributed to a national victory over beer-drinking Germans in the Great War.

The notion of wine, and alcohol more generally, as therapy has had a long history.[3] In making the argument for wine's therapeutic value medical proponents regularly cited opinions from the ancients (Hippocrates) to the early moderns (Rabelais and Montaigne) and to more scientific moderns (Pasteur) to bolster their claims for wine as a healthy drink (*boisson hygiénique*). These arguments became particularly intense at the turn from the nineteenth to the twentieth century.[4] This was the *belle époque* when, according to Michael Marrus, "Frenchmen drank the most."[5] This high level of alcoholic consumption alarmed social critics, and some doctors became involved in the debate when they pointed to alcoholism as not only a social but a medical problem as well. Faced with growing criticisms of alcoholic consumption, certain doctors rallied to the defense of wine as a healthy drink and an exception to the pernicious consumption of hard liquor.

This paper examines how and why the linkage of wine and health emerged at the turn of the last century in France as an argument in favor of wine as "the healthy drink." It discusses a discourse that has as much to do with a constructed social and cultural belief in the importance of wine as part of a distinct French identity as it does with the scientific evidence presented to support the claims of wine's health benefits.

Beginning at the turn of the century a number of doctors wrote theses on the medical benefits that moderate consumption of wine could provide. The chemical composition of wine was scrutinized and data obtained to show that wine-drinkers lived longer and were less susceptible to a wide variety of illnesses. Although some historians of science, such as Harry Paul, have questioned the scientific basis for the exaggerated claims for wine as therapy, the discourse connecting wine consumption and health acquired a national importance within the context of discussions about French national identity. Wine was seen as the national drink and an important part of what it meant to be French.[6] When consumption of alcohol came under attack in the 1890s, a number of doctors rallied to exempt wine from this condemnation, and in 1903 the French Chamber of Deputies proclaimed wine to be a healthy and hygienic beverage.[7]

The prestige of medical science supported the idea that wine could provide an antidote to the illnesses of the individual and could serve as an elixir for a nation concerned about decadence and decline. The authority of science could be invoked to find in wine consumption not a source of degeneration but of regeneration. In this sense the defense of wine consumption as healthy for the individual and the nation was a response to the French cultural crisis of the fin de siècle.[8] Wine as the healthy drink served to reassure that consumption of the national beverage was at once patriotic and good for you.[9]

Why was a "defense"[10] of wine necessary at the turn of the century? One of the principle reasons to defend wine consumption was in response to the anti-alcohol crusade that began in the aftermath of the Paris Commune, which reflected republican, middle-class anxieties about the threatening, revolutionary behavior of drunken Communards.[11] This class fear was part of a broader, culturally driven debate over France's decline in the aftermath of defeat during the Franco-Prussian war and in light of a French static birth rate that also seemed to show a nation that had become "decadent." Signs of decadence and social dislocation could be found in the alarming increase of alcoholic consumption, particularly absinthe, at the end of the nineteenth century. By the 1890s a number of doctors began to recognize alcoholism as a medical as well as a social problem, and some joined the anti-alcohol crusade that had emerged among middle-class reformers.

Faced with criticisms of alcohol abuse within the medical profession, other doctors rose in defense of wine by arguing that moderate wine consumption was not only no social threat or source of alcoholism, but was actually a *boisson hygiénique*. They argued that wine consumption was not only healthy but in moderation served to counteract alcoholism that stemmed from such drinks as absinthe and hard liquor. They claimed to have empirical evidence to back their claims.[12] Wine became an antidote to alcoholism if drunk in moderation.[13] Concern with national decline and the connection between alcoholism and criminality also occurred in Italy at this time.[14] A revealing contrast between the debate over alcoholism and the role of wine is that the anti-alcohol movement in Italy did not separate wine and hard liquor, as did medical defenders of wine consumption in France. The contrast suggests the importance attached to wine as part of a French national identity.

The arguments in defense of wine were several, but the argument about wine as an antidote to alcoholism revealed ways in which its defenders made wine an exception to the implicit dangers of alcohol. During the discussions over alcoholism doctors defended wine consumption on the basis that such practice might produce drunkards but not alcoholics.[15] This distinction became part of an argument that dated from before the Commune when the French believed they were immune from alcoholism.[16] There was a qualitative difference. Those who became drunk from wine were described as being cheerful, *bon enfant*, with an open, lively expression. This "gallic drunkenness" differed from the alcoholism of the 1890s in which the victims were seen to be sullen, hostile, and condemned to an early demise. A later study described the pallid complexion, haggard, closed, and sullen expressions on the faces of those who became alcoholic from hard liquor. Wine drinkers on the other hand, could anticipate long, active, and relatively cheerful lives. Emmanuel Régis, a psychiatrist on the Bordeaux medical faculty claimed "never to have seen an alcoholic who drank only wine."[17] Moderate wine consumption represented no threat to the social order, and it contributed to the formation of a French character.

Even more, the consumption of wine was seen to be a patriotic duty, implying that the anti-alcohol crusaders threatened the French (male) character and what made France distinctively French. According to Dr Edouard Bazerolle, wine "is one of the ingredients from which our race and national temperament was formed." If the French should give up wine, "the French race would lose its true character and become a bland people without any personality."[18] The Gallic rooster, Bazarolle declared, was a rooster who drank wine.

Wine consumption became promoted as a weapon to be used to combat the consumption of industrially produced distilled alcohol. During the phylloxera epidemic, wine became scarce and expensive. Consumers, particularly among the working class, turned to hard liquor, including absinthe or the pernicious "green fairy," which was much less expensive. The consumption of alcohol, particularly distilled liquor, jumped during the 1890s. Wine was promoted as a healthy substitute for what the medical profession generally deplored as the harmful effects of absinthe drinking, which led to degeneration and an alarming increase in alcoholism in the 1890s.[19] The medical defense of wine consumption at a time of growing concern over alcoholism gave wine consumption respectability.[20] Even some doctors who were part of the anti-alcohol movement came to make an exception for wine.

One of the basic arguments was that wine differed from industrially produced alcohol in that it was a natural product, a food that was fermented. As Patricia Prestwich has noted, by 1916 medical research had built a strong case that consumption of industrially produced alcohol was dangerous. The consumption of wine was not, mainly due to the complexity of the constitution of wine.[21] This became a standard argument in favor of wine consumption. The composition of wine provided nutrients and ingredients that had a range of benefits from combating tuberculosis to protection against cancer to calming the nervous system to improving muscular strength or to assuring greater longevity. The different chemical elements to be found in wine, particularly red wine with its tannins, meant that wine also differed from other, naturally fermented drink, cider and beer. The process was less important than the basis, grapes rather than hops or apples, in distinguishing wine as a healthy beverage.

While the medical theses showed some rigor in their analyses of wine, some of the scientific methods employed to support the claims for wine consumption rather than hard liquor were less than rigorous. The use of regional comparisons became standard practice, for example. Each region could defend its own natural product, cider or beer, but the advocates of wine as particularly beneficial used these same regional differences to support wine as the *boisson hygiènique* for France. Not surprisingly inhabitants of the Gironde came out ahead of those from the non-wine-producing areas of France in these comparisons. The medical advocates of wine consumption noted that the incidence of alcoholism was lower in wine regions, such as the Gironde, than in Calvados or Brittany, areas prone to a higher consumption of hard alcohol.[22] Incidence of psychological disorders was shown to be more common north of the Loire than in the wine-drinking areas.

To demonstrate that wine consumption favored longevity, studies looked at vital statistics to show, for instance, that there was a higher proportion of eighty-year-olds living in the Gironde in 1921 than in France as a whole.[23] Another study demonstrated that within France those who drank water had a life expectancy of fifty-nine years while the average life for a wine consumer was sixty-three.[24] The medical proponents considered such methods to be scientific although they suffer from what we would call an "ecological fallacy" since other factors might contribute to relative, regional longevity.[25] Whatever the flaws of the argument wine continued to be recommended to promote better health, including a healthy old age, or *la verte vieillesse*.[26] These were comforting words for an aging population and reassured French readers of the virtues and strengths of French cultural practices.

Regional comparisons suggested differences in health within France, which raised questions about the relevance of this research within the context of wine as a "national" beverage. As wine distribution became national in the latter part of the nineteenth century, wine was more available as the national drink.[27] To show that the healthy effects of wine might be found on a French national level, medical wine advocates readily compared France as a wine-drinking country with Germany, a land of beer drinkers, England, a country of tea-sippers, and the United States with a predilection for cocktails and whisky. Not surprisingly wine was far less harmful. In a widely cited study of soldiers marching after consuming either wine or beer, it was shown that wine drinkers were less fatigued and sang cheerfully as they marched along while beer drinkers were sluggish afoot and exhausted at the end of the day.[28] France had lower cancer rates than countries where hard liquor prevailed, such as the United States. And the French character was much more cheerful than the sober and frigid British. Although a healthier France was identified with winegrowing regions, wine was portrayed as a national resource that contributed to the development of a distinctive national culture.

In this turn of the century debate over wine and health there was always an element of class distinction. Good wine rather than *vin ordinaire* would be more likely to promote health. The wine that was good for people was wine of good quality and consumed in moderation. The middle class, it was assumed, would be more likely to show restraint and have the proper taste to appreciate good wine. Popular consumption of mediocre wine and the nutritionally deficient white baguette, one argument went, was bad for the health of the masses.[29] However, some doctors recognized that consumption of wine might be just as beneficial for the working class as for the bourgeoisie. In recommending "moderate" wine consumption, a number of medical authorities suggested limits on consumption, usually a half or three-fourths liter for those involved in sedentary work and up to two liters for those engaged in manual labor. Just as wine stimulated the intellect, so could a glass of wine provide a "start-up kick" (*coup de fouet*) for the worker.[30]

Yet it was in the trenches of the Great War that the benefits of wine for the ordinary French soldier became apparent. Just before the war one of the leading pro-wine propagandists, Raymond Brunet, claimed that the soldier's *pinard* would provide the *poilu* with the physical and moral strength necessary to assure victory over the *boche*.[31] Thus the *pinard* was considered an essential ingredient of victory and became a defining, almost romanticized, characteristic of the *poilu*. Wine drinkers had prevailed over the guzzlers of beer, and the *pinard* acquired a "mystical status" in the minds of the French with the triumph of 1918.[32] This mystique of the *pinard* would become part of a French legend and would be stressed again as assurance of French strength when the threat of war developed twenty years later.

The *pinard* for the soldier came to be praised in the interwar literature as a positive benefit. No longer was alcohol in the hands of the popular classes seen to be a potential social threat or even a social problem. Insofar as can be determined, the *pinard* was not blamed for the mutinous behavior of soldiers in 1917. In this sense the discourse about wine had escaped any identification with alcoholism as a cause of revolutionary or anti-social behavior as a result of the Great War. If anything the *pinard* reinforced the comradeship of the trenches. There was even a mild revisionism in the interpretation of the relationship between wine consumption and the war of 1870–1. In one of the better theses on wine and health Dr Israel Jager argued that Parisian wine drinkers were better able to withstand the rigors of the siege of Paris in 1870–1.[33] Jager considered wine particularly effective in resisting respiratory diseases.

Wine emerged as a unifying element in the French experience of the war, at least according to one wine advocate, by revealing the value of wine to northerners. Dr Max Eylaud, one of the militant Girondin propagandists for wine, wrote a rather bad novel, *Dans les vignes*, in which the hero, Lieutenant Roger Lansac, distributes "this wine of France (which is) so consoling in moments of weakness" to stir the bravery of his company's soldiers. After the war his companion in arms, René Mongin from northern France became enamored with the healthy life of the vignerons and married Lansac's sister. Even Will Burky, "the worthy son of dry America," became a determined adversary of Prohibition. In the novel Eylaud had nothing but praise for his partner in the interwar campaign on behalf of wine, health, and national identity, Dr Georges Portmann, who was thinly disguised as Dr Lesportes. Portmann/Lesportes was praised for his intellect and his activity as a determined propagandist who "shakes up the apathy of the medical profession" by insisting upon wine "as one of the best elements of physical and moral health."[34]

Support for the soldier's wine ration resulted from the success of the impressive publicity campaign in favor of "natural" alcohol waged between the wars by such wine advocates as Georges Portmann and his ally, Max Eylaud. They participated in a number of organizations to promote wine consumption as a healthy practice. In 1924 the *Office International du Vin* was created, which published its *Bulletin de l'organisation du vin* to promote wine consumption. As a result of American prohibition and the loss of the Russian market, particularly for champagne, after the revolution, French winegrowers again contended with surplus production. The doctors were soon to follow in their campaign linking wine and health. In 1933 the first congress of the *Médecins amis des vins du France* was held. Portmann, Eylaud, and Dr. Georges Fagouet were pioneers in this organization, which met every two years until the outbreak of war in 1939.[35] As its name implies, the organization was intended to promote wine and encourage the medical profession to consider its benefits for maintaining health.

The doctors also published their own journal, *Bulletin des Médecins Amis des Vins*. These voices continued to defend wine consumption against the "so-called" science of those trying to destroy the reputation of wine as the French national drink. Important political connections were enlisted in the cause. A number of doctor-deputies formed a lobby in support of wine producers, and Edouard Barthe, who was a member of the board of the OIV, headed the viticulture group in the Chamber of Deputies. His counterpart in the Senate was Albert Sarraut, seconded by Georges Portmann.[36] Art was enlisted in the cause, as seen in the promotion of the elegant illustrated booklet from Nicolas, *Mon docteur le vin*, and in a series of posters that linked wine with the good, healthy life. Through advertising, such as the elegant booklet from Nicolas, wine consumption increased in the 1930s in France.[37]

During the interwar period Dr Portmann became one of the staunchest advocates for wine consumption, continuing the battles within the medical profession to get acceptance of wine as the healthy drink. He continued to deplore those colleagues who promoted mineral water as healthier for the individual, claiming that these doctors were linked to the mineral water industry. At the same time he denied any connection that he might have to the winegrowers of Bordeaux, despite his staunch advocacy of their interests in the Senate. From his perspective the objective scientific research into wine's healthful properties meant that the propaganda that he and his colleagues pursued was disinterested and concerned only with the welfare and well-being of the French people. In an early intervention in the French Senate, Portmann made his position clear. He called for doctors of good will, who were not connected to any commercial interest, to engage in a propaganda effort on behalf of moderate wine consumption. "This propaganda," he intoned, "more than any other will have an influence because it will be scientific, disinterested, and in the final analysis will be concerned with health."[38] A compilation of his speeches indicates no less than eighty-four interventions on behalf of wine and the wine trade during his political career. Although Portmann's efforts may have had limited impact within the medical profession, as Harry Paul argues, his role as a leading member of the wine lobby within the Senate combined with his medical credentials assured that his views would be influential in a political and economic sense.

With the threat of war and the outbreak of hostilities in the late 1930s the *pinard* became the object of political attention and praised as a boost to morale that would again assure victory. Already in *Mon docteur le vin* Dr Amerlink had argued that the largest, best developed, and most coordinated recruits came from the wine-growing regions of France. Dr Armand Gautier from the Academy of Medicine and the Academy of Science assured readers of *Mon docteur le vin* that moderate doses of wine helped the soldier to make an extra effort. Wine protected him from certain illnesses. Others added their scientific opinions that wine would kill the microbes that caused typhoid fever and cholera and again acted as an antidote to depression.[39] In the Senate, Dr Portmann held forth on the importance of "le vin chaud pour nos soldats."[40]

Armed with these reassurances, the French Army made sure that there would be an adequate supply of *pinard* for the soldier. Supply depots began to fill with abundant supplies of wine from the cheap wine-producing regions of the Midi. Rolling stock was requisitioned to meet the military need for wine. Over 36 percent of the French railroad cars capable of transporting liquid (3,450 out of a total 9,500) were requisitioned to distribute approximately 2 million liters of wine daily to the troops.[41]

During the phony war Edouard Barthe, a deputy from Hérault and an ardent advocate for wine interests, established an organization to promote "le vin chaud du soldat." The campaign of the "Oeuvre du vin chaud" opened with a gala on November 23, 1939 with a large, elegant, and politically connected crowd present, including the Minister for Agriculture, the Labor Minister, the Undersecretary for War, and the military commander of the Paris district. The invited soldiers came forward to be served their *vin chaud* by "femmes du monde en costume noir et bleu ciel" from vats of "fort ordorant" mulled wine according to a report in *Le Temps*. In the aftermath of this kick-off gala, all municipalities were asked to contribute to a fund for the soldier's wine. By March 1940 4.5 million francs had been raised. "Our soldiers will be happy," Barthe boasted.[42]

During the cold days in the Maginot line the soldiers did appreciate warm wine, which caused the anti-alcohol movement to question expending funds to encourage drinking. The wine and alcohol lobby counterattacked. The intrepid Barthe succeeded in getting legislation passed that again designated naturally fermented beverages, wine, beer, and cider, as hygienic drinks. Barthe reassured his colleagues that wine and cider were "antidotes to alcoholism." And the *pinard* would once more assure victory. To a cheering Chamber of Deputies he predicted that the *poilu* would again triumph over those who drank beer. "Wine," Barthe declared, "gives the soldier courage," and added, "wine, the pride of France, is a symbol of strength; it is associated with warlike virtues."[43] The value of the soldier's *pinard* had become politically popular.[44]

A discourse about the healthy benefits of wine that began at the turn of the century had become a political discourse about wine's importance as part of a French identity on the eve of World War II. Much of the language of this discourse was gendered in male terms with reference to the martial, as well as the health benefits that wine consumption provided. There was some discussion of the ways in which wine consumption was also beneficial for women's health, but this was a secondary theme. Champagne, for instance, was recommended for pregnant women and moderate amounts of wine were also suggested for women recovering from childbirth and for daily consumption in more limited quantities than recommended for men.[45] At the 1935 Congress of the International Medical Committee for the Propaganda for Wine, Dr Guénard discussed the usefulness of champagne for women in labor, having the effect of reducing thirst and easing the mother's labor pains.[46]

Alas, the *pinard* did not save France from defeat in 1940, and Marshal Pétain's new, authoritarian government at Vichy blamed alcoholism for France's decline and collapse by undermining the will of the Army.[47] At the Riom trial Professor Heuyer, who was the head doctor for the prefecture of police in Paris, testified that alcoholism caused France's defeat, seen in the panic of May 13 when French troops retreated pell-mell in the face of the German breakthrough on the Meuse.[48] Defeat opened the way for the anti-alcohol movement to influence Vichy legislation, which taxed industrially produced alcohol heavily. However, wine and fermented drinks with an alcoholic content below 16 percent were exempt from this tax.[49]

The success of the wine industry in escaping Vichy's anti-alcohol campaign may be attributed to the continued activities of the wine lobby and its medical advocates. One of the most influential voices at Vichy was Dr Portmann. In the debacle of the 1940 defeat, Portmann was one of a group of conservative and moderate politicians who persuaded President Lebrun not to leave Bordeaux aboard the *SS Massilia* in order to continue resistance from North Africa.[50] After joining those who voted full powers to Marshal Pétain on July 10, 1940, Portmann became a member of the Vichy government when his political ally, Pierre-Étienne Flandin, appointed him Undersecretary for Information in his government. Portmann remained at this post after Flandin was dismissed. He eventually offered discreet assistance to the Resistance, although this was not sufficient to save him from punishment in the purge trials following liberation. Portmann was one of only twenty deputies or senators from the discredited Third Republic to have served Vichy before November 1942. After his mentor and close political ally, Flandin, left France in October 1942, Portmann remained in the government. In the postwar purges he was banished from public life until he was pardoned in 1949.[51] Although there is no direct evidence of Portmann's role, a reasonable assumption is that he pursued his interests and lobbied for wine's protection under Vichy.

Other wine advocates, such as Max Eylaud, argued for the beneficial effect of wine under Vichy. In time of shortage wine was seen to be a source of nourishment and calories.[52] Eylaud also adjusted his writings to the priorities of Vichy's New Order, publishing a pamphlet that demonstrated the value of moderate wine consumption for young people and athletes, again linking wine to national renewal in the spirit of Vichy's call for regeneration.[53] The *Médecins amis des vins de France (MAVF)* continued to publish its *Bulletin* during the first years of Vichy, much to the dismay of the anti-alcohol movement, which asked that public health officials "stop this kind of pro-wine propaganda" but to no avail. In the Free Zone the *MAVF* successfully lobbied to have Radio Santé cease its "unjustified propaganda" campaign against the wines of France, and in December of 1941 French National Radio abandoned its campaign against wine drinking. At the same time doctors on the faculties of Bordeaux and Paris continued to offer courses on "La Vigne plante médecinale" or "Le vin dans l'alimentation."[54]

Not all was smooth sailing, however, in relations between *MAVF* and Vichy. Édouard Barthe, who also had voted full powers to Pétain in 1940, got into trouble with Vichy when he protested the requisition quotas demanded by the Germans. He was imprisoned in Vals-les-Bains from October 1941 to February 1942 for having advised the winegrowers in the Midi not to deplete their stocks. He was subsequently released and placed under house arrest in Nice, but he was banned from any travel in winegrowing regions.[55]

The *Bulletin de la Société des Médecins Amis des Vins de France* also got into trouble despite the presumed protection of Georges Portmann. The *Bulletin* published freely under Vichy until the appearance of the twenty-third issue, which contained a poem in which the *pinard* was praised as the source for France's liberation and renewal.[56] The editorial board decided to cease publication rather than submit to censorship.

The defense of wine resumed after the war. In 1949 the *MAVF* gathered in Bordeaux for its fifth meeting. Once again medical science was invoked against the "so-called" scientific arguments of the doctors who warned against the dangers of alcoholism. "With the same kinds of arguments, we must fight against them and show the inanity of such insults. Our duty as doctors is to rise to the podium … to show why the wine of France, unadulterated wine of good quality, taken in moderate quantities is good for the healthy individual [and] is good for the sick person." Doctor Portmann again pronounced that moderate wine consumption was the best way to combat alcoholism, and it was every doctor's duty was "to defend the healthy drink, which is wine." Technical papers followed this renewed call to arms in defense of wine as a *boisson hygiénique*. Half-century old arguments reappeared to demonstrate the beneficial effect of wine on the health of the cardiovascular system, as a source for valuable vitamins and minerals, as a stimulant for digestion, and an aid in the functioning of the liver and pancreas. The scientific methods that backed such claims became more solidly grounded in the extensive research on wine and health in France and elsewhere than they had been in France at the turn of the century or during the interwar years. Recent research has demonstrated some scientific validity to the claim that moderate consumption of red wine increases longevity and offers some protection against coronary disease. And the superiority of wine over beer or hard liquor has additional scientific backing on the basis of surveys.[57] But the discourse about wine as the healthy drink also continues to be exploited in the commercial promotion of wine consumption.[58]

Notes

1. Gaston Derys, *Mon docteur le vin*, watercolors by Raoul Dufy (Paris: Draeger frères, 1936). An English version of this elegant book has recently been published. Gaston Derys, *Mon Docteur le Vin* (*My Doctor, Wine*) trans. Benjamin Ivry with introduction by Paul Lukacs (New Haven and London: Yale University Press, 2003).

2. Quotation from Gaston Derys, *Mon Docteur le Vin*, preface and cited in Jean-Louis Crémieux-Brilhac, *Les Français de l'an 40*, Vol. 2 *Ouvriers et soldats* (Paris: Gallimard, 1990), p. 463.

3. Harry W. Paul, *Bacchic Medicine: Wine and Alcohol Therapies from Napoleon to the French Paradox* (NY and Amsterdam: Rodopi, 2001), ch. 3; Salvatore Pablo Fucia, *A History of Wine as Therapy*, forward by Sanford V. Larkey (Philadelphia: Lippincott, 1963). The tradition of connecting wine and health may be seen in Ken Albala's essay, "To Your Health: Wine as Food and Medicine in Mid-sixteenth-century Europe," in this volume.

4. Paul, *Bacchic Medicine*, p. iv.

5. Michael R. Marrus, "Social Drinking in the *Belle Époque*," *Journal of Social History*, 7 (1973–4), p. 115.

6. In his article on "La vigne et le vin" in *Les Lieux de Mémoire*, Pierre Nora (ed.) (Paris: Gallimard, 1985), Vol. 3: *Les France 2 Traditions*, p. 796, Georges Durand argues that although Spain and Italy are large producers of wine, viniculture is powerfully associated with France. He also cites a poll conducted by Jean-Pierre Rioux in *Histoire* (May 1987) which revealed that of the qualities that made one French, the liking of good wine was ranked fourth after being born in France, a determination to protect freedoms, and speaking French. Kolleen Guy points out that fermented drinks such as wine, cider and beer were not designated as "alcohol" in the French language. See Kolleen Guy, *When Champagne became French: Wine and the Making of a National Identity* (Baltimore and London: Johns Hopkins University Press, 2003), p. 31.

7. Rod Phillips, *A Short History of Wine* (New York: HarperCollins, 2000), p. 277.

8. Robert Nye, "Degeneration and the Medical Model of Cultural Crisis in the French *Belle Époque*," in Seymour Drescher, David Sabean and Allan Sharlin (eds), *Political Symbolism in Modern Europe* (New Brunswick, NJ: Transaction Books, 1982).

9. This is the formulation of Dr. Frédéric Cayla, *Le vin, le buveur de vin et le buveur d'alcool, les eaux-de-vie et les liqueurs* (Bordeaux: G. Gounouilhou, 1901) p. 9, cited in Marrus, "Social Drinking in the *Belle Époque*," p. 120.

10. Dr. Edouard Bazerolle, *Défense du vin* (Paris: Rousset, 1902).

11. Susanna Barrows calls the campaign against alcoholism a "moral crusade" to reform the working class. Susanna Barrows, "After the Commune: Alcoholism, Temperance, and Literature in the Early Third Republic," in John M. Merriman (ed.), *Consciousness and Class Experience in Nineteenth-Century Europe* (New York: Homes & Meier, 1979), pp. 205–8. Another perspective on alcoholism and the working class may be found in W. Scott Haine, *The world of the Paris Café: Sociability among the French Working Class 1789–1914* (Baltimore: Johns Hopkins University Press, 1996) and on the anti-alcohol campaign, Patricia E. Prestwich, *Drink and the Politics of Social Reform: Antialcoholism in France since 1870* (Palo Alto: Society for the Promotion of Science and Scholarship, 1988).

12. Paul discusses the sharp debate within the medical profession between a few doctors who supported the anti-alcohol crusade and the more numerous but by no means majority of doctors who rallied in defense of wine consumption in *Bacchic Medicine*, pp. 199–207. The pro and con medical arguments were summarized in Dr J.-A. Doléris, *Le vin et les médecins: Le pour et le contre* (Paris: Vigot frères, 1907, 1931). Among the medical theses defending wine as part of the struggle against alcohol were Dr Emile Mauriac, *La Défense du vin et la lutte contre l'alcoolisme* (Bordeaux: Feret et fils, 1901), Louis Izou, *La défense du vin dans la lutte antialcoolique* (Paris: Th. Medical, 1907), and Dr Joseph Vergely, *Quelques chiffres sur l'alcool et l'alcoolisme à Bordeaux* (Bordeaux: G. Gounouilhou, 1902).

13. Dr. Emile Mauriac, *La Défense du vin*; Prestwich, *Drink and the Politics of Social Reform*, p. 50.

14. See Paul Garfinkel's essay, "In Vino Veritas: The Construction of Alcoholic Disease in Liberal Italy, 1876–1914," in this volume.

15. Cayla, *Le vin, le buveur de vin*, pp. 12–14.

16. Barrows, "After the Commune," p. 206 and Marrus, "Social Drinking," p. 117.

17. Bazerolle, *Défense du vin*, p. 32. The citation is from Paul, *Bacchic Medicine*, p. 203. A number of authorities made this claim and would continue to do so into World War I as part of the opposition to the anti-alcohol crusaders. Marrus, for example, quotes Joseph Reinach on the impact of wine on "our character, our abilities [and] our well-being in general," in "Social Drinking," p. 137, fn. 29.

18. Bazerolle, *Défense du vin*, p. 34. Robert-Yves-Jacques Constant, *Le Vin et*

la longevité (Bordeaux: J. Bière, 1935), p. 40–41.

19. Marrus, "Social Drinking," pp. 122, 128–9; Haine, *The World of the Paris Café*, p. 95; Kolleen Guy, "Rituals of Pleasure in the Land of Treasures: Wine Consumption and the Making of French Identity in the Late Nineteenth Century," in Warren Belasco and Philip Scranton (eds), *Food Nations: Selling Taste in Consumer Societies* (New York: Routledge, 2002), pp. 34–47.

20. Haine, *The World of the Paris Café*, pp. 114–15.

21. J. Alquier, "Valeur biologique et hygiénique du vin," *Bulletin de la Société scientifique d'hygiène alimentaire*, no. 17, II (1929) cited in Paul, *Bacchic Medicine*, pp. 223–4.

22. Paul, *Bacchic Medicine*, p. 204.

23. The most detailed statistical analysis for this claim is to be found in Constant, *Le Vin et la longevité*, pp. 29–30, which cited a study showing that the fifty-seven communes of Médoc had 1.981 inhabitants/1000 who were over eighty compared with a figure of 1.053 for all of France. Constant approvingly cited M. Léon Douarche, director of the International Office for Wine (l'Office international du vin), who boasted that these octogenarians "provide a most dramatic illustration that on the blessed soil of Bordeaux's vineyards longevity is stronger than in any other country." Constant compared five departments: Calvados, where the drink was cider, had 6.625% of the population over seventy; Finisterre, where the drink was cider or water, had 6.526% of the population over seventy; Somme and Ardennes, where the customary drink was beer or wine, had 9.94% over seventy; and wine-drinking Gironde, which had 10.76% of its population over seventy. Constant's thesis on wine and longevity was produced under the direction of Dr Georges Portmann whose colleague in wine advocacy, Dr Max Eylaud, used these statistics in their 1936 study of the physiological and therapeutic uses of wine cited by Harry Paul, *Bacchic Medicine*, pp. 233–4 fn. 20. Other works dealing with the favorable impact of (moderate) wine consumption on longevity and in combating senility include, Dr Pierre-Henry Roeser, *Vieillesse et longévité* (Paris: Maloine, 1910) and Dr Alexandre Lacassagne, *La Verte vieillesse* (Lyon: A. Rey, 1920).

24. J. Alquier, "Valeur biologique et hygiénique du vin," *Bulletin de la Société scientifique d'hygiène alimentaire*, no. 17, II (1929), cited in Constant, *Vin et la longévité*, p. 61.

25. As Harry Paul states with a touch of irony, "Although logic was applied with Ockhamite ruthlessness to anti-wine discourse, it played a very small role in the pro-wine arguments." Paul, *Bacchic Medicine*, p. 235.

26. G. Ichok, "Sur la longévité, la sénilité et la vieillesse," *Le Progrès Médical*, 16 mai 1931.

27. Durand, "La vigne et le vin," p. 803, sees this as the point at which attachment to wine became an integral part of French history.

28. Marrus, "Social Drinking," p. 120.

29. Paul, *Bacchic Medicine*, 227.

30. Ibid., p. 230; Prestwich, *Drink and the Politics of Social Reform*, p. 19.

31. Raymond Brunet, *La valeur alimentaire et hygiénique du vin* (Paris: Librairie agricole de la maison rustique, 2nd ed. 1914) cited in Paul, *Bacchic Medicine*, p. 251, fn. 5.

32. Durand, "La vigne et le vin," p. 811. Prestwich, *Drink and the Politics of Social Reform*, p. 172.

33. Israel Jager, *La valeur alimentaire et thérapeutique du vin* (Paris: M. Lavergne, 1938), p. 28.

34. Max Eylaud, *Dans les vignes* (Bordeaux: Delmas, 1934) with a preface by Georges Portmann.

35. Comité national de propagande en faveur du vin, *Véme Congrès national des Médecins Amis du Vin de France*, Bordeaux, 10–12 septembre 1949 (Montpellier, 1951), p. 3. Additional meetings were held in Dijon, Béziers, Algiers (1937) with a fifth scheduled for Reims in September 1939 but not held due to the outbreak of the war.

36. The Office International du Vin had its headquarters on the Place du Bourbon next to the Chamber of Deputies. Paul, *Bacchic Medicine*, p. 254.

37. Lukacs, *Mon Docteur (My Doctor)*, p. x, citing Eugen Weber, *The Hollow Years: France in the 1930s* (New York: W. W. Norton, 1994), p. 71.

38. Georges Portmann, *Son action parlementaire, scientific, social*, Vol. 1 (Bordeaux: Delmas, 1955), p. 51.

39. Crémieux-Brilhac, *Les Français de l'an 40*, Vol. 2, p. 464.

40. Portmann, *Son action parlementaire, scientific, social*, Vol. 1, p. 43.

41. Crémieux-Brilhac, *Les Français de l'an 40*, Vol. 2, p. 464.

42. Ibid., pp. 465–6, 474. Drs Portmann and Roustan leant their authority to the promotion of the soldiers' *pinard* in the pages of the *Revue vinicole*, cited in Prestwich, *Drink and the Politics of Social Reform*, p. 245, fn 10.

43. Crémieux-Brilhac, *Les Français de l'an 40*, Vol. 2, p. 463.

44. Harry Paul observes that Portmann and Eylaud toured France in the 1930s pushing wine consumption to medical audiences that received their message with "condescending smiles and sarcasms." Although the reception was lukewarm within the medical profession, the idea of wine and particularly wine for the soldier, was politically popular. Portmann was one of a number of deputies and senators who formed a lobby in favor of wine consumption generally and promoted the value of wine for the soldier. See Paul, *Bacchic Medicine*, pp. 257, 259.

45. Paul, *Bacchic Medicine*, p. 242.

46. François Bonal, Docteur Tran Ky, Docteur François Drouard, *Les vertus thérapeutiques du Champagne: histoire, traditions, biologie, diététique* (Paris: Artulen, 1990), pp. 24–5.

47. Prestwich, *Drink and the Politics of Social Reform*, p. 247.

48. Crémieux-Brilhac, *Les Français de l'an 40*, Vol. 2, p. 475.

49. Léon Douarche, "Le vin et la vigne dans l'économie nationale française," *Les cahiers de la réorganisation économique*, cahier 2 (janvier 1943): 68. Wine production was not entirely exempt. The Vichy government required those producing more

than five hundred hectoliters of wine set aside 20% of the crop for the production of sugar based upon grapes, producing a loss of four million hectoliters of wine. Another decree ordered that any vineyard over 5 hectares (12.35 acres) had to convert 10% of the land to cultivation of a crop other than grapes as of January 1, 1941.

50. François-Georges Dreyfus, *Histoire de Vichy* (Paris: Perrin, 1990), p. 159.

51. Olivier Wieviorka, *Les Orphelins de la République: Destinées des députés et sénateurs français (1940–1945)* (Paris: Seuil, 2001), pp. 36, 150, 217, 246, 405.

52. The trouble with this argument is that wine was in short supply due to German requisitions, problems of transportation, and a drop in overall production due to the lack of copper sulfate to control diseases and a poor year in 1941. The wine producers, particularly among the grands crus, used this opportunity to dispose of poor quality vintages at the expense of the Germans. Wine became quite expensive and an item for black market commerce placing it beyond the resources of most people.

53. Jean Max Eylaud, *Sports et l'éducation de la jeunesse*, pref. Colonel Duché (Mont-de-Marsan: Jean Lacoste, 1941). He also wrote a novel against Zola, *Le Nouvel assommoir*, cover and illustration by G.-J. J. Hosteins, preface by Édouard Barthe, and introduction by Professor Georges Portmann (Mont-de-Marsan: Jean Lacoste, 1942), and a play in the spirit of Vichy's cultural ideology, "Rétour à la terre: comédie en 1 acte" (Mont-de-Marsan: Jean Lacoste, 1941).

54. Comité national de propagande en faveur du vin, *Véme Congrès national des Médecins Amis du Vin de France*, pp. 7–8.

55. Wieviorka, *Les Orphelins de la République*, p. 289.

56.

"Je suis le vieux pinard versé par Madelon,
Qui faisait trouver beau le sort de la tranchée
Chantaient le coeur d'airain et l'âme empanachée

Seigneur, sans moi demain la France y songes-tu
Ne serait qu'un pays vaincu par la défaite.
Par moi seul elle peut retrouver la vertu
Qui lui rendra l'élan vainqueur qu'elle souhaite.

Cited in Comité national de propagande en faveur du vin, *Véme Congrès national des Médecins Amis du Vin de France*, p. 6.

57. See, for example, the editorial by J.-P. Broustet, cardiologist at *l'Hôpital Cardiologique Haut Lévèque*, Pessac, France in *Heart* 81 (1999): 459–60.

58. A recent wine promotion in a Paris included a pamphlet from *Vin & Santé*, an annual publication since 1995, that informed the public about ways in which polyphenols found in wine were effective in combating cancer and Alzheimer's disease. Several doctors were cited, including Dr Serge Renaud who announced, "Two or three glasses of wine a day reduce by more than 30% the mortality rate from all causes of illness taken together." For the ongoing scientific argument, see Nathalie Vivas de Gaulejac, *Vin et santé: les bases scientifiques du French Paradox* (Bordeaux: Éditions Féret, 2001).

Part II
Sociability

Drinking and Alehouses in the Diary of an English Mercer's Apprentice, 1663–1674

A. Lynn Martin

Recent scholarship on drinking establishments—alehouses, taverns, public houses, and cabarets—demonstrates their importance in the social history of alcohol. In addition to dispensing alcoholic beverages, drinking establishments had manifold functions that reveal their central role in the social life of their customers. A concise expression of this role comes from the definition of a tavern in John Earle's *Microcosmography*, published in 1628: "It is the busy man's recreation, the idle man's business, the melancholy man's sanctuary, the stranger's welcome, the Inns-of-Court man's entertainment, the scholar's kindness, and the citizen's courtesy."[1] The diary of Roger Lowe, an apprentice shopkeeper in the latter half of the seventeenth century, illustrates the importance of drinking establishments, in Lowe's case the alehouse, in the social fabric of both its author and the community. Lowe's comments on alehouses are so informative that both Keith Wrightson and Peter Clark have used the diary in their works on the English alehouse, Wrightson in his article on "Alehouses, Order and Reformation in Rural England, 1590–1660,"[2] and Clark in his book on *The English Alehouse: A Social History, 1200–1830*.[3] However, the diary also demonstrates that Lowe consumed his ale not just in alehouses but also in homes, shops, fields, and streets. The alehouse was important, but the real focus of Lowe's social life was the drinking irrespective of its location. Lowe's diary also makes it clear, however, that drinking was not just a male domain, as the alehouse proved to be just as important a social space for women as for men. In fact, Lowe's evidence indicates that by the second half of the seventeenth century the alehouse had replaced the parish church as the "third place" after the home and the workplace for both men and women.

In 1656 Roger Lowe's master placed him in charge of a shop selling cloth in the market town of Ashton-in-Makerfield, Lancashire. He remained an apprentice until 1666 when he became proprietor of the shop. Lowe supplemented his wages through his skill as a writer, and townspeople regularly called on his services to draft letters and documents. Lowe was a staunch Presbyterian at a time when the newly restored Stuart monarchy was making worship increasingly difficult for dissenters. As a result, he usually spent his Sundays trekking to places where he could hear sermons by preachers whom the government had ejected from their churches.

Despite the failure to attend local church services, as a result of his service to the community as a writer and his shopkeeping Lowe acquired a wide range of friends and acquaintances and became integrated into the life of the town. There he met and courted his wife, Emm Potter, although the date of their marriage is not known, nor are the dates of Roger's birth and death. On April 22, 1679, a Probate Court in Chester granted Emm the authority to administer his property,[4] meaning he had died a few months before, probably aged in his early to mid-forties.

Roger Lowe began his diary on January 1, 1663. The last entry is dated March 12, 1674, but regular entries in the surviving manuscript cease seven years earlier, in October 1667, meaning that the diary covers not quite five years of Lowe's life. The diary is preserved at the Leyland Free Library and Museum in Hindley, Lancashire, and the American scholar William Sachse edited it in 1938. Lowe never explained why he decided to keep a diary, but the practice was widespread among the literate classes in seventeenth-century England. This was especially the case among Puritans, who considered diaries a valuable means of ordering their religious life. Lowe's diary documents his religious feelings, but the entries often deal with the mundane minutia of his life. Typical are the entries for the first four days of January 1666:

> 1. Monday. I went to Nicholas Croft to bid him fetch the cow.
> 2. Tuesday. I went a hunting and the hare took into the rabbits' holes, and I was exceedingly wearied.
> 3. Wednesday. I went to Leigh to speak to Mr Swift, who was come and gone again ...
> 4. Thursday. I got Thomas Harison to go along with me to Peter Lealand's, Hadcocke Wood, to look at a chest for me, which I was to buy.[5]

Included in the mundane minutia of Lowe's life is his consumption of alcohol. For the five-year period covered by the diary, Lowe mentioned his drinking in 170 entries, that is thirty-four times a year, which does not indicate that he was a heavy drinker, even though some entries record more than one drinking session in a single day. However, the total number of entries for these five years is 490, or about eight entries per month. Thirty-five percent of the entries mention his drinking. Lowe might have recorded every one of his drinking sessions, but it seems more likely that the entries only document a fraction of his drinking. As proof of the latter interpretation, the rituals celebrating the rites of passage, christenings, weddings, and funerals were normally occasions for communal drinking.[6] Lowe recorded his attendance at many of these rituals but only occasionally noted the consumption of alcohol. In short, I think it safe to assume that the diary only documents a relatively small portion of his drinking.

The diary primarily records Roger Lowe's occupational and recreational drinking. Hidden from view is the daily drinking that would have formed part of everyone's diet. In the period before safe drinking water, tea, coffee, and other alternatives, most people began their day with a cup of ale or beer with breakfast and continued drinking throughout the day. One of the better indications of this practice is the diary of another English apprentice, Benjamin Franklin, who recorded the drinking habits at the printer's shop in London in the early eighteenth century:

> We had an alehouse boy who attended always in the house to supply the workmen. My companion at the press drank every day a pint before breakfast; a pint at breakfast with his bread and cheese; a pint between breakfast and dinner; a pint at dinner; a pint in the afternoon about six o'clock, and another when he had done his day's work.[7]

On one occasion Lowe's diary does demonstrate the role that drink would have in his diet. On a Sunday in December 1666 he left home without breakfast and walked three miles to attend a funeral. At noon after the burial when everyone was waiting for the customary refreshments, the clergyman in charge came in and prohibited the pouring of drinks until after prayers. Lowe did not wait but returned home "with much vexation … and a hungry belly."[8]

Roger Lowe and his drinking companions drank ale, not beer. Ale was the traditional English drink, made from malted grain, usually barley, yeast, and water. In the late Middle Ages ale brewing had been a domestic industry dominated by alewives. Their brew was usually sweet, sometimes flavored with herbs and spices, and spoiled if not consumed within several days. In the fifteenth century the English began brewing a new type of drink called beer that contained hops. The addition of hops created a bitter drink that was stronger and lasted longer than ale, but the complexities of the brewing process led to the development of large commercial breweries that had no place for the traditional alewife. Precision is difficult, but after gaining reluctant acceptance in the fifteenth century beer replaced ale as England's national beverage by the end of the sixteenth century.[9] In 1587 William Harrison noted in *The Description of England* that ale had become an "old and sick men's drink."[10] However, ale retained its popularity in the north and in some rural areas, as it obviously did in Ashton-in-Makerfield. Lowe's diary does not state if alewives continued to brew ale, or if large commercial breweries had replaced them, although on a few occasions he drank bottled ale,[11] which is probably indicative of commercial brewing.

On occasion Lowe did drink beer; when he called on a woman in a neighboring town, she took him into her parlor and served him spiced beer, and he once offered to buy someone a beer.[12] Just as rare was his consumption of wine, which he had once at a funeral and another time when drinking with a Presbyterian preacher, three drinkers sharing two pints of wine.[13] As for the ale, Lowe never commented on its quality but sometimes mentioned drinking special types, such as bragget,[14] made from fermenting honey and ale together. Although he often dined at alehouses, he recorded few details about the food; once he had a penny's worth of pottage, a thick soup, with his twopenny flagon, and once he ate a hot rye loaf with butter.[15]

Lowe rarely mentioned how much he drank but typically recorded how much he spent or how much others spent on him, which makes it possible to calculate his consumption. A quart of ale, that is a bit more than a liter, was served in a flagon and cost twopence.[16] On two occasions Lowe recorded that he spent one penny, meaning that he drank a half quart of ale. He often drank a twopenny quart. In fact, to ask a friend to spend twopence meant to ask him to go drinking.[17] Almost as often Lowe drank two or even three quarts, and the time he drank five quarts he concluded his diary entry by stating, "at far in night I went to bed."[18] The most he drank was consumed under strained circumstances. When Lowe learned that William Morris had told Emm Potter that he was a bastard, he rode six miles to a neighboring town for the purpose of confronting Morris. Lowe stopped at Izibell Grundie's alehouse, sent for Morris, and when he came proceeded to beat him, stopping only after someone intervened. Lowe then went to another alehouse, Widow Ranicar's, and drank six quarts of ale.[19] On another occasion, while returning from a long ride, Lowe stopped at an alehouse and gave his horse four pence in ale.[20] How strong was the ale? That is impossible to determine. Records indicate that most modern beers would be weaker than many of those produced in the past,[21] but people consumed a large amount of small beer and ale, which were the products of a second brewing and hence quite low in alcohol.[22] They also cost less than normal beer or ale, and Lowe never mentioned that he had saved money by buying small ale. My hunch is that Lowe's ale was comparable in strength to the typical modern beer.

Lowe did most of his drinking at alehouses, often stating that he went to an alehouse without naming it. Even so, he mentioned forty-seven different alehouses, twenty-five in Ashton and another twenty-two in surrounding towns and villages. Most carried the names of their owners. For example, his favorite watering hole was John Jenkins, sometimes referred to as John Jenkinsons, closely followed by Robert Rosbotham's, Tankerfields, and John Robinson's. Of the twenty-five alehouses in Ashton he visited seventeen on only one occasion. Six of the proprietors were women, which is not surprising given the incidence of female alehouse keepers during this period. For example, of the forty-three alehouse keepers listed at Salisbury in 1630, fifteen were women.[23] Throughout England poor widows often received permission to operate alehouses as a means of earning a living and thereby relieving the local poor rates of the burden of their support, and in addition to Widow Raniker's alehouse Lowe mentioned the alehouses of Widow Barker and Widow Heapy in neighboring towns.

Disorderly alehouses could pose a problem for local and national authorities, and Keith Wrightson has argued that "the struggle over the alehouses was one of the most significant social dramas" in early modern England.[24] However, the only case of disorder in an alehouse mentioned in Lowe's diary was the previously mentioned incident when he beat William Morris for slandering him. If violence was rare, disputes were frequent. While drinking at an alehouse, another customer insulted Lowe by attacking the profession of mercer; Lowe's reaction was so angry that it in turn angered the alekeeper's wife.[25] Lowe recorded only one case of drunkenness and this among soldiers guarding an execution at a castle. Although he bribed one of the soldiers with twopence of ale to see the castle, he was glad to get away from them.[26]

Lowe included few details about the alehouses he visited. Some had separate chambers; when Lowe went to Isibell Grundie's alehouse for the purpose of confronting William Morris, he asked for a chamber and got one upstairs. As previously indicated, at least some alehouses served food. The most Lowe had to write about the ambience of an alehouse resulted from his trip with a friend to a neighboring village to hear a Presbyterian preacher on a cold Sunday in December 1666. At noon they went to Humphry Cowley's alehouse, which "was so thronged that we could not obtain a fire to sit by, but we sacrificed ourselves over the twopenny flagon in a cold chamber ... We had each of us a mess of pottage; we spent 3 pence a piece."[27]

In modern societies the consumption of alcohol is usually a social rather than a solitary activity, and drinking has an important role in celebration and in social facilitation and jollification.[28] The socializing and integrating functions of alcohol were even more important in seventeenth-century England. Alcohol was the ubiquitous social lubricant, and Roger Lowe was a social drinker. Of the 170 drinking sessions recorded in the diary, he did not mention any drinking companions on twelve, perhaps thirteen, occasions. The thirteenth might have been a joke, for the gregarious Lowe noted that he "went into alehouse with one Roger Lowe,"[29] perhaps meaning that he had been obliged to drink alone. For the remaining 157 or 158 sessions, Lowe usually named his drinking companions, an amazing total of 129 people. In addition, Lowe often drank with groups of unnamed people. For example, when Thomas Atherton was leaving Ashton to live elsewhere, Lowe joined his neighbors in farewelling him at an alehouse.[30] Other groups included young folk, Mr. Sorrowcold's servants, the men from Rainford, and the townsmen of Ashford.[31]

Studies of modern drinking behavior reveal the importance of alcohol in fostering durable same-sex friendship, camaraderie and solidarity, especially among men.[32] However, some of Lowe's drinking companions proved not so durable. When courting Mary Naylor, Lowe frequently drank with other Naylors, at least some of whom were relatives, but the frequency declined when he began courting Emm Potter. Another frequent drinking partner was John Hasleden, who shared Lowe's Presbyterian faith and often attended dissenting church services with him. However, after August 1665 Lowe no longer mentioned drinking with him. John Potter, possibly Emm's brother, then became his most constant drinking companion. When people came from other towns to see Lowe, they usually headed immediately for the alehouse. For example, when Robert Greinsworth came from London, he "forced" Lowe to go drinking with him at a neighboring village.[33] When Lowe went to other towns and villages to see someone, they invariably drank together, and this included the Presbyterian preachers who were the objects of his Sunday trips.

A significant illustration of the integrating function of shared drinks was the role of alcohol in the reconciliation of disputes. Lowe described his efforts in "endeavoring to rectify some things between old John Jenkins and his son Mathew; ... after a peace was concluded and all things rectified in and among them, we all went to alehouse together."[34] On three occasions Lowe recorded how his own disputes with other persons were settled at the alehouse. Significantly, two of the disputes had their origins during drinking sessions at alehouses. Dick Naylor, probably a relative of Mary Naylor, began a quarrel when he found Lowe drinking at an alehouse with his new sweetheart, Emm Potter. A week later Naylor initiated a reconciliation at John Jenkins's alehouse.[35] Lowe and Emm Potter's former sweetheart, Henry Kenion, had such a bitter quarrel at Tankerfields that Lowe called it "a disaster," but Kenion made amends by asking Lowe to meet him at Tankerfields two days later; "we were both reconciled, and I was somewhat joyful."[36] If drinking together signaled friendship and camaraderie, a refusal to drink could indicate enmity. Lowe described his reaction when an invitation to drink was declined: "I intended to call on Mr Potter, merely out of love, but he would not go to take part of twopence in beer, but seemed as if he were angry, which troubled me very sore. I came home very pensive and sad and not very well."[37]

Another illustration of the integrative function of alcohol was its role in community celebrations, particularly in the rites of passage. These and other drinking rituals fostered communal solidarity. Lowe twice attended christenings as godfather, one of which was for his brother's child. Because he was godfather, both occasions required the expenditure of significant amounts of money on drink.[38] Weddings were likewise occasions for often copious consumption, and moralists had long and loudly complained of the excessive drinking leading to drunkenness that occurred both before and after weddings. After the wedding of Isibell Hasleden, people celebrated at an alehouse, and Lowe spent sixpence on ale at the wedding of Lawrence Pendleberry.[39] The purchase of ale at a wedding was one way of helping the newly-weds establish their households, as was the custom of a bride ale, at which the bride-to-be sold ale. Lowe attended Grace Gerard's bride ale, spent his money, and then left his neighbors and the music to go to bed.[40] Unlike weddings, funerals were occasions for the family of the deceased to provide drinks and other refreshments, partly as a means of assuring a good attendance to pay last respects to the departed. At the funeral of Thomas Taylor, Lowe consumed the wine and biscuits provided and later commented in his diary, "Friends that did much honor this funeral came to attend it to the grave, and there parted."[41] Lowe also attended the celebrations marking another rite of passage when the apprenticeship of Thomas Greene ended.[42]

Not just rites of passages were occasions for celebration. The annual fair days at Ashton were on September 22 and 23, and they could result in more than the usual merry drinking. On September 22, 1663, John Hasleden invited Lowe to drink sixpence worth of ale that came in a jelly bowl.[43] Sundays were likewise days for drinking. Unlike many other dissenters, Lowe was not a puritanical sabbatarian who insisted on the strict observance of Sunday through the closure of alehouses and the prohibition of all recreation so that people could spend the day piously at sermons and in prayer. Lowe did go to sermons on Sundays, sometimes twice, and walked to neighboring villages so that he could attend Presbyterian services. But before, between, and after he often went to alehouses. On an April Sunday in 1665 he and John Hasleden walked over six miles to hear the dissenting minister Roger Baldwin preach and along the way met others with whom they drank. After Baldwin's sermon in the morning, they left before hearing him preach in the afternoon, stopping once again at an alehouse on the way home.[44] On some Sundays he did not make it to church. The only comment in the diary for one Sunday was "I was with Mr Sorrowcold's servants in alehouse, and was merry."[45] On another Sunday three friends came from a neighboring town and asked Lowe to join them at Tankerfields, where they were joined by "wenches." Lowe wrote, 'We were all afternoon in alehouse. The Lord forgive us."[46]

Although moralists considered drunkenness a sin, drinking was not, and, as already noted, alcohol formed a fundamental part of most people's diet. Lowe's Presbyterian faith was sincere—life would have been so much easier for him as a conformist—and on occasion his diary demonstrates strong religious feelings, such as the times he went out in the country and prayed by a ditch.[47] Lowe sought the Lord's forgiveness not for the drinking but probably for the profanation of the sabbath. On another occasion Lowe sought the Lord's forgiveness for time spent in an alehouse, this time for drinking with John Potter and a visitor until late.[48] If moralists found no difficulties in everyday drinking, alehouses were another matter. They characterized alehouses as nests of satan, schools of drunkenness and violence, nurseries of naughtiness and of all riot, excess and idleness, secret dens for thieves, cheaters, and such like, receptacles of all manner of baseness and lewdness, and wombs that bring forth all manner of wickedness. The alehouses patronized by Lowe did not match the descriptions of the moralists, and the conversation was just as likely to be on religion as on any other topic. After spending a night drinking with a minister at Robert Rosbotham's, the minister lent Lowe a copy of Edward Gee's book on prayer, *A Treatise of Prayer and of Divine Providence as Relating to It*.[49] On several occasions Lowe reported that the discussion of religion led to debates, twice with John Potter on episcopacy versus presbytery, and on the first occasion Lowe wrote, "The contention had like to have been hot, but the Lord prevented," but for two or three days afterwards he worried that Potter might still be angry about it.[50] On another occasion he debated with a Catholic at John Jenkins's alehouse, but, unlike the argument with Potter, this time it ended in "love and peace."[51]

Studies of modern drinking behavior reveal that the major consumers of alcohol in most societies are the young men between puberty and their mid-thirties.[52] For the English alehouse Peter Clark believes that the clientele formed two major groups. The first included young unmarried men such as Roger Lowe who were apprentices, journeymen, and servants. The second group comprised young and middle-aged married men. Few old people were patrons, although Clark suggests

that this was a reflection of demography, since the old constituted a small propor-
tion of the population.[53] The vast majority of Lowe's drinking companions were
men, but he usually gave no indications of their age. Lowe did mention "young Mr
Gerard," but this might have been a means of distinguishing him from his father.[54]
He characterized seven of his 129 drinking companions as old, such as "Old
Jenkins" and "Stirrope, my old father," his godfather.[55]

The consensus among historians is that during this period alehouse space was
male space, and women who went there did so at the cost of their reputations.[56]
Nonetheless, women were more likely to visit English alehouses than they were
Continental taverns, and Peter Clark argues that by the late seventeenth century the
stigma attached to women drinking in alehouses had relaxed somewhat.[57] At
Ashton women were free to visit alehouses; single women came with other single
women or with men, and wives came with their husbands or by themselves. Lowe
mentioned twenty-four women with whom he shared a drink, usually at alehouses,
and on two occasions he visited an alehouse accompanied by "wenches,"[58] a
neutral term meaning young women. The occasions of his drinking with women
are instructive in demonstrating the relatively relaxed socializing that could occur
between men and women. On one occasion he and John Hasleden went to an alehouse with Old Izibell "and were merry when we parted."[59] When Ann
Greinsworth came to town, Lowe took her to an alehouse and spent twopence on
her,[60] and when he accompanied Ellen Scott to a church service in a neighboring
town, they spent eight pence at an alehouse before the service began. After church,
they had lunch, did some sight seeing and returned to the alehouse with Ellen's
sister.[61] Finally, one diary entry stated, "John Naylor's wife came to town and
wished me to go with her into an alehouse. I went."[62]

Also illustrating the freedom of women is the role of the alehouse in courtship.
In August 1664 Lowe recorded in his diary, "At this time I had a most ardent affection to Emm Potter, and she was in company at Tankerfields with Henry Kenion,
and it grieved me very much." Lowe went to Tankerfields and sought an opportunity to speak to her; at last she came and had a drink with him but refused to stay,
"and I was in a very sad afflicted state, and all by reason of her."[63] Lowe met Emm
at another alehouse one week later; "there we professed each other's loves to each
other, ... and I promised this night to come see her in her chamber."[64] Despite the
prodigious beginnings, their courtship continued for some time, and eighteen
months later, in February 1666, they had "fallen out." Lowe attempted a reconciliation at an alehouse, of course, but was unsuccessful.[65] Several of Lowe's friends
also courted women at alehouses, and, oddly enough, asked Lowe to accompany
them, perhaps because they were bashful. For example, Henry Low sought his
company at an alehouse for the purpose of courting Ann Hasleden. Ann had previously asked Roger "sundry times" to get Henry to come, so at last they went and
received very good treatment.[66]

Drinking at an alehouse was the principal means of recreation for Roger Lowe,
and he obviously spent many hours in drinking sessions. On January 1, 1663, the

first day of his diary, he recorded that he should have stayed at an alehouse all night but would not and came home instead.[67] Four days later on January 5, Lowe also signaled his good intentions by refusing to stay despite the urging of friends; while coming home by himself in the dark night he nearly drowned.[68] His good intentions did not last long, for the rest of the diary is a record of late drinking sessions, with Lowe frequently stating that he stayed at the alehouse "far in night" or "all night." Lowe also drank during the day. On one occasion he described how he "stayed and drank both bottle ale and common ale and was very merry" at a neighboring village. On his way home he stopped to see Mary Naylor, whom he was courting at the time. "Mary was angry with me [that] I had been out of shop, for folks had been there inquiring for me, which angered her very sore."[69] When old Mr Woods came to Lowe's shop one day, he thought Lowe had been drinking too much ale and warned him to take heed. In his defense Lowe replied that "I could not trade if at sometimes I did not spend twopence."[70]

Lowe's defensive statement could be interpreted in various ways. One interpretation develops from the role of drink in Lowe's diet; ale helped provide the physical energy to transact business. Another interpretation relates to modern studies on the reasons for drinking. One of the reasons men drink is the feeling of power that comes from the consumption of alcohol. As stated by Richard E. Boyatzis, "men drink alcoholic beverages to attain, or regain, a feeling of strength," that is "thoughts about being big, strong, and important, about having more impact on others, [and] dominating."[71] This power could be an advantage in dealing with other people. Another interpretation, one that is more capable than the previous two of empirical verification, is that drinking with customers, what I call occupational drinking, was a requirement for a successful shopkeeper. Just as people courted in alehouses and reconciled disputes in alehouses, so also did they transact business in alehouses. When a mercer from a neighboring town visited Lowe, the two went to an alehouse to talk business.[72] When Lowe traveled to Liverpool to purchase some "commodities" for his shop, he "got his business done" while drinking.[73] On two occasions Lowe wrote that he had to accept drinking invitations from customers for fear of losing their business.[74] As mentioned previously, Lowe sometimes supplemented his income through his skill as a writer, and this could result in further trips to the alehouse, as it did when he was involved in the preparation of a lease.[75] Finally, by drinking with such a large circle of friends and acquaintances he was undoubtedly gaining custom for both his shop and his writing.

Yet another interpretation of his statement that he could not trade without spending twopence focuses on the recreational aspects of Lowe's drinking. The time spent in alehouses might have provided him with psychological energy, recharging his mental facilities as well as providing a temporary release from the cares of keeping shop. The most frequent word used by Lowe to describe a successful drinking session was "merry." For example, when Roger Naylor and Richard Twisse invited him to an alehouse, his only comments on the evening were "very merry we were."[76] Sometimes Lowe explained just what it was that made a drinking session so "merry." Richard Naylor, Henry Low, and he pledged to be as brothers to each other.[77] With other companions he discussed how to be successful in courtship and the meaning of Aesop's fables.[78] They drank toasts, made bets, and engaged in bowling contests, with the loser buying the drinks.[79] And of course there were the wenches, Emm Potter, the jelly bowl of ale, the music, the courtship of friends, the debates on religion, and the celebrations.

Diaries such as that kept by Roger Lowe form a reciprocal relationship with the social historians studying them. On the one hand, historians can apply their general knowledge to the diaries to better understand the life and times of the authors. Examples of this for Lowe's diary are the role of alcohol in diets, the nature of the drinks, the communal solidarity that arises from celebratory drinking, the significance of female and widowed alehouse keepers, and the integrative functions of sharing a drink. On the other hand, the diaries can clarify or reveal little-known features of the society in which they were written. Lowe's diary reveals four significant features of his society. First, beer might have been the beverage of choice in much of England, but ale still ruled in this part of Lancashire. Second, although women elsewhere might have avoided alehouses for fear of compromising their integrity, women in Ashton-in-Makerfield had the freedom to drink in alehouses with men who were not their husbands or their relatives. Third, in this part of England, at least, sabbatarian concerns did not prevent people enjoying a drink at alehouses on Sundays. Finally, despite the concerns of governments and moralists, alehouses were benign institutions rather than nests of satan. For these four conclusions we are indebted to the diary of Roger Lowe, mercer's apprentice, of Ashton-in-Makerfield, Lancashire.

According to André Lascombe, when beer replaced ale as the beverage of choice, the level of violence and disorder increased in English alehouses, which in turn led to concerted government regulations against disorderly and unlicensed alehouses. The addition of hops in the brewing process increased the strength of beer by facilitating the fermentation, so that alehouses which served beer were more unruly than those which served ale.[80] If Lascombe is correct, a possible conclusion is that the consumption of ale in Lowe's alehouses was responsible for making them benign institutions rather than nests of satan, which in turn made them conducive to patronage by women as well as making them suitable for Sunday entertainment. The problem with such a conclusion is that its reductionism is too simplistic; beer might have been stronger than ale, but ale was still strong enough to produce drunken and disorderly behavior, and English brewers had long known how to make strong ale by simply adding less water to the malted barley. A better conclusion focuses on the nature of alehouses. Throughout England alehouses had become the "third place" after the home (first place) and work (second place). As elaborated by anthropologists, the third place is public space that is relatively secure, a place where people can gather, talk, relax, and socialize.[81] The appeal of drinking establishments as a third place was particularly strong to the poor and to men. The poor congregated there because they offered alternative housing, companionship, and even family, while men considered them space that was free from the constraining female influences of the first place, home. However, the alehouse in Lowe's world was a third place for women as well as for men, and it was likewise a third place for the devout dissenters as well as for the poor. At least in this part of England the alehouse was not male space that had a potential for disorderly conduct but an institution that served as an inclusive focal point of popular culture and recreation—a third place for all.

Notes

1. John Earle, *Microcosmography, or, A Piece of the World Discovered in Essays and Characters [1628]*, Harold Osborne (ed.) (London: University Tutorial Press, 1933), p. 32.

2. Keith Wrightson, "Alehouses, Order and Reformation in Rural England, 1590–1660," in Eileen and Stephen Yeo (eds), *Popular Culture and Class Conflict, 1590–1914: Explorations in the History of Labour and Leisure* (Brighton: Harvester, 1981), pp. 1–27.

3. Peter Clark, *The English Alehouse: A Social History, 1200–1830* (London: Longman, 1983).

4. Roger Lowe, *The Diary of Roger Lowe of Ashton-in-Makerfield, Lancashire, 1663–74*, William L. Sachse (ed.) (New Haven: Yale University, 1938), p. 133. When quoting from the diary I have modernized the spelling.

5. Ibid., p. 95.

6. The best illustration of these practices is *The Diary of Henry Machyn, Citizen and Merchant-Taylor of London, From A. D. 1550 to A. D. 1563*, John Gough Nichols (ed.) (London: J. B. Nichols and Son, 1848).

7. Benjamin Franklin, *The Autobiography of Benjamin Franklin: A Genetic Text*, J. A. Leo Lemay and P. M. Zall (eds) (Knoxville: University of Tennessee, 1981), p. 46.

8. *The Diary of Roger Lowe*, p. 109.

9. Judith M. Bennett, *Ale, Beer, and Brewsters in England: Women's Work in a Changing World, 1300–1600* (New York: Oxford University, 1996).

10. William Harrison, *The Description of England [1587]*, Georges Edelen (ed.) (Ithaca: Cornell University, 1968), p. 139.

11. *The Diary of Roger Lowe*, pp. 41, 100.

12. Ibid., pp. 46, 114.

13. Ibid., pp. 66, 68.

14. Ibid., p. 53.

15. Ibid., pp. 109, 116.

16. Lowe twice recorded that he drank a twopenny flagon, ibid., pp. 76, 106; according to Andrew Campbell, *The Book of Beer* (London: Dennis Dobson,

1956), p. 70, a quart of ale cost twopence at this time.

17. *The Diary of Roger Lowe*, pp. 68, 73.

18. Ibid., p. 75.

19. Ibid., p. 105.

20. Ibid., p. 115.

21. G. G. Coulton (trans. and ed.), *Social Life in Britain from the Conquest to the Reformation* (Cambridge: Cambridge University, 1918), p. 376.

22. Clark, *The English Alehouse*, p. 109.

23. Sue Wright, "'Churmaids, Huswyfes and Hucksters': The Employment of Women in Tudor and Stuart Salisbury," in Lindsey Charles and Lorna Duffin (eds), *Women and Work in Pre-Industrial England* (London: Croom Helm, 1985), p. 110.

24. Keith Wrightson, *English Society, 1580–1680* (London: Hutchinson, 1982), p. 167.

25. *The Diary of Roger Lowe*, p. 62.

26. Ibid., p. 118.

27. Ibid., pp. 108–9.

28. David G. Mandelbaum, "Alcohol and Culture," in Mac Marshall (ed.), *Beliefs, Behaviors, and Alcoholic Beverages: A Cross-Cultural Survey* (Ann Arbor: University of Michigan, 1979), p. 17; Mac Marshall, "Conclusion," pp. 451–7 in the same work; Dwight B. Heath, "A Decade of Development in the Anthropological Study of Alcohol Use: 1970–1980", in Mary Douglas (ed.), *Constructive Drinking: Perspectives on Drink from Anthropology* (Cambridge: Cambridge University, 1987), p. 46.

29. *The Diary of Roger Lowe*, pp. 51–2.

30. Ibid., p. 52.

31. Ibid., pp. 41, 71, 74, 82.

32. See the same sources cited in note 28.

33. *The Diary of Roger Lowe*, p. 80.

34. Ibid., pp. 14–15.

35. Ibid., pp. 70–1.

36. Ibid., p. 114.

37. Ibid.

38. Ibid., pp. 74, 96.

39. Ibid., pp. 13, 61.

40. Ibid., p. 45.

41. Ibid., p. 66.

42. Ibid., p. 26.

43. Ibid., p. 34.

44. Ibid., p. 82.

45. Ibid., p. 71.

46. Ibid., p. 26.

47. Ibid., pp. 15, 17.

48. Ibid., p. 120.

49. Ibid., p. 54.

50. Ibid., pp. 52, 89.

51. Ibid., p. 64.

52. Marshall, "Conclusion," pp. 454–5.

53. Clark, *The English Alehouse*, p. 127.

54. *The Diary of Roger Lowe*, p. 104.

55. Ibid., pp. 62, 80.

56. See the discussion in my *Alcohol, Sex, and Gender in Late Medieval and Early Modern Europe* (Basingstoke: Palgrave, 2001), p. 73.

57. Clark, *The English Alehouse*, p. 225.

58. *The Diary of Roger Lowe*, pp. 26, 44.

59. Ibid., p. 42.

60. Ibid., p. 41.

61. Ibid., p. 23.

62. Ibid., p. 56.

63. Ibid., p. 68.

64. Ibid., p. 69.

65. Ibid., p. 97.

66. Ibid., pp. 48–9.

67. Ibid., p. 13.

68. Ibid., pp. 13–14.

69. Ibid., p. 41.

70. Ibid., p. 59.

71. Richard E. Boyatzis, "Drinking as a Manifestation of Power Concerns," in Michael W. Everett, Jack O. Waddell and Dwight B. Heath (eds), *Cross-Cultural Approaches to the Study of Alcohol: An Interdisciplinary Perspective* (The Hague: Mouton, 1976), p. 269; see also James M. Schaefer, "Drunkenness and Culture Stress: A Holocultural Test," in the same work, p. 291.

72. *The Diary of Roger Lowe*, p. 37.

73. Ibid., p. 100.

74. Ibid., pp. 53, 58.

75. Ibid., p. 81.

76. Ibid., p. 15.

77. Ibid., p. 26.

78. Ibid., pp. 37, 42.

79. Ibid., pp. 36, 75, 85.

80. André Lascombes, "Fortunes de *l'ale*: À propos de Coventry, 1420–1555," in Jean-Claude Margolin and Robert Sauzet (eds), *Pratiques et discours alimentaires à la Renaissance* (Paris: G.-P. Maisonneuve et Larose, 1982), pp. 132–3.

81. Dwight B. Heath, *Drinking Occasions: Comparative Perspectives on Alcohol and Culture* (Philadelphia: Brunner/Mazel, 2000), pp. 50–1.

–7–

Taverns and the Public Sphere in the French Revolution

Thomas Brennan

During the hundred years before the French Revolution, public drinking places took on many new forms and became different kinds of public spaces, serving different kinds of publics. In the process, the public drinking place helped to create, and recreate, a number of different public spheres, in which these publics developed distinct patterns of sociability, of identity, and of political awareness. The public drinking place, once merely a wine shop on every corner, suddenly multiplied its forms, functions, and offerings in the late seventeenth century. New kinds of drink, both alcoholic and non-alcoholic, became available and, somewhat more slowly, assimilated as commodities. Coffee is the most famous example of this new trend but certainly not the only one. The introduction of imported drinks, coffee, tea, and cocoa, coincided in the second half of the seventeenth century with growing demand for spirits, principally distilled alcohol in the form of brandy (eau de vie). With a range of new drinks came a range of new shops in which to sell them and a growing differentiation among the customers that drank in them. The introduction of coffee in the middle of the seventeenth century led to the successful foundation of the café as a drinking place, in the late century.[1] These new establishments were awkwardly integrated into an equally new guild, of limonadiers, which also enjoyed the privilege of selling a range of spirits and exotic wines. Spirits were a more familiar decoction than coffee but, until the seventeenth century, had been sold by apothecaries and consumed mostly as a medicine.[2] Thus the new guild of limonadiers at the end of the century was commercializing several fundamentally new kinds of drink and creating new establishments in which to meet and drink. At roughly the same time, wine merchants were setting up new taverns in the outskirts of Paris, beyond the reach of the city's sales tax, to sell wine at a discount. These *guinguettes*, as they were known, were also selling the dance floor and larger crowds that were possible with the extra space available outside of the city. New forms of drinking establishment were proliferating in the eighteenth century, then, some based on new drinks, others on new locations, that transformed the role of the public place in urban society.

The significance of these new establishments lay partly in their being different from the traditional tavern or cabaret. Taverns in Paris had long ago become an integral part of the life of the city's inhabitants, offering wine to take out but, far more importantly, space in which to consume it. Utilitarian in decor, providing little more than tables and chairs in one or two rooms, they served the whole range of the population but were principally neighborhood centers. They could be rowdy and disreputable, but abundant evidence in the archives of the Parisian police paints a rather different picture. The fights and altercations in taverns, which came to the police's attention on a regular basis, were chiefly the result of shopkeepers and artisans contesting and assessing each other's honor and reputation.[3] Although belonging to the level of society that worked with its hands and lived in a simple and sometimes precarious manner, these artisans insisted on having honor and vigorously defended their reputations for having sound credit, producing honest work, and being sober husbands. Their complaints and testimony to the police also depicted their frequent recourse to taverns for the purpose of business discussions, meetings with friends, meals, even occasional family gatherings. Drinking was constant yet unobtrusive, with little evidence of drinking bouts or competitive toasting, and little reference to drink as anything more than background to socializing. In many ways a mundane extension of artisanal life and social patterns, the tavern suffered from being too tied to the populace and too tied to neighborhood life. New establishments were careful to distinguish themselves from these features.

Guinguettes offered cheap wine at an inconvenient distance from most of Paris, yet they turned this handicap into their chief attraction. Away from the familiar scenes of the neighborhood, and with enough space to accommodate dancing and attract crowds, the guinguette offered a new commodity: entertainment.[4] Parisians turned the trip to the guinguette into a Sunday outing; women were more likely to join them there than in the overwhelmingly masculine tavern. Although there had always been periodic entertainment associated with the yearly religious calendar, seasonal fairs, and sporadic royal events, the guinguette offered entertainment whenever one had the time and money to visit; it had become a commodity. This was leisure of a very different sort from the regular drink at the tavern with friends or fellow workers. The guinguette produced a form of glamor, not from any elegance but from a kind of frenzy and festivity, a carnival license that took people away from their normal identities and associations.[5] Yet the crowds here were still the working poor, with only the occasional person of fashion who had come slumming.

Where the guinguette offered a promiscuous mixing of the populace, the café created a different decor and appealed to a more exclusive clientele. Actually, cafés might be found in many guises. Early shops, in the seventeenth century, affected a middle eastern decor. With the amalgamation of coffee sellers into the guild of limonadiers, many cafés became little more than simple beer shops. But at the end of the seventeenth century some cafés adopted a distinctive look that signaled refinement and discrimination. They made a conscious effort to distinguish themselves physically from the tavern and to look more like an *hôtel particulier*. A dictionary of the early eighteenth century described them as "redoubts magnificently decorated with marble tables, crystal mirrors and chandeliers, where quantities of honnêtes gens of the city assemble, both for the pleasure of conversation and to learn the news."[6] Here was a public place where one could avoid rubbing shoulders with the masses. Coffee and tea were touted as sober, intellectual drinks suited to a literate, discriminating clientele. Literary cafés brought famous authors together before an avid audience that could eavesdrop on their conversations. Some of the most famous cafés of the century, the Procope, the Veuve Laurent, or those around the Palais-Royal, were among these magnificent establishments and boasted of a clientele that included the leading lights of the Enlightenment. These cafés became a kind of public salon, where news and ideas were exchanged and conversation, rather than recreation, was prized. The conversation was chiefly literary and, though it could make or break a writer's career, did not particularly challenge the old regime. The café's link to news, however, was more threatening.

For a variety of reasons, cafés became places to hear and discuss the news. Literary cafés appear to have attracted foreigners who were visiting the city, both because the elegant ones were obviously safe and because the middle class of many countries had learned to value cafés in their own metropolises and sought them out in their travels. Already in the late seventeenth century the police were being warned about the "assemblies of all kinds of people and particularly of foreigners" taking place in cafés.[7] The presence of foreigners in turn gave the café's clientele a link to the outside world and to its financial and political news. Police reports spoke frequently of customers reading aloud from letters they had received from abroad, and cafés were a good place to meet foreigners, like the "café of the rue Dauphine where there are ordinarily lots of Englishmen."[8] Some cafés sought locations that gave them better access to news. Those in and around the Palais-Royal profited from proximity to the financial and commercial activities of the Bourse and the Halles, as well as a tradition of gossiping in the Palais' garden.[9] Others, situated near the Parlement, attracted the legal professions and their discussions of constitutional and legal issues. A police spy described one such, the café Maugis, with its "grand assembly of barristers, attorney, book sellers and news mongers, who distribute and read all sorts of defamatory libels. They talk loudly about all sorts of affairs of state, of finance and diplomacy, supported by the book sellers who are in correspondence with England, Holland and Geneva."[10] Patrons brought news from the outside world, often letters received from abroad, to share with other customers. They read and discussed these missives and debated the events of the day. Not surprisingly, they drew the attention of the authorities, for these were men with positions of some prominence and power, with the reputation of challenging the government, either legally or financially, and their opinions mattered. The police spied on their conversations to keep track of "public opinion," an idea gradually gaining importance as a legitimate source of political power. There were probably several dozen of these elite cafés throughout Paris catering to a bourgeois clientele. They were not in the majority, however, for most cafés aimed at the populace and, some, even at the underclass.

Although the populace continued to prefer wine, and the taverns that sold wine, through the eighteenth century, they also drank beer, coffee, and brandy and went to the shops that sold them.[11] An eighteenth-century comedy spoke of "these little cafés which are hardly ever frequented except by artisans who come in the evenings to drink beer and play chequers."[12] Evidence from hundreds of police records confirms that the artisanal population went less frequently than to taverns but were the majority of customers in most cafés. These were not the elegant literary cafés, however, where artisans like the glazier Ménétra (who wrote his memoirs) felt uncomfortable.[13] Places identified as beer and brandy shops catered to a somewhat poorer and more marginal society of day laborers, domestics, and soldiers.[14]

The guild of limonadiers sold far more than coffee, and many of its merchants focused on selling beer and spirits. Through the eighteenth century, a growing number of retailers set up simple shops to sell these drinks. Known sometimes as cafés but often just as spirits shops or dives (*tripots, tabagies*), they had a very different clientele than the cafés of the *honnêtes gens*. Many of these shops appear to have been disreputable places that featured regularly in the police blotter for attracting troublemakers and violating the ordinances. Police patrols throughout the century visited drink shops at night to enforce the curfew and look for prostitutes, *rodeurs de nuit*, and suspicious people. For much of the century, certainly by the second half, the police were almost as likely to find curfew breakers at cafés as at taverns and, much less frequently, suspicious people at both. The cafés in some quarters, for example near the Halles catered to a rough crowd of porters and the women who hung around them. Little distinguished these shops from those of beer or brandy sellers. Although Paris experienced nothing like the panic caused by gin in London, brandy was becoming increasingly popular through the eighteenth century with the lower classes, and the brandy shop seems to have attracted much the same kind of misfits and marginal people that dram shops served in other countries.[15] A commentary near the end of the century spoke of the "recent and deadly taste" for brandy among the working classes, "these laborers who drown their cares with their reason," and their women, "who, like them, drink this dangerous liquor."[16] Thus, at the same time that the police were spying on a few dozen elite cafés to hear what "the public" was saying about domestic and international affairs, the night watch was making the rounds of hundreds of other cafés looking for card players, women, and young roustabouts. Although there were probably only a third as many cafés as there were wine shops, their innovation in public life preoccupied the police disproportionately.

Paris in the eighteenth century, then, experienced a proliferation of public drinking places and, more importantly, a diversification of social sites and clientele associated with them. To the traditional neighborhood tavern serving wine had been added a range of things to drink and places to drink them, with distinctive styles and social roles. Associated with each of the public spaces, new and old, were different social groups, defined less by their class or formal economic function than by their place in a public sphere. The dangerous dives, increasingly identified with spirits shops, catered to those without reputation, passbook, or morals—the "public woman" and disreputable people (*gens sans aveu*). Guinguettes drew many of these same people, as well as artisans who sought the anonymity and novelty of drinking away from their neighborhoods. Then there were the elite cafés, where public opinion was sought and formed by a bourgeois public. And finally the taverns that drew little notice from police spies or the night watch but served the bulk of Parisian society. In addition, each of these public places tells us something about a public sphere—a conceptual arena in which behavior took on public significance. Although the bourgeois public sphere, in which the elite café played a central role, has dominated recent discussions of this concept, it was only one, and the most recent, of these arenas. The emergence of a reading public that discussed and criticized public affairs has been dated back to the seventeenth century, before cafés, but the café clearly provided this public with a forum in the eighteenth century for developing networks of discussion and a sense of its own identity.[17] Yet there were other public spheres associated with other public places, each with its own identity and discursive practices, and they are worth being understood in their own right.

For more than a decade now, historians have been drawn to the notion of publicness as a way to interpret important changes in early modern Europe. They have identified "the public" as an audience—of plays, art, literature, judicial and economic arguments, gossip, and news—whose opinions conveyed legitimacy to various ideas and expressions.[18] The "public" in turn helped to constitute a "public sphere" in which the circulation of opinions and ideas created an autonomously legitimate culture and formed the basis of an emerging civil society. In part, this new culture was capitalist in its growing emphasis on consumption and the commodification of ideas. It was capitalist, too, in being associated with an increasingly powerful world of international commerce and finance, yet it extended far beyond this world to include many elements of old regime society. More generally, however, it was a culture of the Enlightenment, which raised critical reason and the open exchange of ideas to the new standard of legitimacy. The "public sphere" also included new forms of sociability, by which the "public" associated and exchanged ideas. And public drinking was one of the fundamental expressions of this new sociability.

As a heuristic model, the bourgeois or enlightened public sphere has allowed historians to forgo sterile arguments about social class and to focus instead on cultural practices that are more helpful to understanding behavior and attitudes. Yet the hostility to social analysis has carried a price. The "public" was defined by historians and contemporaries alike as literate, urban, informed and right-thinking, middle and upper class, though they have offered little solid evidence for this characterization.[19] In its teleological identification of the public sphere with an emerging modern world, this definition has also marginalized the majority of Europe's population that did not belong to the "public" and largely written them, once again, out of the story. Public drinking, however, was a practice of all levels of society and may, perhaps, allow us to write the populace back in.

Yet the bourgeois public sphere was created, and conceptualized, in opposition to an older, royal public sphere that had long been the monopoly of the king. Public affairs were, by definition, the king's "secret"—his personal privilege.[20] This earlier public sphere included not only matters of international or national significance but also the royal jurisdictions that extended down into maintenance of police in towns and the countryside. Here again, the tavern, and particularly those that were dissolute, were central to this traditional public sphere. But it is the last public, the neighborhood and local community, that mattered to most people yet is most obscure. This was a public sphere because it defined the communal and cultural standards by which the populace judged public authority and by which an artisan created and lived a public reputation. These standards were not simply a quaint vestige of a traditional, communal, or popular culture that was rapidly disappearing in the rise of commercial, cosmopolitan culture.[21] Rather artisanal culture, and its articulation in taverns, was a discursive sphere that claimed a kind of legitimacy in the old regime and would assert it more boldly in the French Revolution and Republic.[22]

In the most mundane sense, all drinking places were public because they were accessible—open to all in society. The edict of 1699 that created the police throughout France explicitly ordered them to "visit the markets, hotels, inns, lodging houses, cabarets, cafés and other public places …"[23] Taverns were prominent among the urban areas for which the police were particularly responsible. A jurist defined taverns as "public places" because they were "devoted to serving the public, their entire house, even their person are engaged in this service," as well as being "open to the first comer." For this reason, he went on to explain, the police had unimpeded access to taverns even if not to other domiciles, which were "immune" and "privileged."[24] The police themselves insisted on their jurisdiction over "cabarets and other places subject to the police." They noted that "police regulations compel wine merchants to open their doors and shops [to the police] as public places … whenever public order and tranquillity require it."[25] Thus the treatise on jurisprudence in the *Encyclopédie* used the tavern to illustrate the realm of urban society that was directly the responsibility of the police, whom the author identified as "uniquely limited to the relations of things and persons with public order."[26] This, then, was one public sphere, as defined by the police in its understanding of the urban landscape and society. It complemented the jurisdiction of royal courts of summary justice, which were responsible outside of the city for "all those [crimes] directly affecting public safety."[27] Both jurisdictions defined places and people whose lack of internal order and privilege left them exposed to the public gaze of the police and the heavy hand of summary justice. The drink shop lay squarely at the center of this public sphere.

Yet the language of police ordinances gave this public character a sinister twist: it spoke of "cabarets and other suspicious places." Edicts warned against "inns, lodging houses, gaming houses, *tabacs* [taverns] and disreputable places," or about "taverns, cabarets and other dissolute houses where vagabonds, [and others] ... are accustomed to retire."[28] Because taverns were public they were accused of being a "retreat for all sorts of swindlers, vagabonds, men and women of evil life ..."[29] In practice the police's surveillance was far more narrowly targeted than its rhetoric might suggest. The police were particularly concerned about those places that catered to the disreputable elements in society, and their patrols led them time and again to the same neighborhoods and the same offending shops. In reports through the century, where the guard noted the public places violating the curfew and, much less frequently, in which they arrested disreputable people, the city's comparatively few guinguettes, cafés bornes, and spirits shops grew to rival the tavern as a site of misbehavior and marginality.[30] Yet the official rhetoric is not simply evidence of the police's misplaced suspicions, although it is easy enough to show that very few taverns misbehaved in this way. The authorities revealed their fundamental assumption that this public sphere was inherently an antiorder, opposed to the rest of society ordered by guild, family, and estate. For behind the threat of public drink shops lay the threat of public people. "Most cabaretiers, limonadiers, [and so forth] ... keep their houses open during the night, and receive people of every estate, and often give shelter to debauched women, soldiers, beggars and sometimes to thieves, who by these asylums find the means of continuing their disorders without concern, and of escaping our searches for them."[31] Although these public people were empirically composed of individual prostitutes, pickpockets, beggars, unemployed servants, and disreputable people, the police harbored an image of a more coherent world of criminality, with its own organization, language, and culture. A literary tradition of a criminal underworld, with its own "beggars' kingdom" and *jargon* that allowed secret communication, joined with important social changes in seventeenth-century France to produce an official view of "cutpurses [who] are joined into a corps in Paris; they have officers and respect a degree of discipline among themselves."[32] Where the police looked for a kingdom, it found a few gangs, and where it looked for gangs it found loosely organized families, but this did not stop it from perpetuating a picture of an underworld that mirrored and threatened the society of orders.[33]

To the traditional definition of public space as enclaves that required public policing was added a new definition. Early in the century, certainly by the 1720s, the police were sending spies into "cafés, promenades, and other public places" that offered a new kind of threat to public order: that of public opinion. For the point of café society was conversation, the polite but pointed discussion of ideas, news and literature that marked an important stage in the spread of civility.[34] The spies reported this conversation in great detail: "some say that ...," "others pretend that ...," "in the cafés a rumor was circulating that ..." News from abroad, broadsheets of scandalous trials, songs mocking those in power, all circulated in these cafés. "I can also report," wrote one spy, "that all the cafés are full of nothing but most satiric songs and verses."[35] Reports spoke frequently of customers reading aloud from letters they had received from abroad, and cafés were also a good place to meet foreigners, like the "café of the rue Dauphine where there are ordinarily lots of Englishmen." Primitive journalists, *nouvellistes*, made the rounds of cafés to hear and record what was being discussed and to pass around informal news sheets (*nouvelles à la main*), like the "bulletin that was distributed in the cafés."[36] The conversations in cafés ranged from wars and foreign affairs, to the rise and fall of members of the government, to the king's personal life, all carefully recorded by the police because the discussion of public affairs was an inherently subversive activity.[37] The growing social, commercial, and political importance of the social groups that made up the café's clientele combined with their avid examination of all kinds of issues in a public forum to create a new political force called "public opinion."

Public opinion, and the places that generated it, became a new kind of public sphere, according to Jürgen Habermas and the many historians who have been inspired by him.[38] As literate private persons increasingly exchanged their ideas about a wide range of public issues, from economic matters on to literary, cultural and political topics, in a public and often published forum, they created a self-conscious identity and culture—a "bourgeois public sphere"—that gradually rose up to challenge the traditional public sphere of the police and the government. Coffeehouses in England and Germany became "centers of criticism" where public opinion was created and recorded and a self-conscious and critical public emerged. Such quasi-private gatherings in public places helped create a public sphere by uniting like-minded people and joining them to larger communities of discourse. The public in Parisian cafés played a more hesitant role, since writing about public matters was heavily censored, and criticism faced severe sanctions when it became too pointed. Nevertheless, the café too helped to create public opinion and a public sphere in France.

Between the two public spaces of the café and the brandy shop, a third has been largely lost to view. We might blame the oversight on the recent historical fascination with texts and those who produced and consumed them. With the "cultural turn" in French revolutionary studies, for example, historians progressively lost interest in the populace and in popular culture. The masses did not belong to the public sphere, which was understood as a Habermasian space of autonomous discourse and legitimacy and closely identified with the polite, commercial society of the coffeehouse. According to Roger Chartier: "The constitution in the eighteenth century of a public space defined as the place of debate and political criticism has been thought to be, in fact, exclusive of all popular participation."[39] This was the sphere that produced discourses; the populace was excluded from politics, from discourses, and from public space.

But the populace also had a public and discourses, and the tavern was a kind of public space.[40] A careful study of police records, available in a city like Paris, makes clear that the tavern's clientele came overwhelmingly from the population associated with the crafts and trades. Although representing only a part of the lower classes, this group was important. Artisans had an income that permitted them to spend money in taverns. They had a community, with which they interacted in taverns. They had stability and drank near home, or if not were respectable enough to remain anonymous and unharassed when the police patrols checked for "gens sans aveu" and those who wandered the city or were suspiciously distant from their lodgings. These artisans expressed a clear sense of a public, their public. One of them, the glazier Ménétra, divided his world between the domestic and his public: "I left her [his wife] to carry the household burdens and I thought only of pleasing my public."[41] His "public" encompassed a wide assortment of friends, both male and female, but more importantly an audience that included neighbors, nobles, guild colleagues, and, occasionally, the authorities. It also invoked a way of behaving that depended on display, competition, and consumption. Ménétra's willingness to spend money on drinking with friends in taverns, as well as on clothing and finery, reminds us that consumer society had its origins as much in popular culture's concerns for social capital as in the middle class's desire for social status.[42] Drinking in taverns with neighbors and colleagues was an investment in this social capital. Like other forms of consumption, it risked excess and was condemned, by wives and peers, when it exceeded cultural limits but was essential to the maintenance of social identity.

The tavern's public character came through clearly in the many cases dealing with slander and reputation in the judicial records. Plaintiffs frequently noted that they were insulted "publicly" or "in the presence of the people who were in the taverns."[43] The insults that a customer in a tavern "had repeated publicly several times ... are too atrocious and scandalous, having been said publicly, for the plaintiff to remain in silence."[44] A plaintiff concluded by saying, "This insult is more dishonoring to the honor and reputation of the plaintiff for having been proclaimed [*publiée*] loudly and publicly in a cabaret in the presence of numbers of people."[45] Several complaints describe women storming into taverns and "loudly" attacking the plaintiff, "causing the neighbors and by passers to assemble" and "even bringing people to put their heads out the window."[46] Thus public calumny in taverns might spill out into the street and involve the whole neighborhood. On the whole, however, slander was less likely to become street theater than it was to remain the public allegations made before one's drinking companion. Several suits described vendettas waged by spreading slander "around the town [*dans le monde*] ... and publicizing such indecent talk in taverns."[47] If an insult was "repeated several times in the presence of people who were in the cabaret," it could not be passed over lightly.[48] As another plaintiff put it, "These are insults spoken publicly in a public place."[49] By being a "public place," the tavern transformed events that happened there into public affairs that required a formal and public complaint.

As the preeminent public space in artisanal culture, taverns helped define a public sphere on a par with the realms of the police and of public opinion that gave public significance to artisanal discourse. Some studies of the working classes have pointed to their politicization in the growing labor unrest in the eighteenth century, much of which used taverns for its headquarters.[50] Neighborhood taverns also contributed to the complex relationship between artisans and public authority. Where the police assumed a responsibility for supervising access to taverns as part of its control of "public places," artisans expressed a clear belief that they had rights to enter and use taverns with little impediment. This attitude led to frequent altercations with tavern owners, some of whom vainly tried to exclude customers when the official closing hour arrived. Other owners willingly cooperated with curfew breakers and refused to open their doors when the night watch came looking or slipped the offenders out a back door. And, although the violators, found by the dozens every night, were sufficiently reputable that very few were ever arrested, they were also willing to contest the state's attempt to regulate this public space. Few challenged the night watch as directly as the customer who refused to identify himself and "took his lack of respect and obedience to the magistrate and officers to an extraordinary point," but many routinely ignored the closing hours and fought bitterly if the tavern owner tried to enforce them.[51] The populace were effectively attempting to transform the tavern from the public sphere given order by the police into one they controlled. The artisanal public sphere emerges most clearly, however, in the discourse of artisanal, communal, masculine interaction in taverns, which, even when insulting, aimed also for a kind of legitimacy. Verbal abuse in public places, particularly the tavern, defined the ideal man, as husband and artisan, and the ideal relationship between employer and employee, and among neighbors and guild colleagues. It prescribed not only the personal behavior of the sociable artisan, but also the political principles of collective rights and social justice. This discourse would become the language of the sans-culottes, which in turn "did some of the work of endowing the language of republicanism with its meaning" and gave the French Republic its original political character.[52] Because "the nature of urban work and social relationships helped shape the distinctive political culture of revolutionary Paris," as a recent history of the city reminds us, it is important to remember that the tavern shaped this society.[53] Thus it is no accident that the Père Duchesne would distinguish the virtuous sans-culotte from the rest of society by distinguishing drinking places: "he'll never be seen either in the Café des Chartres or in the dives [tripots] where conspiracies are hatched and people gamble."[54]

The history of public drinking places is a study not only of the drinks they served but also of the publics they served—the distinct parts of society that constituted themselves through their shared communication and culture. There were at least three different publics in eighteenth-century Paris, associated with different drinking places, but they shared certain features. Each corresponded to a different level of society, each defining itself or being defined, in part, through its consumption of drink, its sociability in drink shops and, to a lesser extent, its communication about public affairs. In the bourgeois café, this communication contained the dangerous seeds of public opinion. In the artisanal tavern, this communication defined the communal expectations of masculine and corporate behavior, with latent political implications. In the brandy shops of the disreputable, no communication is recorded, rather the simple presence of disreputable men and public women constituted a public problem. In each case, the drink shop reveals essential elements of its society. As Scott Haine shows in his discussion of nineteenth-century drinking in this book, the role of public drinking places in artisanal and working-class culture only grew during and after the Revolution. The end of old regime regulations led to the abandonment of the formal distinctions between cafés, taverns, and guinguettes, just as the distinctions between a bourgeois public sphere and a disenfranchised populace began to disappear. As artisanal society gained a legitimate voice in the political world of the nineteenth century, it rehearsed and orchestrated that voice in the public forum of the neighborhood café. But the conflation of public spheres would also undermine that new legitimacy. The state continued to identify the public drinking place as a threat to public order and sobriety and happily equated working class political activism with the sphere of disreputable and dangerous people it had always targeted. The neighborhood café remained the battleground of competing definitions of the public sphere well into the twentieth century.

Notes

1. Jean Leclant, "Le café et les cafés à Paris, 1644–1693," *Annales, économies, sociétés, civilisations* 6 (1951): 1–14.

2. Louis Cullen, *The Brandy Trade under the Ancien Régime* (Cambridge: Cambridge University Press, 1998).

3. Thomas Brennan, *Public Drinking and Popular Culture in Eighteenth-Century Paris* (Princeton: Princeton University Press, 1988).

4. See Robert Isherwood, *Farce and Fantasy: Popular Entertainment in Eighteenth-Century Paris* (New York: Oxford University Press, 1986), for the more general development of entertainment.

5. Thomas Brennan, "Beyond the Barriers: Popular Culture and Parisian *Guinguettes*," *Eighteenth-Century Studies* 18/2 (Winter, 1984–5): 153–69.

6. Savary des Bruslons, *Dictionnaire du commerce* (Paris: J. Estienne, 1723–30) sv. café.

7. Letter from the secretaire d'etat Seignelay to the lieutenant general de police, La Reynie, December 27, 1685, quoted in Jean-Claude Bologne, *Histoire des cafés et des cafetiers* (Paris: Larousse, 1993), p. 43.

8. Bibliothèque de l'Arsenal [BA], ms. 1016, February 9, 1732.

9. Robert Darnton, "An Early Information Society: News and the Media in Eighteenth-Century Paris," *American Historical Review* 105 (2000): 1–35.

10. BA, ms. 10170, fol. 4; quoted in http://www.indiana.edu/~ahr/darnton/cafés_info.html.

11. Figures for beer and brandy consumption are sparse but suggest only a tenth

as much wine consumption; see the discussion in Thomas Brennan, "Towards the Cultural History of Alcohol in France," *Journal of Social History* 23 (1989): 76.

12. "Le café borne" quoted in Bologne, p. 97.

13. Among hundreds of visits to taverns mentioned in his journal, Ménétra, describes only two visits to a "café," once in the company of Jean-Jacques Rousseau; Jacques-Louis Ménétra, *Journal of My Life*, intro. Daniel Roche, trans. Arthur Goldhammer (New York: Columbia University Press, 1986).

14. Brennan, *Public Drinking*, pp. 154–7.

15. Jessica Warner, *Craze: Gin and Debauchery in an Age of Reason* (New York: Four Walls Eight Windows, 2002); Barbara A. Tlusty, "Water of Life, Water of Death: the Controversy over Brandy and Gin in Early Modern Augsberg," *Central European History* 31 (1998): 1–30.

16. Louis-Sébastien Mercier, *Tableau de Paris*, 12 vols. (Amsterdam, 1782–8), Vol. 2: pp. 19–22.

17. Sarah Hanley, "The Jurisprudence of the Arrets": Marital Union, Civil Society, and State Formation in France, 1550–1650," *Law and History Review* 21 (2003): 1–40.

18. James Van Horn Melton, *The Rise of the Public in Enlightenment Europe* (Cambridge: Cambridge University Press, 2001), offers an excellent overview of the current discussion.

19. Mona Ozouf, "'Public Opinion' at the End of the Old Regime," *Journal of Modern History* 60 suppl (1988): S1–21, is astutely critical of contemporary definitions of the public and the political value of keeping the term vague.

20. Keith Baker, "Public Opinion as Political Invention," in K. Baker, *Inventing the French Revolution* (Cambridge: Cambridge University Press, 1990), pp. 167–99.

21. David Garrioch, *The Making of Revolutionary Paris* (Berkeley, 2002); Paolo Piasenza, "Opinion publique, identité des institutions, 'absolutisme'," *Revue historique* 290 (1993): 7–142.

22. Michael Sonenscher, "The sans-culottes of the year II: rethinking the language of labour in revolutionary France," *Social History* 9 (1984): 301–28; Garrioch, *The Making of Revolutionary Paris*.

23. Nicolas Delamare, *Traité de la police*, 4 vols. (Paris: J. et P. Cot; M. Brunet; J.-F. Hérissant, 1705–38), Vol. 1, p. 156. The phrase is "cabarets, cafés et autres lieux publics."

24. *Encyclopédie méthodique: jurisprudence*, 10 vols. (Paris: chez Panckoucke, 1782–91), Vol. 10, pp. 67–70.

25. See in BA, ms. 10129, any of several dozen procès-verbaux for 1751. A police sentence, Bibliothèque Nationale [BN], ms. fr. 21710, 24 July 1720, added to that "the said limonadiers, coffee sellers, which are public," Archives Nationales [AN], Y9538, 21 January 1757.

26. In contrast, "private actions do not regard them [the police], the respective interests of families, of individuals and of *corps* escape for this reason their

considerations," *Encyclopédie méthodique: jurisprudence*, Vol. 10, p. 70.

27. H-F. d'Aguesseau, *Oeuvres* (Paris, 1759–89), Vol. 8, p. 314, cited in N. Castan, "Summary justice" in R. Forster and O. Ranum, *Deviants and the Abandoned* (Baltimore: Johns Hopkins University Press, 1978), p. 113.

28. Delamare, Vol. 1, p. 147, édit du Roi, March 1667; Athanase-Jean-Léger Jourdan, Decrusy, François Isambert, Alphonse-Honoré Taillandier, *Receuil général des anciennes lois*, 29 vols. (Paris: Belin-Leprieur, 1821–33), Vol. 2, p. 269, déclaration du Roi, May 7, 1526.

29. AN, Y9499, June 5, 1733.

30. This is based on weekly reports in 1731, 1751, 1771, and 1781, in AN Y9432, 9452a, 9452b, 9474a, 9474b, 9484a.

31. Duchesne, *Code de la police* (Paris: Prault père, 1767), p. 242, ordonnance de police, 29 October 1760.

32. Roger Chartier, "The Literature of Roguery" in *The Cultural Uses of Print in Early Modern France*, trans. Lydia Cochrane (Princeton: Princeton University Press, 1987), p. 320, is quoting the chancellor, Pierre Seguier,

33. Arlette Farge, *Fragile Lives: Violence, Power and Solidarity in Eighteenth-Century Paris*, trans. Carol Shelton (Cambridge, MA: Polity Press, 1993), pp. 138–67, discusses this world.

34. Lawrence Klein, "Coffeehouse Civility, 1660–1714: An Aspect of Post-courtly Culture in England," *Huntington Library Quarterly* 59 (1997): 30–51.

35. BA, ms. 10161, February 23, 1732.

36. BA, ms. 10169, August 9, 1747.

37. Robert Darnton, *The Forbidden Best-Sellers of Pre-Revolutionary France* (New York: W. W. Norton, 1995), pp. 232–46; Darnton, "An Early Information Society."

38. Jürgen Habermas, *Structural Transformation of the Public Sphere: An Inquiry into a Category of Bourgeois Society*, trans. T. Burger (Cambridge, MA: MIT Press, 1989); see the discussion in Melton, pp. 1–15.

39. Roger Chartier, "Culture populaire et culture politique dans l'ancien régime," in Keith Baker (ed.), *The French Revolution and the Creaton of Modern Political Culture*, 4 vols. (Oxford: Pergamon Press, 1989), Vol. 1, p. 248.

40. Sonenscher, pp. 301–28.

41. Ménétra, p. 191.

42. Colin Jones, "The Great Chain of Buying," *American Historical Review* 101 (1996): 13–40.

43. AN, Y10726, July 1, 1691; Y14066, April 26, 1741; Y11626, October 30, 1691.

44. AN, Y12115, December 28, 1711.

45. AN, Y11933, December 21, 1751.

46. AN, Y14009, August 7, 1732; Y14527, October 17, 1731.

47. AN, Y12925, October 11, 1741.

48. AN, Y15228, June 11, 1721.

49. AN, Y14518, June 4, 1721.

50. Steven Kaplan, "Reflexions sur la police du monde du travail, 1700–1815," *Revue historique* 261 (1979): 17–77; Michael Sonenscher, *Work and Wages: Natural Law, Politics, and Eighteenth-Century French Trades* (Cambridge: Cambridge University Press, 1989); Roger Chartier, *The Cultural Origins of the French Revolution*, trans. Lydia Cochrane (Durham, NC: Duke University Press, 1991), pp. 151–4.

51. BA, ms. 10136, November 22, 1747.

52. Sonenscher, "The sans-culottes of the year II," p. 325.

53. Garrioch, 296.

54. Cited in Albert Soboul, *Les sans-culottes* (Paris: Editions de Seuil, 1968), p. 41.

–8–

Drink, Sociability, and Social Class in France, 1789–1945

The Emergence of a Proletarian Public Sphere

W. Scott Haine

The era between the French Revolution and the end of World War II represents the golden age of public drinking in France.[1] Between the storming of the Bastille (July 1789) and the Liberation of Paris (August 1945), an elaborate and complex working-class café culture developed, centered in Paris but touching every hamlet, village, and city across France. As a result of the extraordinary changes in commerce and communication brought about by the French and Industrial Revolutions, new forms of spontaneous and organized political discussion and working-class solidarity developed. Indeed, what Jürgen Habermas has described as a "proletarian public sphere" emerged not just during the French Revolution of 1789 but also developed across the nineteenth and into the twentieth centuries.[2] Centered especially among the Parisian artisans, this public sphere ultimately became the focus of severe repression after the June Days of 1848 and under the Second Empire but continued to operate well into the twentieth century sustaining the labor movement, the effort to win World War I, the emergence of the French Communist Party after World War I, the political struggles of the interwar period, and the Resistance during World War II. Then, amidst the dramatic transformation of French society in the "thirty glorious years" (1945–75), this café culture disintegrated. By the end of the 1970s the growing affluence of France had turned the café from a target for moralists into an object of nostalgia.[3] The number of cafés by 1980 had dropped to under 200,000 and by 2005 the figure was under 50,000.[4]

The French Revolution and the Industrial Revolution that followed laid the foundations for this working-class drinking and political culture. After the revolutionary parliaments abolished the guild system and instituted freedom of commerce between 1789 and 1791, the number of cafés soared to unprecedented heights. Then with the creation of a national railroad network during the 1850s the working people of France could, for the first time, consume large quantities of wine and spirits. After Third Republic politicians lifted the constraints the Second Empire placed on the café commerce in 1880, the number of drinking establishments achieved a seemingly endless upward spiral until World War I, the same period in which the French urban working class grew ever larger and more self conscious. Lacking adequate housing and drawn by the seemingly "luxurious" cafés of *belle époque* cities (at least compared to older cafés in French villages), working-class family life became more integrated into café life. Entire families, single women, and youth became more conspicuous members of café life and thus nuanced this new proletarian public sphere. Due to the inclusive nature of café life, this proletarian public sphere combined both political contestation with an amelioration of moral life.[5] This combination would have seemed inconceivable to the eighteenth-century administrators and the police that Thomas Brennan has described above who believed that lower-class drinking establishment frequentation produced both political and moral anarchy. Indeed, all indications suggest that the most marginal and demoralized (that is the lumpen) elements of the working class did not play much of a role in this café culture.

The changes French drinking establishments underwent after the 1789 Revolution laid the foundation for this public sphere. At the very heart of the nineteenth-century working-class café culture was an establishment that combined the wine drinking of traditional lower-class taverns with coffee, newspapers, liquors, and often food, which had been the province of upper-class cafés. Cafés had emerged during the reign of Louis XIV. In the last decades of the Old Regime a fusion was already occurring between the working-class tavern and the upper-class café in a form that has been called a Parisian version of "grub street." In inexpensive and inelegant cafés struggling writers poured out their rage at a society that did not recognize or reward their talents. A stream of pornographic pamphlets, books, and journal articles excoriated the French monarchy and the Catholic Church. Some of the leading historians of Old Regime France, such as Robert Darnton, Lynn Hunt, Arlette Farge, and Sara Maza have chronicled the intellectual demimonde.[6] Darnton tellingly cites a contemporary Old Regime loyalist, P. J. G. Gerbier, on their influence: "Where does so much mad agitation come from? From a crowd of minor clerks and lawyers, from unknown writers, starving scribblers, who go about rabblerousing in clubs and cafés. These are the hotbeds that have forged the weapons with which the masses are armed today."[7]

This déclassé culture of café contestation during the 1780s moved into the center of fashionable Paris, the Palais-Royal. The Duke D'Orleans, liberal cousin of the king, built these enclosed arcades in 1781 and it quickly became the center of Parisian café culture as well as a dazzling and dizzying entertainment complex that included theatre, gambling, and prostitution. These arcades were protected not only from the elements but also from the police, as it was private property. The Duke could quite legally bar the police from patrolling and harassing the crowd, and as a result these arcades became a center of free speech.[8] On the eve of the Revolution its cafés—Café de Foy, Café des Milles Colonnes, Café Italien Café de Caveau, and Café de la Regence, as well as about twenty others—facilitated a "convergence between popular and elite culture" in both politics and entertainment. A sociability that had virtually erased social distinctions is recalled by the revolutionary Théroigne de Méricourt at the start of the fateful summer of 1789:

"What most impressed me [about the Palais-royal] was the atmosphere of general benevolence; egoism seemed to have been banished, so that everyone spoke to each other, irrespective of distinctions [of rank]; during this moment of upheaval, the rich mixed with the poor and did not disdain to speak to them as equals."[9]

The Palais-royal cafés facilitated an unprecedented fusion between philosophic, political, and pornographic literature as well as a mass audience that simultaneously read and talked about the material. A young noble, the Marquis de Ferrières, provided a passionate first-hand account of this fusion of literate and oral cultures:

> no Molière comedy could have done justice to the variety of scenes I witnessed. Here a man is drafting a reform of the Constitution; another is reading a pamphlet aloud; at another table, someone is taking the ministers to task; everybody is talking; each person has his own little audience that listens very attentively to him … In the cafés, one is half-suffocated by the press of people.[10]

Amidst this feverish passion and incipient mobilization, James Billington, has traced the emergence of the verb "to politic." A momentous and dramatic moment occurred on July 12, 1789 when the young journalist and revolutionary Camille Desmoulins stood on a café table in the Café de Foy and exhorted the crowd "To Arms!" Two days later the crowds inspired by his words overwhelmed the hated symbol of royal despotism, the Bastille fort on the eastern side of Paris.[11] George Rudé, observes the associate power of the small workshop and adds, in his classic *The Crowd in the French Revolution*, "The wine-shop may have been equally potent as a channel of communication for revolutionary ideas."[12]

Cafés also proved to be spaces of innovation not only in the areas of language and related actions but also through actual organizations. The paradigmatic political club, the Jacobins, first arose at Versailles when a number of Breton deputies developed the habit of meeting regularly at a café to develop their policy. The Parisian club movement, the neighborhood local government assemblies (the sections), and the popular movement of lower middle-class shopkeepers and artisans, the sans-culottes, all had intimate links to café life. The famous red, Phrygian bonnet of the revolutionaries was first worn in the famous left bank Café Procope in December 1792. Sectional meetings often took place in cafés, often under the influence of the red wine so dear to the hearts of Parisians. Petitions to the National Assembly also drew upon the clientele of cafés for signatures.

The centrality of café life to the Revolution is best illustrated by the copious references in the growing number of radical newspapers. The two best journalistic examples are also the two most famous of the Parisian popular press: *L'ami du peuple* (*The Friend of the People*) of Jean Paul Marat and *Père Duchêne* (*Father Duchesne*) of Jacques René Hebert. These and other papers referenced café life constantly either to praise the patriotism of the people or to denounce the machinations of aristocrats. A study of the "verbal violence" of these papers reveals that journalists such as Hebert and Marat assimilated much of the bawdy, ribald, combative vocabulary of the Parisian laboring population into their Rousseauian discourse of popular democracy. The stock and repetitive nature of the insults hurled at "aristos" and counterrevolutionaries was an ideal means by which to fuse popular language with revolutionary politics. By the constant use of such abusive terms as rabble (*canaille*), robber (*brigand*), knave (*coquin*), and murderer (*assassin*), these journalists transformed their insults into political statements. As we shall see, these epithets on the lips of proletarian café habitués will be staple terms of scorn for the police and other agents of governmental authority throughout the nineteenth century. Marat, Hebert, and other radical journalists thus launched a dialectical process between oral and written cultures of café radicalism that would endure throughout the century.

But these journalists did much more. Their writings and actions taught the working people of Paris, especially the small shopkeepers and artisans, that they could now be part of the process of public opinion formation (that is a part of Jürgen Habermas's proletarian public sphere). The daily lives of ordinary people, especially the artisans, their thoughts and actions, were suddenly imbued with a new political purpose and meaning. This is well illustrated in the following passage by Hebert in which freedom to drink and socialize in cafés is tied explicitly to the achievements of the Revolution, in particular the conquest of the rights of citizenship:

> We are finally delivered from all those leeches, those blackguard clerks, those taxmen, that hell has vomited upon the earth to make eternal war on drinkers. What a victory! It is necessary to rejoice today that I do not have to give a damn on any account! I invite all the good lads from all the areas who frequent Courtille and Vaugirard to follow my example … I am going to the Lion d'Or at the Nouvelle France; it is there, damn it, that I let myself drink the quarts [of now untaxed wine after the abolition of royal taxes] … I am bringing Mother Duchesne with me and all the family, along with my friend Jambard, my printer and his workers, and Renard, the drunk, the head of the street sellers who sell my paper. They will all be at this bacchic festival. We will take off our coats and let loosen our suspenders … During this time, damn it, we will do a May dance and we will sing and drink to the health of the National Assembly.[13]

While Hebert specifically refers to the popular actions that abolished the collection of royal taxes on wine, more broadly he is translating the language of political empowerment into the language of the people and showing how the politicization that had started in the "grub street" cafés of the intelligentsia had spread the masses in the eastern Parisian suburbs. Actually, this shift was due to political and economic changes as well.

Due to the Revolution's abolition of the guild system and the proclamation of freedom of commerce, drinking establishment proprietors could now fuse the worlds of the upper class, the literary café, and the popular tavern. Guild restrictions had separated the sales of coffee and wine into two separate types of shops. Now coffee, wine, and other drinks became a staple of Parisian café life across the social spectrum and the reading of newspapers became more generalized. Across France similar sorts of establishments also emerged after 1789 because France now had a uniform system of laws that had smashed the guild system.

During the Revolution evidence emerges of an increasing participation of women in café sociability. This can be seen in the above quotes and has been commented upon by several historians especially since the 1980s. Nevertheless, the evolution of gender relations in cafés from the eighteenth century to the early years of the nineteenth century remains a subject that is highly contested and needs much more research both for Paris and especially for the provinces. By end of the Terror, however, most of this political effervescence had been crushed. First under the Jacobin Terror and then under the Thermidorian and Directory Regimes with the Right-wing gangs known as the *Jeunesse Doré*. By March 1794 the number of drinking establishments stood at 1,685; dramatically lower than the 5,100 or so that were open on the eve of the Revolution.

Although the shifting currents of the Revolution and repression effectively silenced the effervescence of Parisian café life for a generation after 1800, the consequent freedom to open cafés nevertheless brought about a dramatic increase in the number of shops across France between 1789 and 1830. By 1830, the number of drinking establishments in France had soared to 281,847 shops.[14] In the absence of any national statistics for the late eighteenth century, the most reliable figure for the number of drinking establishments in France comes from the work of the pioneer statistician and military engineer Sébastien Vaubin. In a book advocating a new system of taxation published in 1707 Vaubin gave the figure of 40,000, or one shop for every parish in the kingdom.[15] Almost certainly most of the increase between 1707 and 1830 occurred after the Revolution. In any case, the growth in drinking establishments from 1707 to 1830 far outpaced the French population increase from 20 to 35 million over this same period.

Even more remarkable than the increase in the number of cafés and taverns is the fact that this proliferation prompted so little much concern about drunkenness. Indeed, judging from the paucity of statistics or enquiries before the 1830s, this problem simply did not seem relevant to post-revolutionary France. Indeed, reliable statistics on wine and other alcoholic drink consumption start only in 1830s.[16] Instead, as Maurice Agulhon and other historians have noted, this was an age when folklore was flourishing. Almost all the folkloric forms of association—such as the charivari, carnival, 'farandole', and fairs—intersected with café life. The pamphlets, prints, brochures, songs, newspapers, lithographs, and almanacs that catered to popular tastes also circulated in cafés.[17] Across France the number of cafés increased during both the 1830s and the 1840s. The skyrocketing number of closing-hour violations (from around 5,000 in the mid-1830s to just under 16,000 in 1845) reveals the growing fear of the French police about the popularity these establishments.[18]

By the late 1840s this folkloric and festive culture was turning political. In Paris the radicalization that would erupt in February 1848 had been incubating for two decades in cafés, and in the singing societies often attached to them, the goguettes.

Some 400 working-class singing societies existed, with upwards of 10,000 participants.[19] On the Left Bank and especially in the Latin Quarter, the revival of republicanism was supported by a generation of students inspired by Romanticism's
admiration of the people and popular customs and also by a cohort of workers
influenced by the emerging socialist movement. The Banquet Campaign of
1847–8, which helped galvanize the republicans and led to the 1848 Revolution,
took place not only in restaurants but also in cafés. The Revolution erupted during
the traditional holiday celebration of Mardi Gras (February 22–4), and soon barricades went up in and around the popular districts Paris. Often neighborhood cafés
served as command centers of these revolutionary fortifications.

After the triumph on the barricades, Paris remained in a festive atmosphere for
almost a month and the Revolution spread to the rest of the nation. In such provincial cities as Lyon, we also see festivity fusing with revolution. In this city on the
Rhone a drinking society, called the Voraces played a leading role in popular mobilization. In Limoges, café owners painted their marquees in revolutionary red.[20]
During the first two years of the revolution the number of cafés across France continued to grow, reaching 350,424 in 1850, some 70,000 more than in 1830!

Initially the new government liberalized the regulation of social life. As
occurred after the revolutions of 1789 and 1830, drink taxes were abolished, and
newspapers, theatres, assemblies, and associations granted a great measure of
freedom. For example, the Minister of the Interior, the staunch republican
Alexander Ledru-Rollin, believing that café sociability posed no threat to society
(or to the upcoming April elections) abrogated the 1814 law that required that all
cafés and cabarets close on Sunday during church services. He declared that the
law was incompatible with freedom of religion and was also a violation of freedom
of commerce of those "useful" entrepreneurs, café and cabaret owners.[21]

Festivity and political activity at this point was still not associated with excessive drinking or public drunkenness. Indeed, the 1840s had been a time of
declining wine consumption: from 28,020 millions of hectoliters in the 1835–9
period to about 27,310 millions of hectoliters during the 1840s. Consumption of
cider, beer, and alcoholic drinks all increased in that decade, but represented a
much smaller percentage of total consumption than they would after 1860 and thus
did not significantly raise per capita consumption.

Even when the Revolution became more polarized after the "June Days" in Paris
(June 22–6, 1848), the question of drink still did not emerge as an important con-
sideration. Both in Paris and in the provinces cafés became a target of the
emerging "Party of Order" as a source of sedition, not dissipation. Initially the
increasingly conservative government targeted formal political associations and
then, by the summer of 1849, focused on folkloric and symbolic means of expression. Red flags, caps, ties, and belts were now prohibited. Charivari, veillées,
chambrées, and cafés were also subject to increasing harassment or closure.
However, repression often had the paradoxical result of politicizing more effectively these folkloric forms of expression and café life.

Such repressive measures drove the republican movement underground. The era of the clubs was followed by the age of private clubs (chambrées), cafés, cooperatives, and secret societies. By 1850 the leftist republican movement (called *démoc-soc*, that is, democratic) had been largely subdued in urban France. In the countryside, however, the *démoc-soc* party made electoral gains in the legislative by-elections of March and April 1850, alarming conservatives and moderates in the Chamber of Deputies.

This fear of café life was found even within the legislature. After being elected in May 1849, Alexis de Tocqueville was shocked to see how café life, in the speech of the *démoc-soc* deputies, had become part of parliamentary debate:

I felt I was seeing these Montagnards for the fist time, so greatly did their way in of speaking and mores surprise me. They spoke a jargon that was not quite the language of the people, nor was it that of the literate, but that had the defects of both, it was full of coarse words and ambitious expressions. A constant jet of insulting or jocular interruptions poured down from the benches of the Mountain; they were continually making jokes or sententious comments; and they shifted from a very ribald tone of voice to one of great haughtiness. Obviously these people belonged neither in a tavern nor in a drawing room; I think they must have polished their mores in the cafés and fed their minds on no literature but the newspapers.[22]

In March 1851, fearing that the *démoc-socs* might make good on their predictions of winning the 1852 elections, conservative deputies proposed a law to bring cafés under much tighter governmental control. The brief but heated debate showed that de Tocqueville's fears were widely shared. The party of order tried to avoid the question of politics by emphasizing that the law would curb the debauchery and immorality of the rural cafés that the party found politically dangerous. The Chamber's left saw this as a smoke screen and preferred to allow local mayors to close any café that posed a threat to public order or morality. This latter group mounted a strong, eloquent, perceptive, and even profound defense of the café.

Victor Hennequin, a provincial lawyer and Fourierist journalist from the *département* of the Saone et Loire, attacked the proposal as a blow to the freedom of assembly as well as to the inviolability of domicile. The measure, he declared, was an attempt to install the police in every meeting place. Anticipating Foucault's theories in *Discipline and Punish*, Hennequin argued that the ultimate goal of the bourgeoisie was to submit the entire nation to the same cellular system of surveillance found in prisons. He defended the café as a place where news spread, political opinions circulated, and peasants shared newspapers. Drunkenness in such places was minimal; indeed, the only difference between these meetings and ministerial meetings was in the price of the wine. The utopian socialist concluded that a political agenda was being foisted upon the nation under the guise of morality.

Then one of the deputies whose politics had been formed in Parisian cafés, the

Limousin mason Martin Nadaud rose "to defend the café against the salons." He charged that if workers were demoralized, that was due to the economic oppression of the upper classes rather than to café life. In the café the nomadic worker found food, refreshment, lodging, and often advances on their salaries.

During these speeches the Right, after the fashion of de Tocqueville, accused the Left of turning the entire National Assembly into a café. A majority of the deputies then voted to consider the proposition. One of the members of the Left voting with Nadaud against it was Victor Hugo, the writer who would provide copious accounts of café life in his novel written in exile, *Les Misérables*.[23]

Before the Chamber could reconsider the proposal, Louis Napoleon Bonaparte's coup d'état on December 2, 1851 occurred and imposed a much more severe repression of café life than did the National Assembly's proposal. Within the same month, on December 29, Napoleon III enacted a draconian decree that placed café regulation in the hands of the departmental prefects. In the decree's preamble, café sociability, especially in rural areas, stood accused of causing disorder, demoralization, and secret societies. Between 1852 and 1855, combined military and police forces closed more than 50,000 cafés, 40,000 of which were in communes of fewer than 4,000 inhabitants. Clearly the police, gendarmes, and army were targeting the types of small rural communities in which cafés had combined folklore and politics.

Most of these 50,000 shops were shut down in the first two years following the coup. By the end of 1853 even the zealous Minister of the Interior Victor Persigny, who had unleashed the repression, demanded greater care in its application.[24] During these same years the number of closing-hour violations also soared to an average of 24,000 annually. Napoleon III's actions marked the most severe political repression of drinking establishments in nineteenth-century Europe.

While rural and village underwent life faced an overt and severe repression, urban cafés faced a more subtle approach. Urban police forces and administrations well knew that closing a café on a street or in a neighborhood was meaningless if numerous other shops were available nearby. The discretion of the Second Empire vis-à-vis urban drinking establishments is highlighted by the fact that between 1852 and 1855 the number of cafés actually increased slightly in cities above 30,000, from 19,948 to 20,642. In large cities surveillance became more important than repression. Under Louis Napoleon Bonaparte's empire, the beat policing system of London, where the emperor was once a bobby, was brought to Paris and other major cities and enhanced police presence.

The Second Empire's urban renewal programs had a major impact on working-class neighborhoods that had bred revolution. Prefects Baron Haussmann in Paris and Jean-Claude Vaïsse in Lyon effected the most dramatic transformations, destroying the dense central neighborhoods of these two leading cities that had long-standing traditions of contestation in their cafés and on their narrow and sociable streets that had spawned barricades in the turbulence of the previous two decades. The new broad boulevards, fronted by luxurious new apartment

buildings, theatres, department stores, railroad stations, and other public buildings was intended to bring order, opulence and mobility, both physical and social
to French cities.[25]

What was not so quickly realized was that these same wide boulevards also
spawned the modern sidewalk café. These larger and more opulent establishments
emerged not only in the fashionable western side of Paris but also on the working-
class eastern side, which now incorporated such suburban areas as Belleville,
where Hebert had once held forth. Indeed, cafés also sprouted on side streets and
alleyways, especially in the dense and increasingly homogenous working-class
quarters (due to their exodus from the increasingly affluent center and western districts of Paris). By the end of the Second Empire not only had Paris become a city
of wide boulevards but also one swarming with cafés. The number of cafés in Paris
jumped from 4,500 in 1850 to 22,000 in 1870. A comparable increase occurred in
the other large cities of France, such as Lyon and Marseille, but not at the same
rate.

The leniency shown toward the proliferation of Parisian cafés eventually
became imperial policy across France. After 1855 the ministers of the interior permitted the number of cafés to rise. Indeed, the number increased between this date
and 1860 from 291,244 to 306,308. Then, during the 1860s, a period considered
to be the "liberal phase" of the Second Empire, the number of cafés jumped to
351,048 in 1865 and then an all-time high of 372,951 in 1868. At the same time
the empire also permitted the emergence of a new type of establishment, the café
concert, which spawned a new type of mass culture based on such popular singers
as Thérèsa (Emma Valadon), that marginalized the working-class singing society
culture (goguettes) of the earlier decades. This café concert culture, as we can see
in Thérèsa's memoirs and from the iconographic and journalistic data of the era
included both men and women, and often whole families.[26]

This new tolerance, nay, promotion of an emerging mass culture was an attempt
by Napoleon III to gain popularity among the working class. During the 1860s the
Second Empire also liberalized laws regarding assembly, association, and labor
unions. The reason for this shift in political strategy was the growing power of the
republican opposition. But as the vote for imperial candidates fell steadily in the
parliamentary elections between 1857 and 1869 prefects continued to use the
repressive mechanisms of the December 29, 1851 Decree. For example, prefects
might threaten to close a café whose owner displayed republican sympathies or
provide licenses to prospective café owners who promised to support Napoleon III.
Prefects also turned a blind eye when "their" café owners distributed free drinks at
election time or let their cafés become campaign centers for the Empire's candidates.[27]

Napoleon III's strategy of modernizing France—renovating its cities, developing an industrial plant, and extending the railroad network—was meant to
secure his dynasty through creating prosperity. An unintended consequence,
however, of this modernization was a dramatic increase in alcohol consumption.

With a railroad network linking the wine-producing regions in the south with the burgeoning industrial centers of the north, the French population achieved the potential, really for the first time in history, of consuming large quantities of wine and alcohol on a daily basis.[28] It is interesting to note that virtually none of the vitriolic critics of Napoleon III ever accused him of trying to ensure political acquiescence through copious amounts of alcohol (the classic indictment of bread and circuses).

Between 1850 and 1870 French wine consumption more than doubled. From an average of 27,292 million hectoliters of wine consumed during the 1850s, the figures jumped to 39,802 in the period 1860–4 and to 56,112 for the period 1865–9. Other alcoholic drinks had rates of increase almost as impressive. Beer consumption rose from 12.6 liters per inhabitant per year in the 1850–4 period to 19.7 in the 1867–9 period. (Strangely enough cider intake remained constant.) Stronger alcoholic drinks, such as absinthe, did not register quite so impressive an increase: from 651,000 hectoliters during 1850–4 to 983,000 hectoliters in 1865–9.[29]

Such dramatic increases prompted the first intensive discussion of excessive drunkenness in modern French history. This new discourse intersected with the emergence of the medical model of drunkenness, and the actual concept of alcoholism was first presented by the Swedish doctor Magnus Huss in 1853. During the Second Empire the French doctor Benedict Morel, inspired by Huss and Darwin, elaborated on the disease concept of alcoholism, labeling it as heredity and degenerative. Discussions of alcoholism quickly spread from medical institutes to the parliament. In 1861 the imperial senate discussed criminalizing drunkenness. The discussion ended with the senate's decision to turn the question over to the Minister of the Interior, who believed that the December 29, 1851 Decree gave prefects sufficient power, especially through their option to close cafés, to repress drunkenness and café owners who encouraged it.[30]

During the 1860s governmental and popular attention on the cafés remained tied to politics. In this decade various shades of republicanism reasserted themselves. Contemporaries tied the growing power of republicanism at the ballot box to the reemergence of café politics. For example, after the dramatic success of the Republican "list" in Paris in 1863 the writer Ludovic Halévy, most famous for his libretto for Bizet's opera *Carmen*, exclaimed "The cafes have triumphed. The bourgeoisie would not have succeeded without the admirable cafes." Indeed, in the remaining elections of the 1860s, cafés and their owners played a vital role in the growing opposition to Louis Napoleon Bonaparte. Cafés were also a central venue for the public meetings sanctioned in the last years of the Second Empire (1868–70). One wealthy café owner (from the formerly suburban, now Parisian, Belleville area) by the name of Braleret, helped the young Leon Gambetta to win a seat in Parliament in 1869. As in the 1830s, student–worker exchanges on the Left Bank helped prepare the way for rising of republicanism. Writer Alphonse Daudet captured this spirit in his description of Latin Quarter cafés: "In sum, these discussions around beer and pipe smoke prepared a generation and awoke France from its deadened state."

The brief burst of radicalism and utopianism that was the Paris Commune (April–May 1871) altered the political and moral landscape surrounding the subject of cafés and alcoholism. On the one hand, never had café life been so central to a revolution; on the other hand, never had conservatives had a better opportunity to impugn the motives and morality of café life. Contrasting myths rose from the ashes of the burning capital and crushed political experiment. On the Left, from contemporaries such as Karl Marx and the poet Arthur Rimbaud to radicals in the 1960s such as the philosopher Henri Lefebvre and the leaders of the near revolution of May 1968, the Commune has been celebrated as the first instance of a genuinely communist government and as a "festival of the oppressed." On the Right, especially among politicians, moralists, and doctors during the 1870s and 1880s, the Commune was viewed as an "alcoholic orgy." What united these two is the notion of intoxication. The question was how it should be interpreted.

Given the continued imperial repression at the start of the Franco-Prussian War, followed by the suspicion of Parisian radicalism held by the conservatives who took control of the new Third Republic, it was natural and logical that much of the organization and agitation behind the Commune started in cafés. Such cafés could be found throughout Paris but clustered especially in Montmartre to the north, through the *Grands Boulevards* of the central Right Bank to the cafés of Belleville on the eastern side of Paris, across the Seine to the Butte aux Cailles and through to the Latin Quarter. In the north the Café de l'Independence, Café des Vingt Billiards, and the Rat Mort on the streets Chateau d'Eau and the Faubourg du Temple were especially prominent. In the Latin Quarter the most important venues were the Café de la Renaissance, the Café Voltaire, the Café de Serpente, the Brasseries Saint Savarin and Glaser, and the Café Procope.

The habitués of these cafés included prominent Communards. For example, Raoul Rigault and Theophile Ferre became leaders of the Commune's police force; and Emile Duval, Frederic Cournet, Gabriel Ranvier and Gustave Tridon became Commanders of the National Guard and members of the Central Committee. Although notoriously sober, Eugene Varlin, member of Marx's First International and of the Commune's finance ministry, was also part of this café culture. Celebrated artists and café habitués Gustave Courbet and Andre Gill along with songwriter Jean-Baptiste Clement also played prominent roles in the Commune. Courbet's role was perhaps the most infamous since as Minister of Fine Arts he ordered the destruction of the Vendôme Column due to its symbolizing the militarism of the Napoleonic dynasty. Also, as with previous revolutions, a popular press flourished. Indeed, one of the members the of Commune, Eugene Vermersch, rendered homage to Hebert by bringing out a new *Father Duchesne*, which recorded the café slang of a new generation of revolutionaries. Another editor, Maxime Vuillaume, recorded the role of the café in the last desperate week, known

as "Bloody Week" (*La Semaine Sanglante*), as the conservative national government army crushed the revolution in house-to-house fighting.

The Commune and its legacy continued to course through Parisian popular life
for decades after its initial and vicious repression. Despite the fact that crushing
the Commune had cost the lives of approximately 25,000 and had led to another
50,000 being arrested, the Parisian people still resisted the imposition of a monar-
chist- dominated "moral order" government. This contestation is best illustrated by
the sharp jump in the number of people arrested, often in or around cafés, for
insulting police or other government officials. The number of these cases had averaged only 800 annually in the already turbulent 1860s, but then leapt to an average
of more than 3,000 per year in the decade after the Commune, climbing to an
average of 3,467 during the 1880s and then peaking at an annual average of 4,329
in the early 1890s. The link between these insults and the Commune was unmistakable in the first few years, as the insults in about a third of the cases specifically
referred to the Commune. But as the years passed, rather than "Versailles assas-
sins" or "Versailles scum" (in reference to the national government taking up res-
idence in Louis XIV's Versailles palace during the Commune) the epithet would
more likely be "assassin" or "scum." These insults tended to be hurled by the same
types of workers (in metal and the building trades or day laborers) and took place
in the same proletarian districts as had supported the Commune.

Along with keeping the December 29, 1851 Decree in force, the conservative
monarchists who dominated the Third Republic in the 1870s also enacted the first
law in modern French history that punished public drunkenness. The research and
rationale for the law in the parliament, along with its initial implementation,
reflected the trauma of the Commune. But it also reflected the rise of an anti-
alcohol movement in France, which, unlike its counterpart in the Anglophone
world, derived its primary impetus from the medical profession rather than from
religious groups. The scientific base of the French leagues against alcoholism
eschewed teetotalism for temperance. Following Morel, the theory also focused on
intellectual argumentation rather than moral suasion, especially stressing the
potential for the degeneration of the French population over the course of just a
few generations. The movement never created the popular base or passion that the
religiously based prohibitionist movements did in the Anglophone world.

The January 1873 law covered only public drunkenness theorizing that excessive drinking in private could not really be monitored and in any case did not pose
a public problem. The articles of the law aimed to prevent the rise of alcoholism
with a set of graduated fines and punishments for multiple offenders. It was hoped
that early and swift detection of inebriation would dissuade people from continuing to drink heavily, a notion dear to the hearts of doctors focused on fighting
alcoholism. The law also contained several articles proscribing fines and jail time
for café owners who served inebriates. The consensus was that café owners were
as guilty as their clientele for the rise in excessive drinking and public drunkenness.

In practice the 1873 law repressing public drunkenness was never implemented in the fashion intended by the legislators. In Paris, for example, workers who insulted the police were much more likely to be charged with the infraction of public drunkenness (which carried a five franc fine, roughly a day's pay for the average worker) than were abusive husbands, tyrannical fathers, or bullying neighbors whose excessive drinking might later lead to murder. In short, the politically dangerous rather than the chronic drinkers were the ones most likely to be arrested for public drunkenness. In part this was due to the fact that the amount of paperwork necessary to track effectively every person found guilty of public drunkenness was simply beyond the competence of the police and the courts, especially with a highly mobile urban population. As a result the number of convictions for public drunkenness, after rising from 53,613 in the initial year of 1873 to 73,779 in 1874 and 81,486 in 1875, then leveled off to 70,000 in the next two years before falling to 21,712 in 1878. The number would bounce back to 60,714 in 1880 but this figure was only a third of those arrested in Great Britain for the same charge that year. The number arrested annually during the 1880s and 1890s seldom rose above 40,000. Only during the working-class agitation of the period 1906–8 did the Minister of the Interior, the energetic Georges Clemenceau, succeeded in raising the numbers to the levels of the 1870s.[31]

Administrative laxness in fighting drunkenness contrasted with an almost hysterical sensitivity by social commentators, moralists, and doctors to the growing number of cafés and the soaring consumption of alcohol. Indeed, as Robert A. Nye has shown, alcoholism and café life preoccupied French reformers of the late nineteenth century more than any other subject.[32] A declining birth rate, a spike in prostitution, legalization of divorce followed by a rising divorce rate, young men disqualified from military service, an increase in work-related accidents, a growing number of mentally ill, an increase in juvenile delinquency—all of these problems and more were blamed on cafés and the excessive drinking they seemed to encourage. The typical image of café pathology held that young men coming from the countryside to French cities and living in rented rooms were drawn to the café and there succumbed to the temptations of the bottle, the flesh, and radical politics.[33]

After leveling off in the 1870s, the number of cafés increased steadily during the following decades. During the Moral Order regime, the figures declined from 364,875 shops in 1870 to 343,139 in 1877. Of these closures 3,459 occurring around the May 16, 1877 Crisis when the conservatives tried to prevent a republican electoral victory, after which time the number of cafés again increased steadily between until World War I. In 1880 the new republican regime abrogated the December 29, 1851 Decree and reinstituted freedom of commerce.[34] Now cafés could be opened simply by submitting one's intention to the police and paying license fees. The number of shops then climbed from 356,833 in 1879 to 482,783 in 1913.[35] In Paris the figure more than doubled between 1870 and 1885, reaching more than 45,000 before declining to around 30,000 by the time of World War I.

As the number of cafés increased, the consumption of alcohol soared in the late nineteenth and early twentieth centuries. Absinthe, aperitifs, and other distilled drinks gained an unprecedented share of the beverage market as French wine production and consumption plummeted due to the ravages of the phylloxera aphid across French vineyards during the 1870s and 1880s.

The 1865–9 wine consumption figures, 56,112 million hectoliters, were not reached again until 1900, were finally surpassed in the years 1905–9, at 61,537 million hectoliters, and then fell back in the years before World War I to 50,867 hectoliters. Alcohol consumption, in contrast, virtually doubled between 1870 and 1900: from 938,000 hectoliters (1870–4) to 1,751,000 hectoliters (1895–9). Thereafter consumption figures ranged between 1,559,000 hectoliters (1900–4) to 1,676,000 (1910–13). The consumption of beer also shot up steadily from 19.8 liter per person (1870–4) to 32.9 liters (1910–13). Even cider consumption rose smartly from 1.2 liters (1870–4) to 2.3 liters per person (1905–9) before declining to 1.7 liters per person in the last years before the war.

Certainly these statistics seem to indict cafés as a central cause of French social problems. Nevertheless, my study of the Parisian working-class café during the nineteenth century has shown that the supposed etiology is more myth than reality. Even going by the biased statistics of those arrested for the misdemeanor of public drunkenness, certainly not a random sample of café customers, shows that the arrestees were a little less likely than the average Parisian (1) to live in a furnished room, (2) to be an immigrant to Paris, or (3) to be single, young, and unattached. A tabulation of over 4,000 public drunkenness cases between 1873 and 1901, indicating whether a person lived in a *garni*, an apartment, or a house, shows that only 17 percent of the defendants charged with the misdemeanor of public drunkenness were *garni* residents. This is merely seven percentage points higher than lodging residents represent in the Parisian working-class population. Clearly cafés were not simply the antechambers of the *garnis*.

The skewed statistics of the Parisian Correctional Tribunal undermine many other assumptions about café habitués. For example, café customers were no more likely to be immigrants than the general population nor were they primarily young. Most were aged between the mid-twenties and the late forties rather than under the age of twenty-five. Moreover, customers were only slightly less likely to be married than the average Parisian worker: 27 percent for the habitués as compared to 33 percent of Parisian workers. Indeed, since a large percentage of workers chose café owners to witness their civil marriage contracts, it is clear that they did not see café life and marriage as incompatible. Twenty-three percent of brides and grooms in civil marriage contracts in 1860 and 1880 chose a café owner as a witness; 16 percent in 1900 did the same.

A comparison between the occupations of the persons choosing a café owner as a witness to their wedding and those showing up before the courts for drunkenness indicates some important differences and similarities between the two populations in terms of the respectable and disreputable sides of café life. Not surprisingly middle-class, small shopkeepers, and white-collar workers formed a significantly higher percentage of brides and grooms choosing a café owner for their marriage contract than they did as defendants in the courtroom. Conversely, day laborers and other unskilled workers were more likely to be charged with public drunkenness than they were to choose a café owner to witness their wedding. In between, having roughly the same percentage among populations were skilled workers in the metal and building trades.

Women were a minority but still an integral part of café life. As a wife, widow or young entrepreneur, women were often behind the bar and had their own circle of women friends, especially laundresses, other shopkeepers, street merchants, and women in the needle and textile industries. The ages and marital status of these women also spanned a spectrum from the young through those in their fifties and sixties, from single to married, separated, and by the 1890s, the divorced. The question of sexuality in cafés is complex because of the poverty forced many to sell their bodies reluctantly. In many cases women would cease being prostitutes the minute they could find someone to marry. The fact that so many families frequented café life and even chose café owners to witness the baptisms of their children reveals that for the working class these spaces were respectable.

Indeed, judging by the number of working-class families that frequented the café as a unit, one could argue that café life complemented more than contradicted family life. Another indication that café and family life intersected is the fact that café owners, increasingly after 1890, became informal bankers for customers who pooled their salaries to buy sections of farmland and build inexpensive houses in the nearby countryside. This trend of spontaneous working-class suburban development would continue through the 1930s. Often the first commercial establishment built in these new communities was a café.[36]

Although cafés and family life moved closer together at the end of the nineteenth century, the same cannot be said for cafés and the working-class movement. As the French proletariat gained greater rights of assembly and association (to form unions, for example, after 1884 and to create associations after 1901), it also achieved increased institutional solidity. By 1900 most cities had labor exchanges (*bourses du travail*), cooperatives, popular universities (*universités populaires*), and houses of the people (*maisons du peuple*). Gaining such formal spaces meant that workers were less dependent on cafés. Nevertheless, cafés remained important, especially in times of strikes (often as headquarters for strikers near their workshop or factory) or during demonstrations, when cafés often provided a gathering place before a demonstration or a refuge from police actions after it started. It is interesting to note the congruence between the decline of the number of insults reported by the police and the rise in the number of working-class institutions, both tendencies developing in the second half of the 1890s. For example, after the height of insults to the police in the early 1890s, coinciding with the zenith of the anarchist movement in Paris, the average declined to under 3,000 per year for the duration of the pre World War I era. More research will be needed to confirm a connection between the decline of anarchism, the rise of working-class institutions, and a reduction in contestation with the police.

News of the declaration of war with Germany on August 3, 1914 brought cheers from the cafés as part of the general patriotic outburst. Frequently customers, in a state of patriotic zeal, turned in individuals voicing anti-French sentiments. As German armies advanced on Paris in late August, General Joseph Gallieni, recently installed as military governor of "the entrenched camp of Paris" banned absinthe, prohibited cafés from putting out their standard chairs and tables on the sidewalks of Paris, and ordered closing-hours shifted from 2 a.m. to 8 p.m. The French parliament confirmed and generalized his absinthe prohibition the following year but not his other measures. By the time of his death in 1916, cafés were again spread out on sidewalks, the closing hours for cafés were extended, and theaters and cinemas were back in business.[37] Nevertheless, the French temperance movement finally achieved a measure of influence for an extensive government anti-alcohol campaign went into effect even though French wine producers gained a lucrative contract supplying wine to troops in the trenches.[38]

Across the seemingly interminable years of this bloody war of attrition the French parliament debated at great length the role of the café and public drinking in French society. The immediate results were not extensive but did set precedents for the future. The law of November 9, 1915 replaced the 1880 law and created a new regime of café regulation. Reflecting the era's xenophobic fears, Article One stipulated that all café owners must have French citizenship, either by birth or by having lived in France or its colonies for five years. Then the law divided all drinking establishments into two categories: (1) shops exclusively for wine and beer, which establishments could be opened by simple notification and purchase of a license, and (2) shops that sold primarily or exclusively distilled alcohol or aperitifs above 23° proof, but were also required to sell meals along with drinks. In the same year the parliament enacted a new law punishing public drunkenness; this law was neither innovative nor effective. In 1917 the parliament banned prostitutes in cafés as well as employment of women under the age of eighteen except those who were members of the owner's family.[39]

The parliamentary debate on drinking establishments during World War I was one of the most extensive in French history. Repugnance at the number of cafés in France was loudly declared across the entire political spectrum. Deputies expressed shame that France had more cafés per capita than any other nation and that Paris had even more per capita than that Sodom, San Francisco. They looked in envy at Russia, where vodka had been outlawed and the nation had seemed to have become a model of temperance, discipline, and national unity. (No one commented that alcohol taxes had been a vital part of the Russian national budget and that diminished tax revenues severely hampered the war effort.) Turning to the future, many legislators expressed the hope that a new France would eventually emerge from the war and that, thanks to zoning ordinances and urban renewal, a rejuvenated France would have more hospitals than cafés![40]

The effects of World War I on café and drinking issues were neither profound nor long lasting. The number of shops dropped, especially in the devastated war zones of the northeast, from 480,000 in 1914 to 420,000 in 1920. But over the next eighteen years that number climbed to a new high of 509,000 in 1938. In short, neither the Great War nor the Great Depression diminished café commerce. Only in the last two years of the interwar era did the number of shops drop to 455,000.[41]

The consumption of wine and alcohol, as with the number of cafés, declined during the war, then bounced back during the 1920s and 1930s. But while wine consumption reached unprecedented heights in the interwar period, alcohol consumption never returned to prewar levels. Dipping slightly from 50,867 million hectoliters in the period 1910–13 to 47,307 hectoliters in the war years (1914–18), wine consumption then steadily climbed in the following periods (1919–21 and 1922–4) from 58,031 million hectoliters to a consumption higher than ever before: 75,861 million hectoliters. For the rest of the interwar period, wine consumption leveled off at around 69,000 million hectoliters for the periods 1925–9, 1930–4, and 1935–9. In short, the Great Depression did not dampen France's taste for a beverage that seemed the essence of the national identity. Alcohol consumption, on the contrary, fell from 1,676,000 hectoliters for the period 1910–13 to 1,048,000 hectoliters during the war, then fell even further in the immediate postwar period (1919–21) to 813,000 hectoliters. Consumption then rebounded to 1,283,000 hectoliters for the following period (1922–4) and averaged 116,333 hectoliters for the rest of the interwar period. As for beer consumption, it plummeted by about a third during the war and in the immediate aftermath (from 32.9 liters per person per year (1910–13) to 20.3 (1914–18) and 20.7 (1922–4), then jumped back up to prewar levels and even exceed them in the period 1930–4 (at 33.9 liters per person per year). Cider consumption actually increased during the war to its highest rate ever (2.4 liters per person per year), then fell until the period 1935–9 when the rate matched wartime levels.[42]

In short, the hopes of the anti-alcohol movement that the war would bring a permanent change to French drinking habits proved illusory. At least in Paris, however, almost all commentators agreed that postwar public drinking was not as rowdy or disorderly as it had been before the war. Certainly the police, even during the war, arrested fewer workers for public drunkenness or disorderly behavior (including insults). It appears that a tacit "sacred union" was worked out between the police and the Parisian working class. Between the wars, foreigners and vagrants were virtually the only groups charged with drunken and disorderly conduct.[43]

The decline in police prosecution of drunken and disorderly behavior, however, did not mean that café customers no longer engaged actively in politics. The new radical political movements—the French Communist Party on the Left, various proto-fascist parties on the Right, and the French Socialist Party (the SFIO)—if anything, used cafés more systematically for political agitation and mobilization than they had before the war. Evidence for this can be found in abundance in the newspapers of the various political parties during the interwar period.[44]

Much more than before World War I various political parties and groups advertised and reported on meetings held in cafés. For example, on January 8, 1926, the
Socialist paper *Le peuple*, in the section concerning meetings (*convocations*),
reported:

> Natives of Correze—The Paris section of the Natives of Correze has organized, for
> Saturday the 17th, at 8:30 p.m., at Guillet's restaurant at Porte Maillot, a banquet-con-
> ference followed by a dance … Charles Spinasse, the Correze deputy, will preside …
> assisted by citizens J. K. Chastanet, former secretary of the Natives of the Isere
> Department, C. Bebassy, deputy of the Creuse Department, and Fincette, municipal
> consoler of Paris. Price 25 francs.

As the new French Communist Party—formed after its scission from the French
Socialist Party (SFIO) in 1919—assumed editorial control of *L'Humanite*, the
paper founded by Jean Jaures in 1904, café life became more prominently featured. Not only did the paper list meetings as noted in other papers above, it also
closely followed café life after the fashion of Marat's *L'ami du peuple* and Hebert's
Le Pere duchêne. Collections of money to support *L'Humanité*, occurred often in
cafés. In a short article entitled "The Proletariat Defends its Paper" in its
December 2, 1929 issue *L'Humanité*, noted that a party (*goguette*) for *L'Humanité*
had raised 291 franc and 35 centimes: "The defense group of the Pere la Chaise
section had organized this party last Saturday at Charlot's on the avenue Gambetta.
This small festival was a great success because it raised 65 francs, 50 centimes
with the collection as well as the 225 francs, 85 centimes from the party. This is
an excellent amount and represents a great example to follow." This meeting presents a fascinating transformation of working-class culture. In the nineteenth
century the term *goguette* had been used to describe working-class singing groups
in cafés; by the 1930s, the term had taken on a fund-raising role. *L'Humanité* also
frequently reported on small acts of working-class militancy in the café. For
example, on May 3, 1934 *L'Humanité*, in its Paris Region section reported an incident under the title "An example to Imitate":

> Sunday, a group of draughtsmen (*dessinateurs*) of a metallurgical factory in Argenteuil
> went to their usual restaurant at lunch time. Stupefaction! Two policemen are at their
> table. We want to put you on notice, they told the waiters, that if these two clever
> fellows (*lascars*) do not leave this table, we will go eat elsewhere. Confused, the
> manager earnestly entreated … accompanied by the laughter and jeers of the seated
> workers, the two policemen gathered up their equipment and their cutlery and moved
> to a corner. Workers, follow this example.

Communists saw cafés as vital to mobilization for demonstrations on such holidays as May Day (May 1) and Bastille Day (July 14). A circular distributed to the
young communists for organizing on Bastille Day, noted that during this holiday:

Our municipalities have an important role ... The utilization of festivities and their transformation into mass demonstrations must be the grand preoccupation of our municipalities, of our sections (*rayons*) and subregions ... Our sections and subsections equally have to utilize the neighborhood dances organized by the cafés, our street cells, have in this domain a serious work to do, to speak at these various dances, to try, if possible, the launching of a demonstration.[45]

The basic unit of the Communist Party, the cell, often met in cafés.[46] A police report concerning communist activity in the First Arrondissement of Paris quoted a letter as follows: "Camarade, You are invited to be present at the meeting of the committee of '1' which will take place this evening at 6 pm at the ... café de la Grille, 12 rue Montmartre."[47]

Cafés were also a site of both formal and informal speeches. The police reported on July 30, 1930, what the sixth *rayon* of the Communist Party in Paris would do for the August 1 demonstration: "The committee of the 6th *rayon* will meet, before 5 pm, rue St. Charles, at the exits of the Citroen factories ... at 5 pm the speakers, Beaugrand and Croizat, will speak in the neighboring cafés, surrounded by a dozen militants whose task will be to prevent the speakers from being arrested."[48]

Cafés also played a vital role in planning demonstrations. After the demonstration of May 1, 1931 the police reported "among the militants ... the municipal counselor of Saint Denis, Lambert, met with some strikers in a cafe concerning an eventual demonstration." PCF (*Parti Communiste français*) militants often distributed tracts on café terraces. For example, on July 3, 1931 Communist militants descended on the Café de la Rotonde in Montparnasse protesting French repression in Vietnam.[49]

Communists also frequently turned cafés into sites for electoral meetings and used them as a candidate's headquarters. For example *L'Humanité* reported on May 3, 1932: "The headquarters for the candidature of our comrade Montgeauin is in a café on the angle between the boulevard de la Gare and the place Pinel, near the métro station 'Nationale.' It is easily recognized, besides the sign indicating the headquarters, it carries the scars of police brutalities and the panes of the front window are cracked." The article also reports a police charge on the Place d'Italie that resulted in the police overturning the café's tables and chairs and penetrating the café's back room and arresting a group of workers presumed to be ringleaders. The fight lasted until 1 a.m. ending with defiant workers singing in the "Internationale."[50]

The working-class café culture was an anathema to the Vichy regime that took power after France fell to Hitler in June 1940. Whereas the interwar governments had introduced virtually no new laws, Vichy now enacted a wide-ranging overhaul of the drinking establishment regulation. The law of August 23, 1940 prohibited alcoholic drinks in cafés and restaurants on Tuesdays, Thursdays, and Saturdays and to all youths under the age of twenty. Infractions could bring closure of the shop. On November 4, 1940 the regime upheld the power of municipalities (first granted by the July 1880 law and upheld and strengthened by the laws of July 1913 and November 1915) to prohibit cafés within a defined perimeter around churches, cemeteries, hospitals, and schools.

The law of September 24, 1941 elaborated a more complex and restrictive categorization of drinking establishments than the law of November 1915. A fourfold division of drinking establishment licenses emerged (and is still largely in effect), replacing the twofold division established during World War I. The law divided all drinks into five categories: (1) non alcoholic; (2) fermented, not distilled, such as wine, beer, and cider; (3) sweet wines and aperitifs of not more than 18° alcohol; (4) rums and other distilled wines and fruit drinks; (5) all other drinks. In turn these five types of drink could be served in the following four categories of drinking establishment, according to the number of their license: (1) non-alcoholic drinks; (2) "hygienic drinks," serving the first two categories; (3) "restricted license," serving the first three groups on the premises and selling groups four and five to consume off premises or with meals; and (4) the full license, serving the full range of non-alcoholic and alcoholic drinks. Vichy administrators would allow an unlimited number of shops with a license number 1 but no new shops with license number 4. License numbers 2 and 3 could be opened in cities with less than one shop per 450 people but not if this ratio had been exceeded. Clearly the intent was to try to promote non-alcoholic drinking establishments and restrict those that sold the full range of alcoholic beverages.

To ensure enforcement, the law of August 28, 1943 granted prefects and the interior ministry extensive powers. Prefects could close a café for up to three months and the Secretary of the Interior for up to a year either for an infraction to the above laws or to preserve order and health. The law of October 4, 1943 then obliged café owners to post a list of non-alcoholic drinks in their shops.[51]

The repression and privation of the German occupation and these laws of the collaborationist government took a severe toll on café life. The important role that cafés and café owners played in the resistance can be documented copiously and certainly contributed to the fall in the number of cafés.[52] Overall, the number of shops plunged from 455,054 in 1940 to 314,000 by 1946.[53] This was a far larger drop in the number of shops that had occurred during the repression of the Second Empire. Although café life figured prominently in the Resistance, the governments of the Fourth and Fifth Republics, in their striving for national regeneration, were no more sympathetic to the café than Vichy had been. The restrictive Vichy legislation remained in effect and was complemented by rigorous zoning ordinances in the new towns and city districts constructed during the 1960s and 1970s. Today official figures list the number of cafés at merely 46,000, roughly the same number of shops that existed in Paris in the 1880s!

Thus the vision of French parliamentarians during World War I has essentially been realized. The post-1945 consumer culture—with its cars, TV, stereos, spacious homes, vacations, and now the Internet—has essentially killed the proletarian public sphere in the café. Yet the young, the artistic, and the immigrant still gravitate to the café and are reshaping it for the twenty-first century. From philosophical, musical, and cyber cafés, to those with a Muslim, African, Asian, or Latin-American inflection, these establishments may produce a new sort of public sphere, one that is multicultural rather than proletarian.

Notes

1. For early and now classic articles see Michael R. Marrus, "Social Drinking in the Belle Epoque," *Journal of Social History*, 7/4 (Winter 1974): 115–41; Patricia E. Prestwich, "Temperance in France: The Curious Case of Absinthe," *Historical Reflections/Reflections Historiques* 6/2 (Winter 1979); Susanna Barrows, "After the Commune: Alcoholism, Temperance, and Literature in the Early Third Republic," in John Merriman (ed.), *Consciousness and Class Experience in Nineteenth-Century Europe* (New York: Holmes & Meier, 1979), pp. 205–18.

2. Jürgen Habermas, *The Structural Transformation of the Public Sphere: An Inquiry into a Category of Bourgeois Society*, trans. Thomas Burger with Frederick Lawrence (Cambridge MA: MIT Press, 1991).

3. These are the topic of the volumes on twentieth-century café life that I am currently working on for the Johns Hopkins University Press.

4. See my article "Drinking Establishments (France)" in Jack S. Blocker, Jr., David M. Fahey, and Ian R. Tyrrell (eds), *Alcohol and Temperance History: An International Encyclopedia*, Vol. 1 (Santa Barbara, Denver, Oxford: BS Clio, 2003), pp. 203–6.

5. See my *The World of the Paris Café: Sociability among the French Working Class, 1789–1914* (Baltimore and London: Johns Hopkins University Press, 1996, paper 1998). All subsequent references, unless otherwise cited, come from this book.

6. See Robert Darnton, "The High Enlightenment and the Low-Life of Literature," in *The Literary Underground of the Old Regime* (Cambridge, MA: Harvard University Press, 1982), p. 1; Arlette Farge, *Subversive Words: Public Opinion in Eighteenth-Century France* (College Park: Penn State University Press, 1995), Sara Maza, *Private Lives and Public Affairs: The Causes Celebres of Prerevolutionary France* (Berkeley, Los Angeles, London: University of California Press, 1993), and Lynn Hunt, *The Family Romance of the French Revolution* (Berkeley, Los Angeles, London: University of California Press, 1992).

7. Danton, "The High Enlightenment," p. 1.

8. Patrice Boussel, "Cafés," in *Dictionnaire de Paris* (Paris: Larousse, 1964), pp. 76–7.

9. Elisabeth Roudinesco, *Madness and Revolution: The Lives and Legends of Théroigne de Méricourt*, trans. Martin Thom (London: Verso, 1991), p. 5.

10. Jean Robiquet, *Daily Life in the French Revolution*, trans James Kirkup (New York: Macmillan, 1964), p. 4.

11. Still one of most dramatic recounting of this is found in Thomas Carlyle's *The French Revolution* (1837; Oxford: Oxford University Press, 1990) see Book 1. VII The Insurrection of Women chapter 1.7.I "Patrollotism."

12. George Rudé, *The Crowd in the French Revolution* (London: Oxford University Press, 1959), p. 217.

13. Hebert, *Le Père Duchêne* III numeros 41–80, # 51 Le Mai du Père Duchêne, Plante en rejouissance de la liberte des entrees, 2–8.

14. *Annales de l'assembleé nationale, 1871–1876*, Vol. 6, annex 1872, p. 309. All future references to the number of cafés in France from 1828 to 1870 will be from this source.

15. Sebastien Vaubin, Project d'une dîme royale (1707) in Eugene Daire (ed.), *Economistes Financieres dy XVIII siècle* (Paris, 1843), p. 97.

16. Didier Nourrison's *Alcoolisme et antialcoolisme en France souls la Troisième République: L'exemple de la Seine Inférieure*, 2 vols, (Paris: La Documentation francaise, 1986), for example, provides statistics starting from 1830. All following drink statistics from Vol. 2, pp, 903–33.

17. For material on the café and folkloric life from the 1820s through the early 1850s I have drawn upon the entries I did for the *Encyclopedia of 1848 Revolutions*. The entries are as follows: Drinking Establishments, Drink Question, Victor Hugo, Police Regulation Working Class Life, Political Mobilization (France), Popular Culture (France). *Encyclopedia of 1848 Revolutions* is an electronic publication, editor James Chastain, homepage: http://www.cats.ohioedu/~Chastain/index.htm.

18. See *Compte général de l'administration de la justice criminelle en France* (Paris: Imprimerie Royale, Impérial, et Nationale, 1827–1789), section "Nature et number des contraventions jugées par les tribunaux de simple police" for each year.

19. For statistic see Steven E. Rowe, "Inscribing Power, Revising Power: Everyday Acts of Writing among the Working Classes in Nineteenth-Century Paris" New Histories of Writing IV Forms and Rhetorics 2003 MMLA Meeting Chicago Il November 8, 2003 (www.cwru.edu/affil/sce/Texts_2003/Rowe.htm) and Jacques Rancière's article in *Les Revoltes logiques, Cahiers du Centre des Recherches sur les Ideologies de la Révolte*, ed. Solin, Paris No. 1, Hiver 1975, pp. 5–22; and translated as "Good Times or Pleasure at the Barriers," in Adrian Rifkin and Roger Thomas's edited and presented volume *Voices of the People: The Social Life of 'la Sociale' at the End of the Second Empire* trans. John Moor (London: Routledge & Kegan Paul, 1988), pp. 45–96. Edgar Newman, "Workers Remember the French Revolution in Song, 1830–1852," in Boris Blick and Louis Patsouras (eds), *Rebels Against the Old Order, Essays in Honor of Morris Slavin* (Youngstown, OH: Youngstown State University, 1994).

20. John Merriman, *The Agony of the Republic: The Repression of the Left in Revolutionary France, 1848–1851* (New Haven: Yale University Press, 1978), pp. 96, 148.

21. See my "The Regulation of Taverns, Cabarets, and Cafés in France: From the Old Regime to 1800" MA Thesis University of Wisconsin, 1980, passim.

22. Alexis de Tocqueville, *Recollections*, trans. Alexander Teixeira de Mattos, ed. with many additions from the original text and an introduction by J. P. Mayer (New York: Columbia University Press, 1949), p. 112.

23. *Compte rendu des séances de l'assemblée national legislative*, 1849–1851, Vol. 12, pp. 452–60.

24. E. Guerlin de Guer, "Les Débits de boissons," *Revue général d'administration*, 1880, Vol. I, p. 288.

25. Marshall Berman, *All That's Solid Melts Into Air: The Experience of Modernity* (New York: Simon and Schuster, 1982), p. 167

26. Timothy J. Clark, *The Painting of Modern Life: Manet and His Followers* (Princeton: Princeton University Press; revd ed., 1999), chapter 4, see too *Mémoires de Théresa écrits par-elle même* 6th ed. (Paris: E. Dentu, 1865).

27. Haine, "The Regulation," pp. 160–99.

28. Leo Loubère, *Red and White, The History of Wine in France and Italy in the Nineteenth Century* (Albany, NY: State University of New York Press, 1978).

29. Nourrison, *Alcoolisme et antialcoolisme en France*, Vol. 2, pp. 939–43.

30. Haine, "The Regulation," pp. 178–80.

31. Haine, "The Regulation," pp. 200–38.

32. Robert A. Nye, *Crime, Madness, and Politics in Modern France: The Medical Concept of National Decline* (Princeton: Princeton University Press, 1984), p. 135.

33. Haine, *The World of the Paris Café*, pp. 33–44.

34. For the political role of cafés during the 1870s see Jérôme Grévy, "Les cafés républicains de Paris au début de la Troisième République. Étude de sociabilité politique," *Revue D'Histoire Moderne et Contemporaine* 50/2 (2003): 52–72. For Belleville cafés see Fabien Théofilakis, "Mémoire de maîtrise d'histoire contemporaine," *Cabaretiers et marchands de vin à Belleville, 1860–1914*, sd. du Prof. Ronald Hubscher, Université Paris X Nanterre, 1997–1998.

35. Haine, "The Regulation," pp. 200–38.

36. Alain, Faure (ed.), *Les premiers banlieusards: Aux origines des banlieues de Paris (1860–1940)* (Paris: Créaphis, 1991) and Nathalie Graveleau, *Les cafés comme lieux de sociabilité politique à Paris et en banlieue 1905–1913* (Paris: FEN, Cahiers du Centre Confédéral, 1991).

37. See my "Fighting on Two Fronts: The French Campaign to Eradicate Drunkenness in the Army and on the Home Front During World War I." Paper presented at the Kettil Bruun Society, 22nd Annual Alcohol Epidemiology Symposium, Edinburgh, June 3–7, 1996.

38. Patricia Prestwich, *Drink and the Politics of Social Reform: Antialcoholism in France Since 1870* (Palo Alto: SPOSS, 1988)

39. M. D. Dalloz, *Jurisprudence générale* (Paris: Dalloz, 1916 and 1920). See section 4, 144 for 1916 and section 4, 223 for 1920.

40. *Annales de le Chambre des Députés, 1916–1918*, especially the debates during September 28 to October 17, 1916, November 9 to December 29, 1916, October 25, 1917 to December 26, 1917, and February 14–27 and March 6–25, 1918.

41. Jean Dethier, *Cafés, bistrots et compagnie, Catalogue d'exposition* (Paris: Centre Georges Pompidou, 1977), p. 51.

42. Patricia E. Prestwich, *Drink and the Politics of Reform*.

43. See registers of the Correctional Tribunal of Paris for the years 1919–1939. Archives de Paris, D1U6.

44. I analyze these points in more detail, along with exploring the police reports for this era at the archives of the Paris Police in my essay, "A Space for Many Strategies: Parisian-area Cafés and Interwar Political Movements of the Left and Right," Paper presented at the Society for French Historical Studies, Louisville, Kentucky March 21–23, 1997. See too Vanessa Paroux, *Débits et débitants de boissons dans le 18e arrdt de Paris pendant l'entre-deux-guerres*, Maîtrise sous la direction de A. Prost, A. Fourcaut, Paris I, 1994.

45. Archives de la Préfecture de Police, B/a 1646 dossier concerning "manifestation communiste 1er aout 1929" circular from the P.C.F. region parisienne 106 rue Lafayette Paris 5 juillet 1929.

46. Jane Jenson and George Ross, *The View From Inside: A French Communist Cell in Crisis* (Berkeley: University of California Press, 1985), pp. 175–6; Antony Beevor and Artemis Cooper, *Paris: After the Liberation, 1944–1949* (New York: Doubleday, 1994), p. 364, quoting Emmanuel Le Roy Ladurie, *Paris-Montpellier* (Paris: Gallimard, 1982), p. 46.

47. Archives de la Préfecture de la Police, B/a 1852.

48. APP, B/a 1631, 1 aout.

49. See Haine, "Space for Many Strategies."

50. APP B/a 1628, 1er mai.

51. M. D. Dalloz, *Jurisprudence général*, laws found in section 4. The following years and page numbers are as follows: 1940, 353; 1941, 501, 545; 1942, 108, 143; and 1943, 63.

52. Currently I am completing a book on the cafés of the Paris region during World War II based especially on the police blotters, *mains courants*, and the reports "Situation de Paris" and using newspapers and memoirs.

53. Dethier, *Cafés, bistrots et compagnie*, p. 51.

–9–

The Lore of the Brotherhood

Continuity and Change in Urban American Saloon Culture, 1870–1920

Madelon Powers

The saloon was an incubator of working-class culture; the saloon was a snake pit of vice. It promoted working-class organization; it undermined working-class initiative. It was the poor man's club; it was the devil's headquarters on earth. And so the public debate raged over the urban workingman's saloon throughout America's industrializing era of 1870 to 1920, ending with a nationwide prohibition on alcohol sales. What made the saloon so controversial, compared with its antecedents in the colonial and antebellum periods and its successors in the prohibition and modern eras? Why all the fuss over a barroom?

The explanation lies in the historical forces that shaped the saloon, its customers, and its lore. Industrial development wrought great changes in class relations, patterns of work and leisure, and the role of saloons in workers' lives. Concurrently, the stupendous growth of cities increased the demand for practical and recreational services, both of which the saloon supplied, to the dismay of many. Finally, the mass migration of both foreign- and native-born people to US cities vigorously stirred the cultural pot and reshaped American social customs in many venues, including the saloon. The confluence of these trends—industrialization, urbanization, and mass migration—prompted a remarkable flowering of barroom culture as well as an explosion of anti-saloon protest.

During the period of 1870 to 1920, the urban saloon served as a principal center of urban working-class club life. Customers congregated on a regular basis to participate in the rich lore of the barroom, which included drinking customs, games, songs, stories, and the free lunch. Building upon these shared traditions, saloongoers developed collective responses to the historical forces acting on their lives, leading to their involvement in labor activism, machine politics, and ethnic organizing. An analysis of urban workers' barroom lore and the side action that grew out of it will help explain why the saloon was so beloved some and so reviled by others during America's industrializing age.[1]

The term "saloon" was an American corruption (in more ways than one!) of the French "salon," defined as a spacious and gracious social hall. Yet though the average saloon was hardly as genteel as its namesake, it did offer many amenities that appealed to workers. Most contained a large bar counter of oak or mahogany with a brass foot rail to accommodate stand-up drinking. Spittoons and mustache towels were conveniently positioned along its length for communal use. On the wall behind the bar counter were shelves for bottles and glassware, and often a sizeable mirror as well. Some back-bars included massive pillars at each end that were topped with carved cornices. The walls typically displayed pictures of imperious prizefighters, prancing racehorses, or flirtatious femmes fatales. If space permitted, saloons might feature tables and chairs, free lunch counters, gambling machines, or pool tables. Many also offered a backroom for meetings, parties, and free lunch consumers. By custom, female patrons were generally accommodated in the backroom area, while males dominated the barroom proper.[2]

Such amenities were possible on a nationwide scale in this era because of the advent of industrialization. Mass-produced glassware, furniture, gaming equipment, and other items could now be distributed by rail or boat to far-flung markets. The Brunswick Company of Cincinnati, for example, produced many of the elaborate back-bar pillars as well as billiard tables to be found in establishments from the Atlantic seaboard to the Pacific Coast. Similarly, regional food distributors serviced large territories; for example, the William Davidson Company made daily deliveries to saloons in the Chicago area. A bar owner in New York City noted in 1909 that that he procured pretzels from a local firm, sausages and other meats from regional companies, and pork and beans from a supplier in faraway Indiana.[3]

Even more important, alcohol production became big business in the industrializing era. With the rise of large-scale breweries and liquor distilleries, regional brand names increasingly joined local products in the saloonkeeper's larder. Moreover, many breweries tried to gain control of the retail market by buying saloons outright or convincing bar owners to sign exclusive supplier contracts. For a hefty share of the bar profits, breweries provided not only beer, but also foodstuffs, equipment, and decorations for their "tied-houses." Approximately 70 percent of saloons in the United States had such brewery connections by 1909.[4]

The trend toward organization and standardization in the bar business influenced the drinking experience in many respects. Bargoers could enter a new saloon with the confidence of knowing what to expect, for the spatial layout, facilities, and stock would be much the same there as down the street or across the country. Such familiarity was reassuring to customers who were either on the move in search of work or already settled but rattled by urban life's uncertainties. The predictability of the physical environment also brought a measure of order to barroom conduct. Like the regular churchgoer who knows when to stand, sing, and pray, the experienced saloongoer knew to proceed directly to the bar counter, to "assume the position" by slouching casually with one foot on the rail, and to purchase the requisite drink before approaching the free lunch counter or pool table. As saloons became increasingly standardized, such procedures evolved into traditions which smoothed barroom interactions and distinguished the seasoned saloongoer from the novice.[5]

Another important consequence of industrialization was the accentuation of class differences, which in turn had a profound impact on saloons and drink lore.

Distinctions in social rank had of course been evident in bar clienteles before the saloon period. In colonial towns of the seventeenth and eighteenth centuries, the local tavern might have attracted a cross-section of residents, but that did not mean that rich and poor commingled as comrades. As historian Sharon Salinger has observed, "Most taverns drew from all ranks of society, but all ranks were no more equal there than anywhere else." Well aware of their status differences, men drank in clusters within the tavern.[6]

By the early nineteenth century, the rise of the commercial market economy was rapidly changing the age-old reciprocal relations between master craftsmen and their journeymen into the adversarial employer–employee relations of nascent capitalism. With this change, the former practice of classes sharing space within taverns (and workplaces and neighborhoods) soon gave way to that of seeking separate venues. Drinking establishments catered either to elite, middling, or laboring groups, who often further sorted themselves by occupation and ethnicity. From the 1830s to the Civil War of the 1860s, the well-off increasingly forsook taverns for private clubs, drank at home, or abandoned drink altogether for the temperance cause. This left the field of public drinking primarily to laborers, who by the 1870s began calling their favorite haunts "saloons" and cultivating there an ever more self-consciously *working-class* culture.[7]

Many unions made their headquarters in saloons, using them for organizing efforts, chapter meetings, and occasional social events. In the 1890s in Buffalo, New York, sixty-three of the city's sixty-nine unions met in saloons, and a nationwide survey in 1901 showed saloons serving as headquarters for 30 percent of the Brotherhood of Boiler Makers and Iron Shipbuilders and 75 percent of the Amalgamated Wood Workers. The proprietor's welcome was warm compared to the suspicious hostility of hotel owners, municipal building managers, and other guardians of urban public space. The saloon's backroom was usually available without charge as long as union members purchased drinks. Moreover, the saloon was already a principal gathering spot for workers, a place where men engaged in shoptalk and compared notes about working conditions and employment opportunities. It was "the principal place in which ideas underlying the labor movement originate, or at any rate become consciously held," observed journalist Hutchins Hapgood in 1913. "It is there where men talk over, think, and exchange feelings and ideas relating to their labor and their lives." In sum, saloons were convenient and agreeable places to spread the union message.[8]

The saloon also served as an incubator for the lore of organized labor. William "Big Bill" Haywood, a leader of the United Mine Workers and later the Industrial Workers of the World, first became interested in labor issues while listening to the stories of saloongoing workers. He heard hair-raising legends concerning the Molly Maguires, the rebellious Colorado miners of the 1870s who violently resisted oppressive mine owners. These militants of Irish descent were finally undone by a company spy who, ironically, infiltrated their saloongoing circle and used their bar talk against them. On another occasion, Haywood witnessed a group of Cornish miners in a Nevada saloon who, having been wronged by their foreman, Simon Harris, convinced one of their number to stand and utter a few choice words. "Dear Lord, does thee know Simmon 'Arris," the miner intoned. "If thee know en, we wish for thee to take en and put en in 'Ell, and there let the bugger frizzle and fry ..., an' grease en up a bit and turn of en loose. Amen." This curse in the form of a mock prayer was met with great laughter and a hearty toast by the miner's comrades.[9]

Eugene Debs also grew up hearing railroaders' stories of strikes and union politics in the saloons of Terra Haute, Indiana. In the 1880s, Debs himself became part of the lore as saloon storytellers spread the tale of the day he shouted down a Pennsylvania Railroad vice president. As leader of the American Railway Union during the nationwide Pullman Strike in 1894, Debs attained hero status when he was jailed for encouraging the strike at union meetings and saloon gatherings. Little wonder that in Pullman, Illinois, the company town that railcar manufacturer George Pullman named for himself, saloons were banned as fomenters of subversive talk and insubordination as well as heavy drinking.[10]

Labor movement songs constituted another category of lore in the workingman's saloon. In the 1880s, for example, the Knights of Labor were vigorously campaigning for an eight-hour workday and other controversial reforms. Sympathetic saloongoers sang the union's praises to the effect that "The noble Knights of Labor are doing the best they can / To elevate the condition of the noble working man!" By far the most musically inclined labor group was the Industrial Workers of the World (IWW) of the early 1900s. The leaders of this militantly anticapitalist union, including the aforementioned "Big Bill" Haywood, were notorious for their saloongoing habits. Indeed, legend has it that the union was nicknamed the "Wobblies" for the way its hard-drinking members so often wobbled their way from saloon to saloon (a nickname they themselves cheerfully embraced). Equally well known was the group's use of music to unite its largely unskilled and ethnically diverse membership.[11]

In and around the saloon's swinging doors, IWW street bands performed satirical songs composed by members Joe Hill, Jack Walsh, and Harry "Mac" McClintock. The latter man's "Big Rock Candy Mountain," later sanitized into a children's song, originally described a hobo's paradise filled with "cigarette trees" and "little streams of alcohol," where "The box cars are all empty / And the railroad bulls [guards] are blind." Most famous was the Wobblies' parody of the Salvation Army favorite, "In the Sweet Bye and Bye." The IWW musicians serenaded saloongoers with this lilting refrain: "Work and pray, live on hay, / You'll get pie in the sky when you die." Such humorous yet sharp-edged lyrics pointed up the dark underside of the American Dream and reminded saloongoers of their common plight in the urban–industrial marketplace.[12]

Industrialization also brought a sharper division between work and leisure time, greatly affecting the rhythm of public drinking. In the preindustrial era, people had widely engaged in "dram drinking," which entailed imbibing small amounts of alcohol every so often as the day progressed. Even in artisans' workshops, the master, journeymen, and apprentices usually drank a little, worked a little, then drank a little again throughout the workday. With the coming of mechanization and mass production, however, the workplace became increasingly regimented, depersonalized, and sober. Masters-turned-employers not only stopped drinking with employees, but also they forbade their employees to drink with one another while working. The result was that at noontime breaks and shift changes, saloon patronage boomed.[13]

When the factory's mealtime whistle sounded, many workers stampeded to nearby saloons not just for a schooner of beer, but for the famous lunch that came "free" with a five-cent beer. Taverns in the colonial and antebellum eras had of course offered food, some providing a regularly scheduled and fixed-price meal at midday, called an "ordinary." But the saloon lunch was of a different order altogether. When temperance advocates complained in the late 1880s about saloon-goers drinking on empty stomachs, the breweries responded by supplying their tied-houses with meat, vegetables, bread, eggs, and cheese bought in bulk. Reformers sputtered as more workers than ever flocked to saloons for the lunch. By the 1890s, even some respectable female workers were slipping in through the side door or "ladies entrance" in groups to consume the lunch in the backroom. A few workers reported developing a drink habit from the practice, supporting the claims of reformers who forlornly insisted, "There is no free lunch" (now an American proverb meaning all good things have hidden costs). But most workers came to regard the meal as one of the saloon trade's most beneficial and beloved traditions.[14]

Those who brought packed lunches to work might still fetch a pail of saloon beer, a practice known as "rushing the growler." Often a group of workers hired an enterprising young fellow to hang several "growlers" on a pole and "rush" them to the saloon and back. One Chicago saloon reported selling ninety gallons of beer per day in this manner to laborers at a nearby worksite. (Meanwhile, back home in their tenements, wives of such workers were known to chip in for a communal growler of their own on hot summer afternoons.) It was traditional for saloon-keepers to charge only ten cents for a pail of beer, regardless of the pail's actual size, so the practice was understandably popular among financially strapped workers. The beer pail tradition persisted until bottled beer, another innovation of the industrial marketplace, rendered the growler obsolete.[15]

At the end of work shifts, saloons near factories once again sprang to life as the thirsty hordes descended. For men without families, with stark boarding-house rooms awaiting them, this first saloon stop might last well into night. Married men were more likely to have a drink and depart, though a study in New York City in 1913 revealed that most male workers, married or not, spent half or more of their leisure time away from their households. Many men headed home for meals and then went out again to relax with saloon comrades. While some workers used this opportunity to drink excessively, practice infidelity, or behave abusively, the vast majority did nothing of the kind. Instead, their evenings usually consisted of a few beers, some laughs, and perhaps a game of cards, dice, or pool. Their modest expenditures for such pleasures were often regularly planned items in their household budgets.[16]

On Saturday payday, however, many workers let loose to indulge in a rollicking alcoholic frolic. Some laborers brought their womenfolk to backroom parties for which saloonkeepers might hire a band. More often, the Saturday bash was an all-male event in which workers temporarily forgot their grueling factory jobs. This sort of "communal binge" had a long lineage in American drink culture, stretching back to colonial times when whole communities gathered to drink and cavort during militia musters and election days. The great difference in the saloon period, of course, was that the communal binge was now subject to the industrial timetable and was far more class- and gender-specific than in former days. It also contained an element of protest, as workers openly and deliberately defied the middle-class creed of industry, sobriety, and thrift.[17]

Many workers continued their revelry well past Saturday night. Such squandering of Sundays angered religious reformers who campaigned for a sober Sabbath. Some men even failed to show up for work on "Saint Monday" (or "Blue Monday"), as workers had been calling this custom since colonial times. Unions, to their credit, tried hard to stamp out this tradition of Monday absenteeism, noting that it tarnished their efforts to portray the workingman as diligent and deserving of better working conditions.[18]

Constrained and criticized at every turn by employers and reformers, many workers turned to barroom lore to help rehabilitate their wounded sense of manhood. Eschewing cocktails as "sissy" drinks, the saloon regular usually ordered beer or straight whiskey. But he must not be a sloppy drunk; the ability to keep pace with comrades and still "hold his liquor" was essential. If treated to a drink, a bargoer had to buy a drink in return or reciprocate with a cigar, personal favor, or other acceptable substitute. As Jack London observed when he and a friend joined a new drinking circle, "They treated, and we drank. Then, according to the code of drinking, we had to treat." Proper observance of the treating ritual was fundamental to honorable manhood in the barroom where moochers and misers were despised. Not to return a treat "would be the trick of a short-sport, a quitter—unmanly, in fact," according to journalist Travis Hoke. To win basic respect as a man among men, then, a worker had to uphold barroom traditions regarding drink choices, drunken comportment, and the overarching code of reciprocity.[19]

Beyond this, the beleaguered worker might bolster his manly self-image by excelling at various saloon pastimes. Games, made more interesting with modest wagers, afforded many opportunities for small triumphs. Pool and darts tested physical agility; chess and backgammon measured mental acuity; and cards and dice called for a winning combination of skill and luck. Saloongoers also gambled on off-premises sports events such as boxing matches, baseball games, and horse races. The man with the best knowledge of sports lore and betting odds could win both wagers and admiration among his comrades.[20]

The barroom offered musical opportunity in these days before the widespread presence of radios and jukeboxes. Men with good singing voices might join amateur quartets and singing clubs meeting in saloon backrooms. Meanwhile, everyone else could engage in the more raucous songfests that sporadically erupted along the bar. In addition to the labor songs discussed above, saloongoers' repertoires included popular Tin Pan Alley tunes like "Sweet Adeline" and "My Mother Was a Lady," as well as folksongs like the African-American "Frankie and Albert," the German "Ach du lieber Augustin," and the Irish "Wearin' of the Green."[21]

Still another path to barroom stardom involved various forms of verbal lore. Saloongoers often vied to tell the tallest tales of workplace feats, romantic encounters, or personal adventures. Some occasionally recited popular narrative poems such as "Casey at the Bat" and "The Shooting of Dan McGrew." A few customers with more highbrow tastes might utter lines from Shakespeare or recount battle stories from Homer. More commonly, workers engaged in the casual banter of the friendly drinking circle. They told jokes, made jests, and traded ritual insults through humorous toasts such as "Here's mud in your eye" and "Hope you choke." Through sport, song, and story, saloongoers could display their talents, impress their comrades, and counteract feelings of alienation and powerlessness in the industrial workplace.[22]

As the industrializing trend increased, so did the size and complexities of cities, making urbanization another formative force in the saloon period. Manufacturers usually located their enterprises in urban areas where labor and transportation were readily available. In response, the poor poured in from the countryside and from overseas, searching not only for jobs but also for an array of practical and recreational services. While churches and charities dithered over who might be deserving of assistance, the ubiquitous saloon leapt into the breach.[23]

Practical services ranging from employment assistance to bail money were largely the province of political machines like Tammany Hall in New York, whose leaders often used saloons as their headquarters. Barrooms were closely connected to political machines for several reasons. Breweries and saloonkeepers assisted politicians by making campaign contributions and delivering the saloon vote on election day. In return, politicians assisted the bar trade by helping saloonkeepers evade temperance laws and keeping customers happy with personal favors. To seal the bargain, all the workers needed to do was drink and vote, which they dutifully did.[24]

To most saloongoers, machine politicians seemed great benefactors who simply operated according to the familiar code of reciprocity. As the anti-machine reformer Lincoln Steffens reluctantly acknowledged, "Tammany kindness is real kindness, and will go far, remember long, and take infinite trouble for a friend." A man in need of a job, a peddling license, a good word in court, or a reprieve from bill collectors could bring his problem to his ward captain, whose headquarters was often a local saloon's backroom. In San Francisco, for example, Christopher "The Blind

Boss" Buckley could easily be approached at "Buckley's City Hall," which was the backroom of the Alhambra Saloon. In Chicago, the place to go in the first ward was the "Workingmen's Exchange," a saloon owned by boss Michael "Hinky Dink" Kenna. Machine bosses often started out as saloon customers or bartenders or proprietors, so they had firsthand knowledge of workers' needs and drinkers' folkways. Despite their shady dealings in municipal politics, they worked ceaselessly to earn votes by helping ease the pressures of urbanization for their constituents.[25]

Many workers first learned the ways of urban machines through the politician's treat. Building upon the treating ritual already fundamental to barroom lore, politicians would grandly offer to "treat the house" as they pushed through the swinging doors of neighborhood saloons at election time. "And the next thing you know," Jack London recalled from his sailor days in Oakland, California, in the 1890s, "you are lined up at the bar, pouring drinks down your throat and learning the gentlemen's names and the offices which they hope to fill."[26]

Politicians also threw festive parties for the people in their districts. They held semi-annual balls in saloon backrooms, where men and women of the neighborhood drank, ate, and danced to band music. Community gatherings on a grander scale were sometimes sponsored by higher-ups in the machine hierarchy. In New York City in the 1890s, for example, Tammany ward boss Timothy "Big Tim" Sullivan arranged a yearly outdoor "chowder" for his district. These chowder picnics, attended by several thousand people, earned Sullivan great popular support which found political expression on election day.[27]

The pressures of urban life increased the people's demand not only for practical services, but also for recreational opportunities. By the 1890s, workers could choose from an array of leisure institutions including vaudeville theaters, dance halls, poolrooms, penny arcades, and gymnasiums. In its usual versatile fashion, the saloon trade managed to incorporate many elements of these attractions into its lore and thereby hold its own in the expanding realm of urban entertainment.

Many saloonkeepers installed gaming equipment to compete with poolrooms, penny arcades, and gymnasiums. In Chicago's seventeenth ward in 1901, for example, a survey of 163 saloons revealed that 44 (27 percent) contained pool or billiard tables. Some barrooms provided gambling machines, and a few supplied exercise equipment in the backroom. Another strategy was to complement more than compete with gaming establishments. Situated nearby, saloons attracted numerous post-game gatherings, particularly those groups whose wagering involved "playing for the drinks."[28]

Dance halls and cabarets offered opportunities for heterosocial encounters not possible in the heavily homosocial world of the barroom proper. Yet, as previously noted, the saloon's backroom occasionally served as the scene of mixed-gender gatherings such as payday frolics, union parties, and politicians' annual balls. Such gatherings would have cost more to stage in dance halls and would have been decidedly awkward in the often sultry ambience of the cabaret. With its backroom bashes, then, the saloon found its heterosocial niche to fill.[29]

Vaudeville theaters featured an assortment of comedians, magicians, jugglers, skit actors, and "leg shows," as well as singers who introduced Tin Pan Alley's latest sheet music hits. Some "concert saloons," which incorporated elements of the cabaret and the theater, presented smaller and less respectable versions of such shows. A few neighborhood saloons also got into the act by squeezing a stage into the backroom and featuring local talent. Though not as thrilling as the vaudeville theater shows, the saloon's backroom entertainment could often be had for the price of a five-cent beer, compared to ten to twenty-five cents for the ticket alone at its upscale competitors.[30]

Saloon culture was greatly influenced not only by industrialization and urbanization, but also by a third major historical trend of the late nineteenth century: mass migration. Millions of native- and foreign-born migrants left their birthplaces in search of opportunity, often converging on US cities. By the 1890s, African-Americans in the rural South began fleeing northward to escape poverty and racial violence, becoming part of the "Great Migration" that lasted into the 1920s. Poverty-stricken white southerners made the journey as well. Meanwhile, immigrants from around the globe flowed in, Europeans being the most numerous. First came the "Old Wave" from northern and western Europe and the British Isles who predominated until about 1890. Next came the "New Wave" from southern and eastern Europe who continued to arrive until 1924 when strict immigration quotas were imposed. Different though these many migrant groups were, all quickly learned that saloons could serve as congenial shelters for their respective ethnic cultures.[31]

The ethnic saloon was an oasis of familiarity and assistance for the urban migrant. Proprietors cultivated customer loyalty by hiring bartenders of the same ethnic background and serving traditional drinks and food. Customers conversed in their native dialects, swapped news from home, and shared information about work and lodging. Each group had its favorite barroom pastimes. Italians in Boston were especially fond of card games, blacks in Philadelphia played a form of lottery known as "numbers" or "policy," and the Irish staged backroom boxing matches in the coal-mining towns of Pennsylvania. Ethnic groups also celebrated their musical heritages in saloons, including German marching bands in the Pittsburgh area, African-American blues piano in New York's Harlem neighborhood, and Slavic concerts featuring the mandolin-like tamburitza in South Chicago.[32]

Ethnic groups brought their drink preferences to America, where an intricate process of cultural cross-fertilization ensued. In the colonial era, the favored drinks were rum and hard cider. Beginning in the 1790s, however, Irish and Scottish immigrants introduced sophisticated distilling techniques, contributing to a growing national taste for whiskey. Drink preferences underwent another dramatic change after 1840 when German immigrants arrived with their brewing expertise. By the saloon period, workingmen everywhere were consuming beer, with whiskey running a close second. Italians, Jews, and other southern and eastern Europeans, who generally favored wine, soon added beer and whiskey to their drink list. Yet even with this extensive intercultural exchange, drink preferences in heavily ethnic saloons still echoed Old World habits. Beer remained the German favorite, whiskey the Irish preference, and wine the drink of choice for many Italians and Jews.[33]

Ethnic culinary traditions were also evident in the saloon's free lunch. In Chicago and New York, barrooms with predominantly German clienteles offered sauerkraut, wienerwurst, pickled herring, and potato salad. Sanguinetti's in San Francisco was noted for the proprietor's spaghetti and Italian bread, while saloons catering to immigrants from south of the border offered Mexican hot beans. Black and white saloongoers in New Orleans, though often patronizing separate establishments, were united in their fondness for gumbo, a spicy African Creole soup made thick with okra. In New Orleans and many other cities nationwide, saloons offered seafood dishes on Fridays to accommodate Catholic immigrants from France, Ireland, Germany, Italy, and other nations.[34]

To preserve their ethnic identity, many immigrant groups formed fraternal organizations that met in the saloon backroom. These ethnic lodges honored traditional songs and stories of the old country and threw parties on national holidays. Reaching beyond the saloon, they provided assistance to newly arrived countrymen and raised funds for homeland causes. Immigrants also formed mutual aid societies that met in backrooms. Though such societies often had a social dimension, their primary purpose was to collect dues to be used for funeral expenses when a member died. African-Americans formed many such societies as well, a tradition that still survives in New Orleans where many a "Social Aid and Pleasure Club" stages a jazz funeral and a joyous drinking party in fond memory of the departed.[35]

Despite its widespread popularity, the urban saloon also had its detractors in working-class districts. Within ethnic communities, religious and business leaders as well as many upwardly mobile workers joined temperance societies and deplored the saloon as an impediment to group uplift. Further, the exclusivity and clannishness of ethnic barrooms provoked hostile nativist reactions from both working- and middle-class Americans. "The saloon fosters an un-American spirit among the foreign-born population of our country," as prohibitionist John Barker asserted. Immigrants should "assimilate American ideals" and leave behind "any demoralizing custom" from their former lives. The ethnic saloon, by perpetuating alien folkways and facilitating ethnocentric projects, was perceived as a threat to national unity.[36]

Many union leaders saw the saloon as a threat to labor solidarity as well. By emphasizing immigrants' differences, the ethnic saloon could serve to aggravate the cultural clashes that plagued unionizing efforts. Preoccupation with Old World concerns might also make foreign-born workers less committed to the cause of American labor, including the struggle against low wages, long hours, and cutthroat job competition. Beyond this, the unions' efforts to gain more control over the employment process sometimes brought them into conflict with the saloon's machine politicians, who used their own control of jobs to win over working-class voters. To add to the strain, some unionists were temperance advocates, for whom the use of saloon backrooms as meeting space was decidedly awkward. For these various reasons, many labor leaders sought to establish independent union halls by the early twentieth century.[37]

In addition to its working-class critics, the saloon faced ferocious foes in the middle-class progressive movement who pushed for an array of urban reforms from 1890 to 1920. Progressive reformers deplored the drinking in urban barrooms, though they were much more apt to advocate outright prohibition than their working-class allies. They also criticized the side action that had developed out of saloon culture, though they spoke largely from the class-conscious perspective of the bourgeoisie. At their most extreme, these reformers saw unchecked union activism as a subversive challenge to free enterprise, machine politics as a power grab by social inferiors, and ethnic organizing as a threat to the rightful cultural stewardship of Anglo-Saxon Protestants. Through such organizations as the Anti-Saloon League, the prohibitionists finally won the day. In 1920, the Eighteenth Amendment to the US Constitution made it official. The saloon was dead, even if the desire for sociable drinking would live on clandestinely in speakeasies and private homes.[38]

From 1870 to 1920, US cities reeled from the threefold impact of industrialization, urbanization, and mass migration. Saloongoers responded by reshaping existing barroom lore to suit their circumstances and by making their fellowship a foundation for pursuing outside projects, most importantly union activism, machine politics, and ethnic organizing. These latter activities incurred the wrath of anti-saloon crusaders just as much as the leisure time which workers "wasted" on drink and other barroom pastimes. This is not to say that barroom critics did not care fervently about the workers' alcohol consumption, for clearly they did. But it was the extent of the side action that made the saloon different from its predecessors and gave reformers the added ammunition necessary to effect prohibition. They found it insupportable that such disruptive endeavors should be emanating from a drink parlor. They condemned the saloon trade for tolerating such dangerous social experiments and for exploiting workers' needs at this pivotal point in the nation's development. In their estimation, the only solution was annihilation.

The saloon caught a three-capped historical wave in 1870 and, throwing caution to the wind, rode that wave all the way to a final smash-up on the rocky shore of prohibition in 1920. After a fugitive existence underground for thirteen years, drinking establishments reemerged in 1933, but with little of the bravado or the muscle of the old-time saloon. Much of the lore of the barroom survived, but most of the side action had long since been taken over by other institutions. The historical tide that had carried the saloon to unprecedented heights in the industrializing era had receded. Left in its wake was the modern neighborhood bar, which encourages its customers to drink and socialize, but otherwise quietly minds its own business.

Notes

1. On the temperance movement, see Jack S. Blocker, Jr., *American Temperance Movements: Cycles of Reform* (Boston: Twayne, 1989); K. Austin Kerr, *Organized for Prohibition: A New History of the Anti-Saloon League* (New Haven, CT: Yale University Press, 1985); and Barbara Leslie Epstein, *The Politics of Domesticity: Women, Evangelism, and Temperance in Nineteenth-Century America* (Middletown, CT: Wesleyan University Press, 1981).

2. On the term "saloon," see H. L. Mencken, *The American Language*, 4th. ed., abridged (New York: Knopf, 1980), 167; George Ade, *The Old-Time Saloon: Not Wet—Not Dry, Just History* (New York: Long and Smith, 1931), p. 69; Roy Rosenzweig, *Eight Hours for What We Will: Workers and Leisure in an Industrial City, 1870–1920* (New York: Cambridge University Press, 1983), p. 244 n. 36; and Elliott West, *The Saloon on the Rocky Mountain Mining Frontier* (Lincoln: University of Nebraska Press, 1979), pp. 26–40. For a comprehensive description of saloon amenities, see Raymond Calkins, *Substitutes for the Saloon* (Boston: Houghton Mifflin, 1901), chapters 1–3, 7–9. See also Robert E. Popham, "The Social History of the Tavern," in Yedy Israel, Frederick Glaser, Harold Kalant, Robert Popham, Wolfgang Schmidt and Reginald Smart (eds), *Research Advances in Alcohol and Drug Problems*, vol. 4 (New York: Plenum Press, 1978), pp. 225–302.

3. On mass-produced and nationally distributed barroom supplies, see West, pp. 44–5; Perry R. Duis, *The Saloon: Public Drinking in Chicago and Boston, 1880–1920* (Urbana: University of Illinois Press, 1983), p. 55; and "The Experience and Observations of a New York Saloon-Keeper as Told by Himself," *McClure's Magazine* 32 (January 1909): 306.

4. On breweries and tied-houses, see James H. Timberlake, *Prohibition and the Progressive Movement, 1900–1920* (New York: Atheneum, 1970), pp. 104–6. On the alcohol industry, see Peter Park, "The Supply Side of Drinking: Alcohol Production and Consumption in the United States before Prohibition," *Contemporary Drug Problems* 12 (1985): 473–509; and Duis, pp. 25–6, 40–5.

5. Ade, p. 28; Popham, p. 278.

6. Sharon V. Salinger, *Taverns and Drinking in Early America* (Baltimore: Johns Hopkins University Press, 2002), p. 243.

7. On the market economy and taverns, see W. J. Rorabaugh, *The Alcoholic Republic: An American Tradition* (New York: Oxford University Press, 1979).

8. Hutchins Hapgood, "McSorley's Saloon," *Harper's Weekly* 58 (25 October 1913): 15. The saloonkeeper's welcome for unions is noted in Royal L. Melendy, "The Saloon in Chicago (Part 2)," *American Journal of Sociology* 6 (January 1901): 438. For statistics on unions in saloons, see Jon M. Kingsdale, "The 'Poor Man's Club': Social Functions of the Urban Working-Class Saloon," *American Quarterly* 25 (October 1973): 482; and Edward W. Bemis, "Attitude of the Trade Unions Toward the Saloon," in Calkins, appendix I, pp. 307, 311–12.

9. William D. Haywood, *The Autobiography of William D. Haywood* (1929; reprint, New York: International Publishers, 1966), pp. 57–61.

10. Ray Ginger, *Eugene V. Debs: A Biography* (New York: Collier Books, 1962), pp. 47, 124.

11. The Knights of Labor song is cited in Ade, pp. 128–9. On the IWW, see Melvin Dubofsky, *We Shall Be All: A History of the Industrial Workers of the World* (Urbana: University of Illinois Press, 1988).

12. On IWW songs, see Alan Lomax, *The Folksongs of North America in the English Language* (Garden City, NY: Doubleday, 1960), pp. 410–12, 422–4; and Captain Fred Klebingat, *Memories of the Audiffred Building and the Old City Front* (San Francisco: Mills Ryland Company with the National Maritime Museum, 1983), p. 15.

13. On dram versus binge drinking, see Rorabaugh, pp. 149–51, 167–9. The separation of work and leisure is discussed in Eviatar Zerubavel, *The Seven Day Circle: The History and Meaning of the Week* (New York: Free Press, 1985).

14. Popham, pp. 249–50, 258–62, 272–4; Calkins, p. 15; Dorothy Richardson, "The Long Day: The Story of a New York Working Girl," in William L. O'Neill (ed.), *Women at Work* (Chicago: Quadrangle, 1972), pp. 257–59; Melendy, "The Saloon in Chicago (Part 2)," pp. 456–7.

15. Melendy, "The Saloon in Chicago (Part 2)," p. 496; Robert Woods, *City Wilderness* (Boston: Houghton Mifflin, 1898), p. 72; "The Experience … of a New York Saloon-Keeper," p. 305; Duis, pp. 65–7, 103–5.

16. Rosenzweig, p. 51; Calkins, p. 20; Kathy Peiss, *Cheap Amusements: Working Women and Leisure in Turn-of-the-Century New York* (Philadelphia: Temple University Press, 1986), pp. 16–18, 23; Margaret F. Byington, *Homestead: The Households of a Mill Town* (1910; reprint, Pittsburgh: University of Pittsburgh Press, 1974), pp. 154–5; William Kornblum, *Blue Collar Community* (Chicago: University of Chicago Press, 1974), p. 75.

17. Peter Roberts, *Anthracite Coal Communities* (New York: Macmillan, 1904), p. 233; Byington, pp. 37, 149; Herbert G. Gutman, *Work, Culture, and Society in Industrializing America* (New York: Knopf, 1976), pp. 68–74.

18. Gutman, pp. 5, 38; Bemis, pp. 305–6; Rorabaugh, pp. 149–51, 167–9.

19. Ade, pp. 56–8; Jack London, *John Barleycorn: Alcoholic Memoirs* (1913; reprint, ed. John Sullivan, New York: Oxford Univeristy Press, 1989), p. 112; Travis Hoke, "Corner Saloon," *American Mercury* 23 (March 1931): 317–19, 321.

20. On games and gambling, see Calkins, chapters 1, 3, 7. See also Ann Fabian, *Card Sharps, Dream Books, and Bucket Shops: Gambling in Nineteenth-Century America* (Ithaca, NY: Cornell University Press, 1990); and John M. Findlay, *People of Chance: Gambling in American Society from Jamestown to Las Vegas* (New York: Oxford University Press, 1986).

21. Hoke, p. 321; Melendy, "The Saloon in Chicago (Part 2)," p. 437; Ade, pp. 119–20, 125, 191; Lomax, pp. 558, 569–70.

22. James Stevens, "Saloon Days," *American Mercury* 11 (July 1927): 269,

272; London, pp. 56–7; Ade, pp. 32, 110, 130, 152–4; Hoke, p. 319. On narrative poetry in the saloon period, see Russel Nye, *The Unembarrassed Muse: The Popular Arts in America* (New York: Dial, 1970), pp. 117–37.

23. On the charitable activities of saloons versus churches, see Royal L. Melendy, "The Saloon in Chicago (Part 1)," *American Journal of Sociology* 6 (November 1900): 297; and "The Experience … of a New York Saloon-Keeper," pp. 310–11.

24. On swapping drinks for votes, see Jacob Riis, *How the Other Half Lives: Studies among the Tenements of New York* (1890; reprint, New York: Hill and Wang, 1957), p. 66; and George Kibbe Turner, "The City of Chicago: A Study of the Great Immoralities," *McClure's Magazine* 28 (April 1907): 586. For more on the saloon's relationship to political machines, see Duis, pp. 114–42. On Tammany ward bosses, see William L. Riordon, *Plunkitt of Tammany Hall: A Series of Very Plain Talks on Very Practical* (1905; reprint, Boston: Bedford Books, 1994); and Daniel Czitrom, "Underworlds and Underdogs: Big Tim Sullivan and Metropolitan Politics in New York, 1889–1913," in Raymond A. Mohl (ed.), *The Making of Urban America*, 2nd ed. (Wilmington, DE: Scholarly Resources, 1997), pp. 131–51.

25. Lincoln Steffens, *The Shame of the Cities* (1904; reprint, New York: Hill and Wang, 1957), p. 205. See also Jane Addams, "Why the Ward Boss Rules," in Riordon, p. 121. On bosses in the backroom, see William A. Bullough, *The Blind Boss and His City: Christopher Augustine Buckley and Nineteenth-Century San Francisco* (Berkeley: University of California Press, 1979); and Lloyd Wendt and Herman Kagan, *Bosses of Lusty Chicago: The Story of Bathhouse John and Hinky Dink* (1943; reprint, Bloomington: Indiana University Press, 1967), pp. v–xiv. For statistics on saloonkeeper-politicians in New York and Chicago, see Peter Odegard, *Pressure Politics: The Story of the Anti-Saloon League* (New York: Columbia University Press, 1928), p. 248.

26. London, p. 79. For more on the politician's treat, see Riordon, p. 99; and "Martin Kelly's Story," San Francisco *Bulletin*, 19 September 1917.

27. Calkins, p. 9; Melendy, "The Saloon in Chicago (Part 2)," pp. 437–9; Kingsdale, p. 479, 482–3; Kornblum, p. 23.

28. Regarding pool, see Calkins, pp. 13, 156–8, 326; and Melendy, "The Saloon in Chicago (Part 1)," p. 293. On gambling machines, see Calkins, p. 14; Walter Bean, *Boss Ruef's San Francisco: The Story of the Union Labor Party, Big Business, and Craft Production* (Berkeley: University of California Press, 1952), p. 156; Woods, *Americans in Process*, p. 220; Roberts, p. 235; and Duis, p. 248. A photograph of a backroom with exercise equipment appears in E. C. Moore, "The Social Value of the Saloon," *American Journal of Sociology* 3 (July 1897): 11.

29. On saloon backroom parties, see Roberts, p. 233; Byington, pp. 37, 149; Gutman, pp. 68–74; Calkins, p. 9; and Kingsdale, pp. 479, 482–3. On dance halls, see Peiss, pp. 88–114; on cabarets, see Lewis A. Erenberg, *Steppin' Out: New York Nightlife and the Transformation of American Culture, 1890–1930* (Westport, CT: Greenwood Press, 1981), pp. 79–86.

30. Calkins, p. 23: Melendy, "The Saloon in Chicago (Part 2)," p. 447; Timothy J. Gilfoyle, *City of Eros: New York City, Prostitution, and the Commercialization of Sex, 1790–1920* (New York: Norton, 1992), pp. 210, 224–32.

31. On immigration patterns, see Rudolph J. Vecoli and Suzanne M. Sinke (eds), *A Century of European Migrations, 1830–1930* (Urbana: University of Illinois Press, 1991); and Milton M. Gordon, *Assimilation in American Life: The Role of Race, Religion and National Origins* (New York: Oxford University Press, 1964). Regarding African-Americans, see James R. Grossman, *Land of Hope: Chicago, Black Southerners, and the Great Migration* (Chicago: University of Chicago Press, 1989).

32. On the appeal of ethnic saloons, see Thomas J. Noel, *The City and the Saloon: Denver, 1858–1916* (Lincoln: University of Nebraska Press, 1982), p. 11; Woods, *Americans in Process*, pp. 201–6, 220–1; and Rosenzweig, pp. 50–1. On games, see Riis, pp. 40, 80, 117; Fabian, p. 141; and Haywood, pp. 59–60. On music, see Byington, p. 37; Roberts, p. 233; Lawrence W. Levine, *Black Culture and Black Consciousness: Afro-American Folk Thought from Slavery to Freedom* (New York: Oxford University Press, 1977), pp. 200–5; and Kornblum, p. 78.

33. Rorabaugh, pp. 69–74, 109–10, 229–30, and appendix I; Woods, *Americans in Process*, p. 204; Calkins, p. 20; Duis, pp. 163–4. On drinking sprees involving men of various ethnicities and drink preferences, see London, pp. 38, 61–2, 130.

34. Ade, pp. 45–7; Klebingat, pp. 6, 8, 10; Calkins, pp. 16, 381; "The Experience ... of a New York Saloon-Keeper," pp. 305–6; Duis, p. 56.

35. Regarding immigrant lodges and mutual aid societies, see Melendy, "The Saloon in Chicago (Part 2)," p. 434; David Brundage, "The Producing Classes and the Saloon: Denver in the 1880s," *Labor History* 26 (Winter 1985): 32; Noel, pp. 56–7; Peiss, pp. 89–91; and Gilfoyle, p. 231. On jazz funerals, see Jack V. Buerkle and Danny Barker, *Bourbon Street Black: The New Orleans Black Jazzman* (New York: Oxford University Press, 1973), pp. 187–97.

36. On religious and business leaders in ethnic communities who advocated group uplift through temperance and other reforms, see John Bodnar, *The Transplanted: A History of Immigrants in Urban America* (Bloomington: Indiana University Press, 1985), chapters 4–7. On the "un-American spirit" in saloons, see John Marshall Barker, *The Saloon Problem and Social Reform* (Boston: Everett Press, 1905), pp. 49–50. See also Timberlake, pp. 115–19; and Noel, pp. 65–6.

37. On problems with multi-ethnic unionizing efforts, see Bodnar, pp. 92–104; John T. Cumbler, *Working-Class Community in Industrial America: Work, Leisure and Struggle in Two Industrial Cities, 1880–1930* (Westport, CT: Greenwood Press, 1979); and Henry B. Leonard, "Ethnic Cleavage and Industrial Conflict in Late 19th Century America," *Labor History* 20 (Fall 1979): 542–48. On machine politicians in saloons, see Duis, pp. 114–42. Regarding the temperance views of some labor leaders, see Ronald Morris Benson, "American Workers and Temperance Reform, 1866–1933" (Ph.D. dissertation, University of Notre Dame, 1974).

38. Regarding progressives and prohibition, see Kerr, *Organized for Prohibition*. On the Eighteenth Amendment, see Duis, pp. 55, 296–7. On speakeasies and the prohibition era, see Andrew Sinclair, *Era of Excess: A Social History of the Prohibition Movement* (New York: Harper and Row, 1962). Regarding home drinking, see Catherine Gilbert Murdock, *Domesticating Drink: Women, Men, and Alcohol in America, 1870–1940* (Baltimore: Johns Hopkins University Press, 1998).

Part III
State and Nation

–10–

"To the King o'er the Water"

Scotland and Claret, c. 1660–1763

Charles C. Ludington

While popular taste in England took an abrupt turn from French wine to Portuguese wine during the late Stuart and early Hanoverian era, and newly invented luxury claret became the wine for the fashionable English elite,[1] the same was not true in Scotland, where inexpensive, traditionally made claret predominated in aristocratic cellars, political clubs, urban howffs, and Highland taverns for the first half of the eighteenth century.[2] This point, seemingly unremarkable given the very real differences in the cultural practices of the two Stuart kingdoms that were united in 1707, is significant for the fact that one of the principal features of the Treaty of Union was the equalization of duties at the English level for almost all goods, including wine. This chapter will attempt to show how and why the relatively poor Scots continued to drink claret when popular English taste had been coerced by financial considerations and encouraged by a particular definition of patriotism to switch to port.

As in England, Scottish taste for claret was deeply ingrained. In Scotland, claret consumption began no later than the thirteenth century, when English and Gascon merchants found a ready market for wine north of the Cheviot Hills. Soon, however, Scottish fondness for claret was too great to be entrusted to foreign merchants alone, and the Scots themselves ventured south to the Bay of Biscay to retrieve greater quantities and values of wine than any other commodity from their new ally France.[3] Indeed, from an economic standpoint if not from a cultural one as well, claret has aptly been called the "lifeblood of the Auld Alliance."[4] The gradual decline of Franco-Scottish political and economic relations during the sixteenth and seventeenth centuries had little influence upon Scottish taste for wine; between 1660 and 1689, one in ten Scottish vessels was employed in the French trade, which was primarily concerned with "the young wine from the Gironde, shipped mainly from Bordeaux."[5] More extraordinary still, the Parliamentary Union with England was equally ineffective in disrupting Scottish taste for wine. In fact, the Wine Act of 1703, passed by an angry Scottish Parliament, had established French wine—and in Scotland that meant claret—as a commodity with which to defy the English government.[6]

High levels of fraud and smuggling in Scotland, as well as fraud and smuggling at high levels, allowed claret to continue in this symbolic role after the Union of

1707. Scottish administrative disregard and even involvement in illegal importation of claret ensured that the flow of wine from Bordeaux to "North Britain" was not stanched by a legislative Union with France's greatest rival. Instead, patriotic Scots (Jacobites or not) grasped at claret for its potent symbolism. Not only did claret represent Scottish taste prior to the Union but, as such, it represented Scottish grievances within, and resistance to, the Union. This was particularly true in the aftermath of 1745, when Scotland was increasingly brought under Westminster's control. As anglicization increased, so too did the symbolic potency of claret. In short, whether it was consumed by active or passive Jacobites, Unionists or anti-Unionists, Tories or Whigs, Presbyterians, Episcopalians, or Catholics, claret represented something far more than a familiar taste: it represented a nostalgic idea of independent Scotland.

Claret in Scotland Prior to the Union of 1707

In Scotland, as in England, claret was the most popular wine at the outset of the Restoration. Indeed, the celebration of Charles II's return provided a moment for citizens of Edinburgh to revel in their favorite wine. Scotland had not fared well under the Commonwealth or Cromwell's Protectorate. Humiliating military defeats in 1650 and 1651 were followed by loss of sovereignty to a combined British and Irish parliament in which English voices and interests predominated. Moreover, the Scots themselves were still bitterly divided between Covenanting Presbyterians and Episcopalians, neither of whom could imagine a society in which the other was wholly tolerated. The Restoration of Charles II, therefore, provided a moment in which Scots could forget their differences and look forward to the future, if only with the help of wine.

> On 19th June commenced a period of thanksgiving through all the parishes of Lothian, for the restoration of the King. The Magistrates and Town Council of Edinburgh went to church in solemn procession ... After service they went with a great number of citizens to the Cross, where a long board, covered with sweetmeats and wine, had been placed ... Here the healths of the King and the Duke of York were drunk with the utmost enthusiasm, three hundred dozens [3,600] of glasses being cast away and broken on the occasion. At the same time, bells rang, drums beat, trumpets sounded, and the multitude and people cheered. The spouts of the Cross ran with claret for the general benefit.[7]

John Evelyn recorded a similar occurrence in London on the very same occasion; however, he did not mention the type of wine.[8] This detail did not escape the anonymous Scottish observer, despite, or perhaps because of the fact that in Scotland wine and claret were practically synonymous. Claret was the common wine of seventeenth-century Scotland and most especially Edinburgh, whose port, Leith, received roughly two-thirds of all the wine legally imported into Scotland from the Restoration through the eighteenth century.[9]

Leith Customs' accounts for the period from the Restoration to the Union are incomplete; however, for those years in which records do exist, the evidence for claret's popularity is overwhelming. For example, during the fiscal year 1672–3, 96 percent of wine cargoes unloaded at Leith originated from Bordeaux.[10] Uninterrupted Leith Customs' records for the years 1682–6, provide a slightly longer-term view of Scottish wine imports in the late-Stewart era. During these four years, in which the pattern of trade was relatively consistent, Leith received between approximately 900 and 1,250 tuns of wine annually, nearly 85 percent of which was definitely French, and 80 percent of the wine-laden ships arriving into Leith came directly from Bordeaux.[11] The precise percentage of claret within the overall annual figures is impossible to deduce because some of the wine from Bordeaux could have been white, and French wines that came on ships arriving from Rouen, St Mâlo, La Rochelle, St Martin (de Ré), or via Rotterdam and Hamburg might have been claret. Given Scottish taste, much of it probably was.[12] But even without these exact figures it can be estimated that at least three-quarters of all wine arriving in Leith during the 1680s was claret.[13] Customs accounts for Leith in the politically troubled years of 1688–9, concur with the overall picture of Scottish taste for wine: 82 percent of the wine was French, every gallon of which came from Bordeaux. The remaining 18 percent of wine was "sack," or sherry from Spain (see Figure 10.1).[14]

Few complete Scottish cellar records from the seventeenth century exist— perhaps because few were kept—but shards of evidence from one prominent

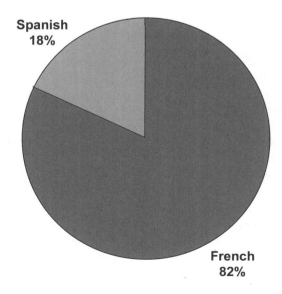

Figure 10.1 Scottish taste for wine, 1688–9
Source: NAS, E72/15/42. Leith Customs' records, imported wine, 1688–9.

household suffice to show that the principal wine being unloaded in Scottish ports was also the dominant wine on Scottish tables. Indeed, so dominant was claret that it served as a reference point for all other wines. When Hugh Campbell wrote to William Douglas, the third Duke of Hamilton on July 22, 1673, informing him that he had sent three tuns of the "best Parisse wine," he explained that "it will not suffer to keep so long as Burdiox wine."[15] Hamilton would have known precisely what that meant.[16] Twenty years later the Duke and Duchess of Hamilton were still fixated on claret. During the 1690s their household consumed "over five hundred bottles of claret, about two hundred bottles of canary, and several dozen of Rhenish and Madeira ... each year."[17]

A principal reason for the popularity of claret in a poor country such as Scotland was not only the weight of tradition, but also its relatively low cost compared to other wines. While ever-increasing duties on French wines helped to push claret to the upper end of the English market in the late seventeenth century, in pre-Union Scotland there were intermittent attempts to hold the price down. To the government and to many Scottish port cities, wine represented the single most valuable import for the revenue that it raised through tariffs. For example, in 1692, £37,000 Scots,[18] or over one third of Edinburgh's income, came from the duty on wine landed at Leith.[19] Generally speaking, the lightest burden was borne by French wines, while Spanish and German wines paid a higher amount. In the 1680s the customs duty stood at £30 Sc. per tun for all wines; however, the excise duty was only £36 Sc. per tun on French wines compared to £54 Sc. per tun on Spanish and German wines. Burghs frequently added their own imposts as a way to raise money, and these also tended to favor French wine as well.[20]

As socially and fiscally privileged as claret was in Restoration Scotland, it was not immune to the effects of King William's wars against Louis XIV. The once cozy political and economic relationship between Scotland and France had been unraveling throughout the seventeenth century and came undone entirely during the 1690s. Scotland was brought into William III's war against France in 1689, and although there was no immediate Scottish embargo on French goods as there was in England, the Scottish Parliament ended its fiscal favoritism for French wine in 1695 by raising the customs duty to £48 Sc. per tun, whereas all other wines paid only £30 Sc. per tun. Additional fees were imposed if the wine was imported via a third country.[21] As French wine was the most popular wine in Scotland, the net effect of the war and the tariff hike was that the volume of official wine imports decreased by a third from their 1680s levels.[22] The tit-for-tat economic warfare that was occurring between Louis XIV and William III's various kingdoms continued when France placed a prohibitive tariff on Scottish woolen goods. In consequence, on January 31, 1701 the Scottish Parliament banned the importation of French wines altogether.[23] Officially the prohibition was effective, because Bordeaux export figures to Scotland declined dramatically from just over 1,000 tuns per year in 1699–1702, to zero tuns in 1702–3.[24] However, a clause in the prohibiting act suggests that Scottish smugglers had already found the loophole so ably exploited by their English equivalents. The act stated, "In case French wine be imported under the name of red wine from St. Sebastian [in Spain]," no such wine could be landed until "the crew swear that the wine is not French."[25] How effective this measure proved in preventing fraud is uncertain.

A new Scottish Parliament was elected in 1703, and it immediately proved to be beyond the control of the Duke of Queensberry, the Crown's Commissioner. Copying a familiar tactic of the English Parliament, the Scottish Parliament refused to vote for financial supply with which to run the Scottish civil government until its grievances were met. It then passed an Act of Security, which asserted that the Scottish Parliament had the right to decide on Queen Anne's successor, and that the two kingdoms would not have the same sovereign unless England granted the Scots freedom of trade with England and all its overseas colonies. Lastly, the act demanded guarantees for the security of Scottish religion, sovereignty, and trade from English interference. If the English still did not get the message that the Scots were dissatisfied with the current political arrangement, the Scottish parliament passed a further act which gave it the right to declare war and make peace on its own if the two nations continued to share a sovereign after Anne's death. The royal government in London found itself in the awkward position of assenting to these acts in the hope that the Scottish Parliament would come into line and vote for the money that the Scottish civil government needed in order to function.

It was at this point that wine became caught in the maelstrom of Anglo-Scottish politics. Having voted in 1701 for an embargo on French wine, the Scottish parliament had outdone even the anti-French English Parliament, whose new ban on French wines did not become effective until 1704. This circumstance pleased both the Crown and Westminster. However, pleasing the English was not the goal of the Scottish embargo; the ban was imposed by an independent Scotland in retaliation for high French tariffs on Scottish goods. However, the Scottish Parliament that convened in 1703 soon found that the wine duty was a double-edged sword. Desperate for money to pay the civil list, the government party in the Scottish Parliament proposed a repeal of the prohibition on French wines in order to collect the revenue brought in by French wine. In other words, the Crown's representatives took the ironic position of advocating trade with the enemy, although only indirectly, while the opposition country party objected to the measure on the grounds that Scotland and France were enemies! As Andrew Fletcher of Saltoun asked in a speech before the parliament on September 13: "are we become greater friends to France now in a time of open war, than we were before in time of peace?"[26] Fletcher's patriotic stance in this instance was disingenuous, or at least underhanded, as his real goal, and that of the country party, was to block any form of supply so that the government would be forced to address the issues raised by the Act of Security.

In the end, the government party was joined by enough Jacobites to overcome the protests of the country party, which suggests that for some members of the Scottish Parliament the Wine Act was not merely about revenue. It was also about the cost and availability of their beloved claret. While Fletcher's point had a certain nationalist appeal, and he was even joined in a formal protest against the act by the claret-loving Duke of Hamilton and the Marquess of Montrose,[27] others saw the Wine Act as a different form of patriotic gesture because it annoyed the English.[28] Fletcher himself understood that point, and stated with bitter sarcasm: "To repeal such a law [that prohibits French wine] in time of war [with France], will sound admirably well in England and Holland: since 'tis no less than a direct breach of our alliance with those nations."[29] But for its supporters, the Wine Act meant that Scots could have their claret and simultaneously send a message to England that Scottish foreign policy was not beholden to English interests. Moreover, it was well known by parliamentarians in Edinburgh and London that French wine coming to Scotland would be smuggled across the border to the detriment of the English Customs revenue. Typically, perhaps, the bombast on either side of the Wine Act debate had nothing to do with the taste for wine among the decision-makers, as a clause in the Act continued to exempt the "peers and barons" of Scotland from paying Customs duty on wine, a privilege they had held since 1597.[30]

Historians have long recognized that the Wine Act of 1703 highlighted problems in Scottish domestic and international relations, and as such was one of the pieces of legislation that helped to precipitate the Union of 1707. In the longer term, however, one effect of the Wine Act has gone largely unrecognized: it helped to establish claret as a symbol of Scottish independence and a commodity with which symbolically to defy the English. More immediately, the Wine Act had the effect of increasing the amount of French wine that was landed in Scotland. Leith Customs records do not exist for the years leading up to the Wine Act; however, Bordeaux records from October 1, 1699 to September 30, 1707 reveal that after 1703 there was an increase to pre-prohibition levels, despite the fact that trade with France was supposedly only indirect.

Table 10.1 Bordeaux wine exports to Scotland, October 1, 1699–September 30, 1707 (in tuns)

1699–1700	1,050	No embargo
1700–1	1,036	"
1701–2	0	Embargo in effect
1702–3	61	"
1703–4	257	Wine Act legalizes indirect trade
1704–5	953	Indirect trade continues
1705–6	853	"
1706–7	1,028	Union begins May 1, 1707
1707–8	48	"

Source: Huetz de Lemps, *Géographie du Commerce*, 147–9.

Just as English merchants and customs officials feared, some of the French wine that was landed in Scotland made its way across the border, either smuggled in directly or sold legally as Iberian wine. This system of "free" or "fair" trading, as it was known in Scotland, was annoying not only to English customs officers; it frustrated Leith administrators as well, because merchants who intended to send their wine to England refused to pay the Leith impost, which was separate from regular Scottish customs and excise duties. However, other than the word of the merchant, there was nothing to guarantee that wine landed at Leith was actually going to England. In this circumstance, some Scottish merchants claimed they were sending the wine south of the border simply to avoid paying the Leith impost. As a result, tensions between Leith officials and merchants rode high until October 26, 1705 when the Leith Council ruled that

> it shall be lawfull to the merchant burgesses of Edinburgh ... to send all sorts of wine from Leith to the south country ... free of impost providing the said wines be carried straight from Leith Wynd up the same and down St. Mary's Wynd without stopping, or lodging in any other place except the waiter's lodge[31]

It is clear from the precise wording of this declaration that a great deal of wine supposedly going from Leith to England was being re-landed just outside of Leith harbor.

How much French wine that actually did make from Scotland to England is unknown, but it was not enough to change the growing belief among Scots that the claret-deprived English drank inferior wine. Writing from London in 1705, William Clelland lamented in a letter to James Erskine, Lord Grange, that "All the wine here is poison'd and all the women pox't at least I would fain fancie so whylst I have no monie."[32] Clelland's opinion aside, the Scottish wine trade with England must have proved lucrative to Scots—and no doubt to some English—traders, because when the terms of the Union were announced in the winter of 1706–7, many merchants scrambled to increase their stocks of claret before the Customs duty on wine was increased to the English level.[33]

Claret in Scotland After the Union of 1707

Despite the Act of Union, which unified tariffs throughout the United Kingdom at the English level, claret remained a tavern wine in Scotland, as well as continuing its role as the wine of the Scottish aristocracy. The wide social range of claret in Scotland is shown by the letters of the English army captain Edward Burt, who in 1725 ventured north to assist General Wade in his massive road-building project to "open up" the Highlands to British Government control. Burt kept an epistolary journal of his travels and, imagining himself something of an epicure, made frequent observations on Scottish food and drink. To be sure, Burt enjoyed regaling his friends in London with hyperbolic tales of the Scottish incivility and the severity of the Highland landscape, but for this reason his testimonies to the ubiquity of claret, his favorite wine, are all the more revealing. On his first night north of the Tweed, Burt was disgusted by the potted pigeons simmering in rancid butter that were presented to him by the innkeeper at Kelso, so he made do with a crust of bread and a "Pint of good Claret."[34] In Edinburgh he was again nauseated, this time by the cook, who was "too filthy an Object to be described." First impressions and exaggerations aside, Burt "supped very plentifully, and drank good French Claret" and all was merry until ten o'clock when Burt was again revolted by the sight of Edinburgh citizens jettisoning their ordure onto the streets from high above in their multistoried "landings."[35] When Burt finally arrived at Inverness, where he was stationed, he found that northern Scotland, although apparently filthy as usual, was not without its creature comforts. "We have one great advantage, that makes amends for many inconveniences," wrote Burt, "that is, the wholesome and agreeable drink—I mean French claret, which is to be met with almost everywhere in Public Houses of any note, except in the heart of the Highlands, and sometimes even there."[36] Burt acknowledged that since the time he and other English soldiers had arrived in Inverness the price of claret had increased from sixteen pence per bottle to two shillings, although "there be no more Duty paid upon it now than there was before, which, indeed, was often none at all."[37] In other words, local merchants knew an opportunity for profit when they saw one. And to English officers stationed in the Highlands, claret was cheap, wholesome and best of all, available, in contrast to what they were used to in England.

The preponderance of claret in the Scottish Highlands held true for the Lowlands as well. An inventory of the third Earl of Leven's wine cellar at Balgonie in 1726 reveals that nearly three-quarters of all his wine was claret, a typical percentage for Lowland aristocrats.[38] Meanwhile, the fact that claret flowed freely in the myriad howffs, or taverns, of eighteenth-century Edinburgh is attested by the vernacular poetry of the day in which the red wine from Bordeaux was the urban bards' elixir of choice. For example, William Hamilton of Gilbertfield (1665–1751) dismissed Scottish whisky for the enlivening virtues of claret:

> The dull-draff drink maks me sae dowff
> A' I can do's but bark and yowff;
> Yet set me in a claret howff
> Wi folk that's chancy,
> My muse may len' me then a gowff
> To clear my fancy.[39]

Allan Ramsay (c. 1685–1758), whose life and work did so much to inspire Robert Burns, was even more effusive about the transcendent qualities of red Bordeaux:

> Gude claret best keeps out the cauld,
> And drives away the winter soon;
> It maks a man baith gash and bauld
> And heaves his saul beyond the moon.[40]

Wine Smuggling and Fraud in Post-Union Scotland

Many historians and wine writers have explained the abundance of claret in relatively poor Scotland, especially when compared to its paucity in England, by claiming that Scottish Customs duties on wine remained lower than English duties even after the Union.[41] As we have already seen, this was not so; after the Union wine duties in Scotland were the same as in any English outport, and thus roughly four pounds per tun less than in London. And yet, the reasons for the continued consumption of claret in Scotland are not straightforward. Indeed, Scottish import records for the first half of the eighteenth century cannot explain the preponderance of claret because officially very little French wine arrived in Scotland. Yet almost no one at the time, and only a few people since have been fooled by what was officially recorded.[42] Claret continued to be the common wine of Scotland long after the Union for the same reason that it could still be found in towns and villages along the south and east coasts of England.[43] Smuggling and fraud kept the cities, towns, and villages from Dumfries to the Orkneys well stocked with red wine from Bordeaux.

From the very outset of the Union, standardization of Customs duties throughout Britain proved exceedingly difficult. In Scotland prior to the Union, as in England and Ireland until the reign of Charles II, Customs duties were farmed. Thus, the Scottish government itself had very little experience in actually gathering the duty on wine.[44] In the spring of 1707 measures were taken to help the Scots conform to both the method of collection and the level of Customs duty taken in England. The Book of Rates, copies of the Acts of Parliament relating to the Revenues of England, standing orders, rules, instructions and five English Customs officers were all sent north,[45] but by July 1707 it was clear that the terms of the Union could not easily be implemented. A letter from the Commissioners of Customs in Edinburgh to the Treasury in London outlined the problems at hand:

> We find all the people and officers here at a loss concerning the computations after the English method, and therefore we shall put such South Britains as are here amongst them, and place the most expert in the ports of greatest business: and all of them shall be attended with plain and full instructions, that so the Comptroller-General and Collectors may agree in their articles, which will prevent the ruin of poor Collectors and their securities, and prove wholesome to the Revenue. We then resolved, that whoever is admitted into the Establishment shall first obtain a certificate that he is affectionate to Her Majesty's Government, Queen Anne; that he is clear of tax-men or late farmers; that he is of sober life and conversation and is not concerned in trade (a thing not hitherto regarded in these parts) nor in the keeping of a public house, or anything else that may divert them from Her Majesty's service.[46]

Nor were confusion and loyalty among Scottish Customs officers the only problems. In many cases they did not have the will or manpower to find and arrest the flow of smuggled goods. The consequence of this was "easy to discern" wrote the

Scottish Commissioners: "goods, Custom free, will by one serpentine stratagem or other, be diffused not only into all parts of the six northern counties [of England] but perhaps to London itself."[47] In other words, Scottish smuggling and fraud would affect the newly created "British" economy, and British government revenue.

Despite the apparent goodwill of the Scottish commissioners and their English assistants, smuggling continued to flourish in Scotland. As T. M. Devine writes, smuggling "became the great growth industry of Scotland during the decades after 1707. This reflected not only a desire to make quick profits but also widespread popular opposition to the new customs and tax regime which had followed in the wake of the Union."[48] As for smuggling wine, "serpentine stratagems" used to circumvent the laws were legion. The most obvious way to smuggle of course, was to "run" the wine past Customs officers and therefore to pay no duty at all. Elaborate sail signals could be used to notify smugglers on shore that the boat full of contraband wine was arriving, which would trigger a signal to proceed to shore if the "coast was clear"; cargo could be unloaded at night, often in a discreet cove or inlet; a ship full of wine could hover off shore and be unloaded slowly by smaller vessels that did not attract the attention of the tide waiters. Ships loaded with cargo were even "wrecked" at a predetermined spot on the coast.[49] When apprehended, ship captains pretended that they had been driven ashore by the weather while on their way to a different country. In the case of Scottish smugglers, this usually meant Norway or a port in the Baltic.[50] "You are to proceed without loss of time to St Martins [St Martin de Ré]," wrote John Steuart of Inverness to Alexander Todd, master of the *Catherine* of Leith in 1726,

> and you are there to address yourself to Mr. Alex. Gordon, Mercht. there, and deliver him the letter herewith given you, who will furnish you in what quantity of salt your ship can taken in, and ye liquor which Mr. Robert Gordon of Bourdeaux is to ship for our accot. which will be about 12 tunns. And sd. Mr. Gordon is to provide you in foreign clearances. Yule endeavour to gett as much as possible, and notice that when, Please God, you return, in case you meet or is taken up by any Coustome House yachtes, to declare yourself bound for Riga in ye Baltick, and be shure you be well furnished with Clearances accordingly. If you gett safe to the firth yule endeavour to calle off Causea [Covesea in Morayshire] where orders will attend you. We beg your utmost care and Dilligence.[51]

There were other methods for running-in wine and other goods as well, all of them risky, because if caught, entire cargoes could be lost without compensation, fines were levied, and punishment, sometimes severe, was exacted on the unlucky smuggler.

A less risky way of illegally importing wine was to engage the Customs official, wittingly or unwittingly, in the act of fraud. There were many, sometimes ingenious, ways of doing this. A general survey of the ports in Scotland, compiled in 1724 for the Lords Commissioners of the Treasury, and specifically for the claret-loving Robert Walpole, stated that the "usual practice at Leith and other ports in Scotland" was to allow "French wines to be entered as from Bilbao and pay dutys under this denomination of Spanish wine." This was certainly a familiar practice to English Customs Commissioners, but the authors of the report stated that it is "at present almost unavoidable, the endeavours of the Commissioners to make the merchants pay up the French dutys for all they import having hither to proved ineffectual."[52] It was difficult enough for Customs officers to prove the provenance of any wine, and in Scotland it could be even more difficult to find a judge who did not sympathize with the "fair traders."[53]

In short, controlling illegal trade was one of the great challenges of the eighteenth-century British state, and controlling it in Scotland was even more difficult than elsewhere. As Rosalind Mitchison explains:

> It was notorious that the Scottish customs were honoured more in the breach than in the observance. Books were not made up, quantities were not checked nor inspections made; if an official was allowed to stay more than a few years in any one customs precinct he would become involved in systematic fraud, receiving fees for non-observance of his duties. All officers belonged to some great man's kin or following and could not easily be sacked.[54]

Indeed, in Scotland, no crime was so respectable as "fair trading," and one of the key items of illicit trade was French wine.[55]

What made wine fraud and smuggling in Scotland so rampant was partly a failure of Westminster adequately to support the Customs officers who were trying to uphold the law, but it was also the involvement of the state's representative in the illicit activities. In one incident in 1716, Archibald Dunbar, Provost of Elgin, was unfortunate enough to have his claret shipment seized by a tide surveyor at Inverness. Elgin used his position to steal the wine back, and when Alexander Erskine, Collector of the Customs at Inverness, protested to him directly, Elgin was unrepentant. Erskine tried to take the matter to a higher authority but the whole affair was ended by the intervention of Charles Eyre, Solicitor to HM Customs, who was himself "a great lover of claret, and probably not averse to accepting cheap contraband wine when it came his way."[56]

For the most part, however, French wine arrived in Scotland through a very simple act. As Writer to the Signet and former Union Commissioner, John Clerk of Penicuik wrote in 1730: "This trade in French wines and brandies [is] founded on notorious perjury for it is well known that since the Union, when high duties in these liquors took place, the wines have been entered on the oaths of the importers as Spanish wines and have all payed the Spanish duties, and the Brandies were run without any duty at all."[57] That this was so is revealed by the surviving Quarterly Customs Accounts for Leith, which begin in 1742, although by that year the so-called "Spanish" wines more often entered as "Portuguese."[58] For example, in the first quarter of 1745, there were nineteen wine cargoes landed at Leith, of which seventeen were supposedly Portuguese, one was French and one was Rhenish.[59] At face value, this quarter was dominated by Portuguese wine imports even more than usual. And yet, of the "Portuguese" wine cargoes, six arrived via Norway in hogshead casks (in other words French casks), and another six are listed as arriving directly from Portugal, but also in hogsheads, and not the actual Portuguese barrel, which was a pipe (equal to two hogsheads). Claiming to carry wine via Norway, usually Bergen or Christiansand, was essentially a form of state-sanctioned deception used by merchants to import French wine.[60] Fake Norwegian documentation of the cargo made the declaration look more genuine because it was supposedly stamped with the authority of another country's port authorities, thus absolving Scottish Customs officers from any involvement should the wine declaration be proven false. This practice also made the fraud more difficult to prosecute, although the use of French casks was no less conspicuous for all that.

More brazen importers did not bother to go via Norway, but simply stated that their French wine was Spanish or Portuguese despite the use of French casks. For example, in one instance in April 1722, John Steuart dispatched the *Margaret* of Inverness to Rotterdam, where it was to pick up "Lisbon salt and about ten tuns of french wine" from Bordeaux, along with two casks of white wine and a hundred flasks of burgundy. More importantly, he asked his Scottish contacts in Rotterdam, the factors Alexander Andrew and Alexander Castairs, to make up invoices and bills of lading for the salt and wine as from Lisbon, "since the ship is to report here as from Lisbon, and the wine to be entered as Portugal wine."[61] In other cases still, what arrived in Scotland as Iberian wine was actually French wine that had been transferred from French hogshead casks to Portuguese pipes and Spanish butts in Guernsey, Jersey, Rotterdam, or again Norway, where these types of Iberian casks were readily available.

Applying this evidence to the Quarterly Customs Accounts reveals a very different picture of the early and mid-eighteenth-century Scottish wine trade. So, whereas the official figures show only one cargo of French wine landed at Leith from January 1 until March 31, 1745, there were probably a minimum of thirteen cargoes of French wine; and instead of seventeen cargoes of Portuguese wine, there were no more than five. The one cargo of Rhenish wine was probably an honest declaration. Because of fraud, precise amounts of wine imported into the Scottish capital can never be known, but rigorous analysis of the Quarterly Customs Accounts in the 1740s reveals that contrary to official evidence, most wine imported into Leith was probably French. Such obvious fraud could not have been committed without the knowledge and involvement of Scottish Customs officers, and if this was the state of affairs in the capital, there is little doubt that fraud was even more rampant in provincial ports.

Indeed, surviving wine bills of Laurence Oliphant, Laird of Gask (1691–1767), help to confirm that claret was readily available outside the capital in the mid eighteenth century. Oliphant had ordered his claret from Perth merchants since at least the 1720s,[62] and this did not change during the Jacobite rebellion of 1745–6, when he fought alongside Bonnie Prince Charlie at Prestonpans and was later appointed treasurer of the Jacobite government in Scotland when the Prince himself ventured south into England. Oliphant held a dinner in celebration of "His Royal Highness the Prince's Birthday" on December 20, 1745, the very day that Charles Edward crossed back into Scotland on his fateful retreat from Derby. The news must not have arrived, because the celebration went ahead and the claret flowed freely. The bill from Ann Hickson, a tavern-keeper at Perth, included 29 bottles of claret, 9 bottles of lisbon, 3 bottles of preignac, 2 bottles of arrack, 1 bottle of rum (for punch), 44 bottles of beer, and only 1 broken glass. That was just for dinner (a mid-afternoon meal in the eighteenth century). The evening supper was somewhat less revelrous, but again the claret flowed far more than any other wine: 11 bottles were served, along with 1 bottle of lisbon, 1 bottle of negus,[63] and 3 bottles of beer.[64] Similar bills exist among the Oliphant of Gask papers throughout 1745–6.[65]

Culloden and After

The Jacobite cause was dealt a mortal blow in 1746 at Culloden, and in the battle's infamous aftermath. But for Scottish traders and Customs officers involved in illicit trade, this was merely the beginning of the end, not the end itself. After the '45, the Hanoverian state slowly began to enforce laws in Scotland that hitherto it had ignored for fear of civil unrest—as had occurred in Glasgow and other towns during the Malt Tax riots of 1725, and in Edinburgh during the Porteous riot of 1736. But the Jacobite army in Derby had put too much fear in the hearts of English and Scottish Whigs for the Hanoverian state to continue to allow Scotland to play by its own rules and pay its own rates. Indeed it was not by coincidence that in 1745, while the Jacobites were in control of Scotland, the duty on French wines was increased by £8 (Sterling) and on all other wines by £4. As before, revenue from wine imports was needed to pay for maintaining a loyal British army. But progress in collecting the new rates was slow, and while direct smuggling of wine was on the decline, fraudulent declarations continued.[66] In a letter to Thomas Barry at Guernsey written on January 14, 1767, the wine merchant Alexander Oliphant of Ayr shows how little had changed since 1707:

> Please ship on board [Captain McGown's] vessel for our account 10 tuns of claret, the best you can afford at about 700 livres per tun and one tun of good malaga white wine. You'll please get the claret rack'd into Spanish casks—one half in pipes and the other in hogsheads[67] and clear it out and ship under the denomination of Spanish Galicia; we must request you'll keep this to yourself, you need not even let the captain into the secret.[68]

In fact, fraud continued in the Scottish wine trade until the 1780s, when it was greatly diminished by Pitt's Customs duty reductions, and then by the outbreak of war with Revolutionary France. But the question remains: Why, prior to that point, did people in Scotland go to such lengths to get their claret?

The most obvious reasons that the Scots smuggled or falsely declared French wine was because claret was their preferred wine and avoiding payment of the high tariffs made economic sense both for the merchant, whose profits were greater, and for the consumer, whose cost was less. From the Treaty of Union in 1707 until 1745 the cost of landing a tun of French wine in Scotland was £46 6s 8 1/2d Sterling, while duty on a tun of Portuguese wine amounted to only £17 13s 9 1/2d. Spanish and German wines paid roughly £1 and £4 per tun more respectively than Portuguese wine. In 1745 and 1763 the duties were increased again, in both cases to help allay the cost of military expenditures. These increases brought the total duty for wines to roughly £62 per tun for French wine, £25 pounds per tun for Portuguese wine, £26 per tun for Spanish wine and £29 for German wine at all British outports; London charges were roughly £4 per tun higher. Given these disparities in wine duties it is no wonder that Scottish merchants chose to pay the lowest duty possible, if any at all.

The Meaning of Claret in Eighteenth-century Scotland

And why did the Scots prefer claret? Partly, because they had been enjoying red wine from Bordeaux since at least the thirteenth century and, as we have seen, by the seventeenth century it had become a national preference. It was therefore logical that, so long as the demand for claret continued, merchants would do their best to supply it. And so long as merchants were successful in supplying claret, whatever their methods, there was little incentive for claret-loving Scots to look for a different wine. Moreover, well-traveled Scots were very aware of the alternative to cheap claret. They had the example of the English to show them. We have seen from William Clelland's letter to Lord Grange in 1705 that already the reputation for common wine in England was debased. Many Englishmen agreed with Clelland, so much so that in 1733 Robert Walpole could write "that far the greatest part of what is sold in publick houses is nothing but a poisonous composition of unknown materials."[69] Walpole had a definite legislative agenda, but evidence suggests he was not grossly exaggerating the truth. Had he been referring to Scotland, he probably would have had a different opinion, as did Captain Burt, who testified in the mid 1720s to the ubiquity and wholesomeness of claret in both Lowland and Highland Scottish taverns. In fact, Burt admitted that for the sake of good wine he was content to be a hypocrite.

> I wish the Reformation [of smuggling] could be made for the Good of the Country (for the Evil is universal); but I cannot say I should even be contented it should extend to the Claret, till my time comes to return to England and humble Port, of which, if I were but only inclined to taste, there is not one Glass to be obtained for Love of Money, either here or in any other Part of Scotland that has fallen within my Knowledge: but this does not at all excite my Regret. You will say I have been giving you a pretty Picture of Patriotism in miniature, or as it relates to myself.[70]

Burt's candid letter inadvertently touches upon the most important reason why the Scots were so determined to get their claret, a reason that was inseparable from the gustatory and economic motivations already mentioned. Whereas Burt self-deprecatingly mocked his own lack of patriotism as an Englishman for preferring smuggled claret to port, Scottish wine drinkers felt themselves patriotic for the very same preference. For one thing, "fair trading" (the ironic term itself is telling) was not merely an economic decision, it was a form of defiance of the Union which was resented by many Scots for the high tariffs that it brought upon formerly inexpensive goods. As T. M. Devine explains,

> Scotland had been accustomed to low taxes and relaxed methods of gathering revenue before the Union, so that the new impositions after 1707 were bitterly resented both on economic grounds and because they were seen as an attempt by London to force Scotland to contribute to the English National Debt, which had swollen hugely to finance the Spanish Succession War.[71]

Furthermore, if the commodity that was clandestinely or fraudulently imported was French, than all the better for the patriotic Scot, because France was not only Scotland's old ally, it was also the home of the exiled house of Stuart (until 1715) and England's greatest enemy.

The link between claret and Scottish patriotism was most commonly manifested in various forms of Jacobite behavior, which were just as likely to be displays of anti-Englishness as they were signs of allegiance to the House of Stuart. Thus, the many Jacobite clubs in Edinburgh, like the National, the Auld Scots, the Anti-Union, the No Surrender, the Scotia's Pride, the Never Give In, the Auld Reekie, and the Anti-English, used great amounts of claret to toast "The Confusion of the Union," "The Cassin' o the Wanchancie Covenant"[72] and most famously of all, "The King o'er the water."[73]

Jacobitism began to die out quickly in Scotland after the '45, while from the same period anglicization of Scotland began to accelerate. This latter process did not entail an immediate or complete transformation of Scotland, and indeed historians of Scottish anglicization continue to debate the time-frame, the primary forces and the degree to which it happened.[74] The evidence from wine suggests that very early under the Union, aspects of what can be termed "English taste for wine" began to penetrate into Scotland. One such example of this trend is that Scottish aristocrats began to prefer fuller-bodied, luxury claret to the "thin," traditionally made claret they had so long enjoyed.[75]

But the real anglicization of Scottish taste mirrored the more profound anglicization of Scotland that began only after 1745. Specifically, this meant a move from traditional claret to port. How substantial this shift was and how quickly it occurred are difficult to ascertain because mid-eighteenth-century Scottish wine import figures are patchy, and where they exist they are less than fully reliable. We have seen that, officially, Portuguese wines were dominant among Leith imports in the early 1740s, but that most of this wine was probably French. In fact, Bordeaux export figures from the same period suggest an annual average of roughly 2,500 tuns of wine to Scotland, far more than the Scottish records acknowledge.[76] But after 1745, and especially during the Seven Years War, there seems to have been a genuine decline in claret consumption. Bordeaux records reveal a shrinking direct trade to the British Isles during this period, and wine import figures for all of Scotland, which were first compiled in 1755, suggest that French wine placed a distant third among Scottish wine imports (Figure 10.2).

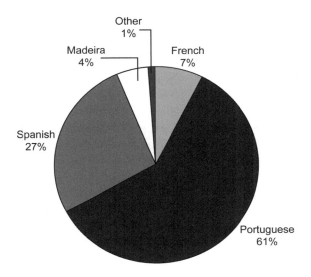

Figure 10.2 Official Scottish taste during the Seven Years War 1755–63
Source: PRO, Customs 14.

Thus, from 1755, when the tremors of war first sounded in the Ohio River Valley, to 1763, when the war ended in an overwhelming British victory in all parts of the globe, French wines officially comprised only 7 percent of all wine imported into Scotland, while, Portuguese wine comprised 61 percent, Spanish wine 27 percent and Madeira 4 percent.[77] How reliable these figures are is impossible to say. Certainly, we know that smuggling and fraudulent declarations still occurred, and therefore, that official statistics are less than fully accurate. Nevertheless, there is evidence to suggest that whatever the actual amount of claret coming into Scotland, that amount was diminishing, and conversely, the amount of port was increasing. For example, heavily anglicized families like the Baillies of Mellerstain seem to have already been consuming more port than claret by the middle of the century.[78] It was this anglicizing trend of Scottish taste for wine that solidified the identification of claret with resistance to anglicization. Most famously, the Scottish dramatist John Home (1722–1808), wrote the following lines sometime after the Seven Years War in response to changing Scottish taste:

> Firm and erect the Caledonian stood
> Old was his mutton and his claret good.
> Let them drink port, the English statesman cried.
> He drank the poison and his spirit died.[79]

The masculine imagery of Home's epigram is clear, as is the supposedly emasculating effect of "English" port. Home, after all, was a proud Scot. However, he was also a Scottish Hanoverian who fought against the Jacobites in 1745–6, and in his politics and prose he was a fervent British patriot.[80] In short, Jacobitism had nothing to do with his claret consumption. Nor is Jacobitism an adequate explanation of the general Scottish zeal for claret during the early and mid eighteenth century. The symbolism of claret was far more expansive than that; it represented resistance to the Union and historic ties to France, but ultimately it stood for an idea of the Scottish past that gradually eroded as Scotland was being subsumed by the Union into a larger British state. Nostalgia for that past was not uniquely Jacobite; it affected all quarters of Scotland, even where Britishness was happily embraced. After all, one can be pulled by both the future and the past, as many proud Scots were. Within this ambivalent state of mind, claret drinking was a decidedly "Scottish" act, even if, like Home, one looked forward to a prosperous British future.

Notes

1. For a discussion of changes in popular and elite taste for wine in England in the seventeenth and early eighteenth centuries, see Charles C. Ludington, "Be sometimes to your country true: The Politics of Wine in England, 1660–1714," in Adam Smyth (ed.), *A Pleasing Sinne: Drink and Conviviality in Early Modern England* (Woodbridge, Suffolk: Boydell and Brewer, 2004), pp. 89–106; Ludington, "Politeness and the Meaning of Luxury Claret in Early-Eighteenth Century England", in A. Lynn Martin and Barbara Santich (eds), *Culinary History* (Brompton, Australia: East Street Press, 2004) pp. 77–86; Ludington, *Politics and the Taste for Wine in England and Scotland, 1660–1860* (Columbia University, Ph.D, 2003), chaps. 1–3.

2. Eighteenth-century clubs in Scotland, most numerous in Edinburgh, were not exclusive gentlemen's clubs; rather, they were informal gatherings of politically like-minded men who usually met in howffs to sing and drink wine. The howffs themselves were urban taverns, which were especially necessary in Edinburgh where kitchens were a rarity. See Robert Chambers, *Traditions of Edinburgh* (1824; reprint, Edinburgh: W. and R. Chambers, 1980); Marie W. Stuart, *Old Edinburgh Taverns* (London: Hale, 1952).

3. Billy Kay and Cailean Maclean, *Knee Deep in Claret, a Celebration of Wine and Scotland* (Edinburgh: Mainstream, 1983), p. 9. For a general background on

medieval Scottish wine trade and consumption, see chaps. 1–6; and S. G. E. Lythe and J. Butt, *An Economic History of Scotland, 1100–1939* (Glasgow: Blackie, 1975), p. 69.

4. F. Marian McNeill, *The Scots Cellar* (Moffat: Lochar, 1992), p. 32.

5. Bruce Lenman, *An Economic History of Modern Scotland, 1660–1976* (London: Batsford, 1977), p. 38.

6. T. C. Smout, *Scottish Trade on the Eve of Union, 1660–1707* (Edinburgh: Oliver and Boyd, 1963), p. 170.

7. Quoted in Robert Chambers, *Domestic Annals of Scotland: from the Reformation to the Revolution*, 2 vols. (Edinburgh: W. and R. Chambers, 1858), Vol. 2, p. 261.

8. John Evelyn, *The Diary of John Evelyn*, 6 vols., ed. E. S. de Beer (Oxford: Oxford University Press, 1955), Vol. 3, p. 281.

9. Bruce Lenman, *Economic History of Modern Scotland*, p. 38, states that between 1660 and 1689, Leith received 60–70 percent of all wine imports, Glasgow a little less than 20 percent, and no other port as much as 5 percent. Leith continued its dominance of the Scottish wine trade long after the Union, consistently accounting for over two-thirds of all legally imported wine; see National Archives of Scotland, Edinburgh (NAS), E501 series, Comptroller General's account of customs, 1707–1830. From the production side of the equation, Bordeaux export figures from 1698 to 1716 reveal that Leith was far and away the principal Scottish destination for wine shipments to Scotland; see Christian Huetz de Lemps, *Géographie de Commerce de Bordeaux à la fin du règne de Louis XIV* (Paris: Mouton, 1975), pp. 110,117.

10. NAS, E72/15/15. Leith Customs records, imported wine, 1672–3. All Customs records in this series begin on Nov. 1 and end Oct. 31 of the following year.

11. NAS, E72/15/27, 29, 33 and 38. Leith Customs records, imported wine, 1682–6.

12. This conclusion concurs with Smout's, *Scottish Trade*, p. 170: most "French wine" was "certainly red wine, and most of the red wine was claret from Bordeaux, the favourite drink of Scotsmen until well into the eighteenth century."

13. This figure is based on the percentage of wines arriving at Leith from Bordeaux, the paucity of seventeenth-century Scottish references to white wine that was not of Spanish origin, and the fact that Bordeaux records from the period show almost all of the exported white wine going to Holland. Huetz de Lemps, *Géographie du Commerce*, pp. 104–15, 181–213.

14. NAS, E72/15/42. Leith Customs records, imported wine, 1688–9.

15. NAS, GD406/1/970, Campbell to Douglas, July 22, 1673.

16. Since at that time almost all wine was made to be consumed within the year of production, it is likely that Campbell was advising Hamilton to drink the "Parisse wine" as quickly as possible. Paris wine was probably wine from vineyards just outside of Paris, which were once plentiful.

17. Rosalind K. Marshall, *The Days of Duchess Anne: Life in the Household of the Duchess of Hamilton, 1656–1716* (London: Collins, 1973), p. 100.

18. At the end of the seventeenth century and just prior to the Union, the Scottish pound stood at 12:1 in relation to the English pound (Sterling). Thus, £37,000 Scots was roughly £3,083 Sterling.

19. Kay and Maclean, *Knee Deep in Claret*, p. 64.

20. *Acts of the Parliament of Scotland* (*APS*) IX, 457.

21. *APS*, IX, 460a–b.

22. Smout, *Scottish Trade*, pp. 170 and 253.

23. I William 8, n. 11 (1701), "Act discharging Wine, Brandy and all other Liquors of the growth of France," *APS*, X, 278–9.

24. Huetz de Lemps, *Géographie du Commerce*, table 7, p. 147.

25. *APS*, X, 278–9.

26. Andrew Fletcher, "Speeches by a member of the Parliament," in *Political Works*, ed. John Robertson (Cambridge: Cambridge University Press, 1997), p. 169.

27. *APS*, X, 102.

28. Rosalind Mitchison, *A History of Scotland*, 2nd ed. (London: Routledge, 1995), p. 306; and Smout, *Scottish Trade*, p. 259.

29. Fletcher, "Speeches by a member of the Parliament," in *Political Works*, ed. Robertson, p. 169.

30. *APS*, XI, 103a, 112a.

31. Quoted in Kay and Maclean, *Knee Deep in Claret*, pp. 74–5.

32. NAS, GD124/15/259/1, Clelland to Erskine, Lord Grange, Nov. 10, 1705.

33. See, for example: National Library of Scotland (NLS), Ms. 1520 (65), *Letter from a Scots Factor at London, to a merchant in Edinburgh, Concerning the House of Commons; to prevent the importation of wines and other Goods from Scotland* (London, April 17, 1707), 1; NAS, GD 124/15/537, Sir Samuel McClellan to the Earl of Mar, April 22, 1707. In this letter McClellan says that almost all wine coming in to Leith was from France.

34. Edward Burt, *Letters from a Gentleman in the North of Scotland to his Friend in London*, 2 vols. (London: S. Birt, 1754), Vol. 1, p. 15.

35. Ibid., pp. 19–20.

36. Ibid., p. 138.

37. Ibid., pp. 138–9.

38. NAS, GD26/6/178, "Inventory of the wine cellar at Balgony, taken the 28th May 1726, and the key delivered up by Mr. Ker to the Earle of Leven."

39. "In praise of Claret," from McNeill, *Scots Cellar*, pp. 158–59: *dull draff-drink*, whisky; *dowff*, dull, spiritless; *yowff*, sharp yelling; *howff*, a haunt, resort, tavern; *chancy*, lucky, bringing luck; *gowff*, blow, hit.

40. From "To the Ph__, an Ode" (1721), in *The Works of Allan Ramsay*, eds Burns Martin and John W. Oliver, 2 vols. (Edinburgh: W. Blackwood and Sons, 1944–5), Vol. 1, p. 223; *gash*, lively, talkative.

41. Kay and Maclean speak of the "reduced customs differential following the Union," *Knee Deep in Claret*, p. 75; however, there was no differential at all; François Crouzet, writing about exports to the British Isles, says, "It was Scotland and especially Ireland that were in fact the principal outlets for wines from Bordeaux; because the customs duties were less elevated, less prohibitive than in England, consumption of French wines was relatively greater." [my translation]. Crouzet, "Le Commerce de Bordeaux," in F.-G. Pariset (ed.), *Bordeaux au XVIIIème Siècle*, vol. V of Charles Higounet (ed.), *Histoire de Bordeaux* (Bordeaux: Fédération Historique du Sud-Ouest, 1968), p. 263. Crouzet's analysis is correct in the case of Ireland but not so for Scotland, where the Customs duty was the same as in England after 1707.

42. For those who have been fooled, see for example, A. D. Francis, who states: "In England Spanish wines were still well to the fore and still more so in Scotland. Scotland was a poor country and perhaps smuggled more than paid customs duty, but in these years it took over 1,000 tuns of Spanish wine, about 90% of its total imports of wine," *The Wine Trade* (London: A. and C. Black, 1972), p. 152. Unfortunately, Francis does not cite his Scottish sources, although in any case his assessment is incorrect. Most Scottish wine imports at the time came directly or indirectly from France. Huetz de Lemps also errs in his analysis when he writes: "Le commerce des vins de Bordeaux vers l'Ecosse semble donc avoir reçu un coup mortel pendant la guerre [1702–13] du fait de l'Acte d'Union avec l'Angleterre. Les Ecossais perdirent l'habitude de boire du vin pour se 'reconvertir' a d'autres boissons comme la biere et le whisky!" *Géographie du Commerce*, 179. This statement is based on official export figures from Bordeaux for the years 1713–16, and not on Scottish import figures or knowledge of Scottish smuggling. In effect, he was speaking of the late eighteenth century, but not the early eighteenth century.

43. Cambridge University Library (CUL), CH (H) 41/18/6, "Of the running of wine," a report to Robert Walpole dated March 1733, shows that most French wine was smuggled into the south coast. See also, André Simon, *Bottlescrew Days: Wine Drinking in England during the Eighteenth Century* (London: Duckworth, 1926), p. 85.

44. For an extensive discussion of Scottish Customs gathering before the Union, see Smout, *Scottish Trade*, pp. 32–46.

45. Parliamentary Report, C. 8706 (LXXXV, 1897), *Customs Tariffs of the United Kingdom from 1800–1897. With some notes upon the history of the more important branches of the receipt from the year 1660*, p. 19. Reprinted letter from the Commissioner of Customs in England to the Treasury, April 22, 1707, and reprinted minute of the Treasury, April 22, 1707.

46. Parliamentary Report, C. 8706, *Customs Tariffs*, pp. 19–20. Reprinted letter from the Commissioners of Customs in Scotland to the Treasury, July 15, 1707.

47. Parliamentary Report, C. 8706, *Customs Tariffs*, p. 20.

48. T. M. Devine, *The Scottish Nation, 1700–2000* (Harmondsworth: Penguin, 1999), pp. 56–7.

49. CUL, CH (H) 40/16, Report of Robert Paul, Richard Sankey and Samuel Kettilby of their general survey of the ports of Scotland to the Lords Commissioners of HM Treasury, Sept. 17, 1724; Kay and Maclean, *Knee Deep in Claret*, chaps. 9 and 12.

50. Simon, *Bottlescrew Days*, pp. 85–9.

51. *Letter Book of Bailie John Steuart of Inverness, 1715–1752*, ed. William Mackay (Edinburgh: Printed at the University Press by T. and A. Constable for the Scottish History Society, 1915), June 22, 1756, p. 258.

52. CUL, CH (H) 40/16, Report ... general survey of the ports of Scotland, Sept. 17, 1724.

53. Ibid.; Kay and Maclean, *Knee Deep in Claret*, chap. 8.

54. Mitchison, *History of Scotland*, p. 324.

55. *Letter Book of Bailie John Steuart*, ed. Mackay, p. xxxiii.

56. Kay and Maclean, *Knee Deep in Claret*, p. 151.

57. Cited in Kay and Maclean, *Knee Deep in Claret*, p. 101.

58. NAS, E504/22, Port of Leith, Collector's Quarterly Accounts.

59. NAS, E504/22/1, Port of Leith, Collector's Quarterly Accounts, Jan. 1, 1745–March 31, 1745.

60. Apparently, Norway's role in this deception went back to the seventeenth century at least. Smout, *Scottish Trade*, p. 158.

61. *Letter Book of Bailie John Steuart*, ed. Mackay, April 5, 1722, pp. 179–80.

62. NLS, Adv. 82.3.3, ff. 23, 147, wine bills from M. Wood to Laurence Oliphant, Laird of Gask, 1723.

63. Negus was a drink made of wine, hot water, lemon juice, sugar, and nutmeg.

64. NLS, Adv. 82.4.1, f. 47, wine and supper bill from Anne Hickson, to Oliphant of Gask, Perth, Dec. 20, 1745.

65. See, for example, NLS, Adv. 82.3.6, f. 154; 82.4.1, ff. 128, 176, miscellaneous wine bills, Oliphant of Gask, 1745–6.

66. Louis M. Cullen, *Smuggling and the Ayrshire Economic Boom of the 1760s and 1770s*, Ayrshire Monograph no. 14 (Darvel, Ayrshire: Ayrshire Archaeological and Natural History Society, 1994), pp. 10, 24.

67. Given the purpose of Oliphant's request, it is surprising that he wanted hogsheads. Since he specified Spanish casks, he probably meant a half-butt, which was roughly the equivalent in volume, although not in shape, to a hogshead. The important thing was that a trained eye could tell the difference between French, Spanish, and Portuguese casks.

68. NAS, GD1/306/1, Oliphant of Ayr to Barry, Jan. 14, 1767.

69. [Robert Walpole?], *A letter from a member of parliament to his friend in the country, concerning the duties on wine and tobacco* (London, 1733), p. 16.

70. Burt, *Letters from a Gentleman*, Vol. 1, pp. 171–2.

71. Devine, *Scottish Nation*, p. 20.

72. The repeal of the unlucky Union.

73. In this toast, two drinkers would toast each other while holding their glasses over a pitcher of water. Thus, a treasonous toast to "the king over the water," i.e. James II or III, could be denied, as the toast could be claimed as being given to "the king," i.e. the Hanoverian king, over the pitcher of water. Chambers, *Traditions*, esp. pp. 142 and 339; McNeill, *Cellar*, pp. 56–75; Kay and Maclean, *Knee Deep in Claret*, chap. 7.

74. The literature here is extensive, but see in particular: Linda Colley, *Britons: Forging the Nation, 1707–1837* (New Haven: Yale University Press, 1992); Colin Kidd, *Subverting Scotland's Past: Scottish Whig historians and the creation of an Anglo-British identity, c. 1689–1830* (Cambridge: Cambridge University Press, 1993); Murray Pittock, *Inventing and Resisting Britain: Cultural Identities in Britain and Ireland, 1685–1789* (New York: St. Martin's, 1997).

75. Ludington, *Politics and the Taste for Wine in England and Scotland*, chap. 4.

76. Archives Nationale, Paris, F12/1500, cited in Crouzet, "Commerce de Bordeaux," 264.

77. Public Record Office (PRO), Customs 14. These figures are based on my own tabulations and are explored in much greater detail in Ludington, *Politics and the Taste for Wine in England and Scotland*, chap. 5.

78. Cited in Kay and Maclean, *Knee Deep in Claret*, pp. 104–5.

79. John Home, *The Works of John Home, Esq., now first collected. To which is prefixed, an account of his life and writings, by Henry Mackenzie, Esq.*, 3 vols. (Edinburgh: A. Constable and Co., 1822), Vol. 1, p. 164. Mackenzie gives no date for the epigram, but writes: "As to the port-wine, it is well known that Mr. Home held it in abhorrence. In his younger days, claret was the only wine drank by gentlemen in Scotland. His epigram on the enforcement of the high duty on French wine in this country, is in most people's hands." Given this evidence, I date the epigram from the 1760s. An alternative date is supplied by James Crichton-Browne, "Claret in Scotland," *The National Review* 80 (1922): 404, who claims that Home wrote the epigram as a "protest against Pitt's Budget" (i.e. sometime in the mid 1780s). This seems unlikely, however, as Pitt's budget reforms actually reduced the tariff on French wines.

80. For Home's Britishness, see for example, act I, scene 1 of his most famous play, *Douglas* (first performed in Edinburgh in 1756).

–11–

Revenue and Revelry on Tap

The Russian Tavern

Patricia Herlihu

Vodka is fascinating because it shows more clearly than any other foodstuffs the links between social history and political history—the extent to which the life of the Russian state and the life of the Russian village were intertwined.[1]

Pre-Emancipation, 1550–1862

Taverns and the State

The Russian tavern has appeared in many forms and under various names. Until the 1550s, taverns where eating and drinking occurred were called *korchma*s, from the word for strong drink (*korchma*). Other sorts of taverns emerged over the next three centuries, notably the *kabak* (tavern), *traktir* (pub or inn), *kruzhechnyi dvor* (tankard bar), *piteinyi dom* (drink house or pub), *pivnaia* (beer hall), *shinok* (illegal saloon), and the *kazennaia vinnaia lavka* (state liquor store).[2]

Like virtually every institution from tsarist to Soviet times drink establishments were subject to state-imposed names, rules, and functions. Rulers inevitably had certain objectives in mind such as to promote alcoholic consumption as a means to raise revenue. At times, however, rulers sought to limit consumption hoping to improve labor productivity or to present a better image of society. The state also tended to discourage any form of free association for fear of political unrest. At times taverns were regulated, limited, or even abolished to prevent potentially dangerous discussions.[3]

Russian rulers understood that by judiciously distributing drinking privileges, they could instill that highly coveted quality—loyalty. Vasilii (Basil) III, who reigned from 1505 to 1533 "built a house for his servants on the far bank of the Moskva River where they could drink beer and mead, which was forbidden to other Muscovites."[4] In a cash-starved society rulers rewarded personal and state service, not with monetary payments or salaries, but with gifts of titles, land, serfs, privileges, medals, and access to feasting and alcoholic beverages.

When Ivan IV (The Terrible), son of Vasilii III, returned to Moscow from conquering Kazan in the middle of the sixteenth century, he closed *korchma*s, establishments where men and women gathered for drinking, eating, games, conversation, music, and singing. In their place, he set up taverns to which he gave the Tatar name *kabak* where only his special secret police (*oprichniki*) could drink vodka. He thus maintained a revenue flow from the sale of vodka while ensuring his royal person fealty from the consumers, his henchmen.[5] Even foreign *oprichniki* had the right to drink in and own *kabaks*. Heinrich von Staden, a German who served from 1569 to 1572, admits in his memoir that he "made a lot of money by keeping a tavern."[6]

To establish a monopoly on all vodka sales, Ivan IV opened *kabaks* to the common people. His trusted officials (*tseoval'niki*) kissed the cross and swore to remit to the tsar all the taxes collected on drink. The Crown jealously guarded this privilege; in one year alone (1563–64) within the jurisdiction of the Moscow Simonov Monastery, four families were accused of "building and operation of *kabaks* ... [and] selling in these *kabaks* many various drinks, such as vodka, beer, and mead."[7] Four years after the death of Ivan IV, Giles Fletcher, a visiting English diplomat, writes:

> In every great town of his Realm he [the Tsar] has a Kabak or drinking house, where is sold *aqua vitae* (which they call Russe wine) mead, beer, etc. Out of these he recruits rent that amounts to a great sum of money. Some yield 800 some 900, some 1000 some 2000 or 3000 rubles a year. Wherein besides the base, and dishonorable means to increase his treasury, many foul faults are committed. The poor laboring man ... many times spends all from his wife and children. Some use to lay in twenty, thirty, forty rubles or more into the Kabaks, and vow themselves to the pot till all that be spent. And this (as he will say) was for the honor of *Hospodare*, or the Emperor. You shall have there that have drunk all the way to the very skin, and walk naked (whom they call *Naga*). While they are in the Kabak, none may call them forth whatever cause there be, because he hinders the Emperor's revenue.[8]

By 1600 the state collected 300,000 to 400,000 rubles annually, or about 21 percent of the total state budget and 37.5 percent of the yearly taxes.[9] Under Boris Godunov, who ruled from 1598 to 1604, the state exerted even greater control over vodka, a monopoly that was codified in the *Ulozhenie,* a law of 1649. In order to protect its monopoly on the production and sale of vodka, the state punished moonshiners severely. Some offenders paid large fines.[10] A visitor to Muscovy during the latter half of the sixteenth century notes, "and if in someone's house they will find as little as a drop of liquor, then his entire house will be demolished, his belongings will be confiscated, the servants and the neighbors living on the same street will be punished, and the owner himself will be sentenced to a life-long prison sentence."[11]

At the end of the sixteenth century nobles could distill spirits and brew beer for themselves, but peasants could not. In 1869 Ivan Pryzhov in his classic history of taverns confirms the policy, "in the *kabak* it was ordered only to drink and only for the masses, i.e. peasants, and common city-folk, for they were forbidden from producing [alcoholic] drinks at home; all of the other people, however were allowed to drink in their houses."[12]

Monks as well as nobles were allowed to produce and consume their own spirits, but they could not sell them. Ivan IV's punishment was the "flogging of monks who produced alcoholic beverages for sale and who operated [drinking houses]."[12] Monks were allowed to impose fines on illicit sales of alcohol within their territories. This income compensated them for their colonizing, economic development, and administration of new territories.[14]

Ivan IV's policy of forcing all but the privileged to drink in *kabaks*—and only to drink, not eat—affected both the treasury and the imbibers. The sale of drink was more profitable than the sale of food. Ivan Pryzhov condemned the absence of food, claiming that it caused drunkenness, whereas 300 years earlier in *korchmas* people were merry but restrained in their drinking. By insisting that food had to accompany drink, Pryzhov was reinforcing an age-old custom. As Robin Milner-Gulland observes:

> A certain ceremoniousness still pervades drinking and to some extent eating in Russia to this day, even at quite a crude or humble level. Vodka tippling in whatever circumstances has it unbudgeable rituals, including toasts (themselves formalized) and the obligatory consumption of some kind of food, however exiguous: Westerners have looked on in wonder to see Russian drinkers, half seas over, stumble out to look for edible herbs in the garden, or carefully cut a boiled sweet into three with a penknife, so as to have a symbolic meal with their drink.[15]

Adam Olearius, a German traveller in Muscovy in the 1630s, relates:

> The pothouses, saloons, and taverns, or kruzhechnye dvory as they are now called, bring the Grand Prince—who now owns all of them through the country—an extraordinary amount of money, since the Russians know no restraint in drinking vodka. Formerly the boyars and magnates had their own taverns in various places, which they leased to different individuals, as the Grand Prince did also. However, the boyars raised the rental charge so high that many of the lessees were ruined. Now the boyars and magnates are forbidden to maintain taverns, for all have been taken over by the Grand Prince. In each town a particular house has been designated where vodka, mead and beer can be obtained, and the receipts go exclusively to His Tsarist Majesty's treasury. In Novgorod there had always been three taverns, each of which turned in 2,000 rubles for a total of 6,000; under the new order, the sum is greater yet. There are around a thousand such taverns in the country, though not all are as profitable.[16]

A major problem, however, was that the managers of the tsar's taverns took as their own much of the profit. By the middle of the eighteenth century a new system was devised to ensure that the state received a reliable stream of revenue from the sale of vodka in taverns. Merchants, called tax farmers, "obtained a concession [*otkup*] from the state to sell a certain amount of liquor at a fixed price over a four-year period. The concession was a monopoly to sell in a specific number of taverns or a given area."[17] The tax farmer (*otkupchik*) pledged his property as security to deliver the agreed upon lump sum to the state each month in anticipation of sales.

Tax farmers known to gouge their customers were highly unpopular.[18] In order to sweeten the deal, the state made them quasi-officials, bestowing on them the right to carry swords, all sorts of privileges and tax exemptions, and declared them under the protection of the Empress Catherine II (the Great). Their taverns were allowed to display the Imperial Eagle. In fact, taverns were state property and the state regulated how many taverns there should be and where they should be placed. The tax farmer had only the concession to sell alcohol and to lease a certain fixed number of taverns. Because the tax farmer could not control the number of taverns or raise the price of vodka, he had to find ways to increase consumption or dilute the product in order to increase his profits.[19]

The tax farming system offered several advantages to the state. It was spared the expense of collecting taxes for every sale; and the tax farmers bore the brunt of policing as well as the criticism and hatred of consumers for the high prices and poor quality of the vodka sold in taverns. Between 1767 and 1863, the government garnered on average one third of its revenue from liquor. In fact, the defence budget that contributed to Russia's status as a great power was largely dependent on the liquor tax farms. As David Christian notes, "if, at any point in the nineteenth century, all Russians had suddenly decided to stop drinking vodka, the government would have faced bankruptcy."[20] Not only the government, it should be added, but also the tax farmers and bribed officials would have lost their livelihood. Not that there was any danger of such a mass renunciation.[21] Tax farmers delivered huge sums to the state and also showered officials with bribes so that they would not enforce any limits on the production and sale of vodka.[22]

Taverns and Society: Urban Taverns

As soon as *kabak*s were founded, they were criticized. In the 1550s one churchman thunders:

> But here we see that in the town called Pskov and in all Russian towns there are taverns and whores. For drunkards never frequent taverns without whores. For if the taverns are not removed—this is known, that there is both drunkenness and whoring for the unmarried and fornication for the married—there shall be retribution for those who grow rich thereby.[23]

In the 1630s Olearius observes:

> While we were there (Moscow), taverns and pothouses were everywhere, and anyone who cared to could go in and sit and drink his fill. The common people would bring all

their earnings into the tavern and sit there until, having emptied their purses, they gave away their clothing, and even their nightshirts, to the keeper, as then went home as naked as they had come into the world.[24]

To combat drunkenness the state ordered *kabak*s to sell vodka only by the jug or tankard and changed the name of the taverns to *kruzhechnyi dvor*. This reform that sought to limit consumption by selling larger containers failed, as did many similar measures over the next nearly 500 years. Olearius explains how drinkers coped:

> However, daily drunkenness has hardly diminished as a result of this measure, for several neighbors pool their funds to buy a tankard or more, and do not disperse until they have emptied it to the dregs. Some of them also buy up large quantities and secretly sell it by the cup. It is true that now fewer people are seen naked, although the number of drunkards wandering about and wallowing in the gutters is not much reduced.[25]

The state made money not only through sales but also by imposing fines.[26] Nikon, the Patriarch in the 1660s, and an ardent reformer and implacable foe of alcohol, sought to put an end to pagan revelry in taverns. He banned musical instruments in taverns and elsewhere and had them confiscated and burned.[27] His influence was so great that he succeeded in abolishing taverns and restricting bulk sales of alcohol to state stores that barred clerics, extended no credit, and were closed on Sundays. The state lost so much revenue, however, that the *kabak*s were back in operation within ten years.

Catherine II, who reigned from 1762 to 1796, changed the name of taverns to *piteinye domy* (drinking houses), but the name *kabak* persisted although it came to take on the pejorative meaning of "pig-sty."[28] Not all *kabak*s were filthy: a charming lithograph made in 1857 depicts two peasants in Moscow visiting a neat tavern; one peasant who has been in the city a little longer than the other, a newcomer, explains how to play billiards and cautions against gambling, although he does not warn about excessive drinking.[29]

Taverns and Society: Rural Taverns

Rural taverns were found along the major roads or at market and fair sites. One entrepreneur opened a tavern in the mid 1800s near the hunting preserve of Alexander II,

> ... where everyone gathered for the hunt and the soldiers' encampment. For the duration of the hunting season he charged thirty kopecks for a small glass of schnapps and a ruble for a finer sort. He charged 30 kopecks for a bread roll and a ruble for a piece of paper on which one could write a petition to the tsar. He charged whatever he saw fit and no one objected. In this way he managed to take in a tidy two hundred thousand rubles, in addition to the sixty thousand rubles his wife earned running a business of her own.[30]

Ivan Turgenev paints an appealing picture of a rural tavern in the mid nineteenth century:

> At the head of the ravine, a few steps from the point where it begins as a narrow crevice, there stands a small, square hut, quite by itself and apart from the others. It is roofed with straw and it has a chimney; one window is turned towards the ravine like a watchful eye, and on winter evenings, when illuminated from within, may be seen afar off through the faint frost-haze twinkling like a lodestar for many a passing peasant. A small blue sign has been fixed above the door of the hut, since this hut is a tavern nicknamed The Welcome. Drink cannot be said to be sold in this tavern below the normal price but it is patronized much more assiduously than all the other establishments of this kind in the locality.[31]

The interior of Turgenev's fictional tavern consists of:

> a dark entrance and a parlor divided in two by a partition, beyond which none of the patrons has the right to go. In this partition, above a wide oak table, there is a big longitudinal opening. The drink is sold at this table, or counter. Labeled bottles of various sizes stand in rows on the shelves directly opposite the opening. In the forward part of the hut, which is given over to the patrons, there are benches, one or two empty barrels and a corner table. Rural taverns are for the most part fairly dark, and you will hardly ever see on the log walls any of those brightly colored popular prints with which most peasant huts are adorned.[32]

Peasants, serfs, and rural factory workers mingled with members of the gentry in that fictional tavern to listen to singing contests, and to have their fill of drink. Although the patrons were often drunk, Turgenev describes no violent outbreaks.

Violence to the point of death, however, results for one unfortunate drinker in a famous story by Nikolai Leskov. A Russian, having won a suit against a German, embarks "on a spree, the gayest and wildest spree of his life."[33] For three days and three nights he pub crawls, treating all his friends, but in the end he mortally wounds himself by falling from a tall ladder in a drunken stupor while vainly attempting to find his way home. More commonly, violence came in the form of drunken brawls on paydays when workers drank to excess.

Women owned taverns as early as the sixteenth century; Pushkin places three monks in a tavern run by a woman in *Boris Godunov*.[34] We also learn from the memoirs of a Jew who lived in the Lithuanian *shtetl* Kamenets, that women ran many taverns in the mid nineteenth century.[35] Kotik also relates that taverns served cheese, herring, and pickled cucumbers along with drink, confirming that *kabaks* had revived the custom of serving food along with drink.[36] In the large Lithuanian village of Kobrin, a Jewish family owned an inn and tavern run by the wife:

> Gentry from all over the district used to put up at her elegantly furnished inn or stop by for drinks at her well-run tavern. The inn's furniture was beautiful, and it also had a

ballroom with a piano for the use of the lords. At one time, before the Polish rebellion, the whole concern had been a virtual gold mine.[37]

Post-Emancipation, 1862–1917

Taverns and the State

To establish a better ethical business climate without corruption and to exert a tighter grip on vodka revenue, the state abolished tax farming on January 1, 1863, part of a series of "Great Reforms," that began with the emancipation of the serfs two years earlier. It gave the state a monopoly on taxation, but not the sale of alcohol. Not able to sink their capital into liquor with a guarantee of large profits, more entrepreneurs chose now to invest in Russia's infrastructure: transportation including railroads and banks and in exploiting natural resources. The new excise system also led to corruption, the adulteration of vodka, and the proliferation of taverns. For example, in St Petersburg in 1863 there were 1,840 *kabak*s, 562 inns, 399 alcoholic beverage stores, 229 wine cellars and several other miscellaneous places where vodka was sold.[38] While it is difficult to assess who, in the immediate aftermath of Emancipation, gained or lost economically, a contemporary observed,

> poverty became widespread, and many Jewish families neared starvation … The only ones that did not feel the pinch were the tavern keepers, who, even before that, had made a good living from the peasants coming on Sundays—market day—to sell their produce and get drunk. Actually, their income increased considerably, for the peasants could now allow themselves to drink more vodka. They no longer feared the lord's flogging if they were still drunk on Monday.[39]

Peasant communes lost revenue, because a village had the power to restrict *kabak*s in its commune and the right to tax them.

In 1894, another reform was effected along with the next big push toward industrialization and railroad building. This time the state created a monopoly on vodka under the leadership of the Minister of Finance, Sergei W. Witte. He argued that if the state became the sole purchaser and seller of all spirits produced for the internal market, it could regulate the quality of vodka as well as limit sales so that people would learn to drink in a regular but moderate fashion. Witte insisted that the monopoly was an attempt to reform the people's drinking habits, not to increase revenue. The result, however, of producing a high quality of vodka and selling it cheaply was that revenue from vodka became the single greatest source of state revenue and also one of the largest industries in Russia.

The new law also closed down taverns and restricted sales of alcoholic beverages as much as possible to state liquor stores where "the salesman or saleswoman hands out through a hole in a netting like that of a telegraph office bottles from long rows of shelves like those in a dispensary, for consumption off the premises."[40] Restaurants would be allowed to sell alcoholic beverages, but state employees in government shops would handle most of the trade. Prices, hours of sale, and the quality of vodka would be determined by the state. The introduction of the monopoly dealt financial loss to Jews who were often proprietors of taverns in Russia, especially in the south. Since the rights of Jews to operate taverns had been curtailed since 1874, the monopoly could be viewed as a culmination of restrictive laws against Jews. Even though Jewish taverns were often looted during pogroms, they provided a livelihood for many Jews.[41]

The new law did favor some women, however, who were willing to buy vodka legally in state stores and resell it illegally in *shinki* (illegal saloons), from their homes or on the street. The more restricted the days and hours of sale in the state liquor stores, the more bootleggers prospered, including women entrepreneurs.[42] As Cherkevskii observes: "the liquor stores profit, bootleggers profit, and the police profit from the small fines." He also notes that of the 1,532 persons arrested for the illegal trade, 1,362 were women, and he claims that "if we continue to have *shinki* for another two or three years, our children will be born drunk."[43] But it was women who protested the legal *traktirs* (pubs that sold food along with alcoholic beverages), saying "we the women and children in Monastyrk village beg with tears to close the cursed *traktirs*."[44] A temperance newspaper laments, "the *kabak* has always been a parasite of the village, sucking away the blood and physical and moral health of men. But the *shinok* does more damage than the official *kabak*s, hidden away as they are."[45] The state monopoly and *shinki* lasted until 1914 when Tsar Nicholas II declared prohibition.

Taverns and Society: Urban Taverns

No reader of Dostoevsky's *Crime and Punishment*, originally entitled *The Drunkards*, will ever forget his description of the taverns in St. Petersburg shortly after the emancipation of the serfs: "Looking around, he [Raskolnikov] noticed that he was standing by a tavern, the entrance to which was downstairs from the sidewalk, in the basement ... He sat down in a dark and dirty corner, at a sticky little table, asked for beer, and greedily drank down the first glass."[46] Like the fictional student Raskolnikov, "students in Kazan', Moscow, and St Petersburg spent many of their non-classroom hours in cavernous pubs [*traktiri*] near the university. There they drank spirits, beer, and wine and smoked to their hearts' content. As part of that process they could affirm their separate group status, both literally and figuratively—as respectable and socially superior— in front of the other tavern denizens. The pub, with its rituals of drunken cele- brations, often served as a launching point of students' more public rowdi- ness."[47]

Workers, usually on paydays, patronized taverns near their factories, where the tavern keepers tended their business at the bar while workers sat at tables in groups to converse, drink, and listen to music and "every profession had a tavern where its workers gathered."[48]

For the male migrants who coursed into Moscow and St Petersburg in the nine-teenth and early twentieth centuries, taverns provided the opportunity to form communities allowing regulars to impart urban ways to the incoming peasant to whom "the new and the strange could be made more familiar and local."[49]

In addition to students and workers, sailors in port cities patronized their favourite taverns and beer halls. Alexander Kuprin's famous short story "Gambrinus" set in the early 1900s has made that name synonymous with Russian beer halls. Down twenty narrow stone steps, unmarked, but well patronized in the port of Odessa, Gambrinus featured Sashka the Jewish musician who played on his fiddle every evening, and who eventually fell victim to a pogrom.

> The beer-shop consisted of two vaulted halls, long but exceedingly narrow. The under-ground moisture always oozed out of the walls in trickling rivulets, and glistened in the light of the gas jets, which burned day and night, since the beer-shop was entirely lacking in windows. On the vaults, however, one could still make out with sufficient distinctness traces of diverting mural painting.[50]

There on any given evening more than 200 patrons would gather, eating sausages and cheese sandwiches, drinking beer and ordering tunes from Sashka and "many—almost half—came with women who wore kerchiefs upon their heads ... Drinking was taken seriously in the Gambrinus."[51] Kuprin describes the various patrons: Greeks from Asia Minor, a group of black sailors, a party of thieves after a heist, doughty fishermen, English sailors, and Georgians, drinking, laughing, singing, dancing, quarrelling, even fighting in the dank smoky beer hall. While this tavern was below ground, it was apparently not typical. "The size and design of prewar taverns in urban Russia were diverse, but most were two-story establish-ments housing a kitchen, a bar, a water closet, a billiard room or two, and several dining rooms."[52]

Ivan Bunin gives us a picture in his story of an entirely different sort of tavern, a refined one called the Prague in Moscow, where a Portuguese string orchestra was playing. Two gentlemen, a retired army doctor and the narrator, drink vodka, wine, and brandy and smoke expensive cigars. They also discuss politics, mostly relating to the Duma, the new parliament allowed by the tsar in 1906. Indeed taverns were undoubtedly forums for political discussion among the rich and poor.[53]

The famous Soviet poet and artist Vladimir V. Maiakovskii shows in one of his paintings a woman with a small boy clutched to her, her arms outstretched against a tavern door, crying out to her ragged husband, "I shall not let you in here." He also drew a vicious critique of the state vodka monopoly, showing the vodka fac-tories in the background belching smoke, and Nicholas and Alexandra sitting on a throne on which the double-headed eagle is a vodka bottle. The royal couple holds bottles of vodka in their arms while pots of coins sit at their feet along with drunk-ards.[54]

Alexander Blok's despairing poem, "The Stranger," takes place in a tavern in the early twentieth century. In part it reads:

> And every dusk, my sole associate
> Is mirrored in my tumbler's sheen;
> Through fumes—astringent and mysterious—
> Like me, both tamed and deafened seems.
> Around me, at the counters neighboring,
> Are drowsy, waiters standing by,
> And drunks, their eyes blood-shot and rabbity,
> In vino veritas they cry.
> Each night—the hour never deviates,
> (Or do I see this in my dreams?)
> A slender form in silken mantelet
> Beyond the misty panes appears.[55]

Taverns and Society: Rural Taverns

The short-story writer Ivan Bunin gives us a picture of a provincial tavern along the Volga:

> A structure on wooden piles, a log barn with windows in crude frames, packed with tables hidden under grubby white tablecloths, with cheap heavy cutlery, where the salt in the salt-cellars is mixed with pepper and the napkins smell of cheap soap; you see a platform of planks, a farcical stage for balalaika-players, accordionists and lay harpists, illuminated along the back wall by kerosene lamps with their blinding tin reflectors.[56]

Although taverns were not supposed to be near churches, one Russian anthropologist recorded that on the way to Sunday services, peasants "may find time to visit a tavern and down a *shkalik* [glass of .06 liters] or two."[57] She also noted "when a new tavern keeper comes to a village, he has to secure a steady flow of customers. To do this he offers to lend peasants from eight to twenty rubles by means of promissory notes that he has notarized."[58] According to Chekhov, the reputation of tavern keepers was generally unsavory: "No matter what kind of a scoundrel the teacher might be, he's always right because he's a teacher, the innkeeper is always wrong, because he is an innkeeper and a *kulak*."[59] Dostoevsky is scarcely more flattering:

> A fire broke out in the village and spread to the church. Presently, the innkeeper appeared on the scene and cried out to the people that if they would cease putting out the fire in the church but would save his pot-house, he would give them a barrel of liquor. The church burned down, but the pot-house was saved.[60]

An informed member of the intelligentsia, A. N. Engelgnidt, who was sympathetic to peasants, wrote that a particular tavern was located in a half-rotted-out hut that was "dirty, dark, filled, with tobacco smoke, cold, damp, close and always full." Nonetheless, he frequented the place, because of the speed by which news and peasant rumors arrived there: "all of this news is transmitted in a completely original fashion, and, besides, not only facts, but also editorials and proposals are presented."[61]

For peasants, in addition to being a locus of sociability, the *kabak* served as a public space, a reading room, a forum for political discussion where various social classes could meet and mingle with travellers, exchange views, express opposition to official policy, and where business was concluded. More than a club and a library, more than a drinking hole, the *kabak* was "the center of village public life."[62]

For camaraderie and relaxation miners sought taverns, for their "conviviality, music, women, and gambling," where they sang "drinking ditties or tearful songs lamenting life's injustices to the accompaniment of an accordion, harmonica, balalaika, or guitar, in a room full of workers all drinking and singing along."[63] Some of the better taverns had colorful wallpaper and white table linens, but most were dirty shacks.

Soviet Period 1917–1991

Prohibition continued until 1925; so there were no legal *kabak*s or liquor stores, but *samogon* (moonshine) was available in abundance. The need for revenue convinced Lenin to reinstate the state liquor monopoly. Stalin urged the vodka industry to increase sales so that his industrialization project could be supported. Dingy stores and unattractive underground drinking establishments that served a *zakuska* such as herring, lightly salted cucumbers, sausage, and bread along with vodka replaced the more colorful and variegated taverns of the tsarist period.

In the early Soviet period when taverns were banned, alcohol found its way into dining halls and workers' clubs. As drinking establishments of all sorts fell to state ownership, men no longer sought news of job openings, engaged in political discussion, or formed tight relationships in public drinking places that had become nameless and numbered substitutes.[64] More and more drinking went on in the kitchens of families and friends where one could speak with relative freedom without being overheard by officials. For "hard core" drinkers, imbibing went onto the street, producing the public drunkenness that so shocked visitors to the Soviet Union. Solitary drinking or sharing a bottle on the street in threes was symbolic of the atomization of Soviet society. Caught in the dilemma of Marxist ideology, the Soviet state could not encourage drinking alcohol because drunkenness was for them a remnant of decadent bourgeois society, yet the state needed the revenue. Liquor stores seemed a discreet compromise: vodka was for sale and what a person did with it subsequently was his own affair.

Alexander Blok saw his lovely apparition, the unknown woman, while imbibing in a convivial tavern before the 1917 Revolution. Venedikt Erofeev in *Moscow to the End of the Line* presents the new Soviet drinker who grabs bottles from stores and dives, drinking their contents on a commuter train while in pursuit of his beloved at the end of the line. In this hallucinatory, haunting, and sadly hilarious "poem," the solitary drunk never reaches his destination unless it is the oblivion he achieves.[65]

President Mikhail Gorbachev in his temperance reforms of 1985–8 attempted to curtail drinking by limiting the hours of sale in state liquor stores and abolishing alcoholic drinks at official functions. While he left pubs open, he attempted to substitute for them alcohol-free restaurants where poetry was read aloud to the patrons or chamber music played. In an effort to dissuade people from drink, he also initiated the promotion of teashops and cafés where only ice cream was sold.[66]

Post-Soviet Union, 1991

Boris Yeltsin, the first President of Russia after the dissolution of the Soviet Union, decreed in May 1992, that the state monopoly on vodka had ceased to exist.[67] A flood of cheap vodka flowed into Russia, resulting in increased consumption and the proliferation of kiosks, pubs, taverns, and modern bars, which dispensed vodka among other alcoholic drinks. From the beginning of the presidency of Vladimir Putin in 2000, there was both a move to centralize the power of the president and to regain control over the production of vodka. Putin created a conglomerate Rosspiritprom that controlled over fifty distilleries in which the government claimed to own a majority of stocks and twenty others in which it was a minority shareholder.[68]

In July 2005, he called for a return to a state monopoly on vodka production, giving as his reason the need to assure a good quality product, the same rationale Finance Minister Sergei Witte had offered a century earlier. Citing 13,000 deaths in four months from illegally produced alcohol, Putin averred the only way to deal with such a problem was to impose a state vodka monopoly.[69] Just as Witte insisted that fiscal considerations were not behind his proposal for a state vodka monopoly, Putin did not mention the inevitability of enhanced state revenue from such a move. While it is true that Putin appears to be concerned with the mounting death rates among productive young men largely because of alcohol-related deaths, it is also true that the pace of oil and gas production is slackening after several years of supplying Russia with 20 to 40 percent of its gross domestic product.[70] The state wants to hedge its prospects by the tried and true method of gathering revenue from vodka. Historically, when the state has gained control over the production of vodka, it also seeks to tighten its grip on consumption. Taverns, or rather, contemporary bars might well come under new regulation.

Conclusion

Soon after the discovery of the art of distilling vodka, Russian rulers used their control over the product to command obedience and loyalty as well as to make as much profit as possible. By designing and redesigning the locus of consumption, the state also shaped the forms and functions of taverns. Just as certainly, consumers found ways to circumvent laws through bribery, bootlegging, moonshining, and otherwise inventing illicit gathering places or using legal venues for illicit purposes. While it is often asserted that Russians have no history of entrepreneurship or are mediocre at exploiting business opportunities, the history of taverns belies such allegations or at least suggests some exceptions. Many a tax farmer made a fortune buying vodka "futures;" many a Jew subleased the right to run taverns and some became wealthy in the process; women tavern owners, managers, or bootleggers had a sharp eye for augmenting the family income and at times accumulating considerable sums for themselves.

Despite the awesome power of Russian monarchs and governments, their vodka monopolies at any time in history were imperfect. Corrupt and clever intermediaries found allies in numerous thirsty consumers and worked singly and together to challenge and thwart total state control over a precious resource. The tighter the controls the state attempted to exercise over the quantity dispensed legally, the more people engaged in bootlegging, moonshining, or using surrogates, not only because of the demand for alcohol, but also because of the money to be made.

Centuries of poverty and oppression made it all the more imperative for people to gather in taverns to celebrate small triumphs and to mark the few but intense joyous punctuations in their lives such as births, christenings, marriages, and successful business contracts. Factory workers, miners, soldiers, sailors, and peasants sought balm in vodka for their aches and pains. Students, as always, had need for association and amusement, the curious for news, merchants for deals, and lovers for rendez-vous. Even losses and grief, chagrin and sorrow needed to be smoothed away through companionate drinking. Politics had to seek a forum, pleas for action shared, and solidarity cemented. The state might take the income from vodka sales and lament the social impoverishment and degradation it caused, but it was as addicted to vodka revenue as some of the imbibers were to alcohol.

Notes

1. R. E. F. Smith and David Christian, *Bread and Salt: A Social and Economic History of Food and Drink in Russia* (New York: Cambridge University Press, 1984), p. 300.

2. For a chronological table of state regulations on the production and sale of alcoholic products in Russia from the sixteenth century to 1999, see I. R. Takala, *Veselie Rusi: Istoriia alkogol'noi problemy v Rossii* (St. Petersburg: Zhurnal Neva,

2002), pp. 304–7. For the most recent survey of the history of Russian taverns, state policy, and drinking, see Igor Kurukin and Elena Nikulina, *Gosudarevo kabatskoe delo: Ocherki piteinoi politiki i traditsii v Rossii* (Moscow: ACT: LIUKS, 2005).

3. I thank Alan Kimball, PhD, George P. Bayliss, MD, and Victor Zaydfudim, MD for sharing their unpublished works with me. Russian authorities were not the only ones to associate taverns with subversive activity: "Public houses have a long history of acting as incubators for revolutionary movements in and outside of Ireland. The British government, reacting to an assertive Irish nationalism, frequently moved to close pubs associate with treasonous activities," Bradley Kadel, "The Pub and the Irish Nation," *The Social History of Alcohol and Drugs: An Interdisciplinary Journal* 18 (2003): 71.

4. Boris. M. Segal, *Russian Drinking: Use and Abuse of Alcohol in Pre-Revolutionary Russia* (New Brunswick, NJ: Rutgers Center for Alcohol Studies, 1987), p. 43.

5. Ivan G. Pryzhov, *Istoriia kabakov v Rossii v sviazi s istoriei russkago naroda* (Moscow: Booth Chamber International, 1991), p. 44. *Korchma*s continued to operate illegally in early modern times. See Takala, p. 39.

6. Heinrich von Staden, *The Land and the Government of Muscovy: A Sixteenth Century Account*, trans. Thomas Esper (Stanford: Stanford University Press, 1967), p. 103.

7. L. I. Ivina (ed.), *Akty feodal'nogo zemlevladeniia i khozaistva: akty Moskovskogo Simonova monastyria 1506–1613 gg.* (Leningrad: Nauka, 1983), pp. 156–7. In 1552 Ivan IV appointed ten guards in the Dvina district to prevent peasants from selling alcohol and anyone attempting to open a tavern should be executed. On the other hand, peasants could purchase permits to brew drink for a religious festival, or to remember their deceased parents, or for a christening, or a birth. Such permits were good for five to seven days (and nights) of revelry, but should the peasants continue to drink, the alcohol would be confiscated and the men punished. See A. I. Kapanev, "Ustavnaia zemskaia gramota krest'ianam trekh volostei," in *Istoricheskii arkhiv,* 8 (Moscow: Izdatel'stvo Akademii Nauk, SSSR, 1953), pp. 17–18.

8. Giles Fletcher, *Of the Russe Commonwealth* (Cambridge, MA: Harvard University Press, 1966), pp. 44–5.

9. Segal, p. 39.

10. Smith and Christian, p. 91.

11. M. M. Sukhman (ed.), *Inostrantsy o drevnei Moskve* (Moscow: Izdatel'stvo Stolitsa, 1991), p. 92.

12. Pryzhov, p. 59.

13. Segal, p. 48.

14. Pryzhov, pp. 48–9.

15. Robin Milner-Gulland, *The Russians* (Malden, MA: Blackwell Publishers, 1997), p. 23. For other customs associated with drink, see Patricia Herlihy, "'Joy

of the Rus': Rites and Rituals of Russian Drinking," *Russian Review* 50 (Apr. 1991): 131–47.

16. Samuel H. Baron, trans. and ed. *The Travels of Olearius in Seventeenth-Century Russia* (Stanford: Stanford University Press 1967), pp. 198–9.

17. John P. LeDonne, "Indirect Taxes in Catherine's Russia: II. The Liquor Monopoly," *Jahrbücher für Geschichte Osteuropas* 24 (1976): 185.

18. Yekhezkel Kotik, *Journey to a Nineteenth-Century Shtetl*, ed. David Assaf (Detroit: Wayne State University Press, 2002), p. 440 n. 9 states that "thousands of Jewish families in the Pale of Settlement were involved in vodka leasing and associated spheres. The lessor ... (*otkupchik*) also exercised a certain amount of influence in the promotion of enlightenment and russification. Thus, he earned the hatred of members of the traditional Jewish society." Jewish tavern keepers also earned the resentment of Ukrainians and Russians who were heavily in debt to them because they often drank vodka on credit. For the many tricky ways the tavern keepers, not only Jews, and tax farmers exploited patrons, see David Christian, " *'Living Water': Vodka and Russian Society on the Eve of Emancipation* (Oxford: Clarendon Press, 1990), ch. 4.

19. See Kotik, pp. 190–7, for a description of how the system worked.

20. David Christian, "A Neglected Great Reform: The Abolition of Tax Farming in Russia," in Ben Eklof, John Bushnell, and Larissa Zakharova (eds), *Russia's Great Reforms, 1855–1881* (Bloomington: Indiana University Press, 1994), p. 105.

21. At times peasants boycotted vodka in protest of high prices. For the most famous occurrence, see David Christian, "The Black and Gold Seals: Popular Protests Against the Liquor Trade on the Eve of Emancipation," in Esther Kingston-Mann and Timothy Mixter (eds), *Peasant Economy, Culture, and Politics of European Russia, 1800–1921* (Princeton: Princeton University Press, 1991), pp. 261–93.

22. David Christian, "Vodka and Corruption in Russia on the Eve of Emancipation," *Slavic Review*, 46, No. 3/4 (1987): 471–488. In the 1870s a British journalist noted, "The 'brandy [vodka] farmers,' for example who worked for the state monopoly for the manufacture and sale of alcoholic liquors paid regularly a fixed sum to every official, from the Governor to the policemen, according to his rank. I know of one case where the official, on receiving a larger sum than was customary, conscientiously handed back the change!" See Donald Mackensie Wallace, *Russia on the Eve of War and Revolution* ed. Cyril E. Black (Princeton: Princeton University Press, 1984), p. 14.

23. Smith and Christian, p. 92.

24. Baron, pp. 144–5.

25. Baron, p. 145. In 1895 and again in 1985 vodka reforms replaced smaller bottles with larger ones, but again, three persons would chip in to buy a bottle to divide the contents.

26. Baron, p. 225.

27. Baron, p. 263. Stalin objected to saxophones as symbols of decadent Western bourgeois jazz and in 1949 in Moscow had them confiscated and destroyed. See S. Frederick Starr, *Red and Hot: The Fate of Jazz in the Soviet Union, 1917–1980* (New York: Oxford University Press, 1983), 216.

28. Joseph L. Wieczynski (ed.), *The Modern Encyclopedia of Russian and Soviet History* (Gulf Breeze, FL: Academic International Press, 1980), p. 15, sv. "kabak."

29. *The Lubok: Russian Folk Pictures 17th to 19th Century* (Leningrad: Aurora Art, 1984), p. 136.

30. Kotik, pp. 128–9.

31. Ivan Turgenev, "Singers," in *Sketches from a Hunter's Album*, trans. Richard Freeborn (New York: Penguin Books, 1967), p. 230.

32. Ibid., p. 235.

33. Nikolai Leskov, *The Enchanted Pilgrim and Other Stories*, trans. David Magarshack (London: Hutchinson International Authors, 1946), pp. 188–202.

34. *The Complete Works of Alexander Pushkin* (Norfolk: Milner and Co., Limited, 1999), vol. 6, pp. 69–77.

35. Kotik, p. 111. For a history of women as barmaids and pub keepers in Australia from the eighteenth century on, see Diane Kirby, *A History of Women's Work in Pubs* (Cambridge: Cambridge University Press, 1997).

36. Kotik, p. 111.

37. Ibid., p. 376.

38. Reginald E. Zelnik, *Labor and Society in Tsarist Russia: The Factory Workers of St. Petersburg, 1855–1870* (Stanford: Stanford University Press, 1971), p. 249.

39. Kotik, p. 341.

40. Harold Whitmore Williams, *Russia of the Russians* (London: Sir Isaac Pitman & Sons Ltd, 1914), p. 340.

41. John Doyle Klier, *Imperial Russia's Jewish Question 1855–1881* (Cambridge: Cambridge University Press, 1995), pp. 311–20.

42. In one village women smashed the windows of huts where bootlegged vodka was sold, but they allowed a woman to continue her illicit trade until she had enough money to buy a cow. Williams, p. 320.

43. V. A. Cherkevskii, *K voprosu o p'ianstve vo vladimirskoi gubernii i sposobakh bor'by s nim* (Vladimir, 1911), pp. 24–34.

44. "Zhaloba krest'ianok," *Nizhegorodskii listok*, 152 (June 6, 1899): 2.

45. "Shinok," *Deiatel'* 17 (Sept. 1912): 205.

46. Fedor Dostoevsky, *Crime and Punishment*, trans. Richard Pever and Larissa Volokhonsky (New York: Vintage Classics, 1992), p. 10.

47. Rebecca Friedman, "From Boys to Men: Manhood in the Nicholaevan University," in Barbara Evans Clements, Rebecca Friedman, and Dan Healey (eds), *Russian Masculinities in History and Culture* (New York: Palgrave, 2002), pp. 40–1.

48. Laura L. Phillips, *The Bolsheviks and the Bottle: Drink and Worker Culture in St. Petersburg, 1900–1929* (DeKalb: Northern Illinois University Press, 2000), pp. 74–5. See also her "Everyday Life in Revolutionary Russia: Working-Class Drinking and Taverns in St. Petersburg, 1900–1929," PhD dissertation (University of Illinois, Urbana-Champaign, 1993).

49. William Arthur McKee, "Taming the Green Serpent: Alcoholism, Autocracy, and Russian Society, 1881–1914," PhD Dissertation (University of California, Berkeley, 1997), p. 56.

50. Alexander Kuprin, *Gambrinus and Other Stories*, trans. Bernard Gulbert Guerney (New York: Adelphi Co. 1925), p. 12. For a general history of sailors' taverns, see Michael Seltzer, "Haven and a Heartless Sea; The Sailors' Tavern in History and Anthropology," *The Social History of Alcohol and Drugs: An Interdisciplinary Journal*, 19 (2004): 63–93.

51. Kuprin, p. 26.

52. Phillips, *Bolsheviks*, p. 73.

53. Ivan Bunin, "The Riverside Tavern", in *The Gentleman from San Francisco and Other Stories* (New York: Penguin Books, 1987), p. 213.

54. Patricia Herlihy, *The Alcoholic Empire: Vodka and Politics in Late Imperial Russia* (New York: Oxford University Press, 2002), cover and photo following p. 68.

55. Alexander Blok, "The Stranger," in *Worlds of Russian Fantasy, Science Fiction and Utopian Thought: From Russian Folk Tales to Space Flight*, trans. Alexander Levitsky and M. Kitchen (New York: The Overlook Press), forthcoming.

56. Bunin, p. 217.

57. Olga Semyonova Tian-Shanskaia, *Village Life in Late Tsarist Russia*, ed. David L. Ransel (Bloomington: University of Indiana Press, 1993), p. 113.

58. Ibid., p. 156.

59. Anton Chekhov, *Stories of Women*, trans. Paula P. Ross (Amherst, NY: Prometheus Books, 1994), p. 48.

60. F. M. Dostoevsky, *The Diary of a Writer*, trans. Boris Brassol (New York: Charles Scribner's Sons, 1949), vol. 1, p. 187.

61. Cathy Frierson (ed.), *Alexandr Nikolaevich Engelgardt's Letters from the Country, 1872–1887* (New York: Oxford University Press, 1993), pp. 142–5.

62. Alan Kimball, "Derevenskii kabak kak vyrazhenie russkoi grazhdanskoi obshchestvennosti v 1855–1905 gg," *Obshchestvennye nauki* (St Petersburg: Academy of Sciences, 2004), p. 4, forthcoming.

63. Charters Wynn, *Workers, Strikes, and Pogroms: The Donbass-Dnepr Bend in Late Imperial Russia, 1870–1905* (Princeton: Princeton University Press, 1992), p. 63.

64. Phillips, *Bolsheviks*, pp. 87–95.

65. Venedikt Erofeev, *Moscow to the End of the Line*, trans. H. William Tjalsma (Evanston, IL: Northwestern University Press, 1992), pp. 13–17.

66. For a detailed study of Gorbachev's reforms, see Stephen White, *Russia Goes Dry: Alcohol, State and Society* (Cambridge: Cambridge University Press, 1996).

67. Herlihy, *Alcoholic Empire*, p. 158.

68. Ibid. p. 161.

69. http://news.bbc.co.uk/http://news.bbc.co.uk/, July 3, 2005.

70. David R. Francis, "To Decipher Russia's Riddle, Watch Its Oil," *Christian Science Monitor*, July 7, 2005.

–12–

Drinking "The Good Life"

Australia c.1880–1980

Diane Erica Kirkby

"Australians are not a nation of Snobs like the English, or of extravagant boasters like the Americans, or of reckless profligates like the French", Marcus Clarke wrote of his fellow-colonists in the later nineteenth century, "they are simply a nation of *Drunkards.*"[1] Clarke was not alone in this view. A few years later visiting English novelist, Anthony Trollope, said similarly of the Australian colonists, that drunkenness was "their one great fault."[2] At that time Australia was six separate self-governing colonies. It was not yet a nation and already the national character was being set in place. A century later Australians seemed determined to live up to this typecasting. Drinking was "probably the most important social activity in Australia," author Craig McGregor wrote in 1966. It was not as important as sex or conversation but, he said, drinking provided the focus for much Australian life, and it was ahead of sport. What a later writer, Michael Thomas, would label a "boozy democracy," to McGregor in the 1960s was "all part of that explosive good humour and companionship which Australians equate with 'the good life'." "Above all," he said, drinking was "a determinedly egalitarian activity, the great social leveler." Except for a crowd of spectators watching a Test cricket match, there was "no more classless place in Australia," he said, than a bar in a hotel.[3]

Three years after McGregor's book was published, another journalist, Cyril Pearl, pointed to the importance of beer drinking in Australia. It was "a religion." he said, more important to the media than other religions, and carrying with it several myths—about the amount that was consumed, about its strength and associated masculinity, "brewed for hairy-chested He-men," and about its patriotic identification with being Australian. Elsewhere Pearl was critical of Australian drinking culture but recognized that it was such an important part of the culture that "becoming part of it made you Australian."[4] On the other hand, another social critic, Donald Horne, said Australians were not "the nation of boozers they imagine themselves to be."[5] It was a misconception to think drunkenness was the national character, and there was more complexity to the history of drinking in Australia than such characterizations allowed. Indeed, Australians were also a nation of "wowsers" (prudes) who deplored "the demon drink" and had heavily restricted its consumption.[6] In the mid twentieth century these two conflicting ideas were circulating as being Australian was redefined.

These books are an insight into the discussion Australians were having in the postwar period about national identity and the place drinking held in the culture and imaginations of Australianness. Not accidentally it was centered on beer. Observers of postwar Australian culture "invariably" saw the pub, "a mecca for drinking and betting" as its center.[7] With some irony, they captured the essence of an Australian drinking culture that was partly a result of past history but was also indicative of a moment of transition.

Australia was transforming from being predominately Anglo-Celtic (98 percent British) to a modern, cosmopolitan, multicultural society. Beer drinking was a mark of an old culture that was disappearing. After two decades of absorbing immigrants from eastern and southern Europe in the aftermath of World War II, Anglo-Australians had become self-conscious about their identity and culture. Similarly at that moment the "perpendicular drinking" (standing at the bar) and discriminatory nature of Australian drinking customs were under sustained attack. The majority of Australians now wanted mixed-sex drinking in more comfortable venues than the old-style pubs. And as cheaper and faster air travel brought in more tourists and lessened the distance between Australia and other parts of the world, Australians also discovered the value of the tourist dollar.

Consequently there were several publications celebrating the Australianness of the beer-drinking culture, not only for a tourist readership but for a more serious audience as well. Architectural historian J. M. Freeland produced a very serious study of the pub in Australia, still the only such study that's been done. Paul McGuire had earlier celebrated the vital role innkeepers had played in Australia's colonial history.[8] Others, like McGregor, Horne, and Pearl, examined the role of drinking in their larger discussions of Australian culture or, like Dunstan, told the history of Australia's attempts to limit drinking and gambling. A few relied on romantic images and anecdotes about outback pubs to capture "the true Australia" in familiar and unproblematized terms.[9] Economic historians studied brewing technology, market share, and consumption patterns.[10] Feminists critiqued the sex-specific character of Australia's drinking customs.[11] Beer's history in Australia, and the drinking culture that grew up with it, was being explored as a national narrative. Drinking beer was celebrated as being Australian but where and with whom you drank your beer depended on what kind of Australian you were. The importance of women to that history was left to a new generation of scholars.[12] The gendered character of Australia's drinking history is now being problematized.[13]

Beer by the 1960s had come to be identified with being Australian because of the nature of Australian drinking practices and the special place the pub played in Australian life. "The pub is one of the most socially significant ... and colourful features of Australian society," Freeland claimed.[14] Australian colonial licensing laws required hotels also to provide meals and accommodation for travelers along with the sale of alcohol, making the Australian pub a different sort of institution from the alehouses, inns, and wine taverns of England. A large number of these pubs came to be owned by the major breweries and run as tied-houses, selling beer as their major product. Even if trade fluctuated somewhat, "the output of beer is always growing per head," the editor of the *Australian Brewer's Journal* claimed early in the twentieth century. "The reason is evident. Beer has been, and always will be, the beverage of the Anglo-Saxon since the day when Hengist (sic.) and Horsa landed in Thanet." This, "the national beverage," was "as dear to the heart of our people as it ever has been."[15]

Over the course of the nineteenth century beer had replaced spirits to become the most popular alcoholic beverage in the Australian colonies.[16] Early colonists— convicts, sailors, and army officers—drank rum and wine but in a climate "conducive to the long cool drink … for those who really wanted to slake a parched throat" fortified wine and spirits would not do.[17] Light, cool, refreshing ales were more suitable as *The Australian Brewer's Journal* told its readers: "Brewers must remember that in this hot climate men often want a long drink rather than a strong one."[18]

It took a while however for a good-tasting local brew to develop.[19] The warm climate was at first a handicap, good quality raw materials and skilled brewers for a time unavailable. Before scientific methods were developed beer production was unreliable and beer could not be transported long distances. The bulk of the beer consumed in the colonies was locally produced but of inferior flavor. Then lager began to be imported from Germany and Australian brewers began to experiment. The first local lagers were produced in the 1880s but a decade later seemed to have been a failure. Sales in the 1890s were lower than expected. While the quantity of colonial beer brewed in 1897 was at its highest for five years, the quantity of lager brewed was at its smallest. Both bulk and bottled lager had decreased so much in such an extremely small time that the *Australian Brewer's Journal* declared disappointedly "The novelty that attached itself to the Teutonic brew has quickly been dispelled."[20]

It was not until major breweries overcame technical difficulties and World War I put an end to the importation of German lager that the Australian product really took off and became "a national phenomenon."[21] Historian Tony Dingle claimed that the use of refrigeration in the early years of the twentieth century provided the final stage in the slow development of "a truly Australian beer," a lager brew fully adapted to local demand and conditions. Bret Stubbs has argued that refrigeration was not enough. Only the largest brewers could afford the expensive equipment and new technology and so concentration of the industry was the key. It enabled the transition to the production of lager and this contributed to further concentration.[22] By the middle of the twentieth century this beer, fully adapted to local tastes and demands, was proudly proclaimed "Best beer in the world" by the patrons of the public bar.[23] It supposedly had a higher alcohol content than some other beers brewed in the UK or the USA, but beer itself was a less alcoholic drink than the spirits or wine consumed in larger quantities in other countries.[24]

A taste for a lager-style chilled beer may have been understandable in Australia's climate but that was not unique to Australia. Its development was part of a worldwide phenomenon at the end of the nineteenth century. The drinking patterns and ethos that accompanied it were more specific. In a survey of Australian drinking rates in the nineteenth and twentieth centuries, economic historian Dingle established that "one of the distinctive features of Australian drink consumption since 1788 has been its variability." Consumption rates have fluctuated with economic fortunes. In periods of prosperity drinking rates were highest, and in periods of economic downturn, they were at their lowest. While this has also been true in other countries, the Australian experience was "exceptional" according to Dingle in "the magnitude of the shifts and their duration." He argued that Australian drinkers had been "volatile" in responding to economic boom and slump.[25]

So it was not what they were drinking so much as how they were that distinguished Australian drinking culture. Such specific historical factors are why historian Elizabeth Malcolm has pointed out that "Drinking patterns ... are almost as characteristic of a nation as its language."[26] In the 1960s Australia was a society that was increasingly prosperous and leaving its rural working-class origins behind. Australians acted out "the good life" they were enjoying with public drinking rituals. In doing so they identified themselves with Australian cultural values of classlessness and a form of male bonding called mateship.

Egalitarianism was much valued by those Australians who believed, before the end of the nineteenth century, theirs was "a working man's paradise." A major contributor to the belief that Australians were a nation of hard drinkers who cherished egalitarianism and mateship was historian Russel Ward who in 1958 published *The Australian Legend*, a historical account of the development of national character. Ward's thesis was that Australia's convict history and the material conditions of bush life and work evoked peculiarly Australian characteristics in pastoral workers, which "spread by osmosis" to the towns and cities, and were taken up by poets and writers as the national ethos. Contemporary accounts from the early and mid nineteenth century suggested, Ward said, that "no people on the face of the earth ever absorbed more alcohol per head of population."[27]

Their observations do not stand up to critical scrutiny, as Dingle convincingly demonstrated. While there have been times in the nation's history when Australians drank more in comparison with other countries, there are more times when they drank less. What was characteristic of colonial drinking was the binges indulged in by pastoral and other rural workers when they finally got to a pub. As Trollope had pointed out, while drunkenness was the colonists' great flaw, "yet they are sober to a marvel ... they will work for months without touching spirits, but their very abstinence creates a craving desire which, when it is satisfied, will satisfy itself with nothing short of brutal excess."[28]

Dingle took up this point. "Because of the great distances which typically separated workplace and pub in the outback, bush workers varied long periods of hard work with short bouts of intensive drinking" when they got to town with a paycheck. Dingle conceded that this practice certainly led to much visible drunkenness but said it did not show up statistically as a high level of annual drink consumption, simply because of the infrequency of such binges.[29] Also the circumstances and actions of bushmen is very partial as an explanation for national drinking patterns. In the mid nineteenth century, almost half, and by the turn of the twentieth century more than half, the population lived in urban centers, usually major cities close to the coast, a trend that accelerated as the century progressed. Urban drinking patterns were more likely to have been shaped by other factors.

One colonist thought that drunkenness was statistically about the same as it was in England, that the quantity of spirits drunk was "appalling", but the difference in the colonies lay in the social class who got drunk. "Here it is not merely the lower classes, but everybody that drinks. Not a few of the wealthiest and most leading citizens are well-known to be frequently drunk, though their names do not, of course, appear in the papers or in the police reports." There seemed to be an acceptance: someone "may be known to be carried to bed every night, for all it affects his reputation as a respectable and respected citizen," for "no social reprobation attaches."[30]

Furthermore the pattern of Australian drinking sounds remarkably like that described for the early national period of the USA, where "public drinking to intoxication ... prevailed wherever groups of Americans gathered" and "practically any gathering of three or more men ... provided an occasion for drinking vast quantities of liquor, until the more prudent staggered home while the remainder quarrelled and fought, or passed out."[31] By the 1820s, these communal and sometimes solitary binges were increasingly replacing the previous custom of taking small amounts at regular and frequent intervals throughout the day. Rorabaugh argues it was the development of this binge-drinking pattern that alarmed observers and led to the organization of the temperance movement.[32]

Again, similarly to Australia, egalitarianism was an important dimension of this early US drinking culture. As Rorabaugh explains "all men were equal before the bottle, and no man was allowed to refuse to drink." To do so was taken as "proof the abstainer thought himself to be better than other people ... To refuse to imbibe gave 'serious offense,' suggesting a lack of respect and friendship."[33] Clarke drew attention to this "egalitarianism" of Australian colonial drinking when he referred to "the notable prevalence of habitual intoxication among all classes" and said of life in the Australian colonies, "no man can hope to succeed in business, profession, or society, unless he is prepared to take his chance of death in an asylum for inebriates."[34] In postwar Australia, to return a "shout" but refuse to drink along was similarly "the worst insult you can offer a man ... Means you don't think he's good enough to drink with."[35]

In the 1960s "the Australian legend" captured the public imagination. It gave historical authority to pub behavior. In the mid twentieth century, drinking among social equals was how Australianness was defined and performed. Drinking "allowed men," as McGregor said, "to indulge in the mateship ritual which has been one of the persistent motifs in Australian history."[36] Being "determinedly egalitarian" nevertheless suggests a tension that McGregor did not examine, although he referred to "the seamy side of Australian egalitarianism, the exclusiveness and racial lunaticism which has always been part of it."[37]

Indeed there was a level of coercion in the expectation that by drinking with mates one endorsed Australian values, and a defensiveness in maintaining social equality in the face of stark evidence to the contrary. Despite the existence of privileged private schools which fostered elitist values, and the demonstrated evidence of high levels of poverty in inner-city metropolitan areas,[38] social inequality was not allowed to be, although it invariably was, knowingly acted out in Australia's drinking practices in the public bar of the local hotel. On the other hand sex difference was manifestly and deliberately so.

Women and Alcohol

Sex-segregation was at the heart of Australia's twentieth century drinking culture. Drinking in the public bar was constructed as a rite of masculinity from which women were excluded. Women drank, either with other women, or with boyfriends and husbands in the "rubberplant-infested" mixed lounges and beer gardens of their local suburban or country pub, or in the women's-only areas known as the Ladies Lounge. They were not allowed to drink in the public bar which was the site of "raucous bon homie" where egalitarianism was at its most pronounced.[39] Similarly at social gatherings women were likely to drink together with other women while men congregated around the beer keg. It was "a tradition," McGregor said, for men to have a few drinks after work. Some city venues , "rather avant-garde 'arty' hotels" and "a few waterfront pubs" allowed mixed drinking or women into "the ordinary bars." Otherwise suburban and rural public bars were still "exclusively male preserves" in the mid 1960s.[40]

In the colonial period drinking had not been so segregated. "Everybody 'drinks'—man, woman, and child," Marcus Clarke wrote.[41] Both men and women drank in pubs, filled jugs to take some home, or brewed it themselves. Authorities and visitors included women in their complaints about drunkenness and the prosecution of women also showed up in the statistics.[42] Women drinkers were nevertheless a minority in a population that was disproportionately male. One crude estimate put the number of women drinkers in Victoria at 30,000 compared with 240,000 men.[43] As women gained more access to paid workplaces outside the restraints of domestic service, and worked in factories where men also worked, the numbers of women wishing to drink in public places also appeared to increase although the numbers of women prosecuted for drunkenness decreased.[44] But by the early twentieth century women's drinking in public places had become less acceptable.[45] The outcome was the establishment of sex-segregated drinking areas.

Women in the postwar period were thus excluded from the egalitarianism and mateship that was the identification of Australianness that public bar drinking created, although this was changing. After World War II women called for mixed drinking venues and by the early 1960s began asserting their right to be included in the culture by drinking alongside men in the public bars of Australia's hotels.[46] The women who initiated these protests were, not unexpectedly, professional women—journalists, academics, and university students—who were working alongside men but unable to join their colleagues in the bar for a drink after work or lectures. The emotional investment that had been made in preserving the sex-segregation of public drinking was revealed in the violence that attended some of these demonstrations.[47]

The culture that had developed, which encouraged a belief that most pubs were "no place for a woman," was a denial of the most significant fact of Australian pub history: the paradox that while women were prevented from drinking in the public bars, they had always been there as workers.[48] Hotels were the largest employer of female labor in colonial Australia both as back-of-house domestic staff or as front-of-house bar staff.[49] This trend continued in the twentieth century as women took up licenses or worked for wages behind the bar. Indeed "the barmaid" was almost as much a national character as the bushman, and her presence was an integral part of the unique drinking culture that had developed in Australia.[50]

Licensing laws and licensing courts in the mid twentieth century were also active in creating this female workforce when they asked both husbands and their wives questions about the provisions and accommodations that were going to be provided before the court granted a license. The license was often then given "on behalf of self and wife." "Many a case appears to have been determined in the applicant's favor because he was able to prove that his wife or manageress or housekeeper was capable of filling the role assigned to her," an editorial in the Victorian hotelkeepers' journal claimed in 1950.[51]

The expectation that a woman would provide this labor was almost as old as the first licensing laws in New South Wales (NSW) and was aptly summed up in 1897 by the parliamentarian who said: "Anyone who lives in a hotel must know that no licensed house can be properly conducted unless there is a good woman in it."[52] The fact that, from early colonial times, licensing laws also required the provision of accommodation and dining facilities in hotels rather than just the provision of liquor, drew women into the trade in substantial numbers as they took advantage of the legal provisions to provide for their own economic well-being. This was particularly so in Victoria where the licensing laws were more liberal in regards to women.[53]

Pubs were important to married women as their workplaces, as well as their domestic residences where they could raise their children and work alongside or in the absence of their husbands (colonial husbands were frequently absent). Running a pub was frequently a family concern, a partnership between husbands and wives, with sons and daughters learning the trade and subsequently continuing in their own house. And once the registration of barmaids was introduced (in Victoria 1916 and South Australia in 1908) it was claimed within the trade that many licensees immediately registered their female children so that in years to come they might be able to work outside the family's establishment, in someone else's premises, thus also perpetuating the tradition of hotelkeeping as a family business.[54] Wartime Australian Prime Minister John Curtin's mother was one such daughter of a publican who subsequently became a publican's wife when Curtin's father took out the license for a hotel in inner Melbourne during John's childhood.[55]

A Culture of Drunkenness

Connected to the fact that this drinking culture was sex-segregated was its celebration of drunkenness. It follows that when women and children are excluded from an activity, that activity becomes identified as a rite of passage for young men entering into adult manhood. Thus drinking beer in the public bar became a boys' own affair where "shouting" mates to another round was indistinguishable from competition to see who could last longest. Nineteenth-century observers of drunkenness drew particular attention to this practice of "shouting."[56] It "had made the present generation of Australians a generation of drunkards ... Men muddle their intellects and waste their money because they must needs do as others do," Clarke had written; "an inability to say NO has allowed the silly and harmful habit of 'shouting' to prevail." Because it was the custom, men "go on drinking themselves into imbecility."[57]

A century later the result of sex-segregation was a drinking culture that left overseas visitors reeling and had Donald Horne commenting that "men stand around the public bar asserting their masculinity with such intensity that you half expect them to unzip their flies."[58] Australians drank usually "with the sole idea of getting drunk," the mark of a good party for young men being when everybody had got drunk, several would have vomited (or "chundered") and others "flaked" (passed out) as McGregor recounted.[59]

That "explosive good humour" that McGregor described, "the jokes, the songs, the poems ... the language, and the whole ... rogue ocker[60] insouciance ..." that was Australian culture "was hatched in the pubs ... [and] rooted in drunkenness" according to a later observer, Michael Thomas. He satirized this culture when he wrote that "when the pubs closed, the streets filled with wild cries and the gutters ran with chunder." Drunken men "came staggering up the street ... Totally blotto, they'd crawl into the car, shut one eye and drive home ... either dead slow or flat out." Flat out was dangerous: you could hit someone or something. 'Limping along ... there was the danger you'd forget where you lived, that you'd blink and fall asleep suddenly." There were road accidents, "multi-car pileups and drunken brawling and grown men on their knees being sick in the street."[61]

Scholars also observed that drunkenness had a level of acceptability in Australia, because "drinking, not abstinence, is usually regarded as desirable behaviour."[62] Drinking to excess, or "the drink problem" as it was called, had caused so much concern in the nineteenth century that a powerful temperance movement had taken hold in Australia, just as it had in the UK, Ireland, the USA and many other countries. Drunkenness "loomed large" as an issue for those who saw alcohol as associated with "poverty, family breakdown, domestic violence, crime and serious illness."[63] Many but by no means all of the "philanthropists, clergy and social reformers," who sought to redress these problems, were women. Beginning as early as the 1830s when white settlement was only fifty years old, the temperance cause grew with the population and became even larger and more powerful with the establishment of various state branches of the Woman's Christian Temperance Union in the 1880s. By then it was also associated with woman suffrage, equal pay and other concerns of the woman's movement.[64]

The prospect of women voting in prohibition thus caused the brewers to oppose female suffrage. "Once a bill to give women the power of voting became a law of the land, there would be an immediate depreciation of property of all sorts connected with the trade …," the Victorian editor of the *Australian Brewer's Journal* wrote in 1896, "giving women votes for the Legislature would mean an immediate and inevitable misfortune to the trade, and a remote, if less certain, chance of its entire destruction." By then women in one state, South Australia, could vote, and those in Western Australia would soon be able to. It was highly likely Victoria would follow. "Every business, even remotely touching on the great liquor traffic, would instantly feel the fatal effects," the editor warned, *"even if the alarm were unwarranted by subsequent events."*[65]

Despite the fear engendered by the power of the WCTU, Australian women succeeded in being enfranchised for both state and commonwealth parliaments earlier than most other nations.[66] Temperance campaigners pursued several strategies: Sunday closing, prohibition, local option legislation, and early closing. Subsequently, and perhaps because of the women's vote, licensing laws introduced into various state parliaments in the early years of the twentieth century reduced the hours of hotel trading and the number of hotels permitted to sell alcohol. The first result of this reduction in the number of licensed premises was, as temperance campaigners had hoped, a reduction in overall consumption.[67]

From the introduction of early closing in 1916 alcohol consumption in the nation as a whole declined, reaching its lowest point in the mid 1930s, during the Great Depression. From the outbreak of war in 1939, however, it began again to increase until it reached the status of national pastime commented on by so many social commentators, and contributed to what, by 1970, was described as "the social problem of alcoholism which pervades Australian society."[68] Rather than reduce drunkenness, the limitations imposed on trading hours actually accelerated the rate of drinking, concentrated it into fewer hours in the day, increased the amount of home consumption, and led to the drinking culture that by mid century was being described as "the most uncivilised drinking practices in the world," and "a most unedifying spectacle."[69]

Being sex-segregated encouraged higher consumption as drinking to excess was part of male youth and pub culture. Yet "Australians" were not universally allowed to join in this culture that Thomas called "adolescence until death." Getting drunk was a male prerogative not equally available to women, but nor was it available to other identifiable groups. Those who were the subject of discussions about drinking and Australian identity were quite specifically white Anglo-Celtic males. Though McGregor and Horne were alert to the sex-segregated nature of Australian drinking, and the "stark unremitting race prejudice of white Australians,"[70] McGregor's depiction of "Australians" and the national drinking culture was used unproblematically. He did not identify or explore the gendered or racialized character of the Australian "good life" he was describing. Not only were women excluded, but restrictions imposed by several state laws meant Aboriginal people for a long time were forbidden to drink alcohol either away from or in pubs.

Alcohol and Aboriginal People

Alcohol was virtually unknown in Australia until Europeans began arriving in the late eighteenth century. The conventional view is that intoxicating liquors were introduced to Aboriginal people by Europeans. Freeland began his pub history stating "the blessings of civilization came to Australia in the form of a flag, gunfire, and alcohol." These "symbols of the European Age of Enlightenment," he said, "marked … the beginning of the building of a nation in New South Wales."[71]

There is however evidence that some Aboriginal tribes used some form of intoxicating drugs or liquor prior to the European introduction of the, ironically described, "civilized blessings." In northern and central Australia anthropologists observed indigenous people in the later nineteenth century commonly using a narcotic herb called "pitchery," a native of that part of the country. Aboriginal people also chewed native tobaccos and made alcohol from pandanus fruit which grew in the Northern Territory. Those living in Tasmania used eucalyptus sap to brew "a potent 'cider'" and Western Australian Aboriginal people fermented nectars to produce "a weak alcohol." Kooris who lived in the southeastern corner of the country later called Victoria also knew how to concoct a form of liquor "from various flowers, from honey, from gums, and from a kind of manna."[72] These and other native plants, "nectars, lerps and sweet acacia gums" were mixed together into a drink that would then be allowed to ferment.[73]

The impact of rum introduced with the convicts and sealers had a devastating impact and various colonies passed laws to prevent the trade in liquor to Aborigines living near settlements. In England in 1837 the House of Commons Select Committee on Aborigines held that local governments in the colonies had a moral obligation to protect indigenous people and it recommended that the sale or barter of spirits to them ought to be prohibited.[74] A year later NSW (which at that time covered the entire east coast and included the states of Victoria and Queensland) prohibited Aboriginal people living within its boundaries from drinking alcohol. This was relaxed for a time but reintroduced in specific legislation in 1867.[75]

Victoria passed legislation of its own in 1855 to prohibit Aboriginal people "from receiving spirits in quantities which produced intoxication."[76] This was followed a few years later by further moves to ban the sale and consumption of alcohol to Aboriginal people who were now being removed to reserves, and placed under "protection" by government-appointed boards. Victoria then followed the NSW legislation and in 1869 forbade Aboriginal people to buy, consume, or receive alcohol. Drinking became their crime, not just drunkenness.[77] These laws were still in place and were only beginning to be overturned in the period in which observers were focusing their attention on Australian drinking culture. The last restriction was lifted in 1972.

Even without exclusionary *laws*, Aboriginal people were not free to binge or breast the bar alongside their mates in quite the way Anglo-Europeans were. Racially discriminatory practices continued informally even after the end of legal prohibitions. Furthermore the meaning of drinking was often different for Aboriginal people. The pattern of drinking was "aggressively Aboriginal in form" and more likely to be on fortified wine.[78] Some scholars have suggested that "prohibition helped to create a drinking pattern which was related to seclusion and fast-drinking … Drinking, therefore, took on an air of secrecy and conspiracy."[79] Once prohibitions were lifted, drinking became identified with the recognition of inclusion in citizenship status and 'the universally recognised rule that all have the inalienable right to drink and get drunk."[80]

There is considerable evidence that Aboriginal Australians actually drank less alcohol than other Australians. However when they did it was more likely to be heavily.[81] Excessive consumption within Aboriginal communities was therefore a subject discussed by government agencies and social researchers, as a "problem" to be solved.[82] It was not seen by social commentators and authors of tourist tracts as a mark of cultural identity to be celebrated as an expression of "the good life."

Immigrants and Wine versus Beer

In the postwar period too, recently arrived immigrants from non-English-speaking backgrounds were not included in "Australian" drinking culture. They had their own cultural practices and drinking preferences, more likely to be wine (or coffee) than beer, and more likely to be in clubs and cafés than pubs. They found Australian red wines to be "terrific" and amazingly cheap. "We could buy a gallon of red wine in a bottle for two and sixpence (that's eighteen litres for a dollar) and it was excellent wine," Italian immigrants reminisced recently about their arrival in Australia in the 1950s and the "great things" they found.[83] To be accepted as "new Australians," not "namby-pamby foreigners"[84] meant abandoning these cultural preferences.

Instead, however, newly arrived Australians from eastern and southern Europe were gradually and imperceptibly teaching the earlier-arrived Anglo-Australians how to drink and enjoy wine. "I used to serve wine with the food without asking them do you want wine or not. And not to make it too obvious, I used to serve it in teacups," one former restaurant-owner recalled. "The white wine ... was accepted as wine. But the red wine, people used to put sugar in it, because they thought it was coffee."[85] The middle decades of the twentieth century were a time of introspection and challenge as Australian culture underwent this reorientation.

Wine consumption in Australia had until then, although on a par or slightly less than beer, been associated with an upper-class sensibility that was not allowed to intrude on the "egalitarianism" of the pub. It was always more European than Anglo-Celtic. Early attempts at winegrowing, such as that begun by German settlers in the 1840s in the Barossa Valley, South Australia, were not particularly successful. Although grapes thrived in the Australian climate, the wine they produced could not be sold in large quantities. Popular opinion thought most of the locally produced wine was "sour and ill-flavoured" and many nineteenth-century wine-growers found that growing edible grapes for the dried fruit industry was more profitable.[86] Dingle pointed to a declining consumption over the nineteenth century although the colonial wine-making industry expanded and locally produced light table wines accounted for a larger share of what was consumed than was imported.[87] In the twentieth century most Australians thought of it as "plonk."[88]

Most of the drinking being done was, as Pearl discussed, of "beer, glorious beer," and the Australian pub was "most of all ... cold beer, beer, beer."[89] McGregor had Australians in 1966 second in the world after the Belgians for beer consumption but other surveys gave different results: in 1952, when seventeen nations were ranked according to their consumption of alcohol, Australia ranked fifth for beer consumption. It also ranked surprisingly fifth for wine, but seventeenth out of the seventeen for consumption of spirits.[90] The early governors of NSW who had first encouraged beer brewing to counteract the trade in spirits would have been pleased with this result.

However less pleasing was the continuing high consumption of alcohol these figures revealed. Although not number one in the world, this was a heavy drinking culture and the proportion of alcoholics in the Australian population was high and sex-differentiated. In a study of the connections between alcoholism and social drinking patterns undertaken in the late 1960s Margaret Sargent concluded that there could be little doubt that alcoholism was a major health problem in Australia. One in fifty Australians over the age of twenty were classified "alcoholic" in 1952. By 1970 Sargent had calculated one in twenty males compared with one in a hundred women was alcoholic.[91]

Most telling was the steep rise in beer consumption that had occurred in the ten years after the end of the war in 1945 as six o'clock closing continued in three states, including the two most populous states, NSW and Victoria.[92] This increase had actually begun earlier but took a steep curve upwards at war's end. In 1935 the average per capita consumption of beer was eight gallons per year. Three years later it was twelve. By 1953 it was more than twenty. In that same period of time, between 1938 and 1953, wine consumption also increased, from a third of a gallon to slightly less than two gallons per head per year. Spirits consumption however, remained relatively fixed at a quarter of a gallon.[93]

One suggestion is that war brought an increase in beer drinking because it brought large numbers of servicemen and war industries workers together in large concentrations in camps and factories away from their own local communities. It also made their drinking very visible.[94] Complaints about excessive drinking in public places, especially by servicemen in uniform, of "drunken soldiers in the streets," echoed similar complaints made during the World War I which had been effective in introducing six o'clock closing.[95] Now these anxieties were added to concerns that liquor was freely available while other, essential, commodities were being rationed for the war effort. These complaints reached the ears of government ministers and a Control of Liquor Order was introduced in March 1942.

This was a Commonwealth government measure to control both the production and sale of alcohol not just its consumption. It was not a system of rationing by coupons which could easily be traded between those customers who drank and those who didn't. It was an effort to control the supply of alcohol which occurred through retail outlets (pubs) owned and run by the major producers (the breweries). Retailers this way could be guaranteed continuation of their beer supplies because breweries would not just channel their reduced production to their own tied outlets. And customers could not turn to using other types of alcohol because control was also over sales of imported wines and spirits normally provided to retailers in bottles.[96]

The local wines however had some reprieve. At that time half of Australia's wine production was exported, as port and sherry, but the outbreak of war meant it had lost markets in Southeast Asia due to the Japanese advance and in England because of a decision taken by the British Government to ban all imports of wine. Facing disaster the wine industry succeeded in having wine removed from the reduction in sales required under the Control of Liquor Order. Consequently the war was good for winemakers. As sales of beer and spirits were reduced, wine sales in Australia almost doubled as domestic consumers replaced export markets.[97] Drinkers who discovered a taste for wine (and an appreciation that it was cheaper to drink) during the war years, continued to enjoy it afterwards.

Beer drinkers also increased in number during and after the war. Between 1946 and 1955 they were joined by a million newcomers migrating from Europe as Australia embarked on a major immigration program. The 1960s brought further substantial migration from the Mediterranean countries of Italy and Greece while a younger generation of Australian-born travelers holidayed or worked overseas and learned other drinking customs. Australian men's beer-swilling practices were beginning to look increasingly unacceptable. Although the Control of Liquor Order ended in 1946 the major breweries continued to regulate the supply of beer to retail outlets through a quota system. This, together with licensing laws that in some states kept the trade restricted to drinking before 6 p.m. helped shaped the peculiar character of Australia's postwar drinking culture.

Demand was increasing and the breweries claimed they could not meet it. Yet there was more to the story. To investigate the problem the NSW government set up a Royal Commission to examine drinking in pubs and clubs throughout the state. Its terms of reference were to examine the breweries' financial interests in the ownership and control of hotels, and the adequacy of the present liquor licensing laws in controlling licensing; whether the distribution of liquor was reasonable, and whether the meals and accommodation being provided by hotels was adequate for the needs of the public. The Commission was also required to consider the provision of additional club licenses, and the desirability of reintroducing the temperance advocates' goal of local option provisions into the matter of granting new licenses.[98]

The Commission began hearing evidence in July 1951 and the Commissioner, Justice Maxwell handed down his report in March 1954. "I am satisfied ... that there are evils associated with 6 o'clock closing which ought not to be tolerated in a civilised community," Maxwell reported. He described drinking conditions in the metropolitan area as "deplorable" and early closing also as an encouragement to the practice of sly grog and after-hours trading at black-market rates. Maxwell thus recommended legislation should be introduced to extend trading hours, allowing for staggered and later hours in metropolitan areas, and added hours in rural areas where the need was "markedly greater."[99]

The government followed his recommendations and quickly brought in new legislation. The early closing era was over for NSW. Other states also began investigating drinking in their state. Western Australia, which had 9 o'clock closing, also held a Royal Commission in 1957 because of the findings of Maxwell's Commission in NSW. Victoria undertook a referendum in the hope of changing the licensing laws in time for the 1956 Olympics being held in Melbourne. However it failed to achieve an affirmative result and Victoria too had to go the way of a royal commission followed by legislation.[100] It thus took another ten years before Victoria (1966) and finally South Australia (1967) followed NSW and abandoned the era of six o'clock closing which had been in place for fifty years.

With these changes in pub trading hours and an expansion of liquor licensing to restaurants, Australian drinking culture began to change. Even more important than extending trading hours was the breakdown in sex-segregated drinking which accompanied it.[101] Sargent suggested somewhat tentatively, "It seems ... that it is the presence or absence of women which influences the amount of drinking in men." Her research found that more drinkers in the "high amount and moderate-frequent" categories had drunk most recently in the absence of women, and were more likely than lighter drinkers also to have drunk in a hotel rather than either their own or someone else's home. She concluded that it was the absence of social controls provided by relatives and community groups that spurred on drinking in locations like the public bar, where women didn't drink. One-third of the men in her study came into the category of high amount drinking, and virtually 5 percent were possibly problem drinkers.[102]

Sargent also found that the amount of drinking among Australians, unlike other cultural groups in her study, varied with age. Her findings indicated that Australian drinking symbolized a change in status; the achievement of adult status for boys, which occurred with "membership of an adult male drinking group."[103] From now on they were to do this in mixed company. Public drinking places, most notably the public bar of the local hotel, was no longer the place where men drank only in the company of other men. Justice Maxwell specifically said that it was no longer acceptable for women to wait outside on the footpath while their husbands drank in the bar with their mates. He advocated changes that meant "both sexes would be permitted to partake of liquid refreshment prior to attending the evening shows."[104] Nor were pubs any longer going to be the only place to drink as licensing provisions were extended to restaurants and theaters.

Licensing laws were clearly very significant in bringing about changes to drinking patterns, but the changes to the licensing laws were part of larger social changes occurring at this time. High alcohol consumption had always accompanied prosperity, Dingle said. In the early 1970s the long period of prosperity following the war finally came to an end. At that time too Australia also officially abandoned its identification as Anglo-Celtic and adopted a policy of multiculturalism. Being Australian was now to be defined by a willingness to accept Australian laws not by where you had come from. Almost simultaneously the self-conscious nationalism that celebrated beer and male drunkenness emerged for a time as Ocker Chic among a group of urban professionals busy selling the old-style Australian culture. However it was clear it failed to reflect a majority reality.[105] "It's all a dream. It's not there anymore," Michael Thomas declared in 1987. Australia was multicultural, part of a global economy, and in the new hybrid society, the old "white, English-speaking culture [had] retreated into truculent pockets of resistance."[106]

Although beer consumption continued to increase after the licensing changes, moving Australia in 1970 to fourth on Sargent's international table, it slowed the pace considerably. Now wine consumption was on the steep curve upwards.[107] The change was evident precisely at that moment in the mid 1960s when Horne, Dunstan, Pearl, and McGregor published their books and the last states capitulated on early closing. Leading this charge were "sweet, white sparkling wine[s]," which, largely drunk by young women, were, as McGregor called them, "a sort of feminine substitute for beer." Nevertheless they were reflective of what he saw was "the growing sophistication of Australians" drinking habits' now becoming apparent.[108]

By the 1980s there was "nobody out there in navy blue singlets any more," Thomas said. "They're all wearing alligator shirts and running shoes … sitting around … eating guacomole quiche and drinking low-alcohol beer."[109] Indeed beer sales were dropping dramatically as Australian table wine was being routinely drunk at home, in restaurants and pubs as well as being exported around the world. The most famous Australian brew of all, Foster's lager, for so long identified with the Australian "good life," was now just one of several products of Foster's Brewing Group, which, early in the new century, promoted wine as its primary beverage. Drinking "the good life" no longer meant celebrating drunkenness as Australians embraced a new urbane, cosmopolitan culture of Chardonnay and café latte.

Notes

1. Marcus Clarke, "The Curse of the Country," *Humbug,* September 15, 1869, reprinted in L. T. Hergenhan (ed.), *A Colonial City High and Low Life: Selected Journalism of Marcus Clarke* (St. Lucia: University of Queensland Press, 1972), p. 195.

2. Anthony Trollope, *Australia and New Zealand* (London: Chapman and Hall, 1873; reprinted by St. Lucia: University of Queensland Press, 1967: 1876), p. 202.

3. Craig McGregor, *Profile of Australia* (London: Hodder & Stoughton, 1966), pp. 131–5; Michael Thomas, "The Decline and Fall of Ocker Chic," *Australian Playboy* (April 1987), p. 50.

4. Cyril Pearl, *Beer, Glorious Beer* (Melbourne: Nelson, 1969), pp. 3–12; Cyril Pearl, *So You Want To Be An Australian* (Sydney: Ure Smith, 1959).

5. Donald Horne, *The Lucky Country: Australia in the Sixties* (Ringwood, Vic.: Penguin, 1964), p. 40.

6. Keith Dunstan, *Wowsers* (Melbourne: Cassells, 1968).

7. Stella Lees and June Senyard, *The 1950s – How Australia Became a Modern Society and Everyone Got a House and Car* (Melbourne: Hyland House, 1987).

8. J. M. Freeland, *The Australian Pub* (Melbourne: Melbourne University Press, 1966); Paul McGuire, *Inns of Australia* (London: Heinemann, 1952).

9. John Larkins and Bruce Howard, *Australian Pubs* (Adelaide: Rigby, 1973); John O"Grady, *It's Your Shout, Mate! Australian Pubs and Beer* (Sydney: Lansdowne Press, 1972); Douglass Baglin and Yvonne Austin, *Australian Pub Crawl* (Sydney: PR Books, 1977).

10. A. E. Dingle, "'The Truly Magnificent Thirst': An Historical Survey of Australian Drinking Habits" *Historical Studies* 19, no. 3 (1980): 227–49; T. G. Parsons, "Technological Change in the Melbourne Flour-milling and Brewing Industries, 1870–90," *Australian Economic History Review* 11, no. 2 (September 1971): 133–46.

11. Ann Summers, *Damned Whores and God's Police: The Colonisation of Women in Australia* (Ringwood, Vic: Penguin, 1975).

12. Diane Kirkby, *Barmaids: A History of Women's Work in Pubs* (Cambridge: Cambridge University Press, 1997); Clare Wright, *Beyond the Ladies Lounge: Female Publicans in Australia* (Melbourne: Melbourne University Press, 2003).

13. Diane Kirkby, "'Beer, Glorious Beer': Gender Politics and Australian Popular Culture," *Journal of Popular Culture* 37, no. 2 (2003): 244–56; Jill Matthews, "Normalising Modernity," *UTS Review* 6, no.1 (2000).

14. Freeland, *Australian Pub*, p. 1.

15. Editorial, "Beer and Prosperity," *Australian Brewer's Journal* 24 (April 20 1906): 381.

16. Brett J. Stubbs, "A New Drink for Young Australia: From Ale to Lager Beer in New South Wales, 1880 to 1930", in Robert Dare (ed.), *Food, Power and Community* (Adelaide: Wakefield Press, 1999), p. 126.

17. Freeland, *Australian Pub*, p. 28.

18. *Australian Brewer's Journal*, 1882, quoted in Stubbs, "From ale to lager," p. 132.

19. Told in Stubbs, "From ale to lager," pp. 126–41.

20. Victorian Beer Statistics for the Years 1893 to 1897, *Australian Brewer's Journal* (May 20, 1898): 251.

21. Stubbs, "From ale to lager," p. 136; Dingle, "Truly magnificent thirst," p. 236.

22. Stubbs, "From ale to lager," p. 139.

23. See e.g. the incident in the bar recounted in the satirical novel by Nino Culotta [pseud.] *They're a Weird Mob* (Sydney: Ure Smith, 1957), p. 26.

24. McGregor, *Profile of Australia*, p. 131, reported 8.5% alcohol content compared with 7.7% in Britain and Germany; but one of the myths Pearl debunked was this one about the comparative alcoholic strength of Australian beer: *Beer, Glorious Beer*, pp. 5–7.

25. Dingle, "Truly magnificent thirst," p. 234.

26. Elizabeth Malcolm, *"Ireland Sober, Ireland Free": Drink and Temperance in Nineteenth-century Ireland* (Dublin: Gill & Macmillan, 1986), p. ix.

27. Russel Ward, *The Australian Legend* (Melbourne: OUP, 1958, 2nd ed. reprinted 1970), p. 35.

28. Trollope, *Australia*, p. 202, quoted in Dingle, "Truly magnificent thirst," p. 237.

29. Dingle, "Truly magnificent thirst," pp. 236–7.

30. Richard Twopeny, *Town Life in Australia* (London: Elliot Stock, 1883; facsimile reprint Penguin, 1973), p. 70.

31. W. J. Rorabaugh, *The Alcoholic Republic: An American Tradition* (New York: OUP, 1979), p. 149.

32. Ibid., p. 169.

33. Ibid., p. 151.

34. Clarke, "Curse of the country," pp. 195–8.

35. A custom captured in the novel by Culotta, *They're a Weird Mob*, p. 27.

36. McGregor, *Profile of Australia*, p. 134.

37. Ibid., p. 295.

38. Ronald Henderson, *People in Poverty: A Melbourne Survey* (Melbourne: Institute of Applied Economic Research, 1970).

39. These quoted phrases are McGregor's; see a similar description in Freeland, *Australian Pub*, p. 2; for an exploration of women's separate drinking culture see Clare Wright, "Doing the Beans: Women, Drinking and Community in the Ladies Lounge," *Journal of Australian Studies* (Jan. 2003): 7–22.

40. McGregor, *Profile of Australia*, p. 133.

41. Clarke, "Curse of the Country," pp. 195–6.

42. See, for example, as quoted in Ward, *Australian Legend*, p. 35 and Dunstan, *Wowsers*, pp. 40, 50.

43. *Bulletin*, 26 October 1889, quoted in Dunstan, *Wowsers*, p. 43.

44. See evidence provided to New South Wales. Parliament. Intoxicating Drink Enquiry, 1887, Legislative Assembly, Votes and Proceedings, vol. VII, 1887–8 (Sydney: Government Printer, 1888).

45. A point also made about Canadian women, see Cheryl Krasnick Warsh, "'Oh, Lord, pour a cordial in her wounded heart': The Drinking Woman in Victorian and Edwardian Canada," in Cheryl Krasnick Warsh (ed.), *Drink in Canada: Historical Essays* (Montreal: McGill-Queen's University Press, 1993), p. 71.

46. Told in Kirkby, *Barmaids*, pp. 196–200.

47. For further elaboration see Diane Kirkby, "Barmaids, Feminists, Ockers and Pubs, 1950s–1970s," in Patricia Grimshaw and Diane Kirkby (eds), *Dealing With Difference: Essays on History, Gender and Culture* (Melbourne: University of Melbourne Conference and Seminar Series, 1997), pp. 130–45.

48. This phrase was used ironically by a former publican in her autobiography, Mayse Young, *No Place For a Woman: The Autobiography of an Outback Publican* (Sydney: Pan Macmillan, 1991) and the irony was explored in Kirkby, "No Place for a Woman? Pubkeeping in Colonial Times," *Barmaids*, pp. 19–42; for an extended account of women as publicans see Wright, *Beyond the Ladies Lounge*.

49. This was first pointed out in Diane Kirkby, "Women's Work as Barmaids: Some Thoughts from a Research Project," *Lilith: Journal of Women's History* 6 (Spring 1989): 94–9; and Diane Kirkby, "Writing the History of Women Working: Photographic Evidence and the 'Disreputable Occupation of Barmaid'," *Labour History* 61 (November 1991): 3–16; and pursued further in Diane Kirkby, "'Barmaids' and 'Barmen': Sexing 'Work' in Australia, 1870s-1940s," in Helen Brash, Jan Gothard, and Jane Long (eds), *Forging Identities: Bodies, Gender and Feminist History* (Nedlands: University of Western Australia Press, 1997), pp. 161–80.

50. Discussed in Kirkby, *Barmaids*, pp. 200–3; for a parody which is also a manifestation of this view see John Hepworth and John Hindle, "In Praise of Splendid Gels Behind Bars," *Boozing Out in Melbourne Pubs* (Sydney: Angus & Robertson, 1980), pp. 11–13.

51. *Vigilante* (1950).

52. NSW Parliamentary Debates, Series 1, vol. 89 (1897), p. 2984.

53. Explored in Diane Kirkby, "'The Barmaid', 'The Landlady', and 'The

Publican's Wife': History, Law and the Popular Culture of Women's Work in Pubs," in Margaret Thornton (ed.), *Romancing the Tomes* (London: Cavendish, 2002), pp. 167–83.

54. Reported in the *Vigilante* (Feb. 4, 1971), p. 3.

55. David Day, *John Curtin: A Life* (Sydney, Harper Collins, 1999).

56. Neeute [pseud.] "Colonial 'Shouting'," *Victorian Review* 6 (June 1882): 239–44.

57. Clarke, "Curse of the Country," p. 196.

58. Horne, *Lucky Country*, p. 36.

59. McGregor, *Profile of Australia*, p. 132.

60. "Ocker" is defined in the *Macquarie Australian Dictionary* as "typical Australian male".

61. Thomas, "Ocker Chic", p. 50.

62. Margaret J. Sargent, *Alcoholism as a Social Problem* (St. Lucia: University of Queensland Press, 1973), p. 2.

63. Stephen Garton, "'Once a Drunkard, Always a Drunkard': Social Reform and the Problem of 'Habitual Drunkenness' in Australia, 1880–1914", *Labour History* 23 (1987): 38–53.

64. Anthea Hyslop, "Temperance Christianity and Feminism," *Historical Studies* 17, no. 66 (April 1976): 27–49 was probably the first to point to these connections; the ambivalence in the temperance women's campaign against women workers in pubs is discussed in Kirkby, *Barmaids*, pp. 92–134.

65. *Australian Brewer's Journal* 14, no. 12 (Sept. 21, 1896): 1.

66. Audrey Oldfield, *Woman Suffrage in Australia: A Gift or a Struggle?* (Cambridge: Cambridge University Press, 1992).

67. See graph in Sargent, *Alcoholism as a Social Problem*, p. 24.

68. Sargent, *Alcoholism*, p. 1.

69. Novelist Dymphna Cusack in her introduction to *Caddie: A Sydney Barmaid, Written By Herself* (London: Constable, 1953); and Justice Maxwell, Report, New South Wales. Royal Commission on Liquor Laws in New South Wales (Sydney: NSW Govt. Printer, 1954), p. 86.

70. McGregor, *Profile of Australia*.

71. Freeland, *Australian Pub,* p. 9.

72. John Albanis, "Drink and Drinkers," PhD thesis (La Trobe University, 1998), p. 131.

73. See also Tim Low, *Wild Food Plants of Australia* (Sydney: Angus & Robertson, 1988, rev. ed. 1991), p. 4.

74. Albanis, "Drink and Drinkers," p. 132.

75. Richard Broome, *Aboriginal Australians: Black Response to White Dominance,* first pub. 1982, 3rd ed. (Sydney: Allen & Unwin, 2001), p. 59.

76. Albanis, "Drink and Drinkers," p. 137.

77. Ibid., p. 142.

78. Point made by Ian Pitman, former Chairman, Northern Territory Liquor

Commission, in the "Preface" and further developed by the authors, Maggie Brady and Kingsley Palmer, *Alcohol in the Outback: Two Studies in Drinking* (Darwin: Australian National University North Australia Research Unit Monograph, 1984), p. vii.

79. Discussed in Brady and Palmer, *Alcohol in the Outback,* p. 14.

80. Brady and Palmer, *Alcohol in the Outback*, p. 19.

81. Broome, *Aboriginal Australians*, p. 270.

82. Australia. Parliament. Standing Committee on Aboriginal Affairs. Final Report. Alcohol Problems of Aboriginals (Canberra: Australian Government Publishing Service, 1977).

83. Guiseppe De Carlo in Will Davies and Andrea Dal Bosco, *Tales from a Suitcase* (Melbourne: Lothian, 2001), p. 157.

84. An explicitly satirical comment on Australian macho beer-drinking by Pearl, *Beer, Glorious Beer,* p. 7.

85. Beppi Polese in Davies and Dal Bosco, *Tales from a Suitcase,* p. 157.

86. *Sydney Morning Herald* (July 1, 1854): 4; Jury Report, *Official Report of Melbourne Exhibition,* 1866–7, Wine Section, 1 quoted in Ian Philip, "The Development of Brewing and Beer Drinking in New South Wales in the Nineteenth Century," BA Hons. thesis (Australian National University, History Department, 1979), p. 15.

87. Dingle, "Truly Magnificent Thirst," p. 232.

88. Australia, Parliament. Debates, vol. 171 [1942] 1654, cited in K. G. Laycock, "Government Interference With the Australian Way of Life: The Control of Liquor Order of 16 March 1942 (An Administrative History)," unpublished essay for Bachelor of Letters (History Department, Australian National University, 1981), p. 20.

89. Freeland, *Australian Pub,* p. 2.

90. Reported in Sargent, *Alcoholism,* p. 23.

91. Sargent, *Alcoholism,* p. 25. These figures differ somewhat from those produced by the Alcoholism Research Foundation in Canada, which on 1947 figures placed Australia tenth out of twelve countries, perhaps because of differing definitions or ways of measuring alcoholism, see Robert E. Popham and Wolfgang Schmidy, *Statistics of Alcohol Use and Alcoholism in Canada 1871–1956* (Toronto: University of Toronto Press, 1958), p. 120.

92. See graph in Sargent, *Alcoholism*, p. 24.

93. Laycock, "Control of liquor order," p. 10.

94. Ibid., p. 9.

95. Walter Phillips, "'Six o'clock Swill: The Introduction of Early Closing of Hotel Bars in Australia," *Historical Studies* 19, no. 75 (October 1980): 250–66.

96. Laycock, "Control of Liquor Order," pp. 8–9.

97. Ibid., p. 20.

98. Maxwell Royal Commission, p. 4.

99. Ibid., pp. 87–8.

100. Western Australia. Parliament. Parliamentary Committee Appointed to Enquire into the Licensing Act, 1958. Report. WA Parliamentary Papers, vol. 3, 1959; Victoria. Parliament. Royal Commission into … Liquor in Victoria, 1964–5, Victoria Parliamentary Papers, 1965.

101. Changes that occurred in pubs are discussed by Tanja Luckins, "Time, Gentlemen, Please: The End of Six o'clock Closing and the 'Post-swill Pub'," in Tanja Luckins & Seamus O'Hanlon (eds), *GO! Melbourne in the Sixties* (Melbourne: Circa, 2005), pp. 146–59.

102. Sargent, *Alcoholism*, p. 108.

103. Ibid., p. 105.

104. Maxwell Royal Commission Report, 86.

105. Discussed in Kirkby, "Beer Glorious Beer".

106. Thomas, "Ocker Chic", p. 50.

107. See graph in Sargent, *Alcoholism*, p. 24.

108. McGregor, *Profile of Australia*, pp. 132–3.

109. Thomas, "Ocker Chic," p. 50.

–13–

Kaleidoscope in Motion

Drinking in the United States, 1400–2000[1]

Jack S. Blocker Jr.

Drinking in that portion of the North American continent now occupied by the United States has changed in virtually every possible way since the last century before the arrival of Europeans. Native societies, in most of which alcoholic beverages were unknown before European contact, were forced to share the continent with invaders whose cultures incorporated many forms of liquor, and the alcoholic interactions that resulted produced devastating outcomes for the land's First Nations. Among the European settlers and their descendants, production of alcoholic beverages moved from the home to the factory and from the hands of a large number of domestic artisans into the grip of a few highly industrialized corporate producers. Beverage choice shifted, as the early favorite type, distilled spirits, gave way to various fermented beverages—first lagers, and then more recently, wines. Drinking moved from the home to the public drinking place and back again to the home. The drinking population expanded and contracted, and its composition changed as various groups defined by social class, age, sex, racial identification, region, and ethnicity entered or left its ranks. The level of per capita consumption rose and fell as a result of shifts in preference and alteration of the drinking population, as well as cultural and economic variation. Few, if any, of these changes have been linear. For example, during National Prohibition (1920–33) amateur domestic producers regained a significant share of production from the corporations which had previously come to dominate the manufacture of alcoholic beverages.

Although the subject has been studied extensively, much remains to be discovered about American drinking. What we now know about historical patterns of alcohol use reveals a complex and variable phenomenon. In short, drinking in the United States has a history, and the historical turns in the production and consumption of alcohol often reflect changes in American economy and culture. Shifts in drinking behavior in turn have stimulated transformations in public discourse, social movements and public policy.

Alcohol is Everywhere: From European Colonization to the New Republic

When Europeans first reached the shores of the New World, a culture in which alcoholic beverages were deeply embedded encountered a set of cultures in most of which alcohol was nonexistent. If native societies did use alcoholic beverages, they did so in forms, such as cactus and persimmon wine or corn beer, having a far lower alcohol content than the distilled spirits brought by Europeans.[2] Beginning as ritual gift exchange, the passage of high-alcohol liquor from settlers to native peoples expanded into a central channel of commerce; by the middle of the eighteenth century, the liquor trade became a tool of both French and English colonies in their rivalry for native alliances.[3] European observers of native drinking created a stereotype of the drunken Indian, but this image owed more to the observers' belief in Indian inferiority than to native peoples' behavior, which was far more contingent and varied than the stereotype allowed. Some First Nations people did not drink at all, and others drank moderately. Some incorporated drinking into various rituals; others drank to escape temporarily from the disease, dispossession, and defeat that also came with the Europeans.[4] Colonists' supplying of liquor to native peoples coexisted with frequent official disapproval and generally unenforced prohibition of the trade, a pattern that was to outlast the colonial period.[5]

Prohibition of sales to Indians represented one of the few novel elements in colonial laws pertaining to drinking, which usually repeated Dutch and English legislation, as well as reflecting the prevailing attitudes of their respective metropolitan worlds.[6] The principal goal of such laws was social order, not the drinker's health or salvation. Public drinking was viewed as a uniquely potent source of disorder. On the other hand, the taverns in which most public drinking took place were regarded as indispensable institutions for the lodging and feeding of travelers. Colonial laws therefore sought to regulate drinking and drinking behavior, but not to eliminate drinking or to hedge tavern-keepers about with so many restrictions that they could not carry out their necessary and desired social function.[7] In rural America, taverns were so important as social centers as well as providers of lodging that local authorities seem not to have cared whether they were licensed or not.[8]

Not all drinking, however, took place in public. Most of the alcohol consumption of colonial America occurred in the home, where in fact much of it was also produced. The great exception was distilled spirits. The favorite hard liquor was rum, whose upsurge in popularity in the Atlantic world of the seventeenth and eighteenth centuries was part and parcel of Europeans' and European colonists' growing addiction to sugar. Sugar came from the West Indian islands colonized by the European powers and was produced by the vast slave labor forces of those islands, maintained by the booming slave trade from West Africa. The sugar planters of the islands could make themselves rich simply by growing sugar cane, or at most adding basic processing of the cane into molasses. Rum-making was left to mainland colonial distillers. On the eve of the American Revolution, rum bubbled out of 140 distilleries in Britain's mainland colonies.[9] From Boston, Newport, New York City, Philadelphia, and other centers, the rum flowed in several directions: mainly to consumers in the colonies and in Indian country, but also to European drinkers.

The other popular alcoholic beverages of the time, however, were most commonly made in the home. Housewives in the northern colonies brewed beer every few days, since their product had a short shelf life.[10] Cider was also widely produced wherever apples grew.[11] Commercial breweries existed, but all of them brewed English-style ales made from top-fermenting yeasts, and these brews would eventually prove unable to survive the conquest of the American palate by the lager beers that were to arrive in the mid nineteenth century with the first big wave of German immigration. None of the colonial-era breweries lasted into the late twentieth century.[12] Nor did any of the colonial rum distilleries, as rising nationalism in the post-revolutionary years led American drinkers to switch from rum, a product dependent on supplies from Europe's Caribbean colonies, to whiskeys distilled from domestically produced grains. Nationalistically inspired changes in beverage preference were pushed along by higher taxes on imported rum and the closing of former American markets in the Caribbean by the European empires.[13] Home brewing, in contrast, was to outlast the colonial period and to revive during National Prohibition and again in the late twentieth century.[14]

In the American colonies and in the early years of the new republic, then, what alcoholic beverage was drunk depended on who was drinking and where drinking took place. Wine was consumed mainly by the upper class, and much of the wine consumption took place in upper-class homes. When upper-class men left home to drink, however, they moved from class-segregated but gender-inclusive company into gender-segregated but class-inclusive surroundings. In the colonial metropolis of Philadelphia, until the opening of the City Tavern in 1773, upper-class drinkers had no retreat they could call their own. Before then, their numbers and wealth were insufficient to justify opening separate quarters, and so they drank in public, and socialized and argued, cheek by jowl with those they considered their social inferiors.[15] Rum was widely popular before the American Revolution, but its principal market was probably the colonial cities, which held only a small proportion of the population. In the vast reaches of the American countryside, domestically produced ale and cider held sway. In both urban and rural homes, however, neither age nor sex defined the drinking population. This was a world in which coffee and tea were expensive, and sugar was too costly to be routinely added to water. Water, in any case, was considered to be unsafe to drink without the addition of alcohol (and, in cities at least, frequently was). Often the best that could be said of water was that "It's very good for navigation."[16] Everyone drank, even infants, who were given a "toddy" to keep them quiet. Americans did not drink all the time, but they drank liquor on every occasion when they drank anything, including not only celebrations and social gatherings, but also during working hours and at meals. At the close of the eighteenth century, total annual consumption of absolute alcohol (the alcoholic content of all beverages) is estimated at 3.5 US gallons per capita (13.2

liters).[17] Of this total, distilled spirits provided about one-half. In Americans' lives, alcohol was literally omnipresent.[18]

Becoming Sober: The Nineteenth Century

During its first twenty-five years, the drinking scene in the nineteenth century pre-served, and even heightened, the colors and patterns established during the previous 200 years. Except for the failing rum distilleries of the northeastern port cities, pro-duction continued to be largely home-based. This had always been the case for ale and cider, but now the whiskey that was displacing rum in American tastes offered new opportunities for home producers, as small-scale distilling equipment hissed and dripped on ordinary farms, especially those on the new western frontiers.[19] Indeed, the abundant crops springing from the productive soils of the Ohio Valley, together with the high cost to transport the bulky product to eastern cities, produced a whiskey glut before the Erie Canal (completed in 1825) and its imitators brought shipping costs down and thereby created a national grain market. At the height of the whiskey glut in the early 1820s, a gallon of whiskey could be purchased for as little as 25 cents, easily affordable by an agricultural worker making one dollar a day. Riding a rising curve of spirits drinking, per capita consumption reached an historic peak of 3.9 US gallons (14.8 liters) in 1830.[20]

Drinking remained omnipresent in Americans' lives. A critical observer in 1814 summed up prevailing attitudes:

> Strong drink in some form is the remedy for every sickness, the cordial for every sorrow. It must grace the festivity of the wedding; it must enliven the gloom of the funeral. It must cheer the intercourse of friends and enlighten the fatigues of labor. Success *deserves* a treat and disappointment *needs* it. The busy drink because they are busy; the idle because they have nothing else to do. The farmer must drink because his work is hard; the mechanic because his employment is sedentary and dull. It is warm, men drink to be cool; it is cool, they drink to be warm.[21]

During the second quarter of the nineteenth century, however, converging forces changed drinking on every front. The transportation revolution initiated by the new canal network and later completed by the railways, which made it feasible for mid-western farmers to ship their grain to eastern cities rather than distilling it into whiskey, also facilitated consolidation in the business of spirits production. The number of distilleries in New York state, for example, dropped from more than 1,100 in 1825 to 77 in 1860, while total output grew.[22] Expansion of the trans-portation network also encouraged apple growers to find more profitable markets for their crops than in the form of cider.[23] Regional specialization turned north-eastern farm folk into industrial workers and midwestern farmers into focused pro-ducers for the market. The growth of urban populations created consumers who were no longer producers of the liquor they drank and retail establishments—

saloons—from which most of the multiple functions of rural taverns had been stripped away by other urban institutions. Industrialization both produced new anxieties that induced drinking to assuage them and required a new discipline among both agricultural and industrial producers to meet the demands of the market.[24] In response to such demands, a new code of manly conduct gave sobriety a favored place among male virtues.

As men's work increasingly took them out of the household, women's work remained behind. An ideology of separate spheres took shape, operating both to justify the growing distance between male and female worlds and to prescribe new norms for "proper" denizens of woman's sphere. These norms assumed a finer, more spiritual character for "true" women, a nature incompatible with the loss of control that alcohol threatened (or promised). Probably women had always consumed less than men and had historically been less likely to drink in public, but now these behavioral gaps widened into a chasm. Women did not cease drinking altogether, but their drinking was now more confined to the home, and their consumption was likely to be in the form of patent medicines—many of which were extremely potent— liquor used in cooking, and wine, champagne, or cordials consumed at "precisely defined social events". As Catherine Murdock has argued, women's drinking presented a model of respectable consumption that coexisted with the model of alcohol abuse in all-male public settings which dominated temperance rhetoric from the early nineteenth century onward.[25] Yet even if women never became as abstemious as the cult of true womanhood implied, their respectable mode of drinking shrank the place of alcohol in women's lives compared to earlier times.

As changes in norms of female behavior reduced women's alcohol consumption, the drinking population was augmented by a new wave of immigration. During the 1840s and 1850s, immigrants from Ireland and the German states entered the United States, bringing with them the drinking customs of their homelands. The Irish more than matched existing American preferences for whiskey, while the Germans brought a new taste for beer, plus a new kind of beer. German brewers produced lager, using a bottom-fermenting yeast and a cooler fermentation process that yielded a lighter, more carbonated drink than the traditional English-style ales. Lager was actually a newcomer to commercial brewing in Europe when the new immigration to the United States began, so the German brewers in the USA, such as Bernard Stroh, Eberhard Anheuser, Adolphus Busch, Frederick Pabst, Frederick Miller, Joseph Schlitz, and Adolph Coors, became pioneers of the new product. When they began adding maize (corn) and rice to the traditional barley in the fermentation process, they created a distinctive American-style beverage, "very pale, stable, easy drinking beers of unrivaled blandness."[26] Lager soon caught on, not only among the rapidly growing numbers of their fellow immigrants, but among native-born drinkers as well. The companies these men founded would dominate American brewing from this time forward.[27]

Counter-pressure to the importation of immigrant drinking customs and the popularity of a new alcoholic beverage came from the temperance movement, another innovation of the early nineteenth century. Temperance sentiment had appeared occasionally before, but temperance only became a mass movement in the 1820s. When it did, the movement spread with striking rapidity across society, focusing its considerable energies on a demand for total abstinence from distilled spirits, then, radicalizing by the 1830s, on the goal of total abstinence from all intoxicating beverages. One of the most widespread, tenacious, and powerful social movements of the century, temperance dovetailed with larger social changes to bring about a remarkable change in drinking behavior. By 1840, alcohol consumption had suffered its most rapid decline in American history, from nearly four gallons of absolute alcohol per capita in 1830 to about two gallons.[28] Men and women of all classes drank less or became abstainers; except in medications, children were now less likely to be given alcohol.[29]

Continued temperance pressure—now in the form of demands for legal prohibition of the liquor trade—and the growing popularity of lager beer, which began to substitute for spirits in the American diet, cut per capita consumption even further by 1850, to about one US gallon of absolute alcohol per capita (3.8 liters), and there it stayed, with occasional but short-lived fluctuations, for the rest of the nineteenth century. Behind this portrait of stability, however, lies an underpainting of drastic change in American tastes. In 1850, 90 percent of the alcohol consumed by drinkers was in the form of distilled spirits; fifty years later, spirits contributed less than half of total consumption. In 1850, beer consumption averaged about two US gallons per capita (7.6 liters); fifty years later, it approached fifteen gallons (64.3 liters). Two major changes in American drinking behavior had occurred: first, a reduction in overall consumption; and, second, a partial but substantial replacement of spirits by beer in American preferences. While the shift to beer had contributed to the latter stages of the reduction in consumption, otherwise the two historic changes were distinct chronologically.

Pervasive temperance pressure probably contributed to both trends, but larger structural changes in American society also played a role in drinkers' turn to beer. These become evident when data on liquor availability are brought together with a time series measuring consumption. Statistics on the number of retail liquor outlets are available only since 1862, when the federal government first taxed dealers. In 1873, official records counted nearly 205,000 retail liquor sellers, which meant there were 4.2 dealers per 1,000 population, but their numbers fell regularly after that. By the end of the century, this ratio had been cut nearly in half. As the United States urbanized, fewer dealers were needed to serve a more geographically concentrated population, and distilled spirits, less costly to transport and store, lost the advantage they had held over fermented beverages in a more rural world. Beer, in other words, was the preeminent urban beverage.[30] And beer, which in the form of lager required cool storage in an age before home refrigeration became common, was drunk mostly in saloons. The popularity of the saloon reflected an increasingly tight linkage between liquor and leisure for workingmen; the reason why saloons clustered around factory gates is that the combined pressure of temperance reformers and bosses made liquor no longer acceptable in the workplace.[31]

The latter half of the nineteenth century became the golden age of the saloon. They became bigger operations: in 1875 the average outlet did a year's business of nearly 400 US gallons of distilled spirits (1,514 liters) and about 1,700 gallons (6,400 liters) of beer; by 1910 those figures had risen to 600 gallons of spirits (2,270 liters) and more than 8,300 gallons of beer (31,400 liters).[32] They also became male preserves, and often, ethnic social centers, for the Irish and German immigrants of the antebellum years and their sons, but also for the new immigrants from southern and eastern Europe who began arriving in large numbers during the 1880s.[33] The Irish saloon in Pittsburgh, for example, 'was the center of neighborhood news and gossip, an informal hiring hall, a source of loans, the locus of business transactions, and hub of trade union, ward, and Irish-American nationalist activities.'[34] For their proprietors, saloonkeeping became a potential avenue to self-employment and possibly social mobility from the manual labor that employed most new arrivals.[35] As a way to wealth, however, saloonkeeping during the late nineteenth century was becoming less attractive, since the expanding major breweries—another beneficiary of the transportation revolution—sought to control saloons as a means of multiplying outlets for their products.[36] Brewers' willingness to provide start-up capital, in conjunction with workingmen's thirst, which yielded a steady flow of consumers, and workingmen's aspirations, which produced ranks of eager saloonkeepers, made the saloon a central institution during the urban era of the late nineteenth and early twentieth centuries. The saloon's presence at the heart of America's booming cities meant that it became a highly visible institution, and its visibility in turn made it the prime target of temperance reformers; the organization that took the lead in bringing about National Prohibition was named the Anti-Saloon League. The notoriety conferred on the saloon by prohibitionists has too often masked the fact that its golden age was also a period of depressed alcohol consumption following the national binge of the early nineteenth century.

Prohibition, Normalization, and Health Consciousness: The Twentieth Century

Drinking entered the twentieth century a fiercely contested act. As a result of seventy-five years of temperance advocacy, few respectable publications dared to show drink in a positive light, and the same was true of the fledgling film industry.[37] Since the 1890s, however, night clubs, first in New York city and later in other major cities, had been pioneering a novel style of expressive and participatory entertainment in which drinking played a central role; part of the attraction of the night-club experience no doubt stemmed from the "naughty" image given to drinking by the temperance movement.[38] During the new century's first decade, the cultural war over drinking gained greater intensity from the onset of a new, larger wave of immigration, bringing reinforcement to the wet side from the drinking cultures of southern and eastern Europe. Reinforcing this trend, African-Americans, previously among the most abstemious of ethnic groups, adopted urban drinking cultures as they began to migrate in large numbers from the rural South to cities in both North and South.[39] Buoyed both by immigration and by internal migration to the cities, beer consumption continued to rise, and even per capita spirits consumption began to inch upward.[40] During the period 1906–14, per capita consumption of absolute alcohol peaked at about 1.6 US gallons (6.1 liters), about 50 percent higher than the turn-of-the-century level. This upsurge gave added impetus to the dry cause and contributed to the political swing that produced adoption of wartime measures to curb liquor production and then the Eighteenth Amendment, which brought on National Prohibition[41]

National Prohibition changed drinking in three major ways. First, it seems to have significantly lowered per capita consumption. Obviously, we can never know definitively how much alcohol Americans consumed during Prohibition, and the existing estimates, derived by extrapolation from measures of associated phenomena, depend heavily on their supporting assumptions. The more straightforward estimates show consumption dropping significantly during 1917–18, as the effects of spreading state prohibition laws and federal wartime restrictions on liquor production began to bite. Consumption remained low during the first half of the 1920s, then rebounded somewhat afterward, although still falling short of the pre-Prohibition level. Indices of alcohol-related medical disorders also fell. At the same time, consumption of alternative beverages—milk, coffee, carbonated drinks, and fresh fruit juices—increased. Prohibition therefore wrought a significant change in American drinking habits.[42] The era of diminished consumption was to outlast the end of National Prohibition.

Second, Prohibition altered beverage choices. For nearly three-quarters of a century prior to Prohibition, beer had been steadily replacing distilled spirits in American glasses. When the Volstead Act (the Eighteenth Amendment's enforcing law) embargoed all beverages having an alcohol content greater than 0.5 percent, beer was placed at a marked disadvantage relative to spirits because of its lower ratio of cost to weight and higher ratio of price to alcohol content. To a bootlegger, in other words, a choice of spirits made better economic sense. Reversing a historic pattern, hard liquor took the place of beer, contributing about two-thirds of total alcohol consumption by the end of the 1920s.[43] Although winemaking was illegal, production of grape concentrate was not, and California wine-grape growers gleefully discovered a booming market in home vintners.[44]

Finally, the drinking population changed in size and composition, in part reflecting the shift in beverage availability. Beer was the preeminent working-class beverage, and the closing of the saloons and the shortage of beer left many working-class drinkers high and dry. Meanwhile, rebellious youth—mainly middle-class students in colleges and universities—began to use alcohol as a badge of modern, cosmopolitan tastes.[45] Their models were found in the writings of the "Lost Generation" of American intellectuals and on the movie screens of the

1920s; both media portrayed drinking in a radically different light than their pre-World War I counterparts. To present drinking as fashionable was to normalize it, to free it from the negative associations affixed by a century of temperance rhetoric—and at the same time to draw on those associations and that rhetoric for the flavor of cultural rebellion.[46]

Of National Prohibition's three achievements, one—the shift from beer to hard liquor—was destined to be short-lived. The other two, however—the reduction in consumption and the normalization of drinking among middle-class youth—outlasted Prohibition and thus made the 1920s a watershed in the history of American drinking. Because middle-class acceptance of drinking showed greater staying power than Prohibition's induced sobriety, the conventional view of the Prohibition era has emphasized the former while forgetting the latter.[47]

After repeal of the Eighteenth Amendment in 1933, the work of the movies in normalizing drinking was enthusiastically reinforced by the revived liquor industry. "In the post-Prohibition era, advertisers used images of glamour, wealth, and sophistication to promote public drinking and those of domesticity and companionate marriage to encourage household consumption."[48] Women became a prime target for liquor advertising, since they represented the industry's largest untapped market. But other players than drink executives and Hollywood screenwriters also contributed to changing perceptions of drinking. Prohibition had killed the inebriate asylums which had previously provided the institutional foundation for alcohol research; after repeal, a new set of scientists emerged to take the lead in alcohol studies. Their institutional base was Yale University, in particular its Center of Alcohol Studies, and its principal spokesman was a scientist of considerable ability though uncertain credentials, E. M. Jellinek (1890–1963). Jellinek developed and publicized a new view of habitual drunkenness whose central claim was that "alcoholism is a disease." The principal aim of those who formulated the disease concept of alcoholism was to support therapy rather than censure for "alcoholics." The disease concept implicitly opened the door to moderate drinking in the population at large. Howard Haggard, Jellinek's sponsor at Yale, hoped that habits of moderation would prevent drinkers from falling into excess. Basic to the disease concept was the belief that alcoholics suffered from a physiological disorder that rendered their drinking pathological; it followed that those who were not thus afflicted could drink safely, without risking descent into alcoholism.[49] Other scientists independently furnished supportive conclusions. Biologist Frank B. Hanson closed down the long-flourishing line of research into the effects of alcohol on reproduction by claiming persuasively that animal experimentation revealed no genetic consequences whatsoever.[50] Physiologist Yandell Henderson taught Americans to perceive alcohol in the same light as toxic chemicals, namely, as a substance that "could, like [carbon] monoxide, be managed in such a way as to be innocuous."[51] Since alcohol's role in various disorders was supported only by epidemiological rather than clinical evidence, medical scientists in general downplayed its effects.[52]

Scientific arguments converged neatly with the thrust of a new approach to the treatment of alcoholism. Founded in 1935, by the early 1940s Alcoholics Anonymous (AA) was spreading across the United States. AA played a key role in promulgating the disease concept of alcoholism, adding to scientific claims what appeared to be convincing evidence for the therapeutic value of a treatment strategy premised upon it.[53] Further support came from the National Council on Alcoholism, an advocacy group devoted to spreading the new gospel.

Governments also played a crucial part in normalizing drinking as well as in directing it into particular channels. Immediately following repeal, the federal government played a key regulatory role through the New Deal's National Recovery Administration (NRA), but after the Supreme Court struck down the NRA in 1935, state governments took over primary responsibility for regulation. Those that abandoned their state prohibition statutes generally created their own liquor-control agencies, which preempted the return of licensing into local hands. Licensing regimes were structured to favor off-premise sales, and many states, while establishing government monopolies over spirits sales, now permitted grocery stores to sell beer and, by the 1960s, wine as well. Home consumption was facilitated further with the arrival of the aluminum beer can in 1934 and the spread of home refrigerators beginning during the 1930s.[54] The new regulatory regime aimed to prevent both the return of the saloon and continuation of the lawlessness and disorder that were perceived to have accompanied Prohibition. In a return to the spirit of the colonial period, laws governing alcohol sale and consumption sought to produce social order rather than to foster public health.[55] As a result, drinking returned to the home and surfaced publicly in the new cocktail lounge, in both of which women's drinking was more acceptable than in the old-time saloon.

By the late 1940s, writes cultural historian Lori Rotskoff:

> Americans generally viewed drinking as a matter of individual choice and alcoholism as a matter of individual or familial concern ... [T]he ideological distinction between moderation and alcoholism allowed for the further domestication of drink in the postwar period. By the late 1940s and 1950s, cocktail rituals were woven into the fabric of the dominant culture, both absorbing and reflecting anxieties that accompanied such trends as consumerism, status seeking, social conformity, and the bureaucratization of the corporate workplace.[56]

The main contours of the post-repeal world were profoundly shaped by the historical experience of Prohibition and the century of temperance agitation which preceded it. The liquor industry's fervent efforts to make drinking an integral part of everyday life stemmed of course from fear of Prohibition's return. Jellinek and his co-workers explicitly distanced their "scientific" approach from the "moralism" of the temperance movement. State liquor-control agencies were intended to remove the liquor issue from local communities, where it had troubled the waters for more than a century, and thus to depoliticize what had recently furnished the nation's most divisive political issue. The alcohol-control regimes they created sought to prevent at all costs the return of the saloon.

Prohibition also shaped another major aspect of American drinking during the quarter-century that followed repeal: diminished consumption compared to the immediate pre-Prohibition years. Hard times during the Depression kept consumption low, and the federal government's encouragement of the liquor industry (compared to World War I) helped to boost consumption somewhat during World War II years.[57] But despite the unprecedented prosperity of the late 1940s and 1950s, and despite the normalization of drinking that was occurring since repeal—despite the arrival of the cocktail hour—per capita consumption stubbornly refused to rise significantly until the 1960s.[58] During the entire period from repeal to the election of John F. Kennedy to the presidency, about two-fifths of the adult population reported themselves to be abstainers.

The drinking scene changed as the baby-boom generation began to reach the older teenage years. Compared to 1960 levels, spirits consumption per capita rose during the ensuing years by about 30 percent, beer by 40 percent, and wine by 75 percent. These significant changes do not, however, seem to have been caused by major alterations in drinking behavior. Survey data show no noteworthy growth in the proportion of drinkers in the male population and only a slight increase in the percentage of women who drank. The key change seems to have been a modification in drinking habits, and one that took place in other Western societies than the United States. Fewer men and women drank only once a month, and more reported drinking daily. Heavy drinking occasions were infrequent, however, and apart from these the amounts consumed were moderate.[59] Drinking, that is, began to shift from an occasional, often public, act to one that was incorporated into daily life in the home as a marker and accompaniment of leisure.[60] Such small alterations in lifestyle were facilitated by the affluence of the period and amplified by the impact of the baby-boom generation, among whose members the changes occurred most notably.[61]

Drinking's upward climb, however, barely outlasted the 1970s. Per capita spirits consumption peaked in 1969 and by 2000 had fallen by more than 40 percent. Beer and wine consumption peaked in 1981 and 1986 respectively, and fell by 12 and 20 percent by 2000.[62] This period of sobering-up is attributed to a spreading health consciousness, aided by concern about drunken driving that led to legislation mandating placement of warning labels on drink containers.[63] Medical scientists' discovery of fetal alcohol syndrome in 1973 may also have helped.[64] Those involved in institutions for treatment of alcoholics, which had blossomed with growing acceptance of the disease concept of alcoholism, by the late 1970s began to engage in an effort to raise societal consciousness about problems caused by drinking. Such concerns received further impetus from the spread of a new self-help therapeutic movement directed at the grown children of drinkers, which took institutional form as the Adult Children of Alcoholics.[65]

As the baby-boom generation aged, at least some of its members became somewhat more selective about what they drank. The background to this recent development is the massive concentration that occurred in the liquor industry during the period since repeal. By the end of the 1930s, four corporations dominated the distilling industry, and these four produced more than three-quarters of the liquor distilled in the USA. In 1935, there were more than 700 brewing companies operating; by 1979 their number had dropped to 45, and by 1984 the four largest firms held a market share of 94 percent. By 1972, led by the vertically integrated Ernest and Julio Gallo Winery, the four largest wineries controlled 53 percent of US wine and brandy shipments. Following the lead of other industries, the liquor industry since the late nineteenth century embraced mass production. Beer was not only brewed in larger batches in massive new breweries, but the brewing process was also accelerated.[66] For the wines and beers that together contributed 70 percent of the alcohol they consumed, some American drinkers increasingly turned to imports and to microbreweries and brewpubs. In 2000, there were more than 1,000 brewpubs and 3,000 microbrew labels in the US. Although microbreweries controlled only 2 percent of the beer market, their segment is a lucrative one, and their growing popularity caused major brewers to diversify their offerings.[67] Another sign of discontent with bland, indistinguishable beer is a rise in home brewing, enabled by federal legislation in 1979. Like drinking at home, where two-thirds of consumption takes place, home brewing closes a circle first inscribed in the early years of American history.[68]

Notes

1. The author thanks Robin Room for his comments on an earlier version of this essay.

2. Kathryn A. Abbott, "Native Americans: Drinking Patterns and Temperance Reform," in Jack S. Blocker Jr., David M. Fahey, and Ian R. Tyrrell (eds), *Alcohol and Temperance in Modern History: An International Encyclopedia*, 2 vols (Santa Barbara, CA: ABC-Clio, 2003), Vol. 2, p. 446.

3. Peter C. Mancall, *Deadly Medicine: Indians and Alcohol in Early America* (Ithaca, NY: Cornell University Press, 1995).

4. Abbott, "Native Americans," pp. 446–8; Mancall, *Deadly Medicine*; Craig Heron, *Booze: A Distilled History* (Toronto: Between the Lines, 2003), pp. 43–5.

5. Mancall, *Deadly Medicine*, pp. 101–29; William E. Unrau, *White Man's Wicked Water: The Alcohol Trade and Prohibition in Indian Country, 1802–1892* (Lawrence: University of Kansas Press, 1996).

6. Jack S. Blocker Jr., *American Temperance Movements: Cycles of Reform* (Boston: Twayne, 1989), pp. 5–7.

7. Sharon V. Salinger, *Taverns and Drinking in Early America* (Baltimore: The Johns Hopkins University Press, 2002); David W. Conroy, *In Public Houses: Drink and the Revolution of Authority in Colonial Massachusetts* (Chapel Hill: University of North Carolina Press, 1995).

8. Daniel B. Thorp, "Taverns and Tavern Culture on the Southern Colonial Frontier: Rowan County, North Carolina, 1753–1776," *Journal of Southern History* 62 (1996): 661–88.

9. Mancall, *Deadly Medicine*, p. 41.

10. Mary E. Saracino, "Household Production of Alcoholic Beverages in Early-Eighteenth-Century Connecticut," *Journal of Studies on Alcohol* 46 (1985): 244–52.

11. W. J. Rorabaugh, *The Alcoholic Republic: An American Tradition* (New York: Oxford University Press, 1979), pp. 9–10, 110–13.

12. Stanley Baron, *Brewed in America: A History of Beer and Ale in the United States* (Boston: Little, Brown, 1962).

13. Frederick H. Smith, "Rum," in Blocker, Fahey, and Tyrrell (eds), *Alcohol and Temperance in Modern History*, Vol. 2, p. 526; Peter Park, "The Supply Side of Drinking: Alcohol Production and Consumption in the United States Before Prohibition," *Contemporary Drug Problems* 12 (1985): 486–9; Rorabaugh, *Alcoholic Republic*, pp. 65–9.

14. Stephen R. Byers, "Home Brewing," in Blocker, Fahey, and Tyrrell (eds), *Alcohol and Temperance in Modern History,* Vol. 1, pp. 297–8.

15. Peter Thompson, *Rum Punch and Revolution: Taverngoing and Public Life in Eighteenth-Century Philadelphia* (Philadelphia: University of Pennsylvania Press, 1999).

16. Quoted in Rorabaugh, *Alcoholic Republic*, p. 97.

17. In all per capita consumption statistics given in this paper, the reference group is the total US population, not the population of presumptive drinking age.

18. Rorabaugh, *Alcoholic Republic*.

19. Park, "Supply Side of Drinking," pp. 483–6.

20. Rorabaugh, *Alcoholic Republic*.

21. Quoted in Carol Steinsapir, "The Ante-Bellum Total Abstinence Movement at the Local Level: A Case Study of Schenectady, New York" (Ph.D. dissertation, Rutgers University, 1983), pp. 266–7.

22. Park, "Supply Side of Consumption," pp. 483–4; Rorabaugh, *Alcoholic Republic*, p. 87.

23. Park, "Supply Side of Consumption," p. 492.

24. Heron, *Booze*, pp. 51–77; Blocker, *American Temperance Movements*, pp. 35–7.

25. Catherine Gilbert Murdock, *Domesticating Drink: Women, Men, and Alcohol in America, 1870–1940* (Baltimore: Johns Hopkins University Press, 1998), pp. 52–69.

26. Raymond G. Anderson, "Beer," in Blocker, Fahey, and Tyrrell (eds), *Alcohol and Temperance in Modern History*, Vol. 1, pp. 94–5.

27. K. Austin Kerr, "The American Brewing Industry, 1865–1920," in R. Wilson and T. Gourvish (eds), *The Dynamics of the International Brewing Industry Since 1800* (London: Routledge, 1998), pp. 176–92.

28. Blocker, *American Temperance Movements*, pp. 28–9.

29. Cheryl Krasnick Warsh, "Medicine, Alcohol as," in Blocker, Fahey, and Tyrrell (eds), *Alcohol and Temperance in Modern History*, Vol. 2, pp. 407–9.

30. Jack S. Blocker Jr., "Consumption and Availability of Alcoholic Beverages in the United States, 1863–1920," *Contemporary Drug Problems* 21 (1994): 631–66.

31. Heron, *Booze*, p. 72.

32. Blocker, "Consumption and Availability," pp. 652–3.

33. Stephen R. Byers, "Saloons and Taverns (United States)," in Blocker, Fahey, and Tyrrell (eds), *Alcohol and Temperance in Modern History*, Vol. 2, pp. 537–40; Madelon Powers, *Faces along the Bar: Lore and Order in the Workingman's Saloon, 1870–1920* (Chicago: University of Chicago Press, 1998); Ron Rothbart, "The Ethnic Saloon as a Form of Immigrant Enterprise," *International Migration Review* 27 (1993): 332–58; Perry R. Duis, *The Saloon: Public Drinking in Chicago and Boston, 1880–1920* (Urbana: University of Illinois Press, 1983).

34. Victor A. Walsh, "'Drowning the Shamrock': Drink, Teetotalism, and the Irish Catholics of Gilded-Age Pittsburgh," *Journal of American Ethnic History* 10 (1990–91): 60–79.

35. Jack S. Blocker Jr., "Artisan's Escape: A Profile of the Postbellum Liquor Trade in a Midwestern Small Town," *Essays in Economic and Business History* 12 (1994): 335–46; Rothbart, "Ethnic Saloon".

36. Kerr, "American Brewing Industry".

37. Joan L. Silverman, "'I'll Never Touch Another Drop': Images of Alcohol and Temperance in American Popular Culture, 1874–1919" (Ph.D. dissertation, New York University, 1979).

38. Lewis A. Erenberg, *Steppin' Out: New York Nightlife and the Transformation of American Culture* (Westport, CT: Greenwood Press, 1981).

39. Denise Herd, "A Review of Drinking Patterns and Alcohol Problems Among U.S. Blacks," in *Report of the Secretary's Task Force on Black & Minority Health: Black and Minority Health, Vol. VII: Chemical Dependency and Diabetes* (Washington: US Department of Health and Human Services, 1986), pp. 77–140.

40. Blocker, "Consumption and Availability".

41. Blocker, *American Temperance Movements*, pp. 111–19.

42. Angela K. Dills and Jeffrey A. Miron, "Alcohol Prohibition and Cirrhosis," *American Law and Economics Review* 6 (2004): 285–318; Jeffrey A. Miron, "An Economic Analysis of Alcohol Prohibition," *Journal of Drug Issues* 28 (1998): 741–62; Miron, "The Effect of Alcohol Prohibition on Alcohol Consumption," National Bureau of Economic Research Working Paper #7130 (1997); Miron and Jeffrey Zweibel, "Alcohol Consumption During Prohibition," *American Economic Review* 81 (1991): 242–7; Blocker, "Consumption and Availability"; John C. Burnham, "New Perspectives on the Prohibition 'Experiment' of the 1920's," *Journal of Social History* 2 (1968): 51–68; Clark Warburton, *The Economic Results of Prohibition* (New York: Columbia University Press, 1932).

43. Warburton, *Economic Results of Prohibition*.

44. John R. Meers, "The California Wine and Grape Industry and Prohibition," *California Historical Society Quarterly* 46 (1967): 19–32.

45. Paula S. Fass, *The Damned and the Beautiful: American Youth in the 1920's* (New York: Oxford University Press, 1977).

46. John C. Burnham, *Bad Habits: Drinking, Smoking, Taking Drugs, Gambling, Sexual Misbehavior, and Swearing in American History* (New York: New York University Press, 1993); Robin Room, "'A Reverence for Strong Drink': The Lost Generation and the Elevation of Alcohol in American Culture," *Journal of Studies on Alcohol* 45 (1984): 540–6; Room, "The Movies and the Wettening of America: The Media as Amplifiers of Cultural Change," *British Journal of Addiction* 83 (1988): 11–18.

47. Ian R. Tyrrell, "The US Prohibition Experiment: Myths, History and Implications," *Addiction* 92 (1997): 1405–9.

48. Cheryl Krasnick Warsh, "Smoke and Mirrors: Gender Representation in North American Tobacco and Alcohol Advertisements Before 1950," *Histoire sociale/Social History* 31 (1998): 220.

49. Blocker, *American Temperance Movements*, pp. 144–50.

50. Philip J. Pauly, "How Did the Effects of Alcohol on Reproduction Become Scientifically Uninteresting?" *Journal of the History of Biology* 29 (1996): 1–28.

51. Philip J. Pauly, "Is Liquor Intoxicating? Scientists, Prohibition, and the Normalization of Drinking," *American Journal of Public Health* 84 (1994): 305.

52. Brian S. Katcher, "The Post-Repeal Eclipse in Knowledge about the Harmful Effects of Alcohol," *Addiction* 88 (1993): 729–44.

53. Ernest Kurtz and William L. White, "Alcoholics Anonymous," in Blocker, Fahey, and Tyrrell (eds), *Alcohol and Temperance in Modern History*, Vol. 1, pp. 27–31; Kurtz, *Not-God: A History of Alcoholics Anonymous* (Center City, MN: Hazelden, 1991).

54. Blocker, *American Temperance Movements*, pp. 133–36; David Fogarty, "From Saloon to Supermarket: Packaged Beer and the Reshaping of the U.S. Beer Industry," *Contemporary Drug Problems* 12 (1985): 541–92.

55. Harry Gene Levine, "The Birth of American Alcohol Control: Prohibition, the Power Elite, and the Problem of Lawlessness," *Contemporary Drug Problems* 12 (1985): 63–115.

56. Lori Rotskoff, *Love on the Rocks: Men, Women, and Alcohol in Post-World War II America* (Chapel Hill: University of North Carolina Press, 2002), p. 210.

57. Jay L. Rubin, "The Wet War: American Liquor Control, 1941–45," in Jack S. Blocker Jr. (ed), *Alcohol, Reform and Society: The Liquor Issue in Social Context* (Westport, CT: Greenwood Press, 1979), pp. 235–58.

58. National Institute of Alcohol Abuse and Alcoholism (NIAAA) (2002), "Apparent per capita ethanol consumption for the United States, 1850–2000," available online at http://www.niaaa.nih.gov/databases/consum01.htm (consulted August 2004).

59. Michael E. Hilton, "Trends in U.S. Drinking Patterns: Further Evidence from the Past 20 Years," *British Journal of Addiction* 83 (1988): 269–78.

60. Klaus Mäkelä, Robin Room, Eric Single, Pekka Sulkunen, and Brendan Walsh, *Alcohol, Society, and the State, Vol 1: A Comparative Study of Alcohol Control* (Toronto: Addiction Research Foundation, 1981), pp. 27–30.

61. Andrew J. Treno, Robert Nash Parker, and Harold D. Holder, "Understanding U.S. Alcohol Consumption with Social and Economic Factors: A Multivariate Time Series Analysis, 1950–1986," *Journal of Studies on Alcohol* 54 (1991): 146–56.

62. NIAAA, "Apparent per capita ethanol consumption".

63. Pamela Pennock, "The Evolution of U.S. Temperance Movements Since Repeal: A Comparison of Two Campaigns to Control Alcoholic Beverage Marketing, 1950s and 1980s," paper presented to the International Conference on Drugs and Alcohol in History, London, Canada, 2004, cited by permission; Ruth Engs, *Clean Living Movements: American Cycles of Health Reform* (Westport, CT: Praeger, 2000).

64. Janet Golden, "'An Argument That Goes Back to the Womb': The Demedicalization of Fetal Alcohol Syndrome, 1973–1992," *Journal of Social History* 33 (1999): 269–98.

65. Robin Room, "Changes in the Cultural Position of Alcohol in the United States: The Contribution of Alcohol-Oriented Movements," unpublished paper in author's possession, 1987. Cited by permission.

66. Rod Phillips, "Wine," in Blocker, Fahey, and Tyrrell (eds), *Alcohol and Temperance in Modern History*, Vol. 2, pp. 670–1; Anderson, "Beer," in ibid., Vol. 1, pp. 97–100; A. M. McGahan, "The Emergence of the National Brewing Oligopoly: Competition in the American Market, 1933–1958," *Business History Review* 65 (1991): 229–84; Blocker, *American Temperance Movements*, p. 136; Robert McBride, "Industry Structure, Marketing, and Public Health: A Case Study of the U.S. Beer Industry," *Contemporary Drug Problems* 12 (1985): 593–620; Fogarty, "From Saloon to Supermarket"; Richard Bunce, "From California Grapes to California Wine: The Transformation of an Industry, 1963–1979," *Contemporary Drug Problems* 10 (1981): 55–74; Thomas C. Cochran, *The Pabst Brewing Company: The History of an American Business* (New York: New York University Press, 1948).

67. Amy Mittelman, "Microbreweries (United States, United Kingdom, and Canada)," in Blocker, Fahey, and Tyrrell (eds), *Alcohol and Temperance in Modern History*, Vol. 2, pp. 416–17; Wes Flack, "American Microbreweries and Neolocalism: 'Ale-ing' for a Sense of Place," *Journal of Cultural Geography* 16 (1997): 37–53.

68. Byers, "Home Brewing".

Index